Under Divine Auspices

This book explores how deities were used to communicate and negotiate imperial power under the Severan dynasty (AD 193–235). Septimius Severus connected his reign to the divine support of Liber Pater and Hercules, while Caracalla placed a particular emphasis on the gods Apollo, Aesculapius and Sarapis. Elagabalus' reign was characterised by the worship of the Emesene deity Elagabal, which resulted in a renewed emphasis on the cult of Jupiter under Severus Alexander. Numismatic evidence is reintegrated into the wider material culture of the Severan period in order to bring new insights into the use of the divine in this period, as well as the rôle played by the provinces in the formation and reception of this ideology. By taking a dynastic approach, this book demonstrates the dynamic nature of the imperial public image and the complex dialogue that existed between Rome and the wider empire in this period.

CLARE ROWAN is Research Fellow in Numismatics in the Department of Classics and Ancient History, University of Warwick. She has been a junior fellow and research officer at the Australian Centre for Ancient Numismatic Studies, and she was the Macquarie Gale Fellow at the British School at Rome. She works on visual culture, Roman history and the Roman economy and was part of the student-mentoring group Telemachus, which was awarded an Australian Learning and Teaching Award in 2010.

Under Divine Auspices

Divine Ideology and the Visualisation of Imperial Power in the Severan Period

CLARE ROWAN

CAMBRIDGE
UNIVERSITY PRESS

CAMBRIDGE
UNIVERSITY PRESS

University Printing House, Cambridge CB2 8BS, United Kingdom

One Liberty Plaza, 20th Floor, New York, NY 10006, USA

477 Williamstown Road, Port Melbourne, VIC 3207, Australia

314-321, 3rd Floor, Plot 3, Splendor Forum, Jasola District Centre, New Delhi-110025, India

79 Anson Road, #06-04/06, Singapore 079906

Cambridge University Press is part of the University of Cambridge.

It furthers the University's mission by disseminating knowledge in the pursuit of education, learning and research at the highest international levels of excellence.

www.cambridge.org
Information on this title: www.cambridge.org/9781107020122

First published 2012

A catalogue record for this publication is available from the British Library

Library of Congress Cataloging in Publication data
Rowan, Clare, 1982–
Under divine auspices : divine ideology and the visualisation of imperial power in the Severan period / Clare Rowan.
p. cm.
ISBN 978-1-107-02012-2 (hardback)
1. Rome – Religion. 2. Rome – History – Severans, 193–235. I. Title.
BL803.R69 2012
292.07–dc23

2012020513

ISBN 978-1-107-02012-2 Hardback

To my fellow students of history, past and present

Contents

Figures

Preface

When I began work on this project, it was not my intention to produce a book so heavily focused on numismatic evidence. At that time I was not trained as a numismatist and had little idea about the potential uses of this often neglected type of evidence. But the more I learnt about the Severans the more I became convinced of the importance of addressing the numismatic evidence and examining it in a proper manner. It was from coinage, I believed, that we could make great advances in our understanding of the public image of the Severan emperors and the image of the principate in general. I believe that the final result has more than justified the deviation from my intended course.

This book derives from my doctoral thesis *Under Divine Auspices: Patron Deities and the Visualisation of Imperial Power in the Severan Period*, completed at Macquarie University in 2009. The conversion of this work into a book took place under the kind advice of the anonymous readers from Cambridge University Press, and was assisted by the tireless efforts of Michael Sharp, Josephine Lane and Gillian Dadd. The adaptation of my raw doctoral work into publishable form was made possible by a postdoctoral grant to the British School at Rome. The school and its staff provided an ideal environment in which to write, and living in Italy informed my ideas about Severan Rome in a way I had hardly thought possible. Enormous thanks are due to the stimulating community housed in the British School, particularly the scholars and artists in residence. A debt is also owed to Mrs Janet Gale for her continued funding of the Macquarie Gale Scholarship.

The genesis of this study and its metamorphosis could occur only with the sage advice of my doctoral supervisors, Professor Samuel Lieu, Associate Professor Andrew Gillett and Dr Ken Sheedy, who each provided a complementary area of expertise and unflagging support. My research was funded by an Australian Postgraduate Award and supported by a generous travel allowance granted by Macquarie University. I got my first taste of numismatics as a fellow at the Australian Centre for Ancient Numismatic Studies and this Centre went on to form a home for my research. Thanks are due here to Dr Bill Gale and Janet Gale, not only for establishing the Centre, but providing the monetary support for research and training.

In 2007 I participated in the American Numismatic Society Summer School, where I did much of my research on Severus Alexander. The seminar and its participants taught me more than I can express, and so a hearty thanks to the ANS staff, guest lecturers and my fellow students, particularly to Professor Dr Bernhard Weisser, Dr Andrew Meadows, Rick Witschonke, and Dr Peter van Alfen, who continued to encourage me well after the seminar was over.

Thanks are also due to my parents, who have provided emotional, economic and culinary support over the years. Finally, I acknowledge the enormous debt this work owes to my fellow students, both at Macquarie and abroad, who have continually engaged and challenged me, and have provided support and friendship. Much of this thesis has been shaped by their intelligent questioning, and by their patience in listening to various numismatic problems and topics. This book is dedicated to them.

Abbreviations

Unless otherwise stated, all translations are those of the Loeb Classical Library. Ancient authors and their works are abbreviated according to the style laid out in the *Oxford Classical Dictionary*. Journals are abbreviated according to *L'Année Philologique*.

Since it is anticipated this work will have an audience without specialist numismatic training, I have attempted to be as clear as possible in referencing ancient coins. References to the *Roman Imperial Coinage* (*RIC*) or *Coins of the Roman Empire in the British Museum* (*BMCRE*) provide the relevant volume as well as the emperor concerned. References to the catalogue series *Greek Coins in the British Museum* (*BMC*) provide the standard name by which the volume is known, as well as the particular city concerned in parentheses. References to Gnecchi's *I Medaglioni Romani* (Gnecchi 1912) provide the volume number, followed by the page number and medal number. These conventions were deemed necessary since the work switches rapidly between emperors and cities, and it is hoped this system will keep confusion to a minimum.

Other abbreviations used frequently throughout are as follows:

ANS — American Numismatic Society

ANSMN — *American Numismatic Society Museum Notes.*

BMC — Poole, R. S. et al. (1873–1972). *A Catalogue of Greek Coins in the British Museum* (29 vols.). London.

Bull. Épigr. — *Bulletin épigraphique.*

BCTH — *Bulletin archéologique du Comité des travaux historiques et scientifiques.*

CHRB — *Coin Hoards from Roman Britain* (1975–). London.

Cohen — Cohen, H. (1880–1892). *Description historique des monnaies frappées sous l'Empire romain communément appelées médailles impériales* (8 vols.). Paris.

Crawford	Crawford, M. H. (1974). *Roman Republican Coinage* (2 vols.). Cambridge.
Emmett	Emmett, K. (2001). *Alexandrian Coins*. Lodi.
FMRD	*Die Fundmünzen der römischen Zeit in Deutschland* (1970–). Berlin.
FMRSlow	*Die Fundmünzen der römischen Zeit in Slowenien* (1980–). Berlin.
FMRÖ	*Die Fundmünzen der römischen Zeit in Österreich* (1970–). Vienna.
IRT	Reynolds, J. M. & Ward Perkins, J. B. (eds.) (1952). The *Inscriptions of Roman Tripolitania*. Rome.
IvE	Wankel, H., ed. (1979–1984). *Die Inschriften von Ephesos* (8 vols.). Bonn.
LCL	Loeb Classical Library
Mionnet	Mionnet, T. E. (1806–37). *Description de medailles antiques, grecques et romaines, avec leur degré de rarité et leur estimation* (16 vols.). Paris.
Mouchmov	Mouchmov, N. A. (1912). *Ancient Coins of the Balkan Peninsula and the Coins of the Russian Czars*. Sofia.
PL	*Patrologia Latina*.
RIB	Collingwood, R. G. and Wright, R. P. (1965–). *The Roman Inscriptions of Britain*. Oxford.
RIU	Barkóczi, L. (ed.) *Die römischen Inschriften Ungarns*. (1972–1991). Amsterdam and Budapest.
RMRVe	*Ritrovamenti Monetali di età Romana nel Veneto* (2006–). Padua.
RPC	*Roman Provincial Coinage* (1992–). London.
SIRIS	Vidmann, L. (1969). *Sylloge inscriptionum religionis Isiacae et Sarapiacae*. Berlin.
SNG	*Sylloge Nummorum Graecorum* (1931–).
Strack	Strack, P. L. (1931–1937). *Untersuchungen zur römischen Reichsprägung des zweiten Jahrhunderts* (3 vols.). Stuttgart.
TM	*Trésors Monétaires* (1979–). Paris.
Varbanov	Varbanov, I. (2005–2007). *Greek Imperial Coins and Their Values* (3 vols.). Bourgas.

1 Introduction

After the murder of the emperor Pertinax in AD 193, Septimius Severus was proclaimed ruler of the Roman Empire. The rise to power of this Pannonian military commander, who had been born in Lepcis Magna in North Africa, heralded the beginning of a dynasty that would last until AD 235. In AD 194, a year after Severus assumed power, a coin was struck for the new emperor showing Liber Pater and Hercules with the accompanying legend *DIS AVSPICIB* ('under divine auspices', Figure 1).[1]

The character of imperial rule for the next forty-one years had been announced: the Severan emperors would rule with the support of deities whose cultic centres lay both in Rome and in the provinces of the empire. The marked Lepcitanian imagery of this coin type (Liber Pater paired with Hercules) marks the beginning of an era in which local provincial cults would come to have a close association with the princeps. Septimius Severus and the succeeding members of the Severan dynasty would all emphasise a special connection with the divine. The form this connection took was unique to each emperor and his particular circumstances, a reflection of the potential for each emperor to shape his own image within wider imperial ideology.

The visual expression of one's *patria* (native city) was not unusual. Republican moneyers had often placed specific deities on their coinage as an expression of their identity and heritage. For example, Roman monetary officials (*monetales*) from Tusculum displayed imagery recalling the regional cult of the Dioscuri and those from Lanuvium placed the local goddess Juno Sospita on their coinage.[2] This practice continued under the empire: Spanish-born Trajan and Hadrian included images of the local cult of Hercules Gaditanus on their coinage.[3] Juno Sospita appears on the coinage of the Lanuvium-born Antoninus Pius.[4] Clodius Albinus had the Hadrumentine

[1] *RIC* IV.1 *Septimius Severus* 25, 31, 661, 666, 669. [2] Crawford 307/1, 412/1.

[3] *RIC* II *Trajan* 49–51; *BMCRE* III *Trajan* lxvii–lxviii, 56–9, 81–93, 1058–9; *RIC* II *Hadrian* 56–8, 125. On the temple of Hercules Gaditanus in Spain see Mierse 2004: 545–75.

[4] *RIC* III *Antoninus Pius* 608; *BMCRE* IV *Antoninus Pius* p. 210*.

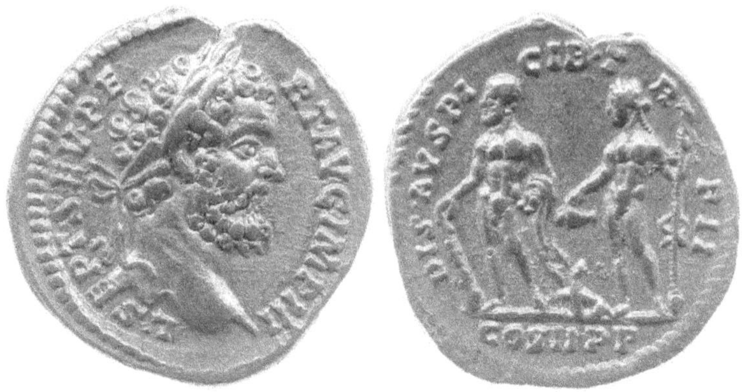

Figure 1: Aureus of Septimius Severus with Liber Pater and Hercules and the legend DIS AVSPICIB TR P II COS II P P.

deity Baal Hammon displayed on his coinage.[5] The existence of this practice under the Severans can thus be seen as the continuation of a wider tradition.

The Severan dynasty forms a period of transition between the ideology of virtue that characterised emperors who ruled the 'Golden Age' of the second century, and the divine *comes* or companions increasingly associated with rulers from the second half of the third century.[6] The shift in the articulation of the emperor's power during these periods is best illustrated by a comparison of the reverse types of each emperor's coinage. Whether the emperor was responsible for the images on his coinage or not (an issue discussed in the following chapter), coin types nonetheless reflect the ideology of rule in a particular period. Unlike modern day coinage, the images which graced the reverse or 'tails' of an emperor's coinage changed to reflect current ideologies and situations, forming part of a wider monumental dialogue. But while an imperial arch or sculptural monument may have been erected in Rome every few years (if that), imperial coinage was issued by the mint *several times a year*. In a large number of instances these coins are dated to a specific year, or even to a period of a few months. This allows the historian to place the imagery within specific political, martial or social contexts, and allows us to trace the shifting emphases of ideology over the course of a year, or over several years. The information offered by numismatic evidence can thus provide a more nuanced picture than that provided by other media.

[5] *RIC* II *Hadrian* 10 (where the figure is identified as Saeculum Frugiferum); Birley 1988: 169; Xella 1991: 177.

[6] The expression *comes* first appears under Commodus, but becomes more frequent from the reign of Gallienus. See Nock 1972: 653–75, and de Blois 2006: 274–5.

That the Roman mint consistently released coinage bearing official imagery several times a year, every year, means that coinage forms an ideal medium to study the image of the princeps from a long-term perspective. Few other sources offer such research possibilities: the same genre (coinage) was utilised again and again under each emperor (however short-lived), and the record of these coins in the present day is impressive (one may say it is almost complete). Textual evidence carries with it the inevitable perspectives of individual authors, and its survival rate is patchy at best. Epigraphic evidence comes closer to the numismatic record in terms of quantity, but the damage suffered by many inscriptions leaves us reliant on restorations and speculations in many cases. Papyrological evidence is inevitably weighted towards those areas where it is best preserved, like Egypt. And here the extremely good survival rate of numismatic material must be emphasised – coins buried in hoards, deposited in votive contexts or in other contexts survive in enormous numbers in the present day. Even emperors who suffered *damnatio memoriae* are well represented within the numismatic record, offering a rare glimpse of the public image of these rulers before it was intentionally obliterated. Numismatic evidence survives in bulk, and its potential has yet to be fully exploited.

Alongside the imperial coinage issued under the authority of the emperor, smaller cities in the east of the empire produced their own coinages, albeit on a more sporadic basis. But here the numismatic evidence offers a glimpse of the cultures, ideologies and festivals of smaller cities as they negotiated their place in the changing Roman empire. In many instances coins remain our only evidence for the celebration of civic festivals and the adoption of emperor cults or *neokoroi*. Provincial coinage also offers a glimpse into how the public face of the emperor was negotiated at a local level. With provincial coinage we also have the possibility of studying a single medium (coinage) across a wide geographical and chronological time span.

The enormous scale on which Roman imperial coinage was produced and the large quantities that survive to the modern day enable us to undertake something rarely possible with other ancient media: a quantification of ideology. Within the discipline of ancient history, a single coin type is often cited as evidence for a particular event or ideology. But rarely do we pause to consider just how common this coin was in antiquity, and how many people might actually have seen it. Different coin types (and their associated imagery) were produced in different quantities in the ancient world, and before we can discuss the impact of a particular image we need to know whether this imagery flooded the marketplace, or whether it was specifically designed and produced in small numbers to be given as gifts to elite groups.

What coin types were common in each year, and why? Although a particular coin might be relevant to a particular historical event, this coin was just one amongst thousands circulating throughout the Roman world. In view of this broader context, we should consider what image was conveyed by an emperor's coinage in its *entirety*: what general impression would users have obtained from the coins they received? Here the reading of the numismatic evidence (in its entirety) in conjunction with other textual and archaeological sources can lead us to new conclusions. Why was a coin type discontinued, or why did it suddenly become less popular? Can we trace a shift in coin imagery between emperors, and what does this suggest about the changing public image of the Roman ruler? We can begin to answer these questions by examining numismatic iconography from a quantitative perspective.

Quantification, identifying in what numbers different numismatic types were produced, provides us with a more nuanced perspective of the imperial image, and offers the opportunity for long-term comparisons.[7] Such a perspective is not yet offered by most numismatic handbooks, which list coin types with little regard for (or an inaccurate representation of) quantity. Consequently, the impression gained from flicking through the pages of the *Roman Imperial Coinage* can be very different to the reality of imagery and ideology in the empire.

The potential of numismatic evidence for the study of ancient history can only be realised if the material is reintegrated into the discipline and the wider material culture of the Roman empire.[8] Too often numismatic imagery is used to 'illustrate' a historical work (for example by supplying a nice image of an otherwise obscure emperor) without its true informative potential being acknowledged, or the wider context of its production mentioned (just how common *was* this image?). Likewise numismatic works are often somewhat removed from the wider material culture of the Roman empire. This book seeks to overcome many of these barriers, and demonstrates what can be achieved if coinage, viewed as a whole, is studied in conjunction with the textual and archaeological data available.

The Romans themselves viewed coinage as a communicative tool, similar to arches, imperial letters and other monumental architecture. This is clearly demonstrated by the imperial practice of 'audience targeting': the production of a particular coin series, with a particular message, sent to a particular

[7] Already highlighted by Noreña 2001: 146–68.

[8] A similar problem is encountered in the separation of numismatics from archaeology. See Kemmers and Myrberg 2011: 97–108.

audience (for example, coins bearing ideologies of military prowess and victory were sent to Roman camps, and coins advertising the benefits of Pax sent to civilian settlements).[9] As one of many imperial communicative tools, numismatic evidence can inform sculptural and architectural remains, and wider material culture can clarify numismatic imagery.

The reason that coins survive in such quantity and provide such a full record is that often coins were buried in hoards that remained hidden until the modern day. Buried at a particular moment in time, these hoards provide a glimpse of coin circulation at a particular period, and allow us to gauge how frequent different coin types actually were. A coin type that occurs only once in a hoard in Britain, for example, must be treated very differently to a coin type that is found in quantity in hoards all over the empire. By examining these hoards as evidence, we can see which images were employed more frequently than others, and we can begin to gain a better idea of the *overall* numismatic image produced by an emperor. Then we can contextualise this through comparison with other emperors, and gradually long- and short-term shifts in imperial ideology can be identified. This approach is discussed more fully in the following chapter.

We return to the statement that the Severan dynasty saw a shift in ideology from the 'Golden Age' of the Antonines to a dynasty based more on the idea of divine support. This shift can be identified through a quantitative comparison of the reverse types employed by the imperial mint. For a quick demonstration, the Reka-Devnia coin hoard forms an excellent sample. Buried some time after AD 251 in Marcianopolis (modern day Bulgaria), the hoard contains more than 80,000 silver coins from a variety of emperors.[10] Using the Reka-Devnia hoard we can trace changes in the representation of the emperor on Roman currency. For Trajan, Hadrian, Antoninus Pius, Marcus Aurelius and Commodus, personifications and virtues constitute a substantial part of the emperor's reverse types (52%, 61%, 67%, 56% and 60% respectively, Appendix 1, Figures 85–9). These

9 The best demonstration of this is Kemmers 2006.

10 The Reka-Devnia hoard provides a large sample that largely reflects the composition of other hoards. This can be illustrated by an overview of the coinage of the Severan dynasty. The composition of Severan coinage as it is found in the Reka-Devnia hoard compares favourably to the composition of other hoards of smaller size. For example, 18% of the reverse types of Septimius Severus' silver coinage in the Reka-Devnia hoard display deities, 25% portray military themes, 39% personifications and virtues, while 13% display other images. Smaller hoards consulted in the course of this research suggest 22% of Severus' reverse types displayed images of deities, 25% had military themes, 33% portrayed personifications and virtues and 20% displayed other types. A similarly rough correlation can also be seen for the other Severan emperors. The date of the hoard is given by the coins of Decius found in the sample, though Metcalf 2002: 145–50 suggests a more accurate date may be the reign of Gordian III.

types communicate the idea of a virtuous ruler whose reign brought manifold blessings to Rome and the empire. By contrast, deities had a smaller role in the emperor's numismatic image, constituting 12%, 4%, 13%, 16% and 19% respectively (Appendix 1, Figures 85–9). If we compare these ratios to those present under the Severan emperors, we can see a greater emphasis on the divine, perhaps already heralded on Commodus' coinage. Indeed, Commodus' public image may be better understood within the context of the Severan period. Deities constitute 18% of Severus' silver reverse types, 73% of Caracalla's types while he was sole emperor, 36% of Elagabalus' types and 34% of the silver coinage of Severus Alexander (Appendix 1, Figures 90–3). Through this quick comparison we can quantify the shifting ideology associated with the emperor on coinage: the power wielded by the princeps was increasingly expressed in terms of divine support and divine sanction.[11] This is not to suggest that the divine played no role in the articulation of power in the second century, or that virtues had no role in the third. But the results suggest a development in imperial ideology, in the ways in which virtues and deities were used in the construction of the image of the emperor and his power. The large proportion of personifications under Elagabalus and Severus Alexander highlights the fact that imperial virtues retained a central role in the conceptualisation of the emperor in the Severan period, but the large proportion of types relating to the divine highlights changes to the dialogue of power.

The second half of the third century following the death of Severus Alexander sees a sharper definition of this divine support. Though we should not classify this as a simple linear development, coinage in this period increasingly casts deities as the companions or *comites* of the emperor.[12] Fears' study of this phenomenon has suggested that the Persian threat (particularly the capture of Valerian by the Persians in AD 260), in conjunction with the failure of emperors in the later third century to establish a dynasty, meant that divine election and divine support became key in the legitimisation of power.[13] The use of the divine in the Severan period can be seen as a precursor to the more clearly articulated relationship between the emperor and the gods in late antiquity. Septimius Severus, like many emperors in the later third century, came to power through war and thus could not claim an ancestral right to the throne. The strong assertion of divine support under Severus and his successors was a reaction to this circumstance, and is a key phase in the development of imperial ideology.

[11] This conclusion is similar to that reached by Manders 2008: 35–6.

[12] de Blois 2006: 274; Hedlund 2008: 213; Nock 1972: 653–75; Possenti 1995: 141–70; Turcan 1978: 1022–5.

[13] Fears 1977: 279–305.

2 Contextualising a 'foreign' dynasty

> My belief that his origin mattered has led me to call the story of his life *The African Emperor.*[1]

The title of Birley's biography of Septimius Severus highlights an ever-present factor in many modern studies of the Severan emperors: their provincial origins. The provincial origins of this dynasty, particularly Septimius Severus, have shaped modern ideas about Severan culture, Severan politics and Severan religion.[2] Much of this discourse tells us more about the modern colonial and postcolonial worlds than about the Roman empire in the third century. The modern political and cultural contexts that have informed our ideas surrounding the identity of one Severan emperor, Septimius Severus, are detailed below. This is followed by an introduction to the ancient material of the Severan period and the ways in which it can be approached.

Interest in the cultural identities of the Severan emperors has not remained confined to the academic world. In 1963 a member of the US Congress mentioned the origins of Septimius Severus during a debate on the capacity of various countries containing 'African' populations (Haiti, Liberia and Ethiopia) for self-government.

> Mr. Speaker, I must take issue with a colleague of mine in the 88th Congress in the statement attributed to him that the Africans had never shown any ability to build and govern. I would suggest to him that when his ancestors and my ancestors may have been wandering around in the darkness, reaching out for a better life, that an African was Emperor of Rome and according to John Gunther[3] was of Negro blood.[4]

Congressman O'Hara's comments on this occasion sent the opposing party scuttling towards their history books in an attempt to defend their beleaguered colleague. Two weeks later came the declaration that there was

[1] Birley 1988: xi. [2] For example, Hammond 1940: 137–73 and Haywood 1940: 175–85.

[3] John Gunther was a journalist and author of popular books, notably an *Inside* series of continental surveys.

[4] Comments of Mr O'Hara of Illinois, *Proceedings of the 88th Congress of the United States of America*, page 11,498.

'no indication that he [Severus] was a black man', and Gibbon was triumphantly produced to show that Septimius, in any case, was a poor ruler.[5] This strange chapter in US politics highlights the fact that questions of identity in the ancient world remain loaded with modern concerns.[6] More than fifty years after this incident the election of Barack Obama to the US presidency revived the 'African' debate surrounding Septimius Severus after an eminent classicist drew a parallel between the two.[7] The release of the song '*Barack Obama Is Septimius Severus: Change You Can Believe In*' by the Ghanian artist Heru once again casts Septimius as a 'black' emperor of Rome.

During a trip to Italy in 2009, the Libyan leader Muammar Al-Gaddafi took advantage of his presence in Rome to claim descent from Severus, the 'Libyan' emperor.[8] Gaddafi's statement takes on a particular irony when one considers the relationship between Italy and Libya in the modern era. During the Italian occupation of Tripoli, archaeology and Roman history played an important ideological role, highlighting the connectedness of the two regions. The excavation (or 'liberation') of the archaeological remains of the area, particularly the city of Lepcis Magna, was one of many ways in which the Italians sought to bring their new conquest under control. In a 1926 work detailing to the Italian people the work done in Tripolitania under the Governor Count Volpi, archaeological excavations are summarised under the larger heading *La Conquista Morale*.[9] As part of the renovation of the Piazza Castello area (a region that formed the civic and cultural centre of Italian Tripolitania), a bronze statue of Septimius Severus was erected at the entrance to the old city, a reminder of Italy and Libya's common heritage and Rome's imperial mission.[10] This statue is now placed at the entrance to the archaeological area of Lepcis Magna, and features on postcards.[11] The statue also features in the political pieces of the Libyan cartoonist

[5] Comments of Mr Waggonner of Louisiana, *Proceedings of the 88th Congress of the United States of America*, page 12,198, quoting Gibbon: 'He promised only to betray; he flattered only to ruin; and however he might occasionally bind himself by oaths and treaties, his conscience, obsequious to his interest, always released him from inconvenient obligation.'

[6] The same postcolonial climate has given rise to other Afrocentric ideas about the ancient world, notably Bernal 1987–2006, and the debate *Black Athena* has created. On this see Bernal 2001; Howe 1999; Keita 2000: 337–45; Lefkowitz 1996; and Lefkowitz and Maclean Rogers 1996.

[7] www.timesonline.typepad.com/dons_life/2008/11/barack-obama–.html.

[8] www.news.bbc.co.uk/2/hi/programmes/from_our_own_correspondent/8098681.stm.

[9] Piccioli 1926: 337–52. The work comments that Lepcis Magna is distinguished above all other African cities by a single event: the birth of the 'grande Imperatore romano: Settimio Severo' (p. 345). Severus is described as a 'barbarico' (p. 345) and 'bruno' (p. 346).

[10] von Henneberg 1994: 141. [11] Munzi 2001: 129.

Muhammad az-Zwâwî: in one such piece Severus writes on the base of his statue 'I am an Arab and a Muslim.'[12]

The French occupation of Algeria also led to interest in Roman North Africa. Having connected their own origins to ancient Rome, the French saw themselves as saving and reclaiming a lost past, and believed themselves to be the 'rightful' owners of the region.[13] But while scholars in the colonial world stressed the 'Africanity' of Severus, those in the postcolonial world were more reluctant.[14] A notable example here is Marcel Benabou, an African scholar who reacted against French dominated scholarship by suggesting that people in Africa led a passive resistance to Roman conquest through local culture. In his *La résistance africaine à la romanisation*, Benabou argued that Septimius did not possess any African patriotism or partiality.[15]

In modern scholarship Septimius' African origins have been seen as a motivating force for the embellishment of Lepcis Magna, Carthage and other parts of Africa, as a reason behind an 'African' faction of politicians under his reign, and as a factor behind several of his building projects, notably the Septizodium.[16] However the area in which this perceived expression of non-Roman identity was considered especially prominent was in the religion of Severus and his successors.

> The elevation of the provincial Septimius Severus of Libyan birth to the imperial power brought to the fore a dynasty of non-Italians who wrought considerable changes in the facade of the principate by encouraging the development of customs drawn from their African and Oriental ancestry and experience. Nowhere is the change more marked than in the dynasty's religious proclivities.[17]

There is no denying the provincial origins of these emperors, yet examinations of their religious activities have lacked historical context and have been largely piecemeal. The last published monograph exploring religion during

[12] Munzi 2001: 130. [13] Lorcin 2002: 295–329.

[14] Reinforcing the idea that terms like 'Orientalism' formed a mechanism of cultural domination (Ghazoul 2004: 123–7). The idea of Severus as a 'traitor' to his own culture is also apparent in Heru's lyrics: 'Severus we had high hopes for you, every African man, woman and baby, but you became the metaphor of a weeping willow tree so shady, you went along with their brutality, you went along with their insanity, and disregard for non-Roman humanity, you rejected your own history, and adopted a Roman identity.'

[15] Benabou 1976: 166. For a discussion of the context of Benabou's work see Mattingly 1996: 49–69.

[16] Embellishment of Lepcis Magna: Babelon 1903: 157–74; Haywood 1940: 177. African politicians: Birley 1969: 271–80; Birley 1988: xi; Lo Cascio 2005: 137 (against which Barnes 1967: 87–107). Septizodium: Palmer 1978: 1117; Thomas 2007: 334.

[17] Palmer 1978: 1085–6.

the entire Severan dynasty (from Septimius to Severus Alexander) was published by the French Protestant theologian Jean Réville in 1886, entitled *La religion à Rome sous les Sévères*. Réville was the son of Albert Réville, founding president of the religious studies section in the École des hautes études at the Sorbonne, where Jean would later go on to become professor of patristic literature. The section was founded in the hope of pursuing *sciences religieuses*, a combination of science and theology pioneered by F. M. Müller and C. P. Tiele.[18] Strict, 'scientific' procedures were employed to search for evidence of a natural human religion, a concept connected to theological concerns of French Protestantism at the time. Mankind was believed to possess a 'natural', primordial monotheistic revelation that was lost after the fall from Paradise.[19] Jean Réville, like his father, believed strongly in this concept, arguing that mankind had an innate religious mental faculty that could not be quashed.[20] This has a strong bearing on his work on the Severans, whom he studied in the hope of tracing the rise of Christianity.

Réville saw a religious renaissance in third century Rome, born of man's desire and demand for religion, a renaissance that by its very existence proved man could not exist without belief.[21] In Réville's interpretation of the third century, the Romans rebelled from the skepticism of earlier periods and demanded the reinstitution of religious belief.[22] The seeming 'Neopythagorean reform' witnessed in the publication of Philostratus' *Life of Apollonius of Tyana*, a perceived increase of 'orientalism' in Roman religion (culminating under Elagabalus), and an alleged increase in syncretism (culminating under Severus Alexander) were all believed by Réville to have contributed to a society in which paganism and Christianity became so similar that one could be mistaken for the other.[23] From this confusion, according to Réville, Christianity emerged triumphant. *La religion à Rome sous les Sévères* later influenced Cumont and other scholars working on the Severan dynasty.[24] Réville's work can only be assessed within the boundaries of nineteenth-century scholarship: its dependence on French theological debates, its belief in the inevitable rise of Christianity, and its uncritical acceptance of passages from the *Historia Augusta* mean that it can be of little use outside the realm of historiography.

18 Strenski 2002: 161–76. 19 Strenski 2002: 157. 20 Strenski 2002: 161.
21 Réville 1886: 18. 22 Réville 1886: 17.
23 Réville 1886: 294. See also the review of the book, Gardner 1886: 553.
24 Cumont 1911: 199; Scheid 1987: 312. For examples of the impact of Réville in later Severan studies see (by way of example) Hijmans 1996: 121–2; Mader 2005: 171; McCann 1968: 58; Pietrzykowski 1986: 1823; Platnauer 1965: 143 n.5; Turcan 1997: 154–5.

Recent work done on the transmission of imperial ideology through architectural, archaeological, and literary material provides a new basis for the examination of the Severan dynasty. Like rulers and leaders before them, the Severans sought to legitimise their power and to justify their rule. Divine ideology formed an important aspect of this, and by connecting themselves with the gods the Severans continued a tradition that had been developing since the Roman Republic.

Power and divine support in the Roman world

Rather than constituting an 'outside' force, the use of divine support by the Severan emperors continued a well-trodden Roman tradition. In the Roman world deities, divine qualities, omens and prodigies were constantly employed and re-deployed in contests for power and legitimacy. This dialogue manifested itself in the erection of temples, on coins, in historical works and other material, and its output only grew in size as individuals gained more power and more resources. Under the empire, the enormous resources held by the princeps meant that this phenomenon reached new heights.

Clark's examination of divine qualities under the Republic traces the increasing claim to the divine by individuals in this period. Booty from the Samnite Wars (343–290 BC) funded some of the first temples erected on the initiative of individuals (for example, Brutus' temple to Salus on the Quirinal).[25] The rôle of these temples and other manifestations of divine support in the contest for power and status in the Republican period are highlighted by the activities of Marius and Sulla. During the Cimbric campaign (102/101 BC), Marius vowed a temple to Honos and Virtus, which he then built in Rome near the forum (and possibly also near his own house).[26] The victory over the Cimbri, however, was contested, and Marius' rival general Catulus countered Marius' creation with a temple to Fortuna.[27]

Marius' contemporary Sulla also employed divine support to communicate and justify his eminence. The omens, oracles, prodigies, dreams and other phenomena that accompany the portrayal of Sulla and his activities in the ancient literature foreshadow the *omina imperii* (omens of power) that Dio would later publish concerning the rise of Septimius Severus.[28] Plutarch records that Sulla's trophies in Greece were inscribed with the names of

[25] Clark 2007: 49–52. [26] Clark 2007: 123–6. [27] Clark 2007: 126–30.

[28] On omens under Sulla, many of which were likely to have been published in his memoirs, see Balsdon 1951: 2; Ramage 1991: 95–102; and Sumi 2002: 414.

Mars, Victory and Venus, since he believed his victory in war was as much due to good fortune as to military skill and strength.[29] Sulla associated himself with Fortuna and emphasised his close relationship with Aphrodite, indicated by his two epithets *Felix* and *Epaphroditus*.[30] For a period Sulla also had a military mint under his control, and thus was also able to use coinage to express his divine favour. Coins were struck with a Venus portrait accompanied by cupid on the obverse, imagery juxtaposed with the legend L SVLLA.[31] The reliefs excavated from Sant'Omobono in Rome hint at the communication of this ideology through larger monuments.[32] Sulla rebuilt the Temple of Hercules Custos in Rome, as well as other Herculean shrines outside the city (Plutarch reports that Sulla gave a tenth of his booty to Hercules).[33] In order to legitimise his activities, Sulla publicly emphasised his favour with the gods and higher powers.

Displays of divine support grew as the resources and power of individual Roman generals grew under Julius Caesar and Pompey. Pompey continued Sulla's patronage of Hercules: he probably dedicated a temple to Hercules Invictus that became known as the *aedes Herculis Pompeiani*.[34] He also highlighted his connection to Sulla's other patroness by incorporating a temple to Venus Victrix in his new theatre.[35] Julius Caesar also proclaimed the special support of Venus by claiming descent from Aeneas and by constructing a temple to Venus Genetrix in the Julian Forum.[36] The rôle of Venus in articulating the struggle for power between Caesar and Pompey is reflected in accounts of the battle of Pharsalus. Both leaders promised dedications to Venus Victrix if successful, and Plutarch goes as far as to comment that Pompey feared Caesar's superior claim to the goddess.[37] The political and military contest for supremacy was also played out in a spatial context with the erection of buildings and other structures, and was recorded on the coinages of the competing generals. Caesar's coinage highlighted his connection to Venus and Aeneas (though notably these coins were not struck until after the defeat of Pompey). The supporters of Pompey struck coinage that connected the general to both Venus and Hercules.[38]

After Caesar's death, the new power brokers also articulated and negotiated their claims for power through divine ideology. Pompey's son Sextus

[29] Plut. *Sull.* 19.5. [30] Plut. *Sull.* 34.1–3; Santangelo 2007b: 204–7.
[31] Crawford 359/1–2; Ramage 1991: 102; Santangelo 2007b: 204. [32] Ramage 1991: 112–13.
[33] Plut. *Sull.* 35.1; Ramage 1991: 113–14. [34] Rawson 1970: 30.
[35] Rawson 1970: 30–6; Santangelo 2007a: 228. [36] Suetonius, *Div. Iul.* 6.
[37] Plut. *Pomp.* 68.2, App. *BC.* 2.10.6.
[38] Caesar: Crawford 458/1, 463/1, 463/3, 463/5, 463/6, 468/1, 468/2. Pompey: Crawford 424/1, 426/3, 426/4a. See discussion in Crawford 1974: 733–44.

advertised a particular connection to Neptune, going so far as to align his dead father with the god.[39] Antony highlighted his connection with Dionysus, and Octavian touted the special support of Apollo.[40] This last echoes the claims of Caesar's assassins, Cassius and Brutus, who communicated the restored *libertas* of the Republic after Caesar's death through an allusion to Apollo, from whom the oracle had been received to expel the Tarquin kings from Rome.[41]

Thus the competing claims for power and status in the Republic were often voiced and contested through claims of divine support and affiliation. With the creation of the Empire under Augustus, the ability of one individual to proclaim a connection with the divine reached a new level. Augustus' temple to Apollo on the Palatine, intricately connected to his own house, echoes (with some differences) the earlier juxtaposition of temple and residence seen under Pompey, Caesar and perhaps also Marius.[42] This layout reappears under the emperor Elagabalus. After the settlement of 27 BC, the dialogue of divine ideology shifted. Instead of forming part of a wider contest for superiority and status amongst the Roman élite, divine support was used to legitimise the rule of one man. Divine support indicated that the gods wanted Augustus to rule as emperor, and divine support became a sphere in which others could discuss and negotiate this new power.[43] Though Augustus emphasised his connection with Apollo, he also claimed the support of other deities in different contexts. A particular connection to Mars Ultor, for example, was monumentalised through the placement of a temple to the god in Augustus' forum. The temple to Mars Ultor communicated Augustus' divine support in the war against Caesar's assassins and celebrated the recovery of the Parthian standards from the east. In this shifting use of divine support (highlighting a strong connection to Apollo, but also underscoring the support of other deities when appropriate) Augustus formed a precedent for later rulers, including the Severans.

Just as each Severan emperor would communicate a particular brand of divine support, so too did the divine ideology of earlier emperors shift and change according to circumstance and personal preference. One of the better examples of the way an individual princeps could influence the image of the emperor is provided by the reign of Domitian. Dio records

[39] Crawford 511/3a; Pollini 1990: 340; Zarrow 2003: 123–35. On the continuing claims to divine qualities in this period see Clark 2007: 233–43.

[40] Lange 2009: 39–45. [41] Hollstein 1994: 113–33.

[42] Clark 2007: 240, 265. For Augustus and his ideology see Zanker 1988.

[43] On the use of Apollo in the literature of this period see most recently Miller 2009.

that Domitian honoured Minerva above all the gods; the emperor's coinage shows little else.[44] The emperor's new forum, completed by Nerva, contained a temple to Minerva.[45] There are hints that such exclusive patronage of one deity was not looked upon favourably in the Roman world: Minerva is noticeably absent from the coinage of Domitian's successors.[46] No Severan emperor, even Elagabalus, was so exclusive in his devotion. But Domitian illustrates the capacity for expressions of religious individuality within the office of the principate. This is seen again from AD 190 with Commodus' alignment with the god Hercules, a new development in divine authority and ideology.[47] No Severan emperor went to such lengths. In the adoption of an individualised ideology of divine support, the Severan emperors were following Roman precedent.

Under the Severans the role of the divine seems to take on a greater visual presence, heralding the divine *comes* of late antiquity. The discourse of divine support was negotiated and communicated in a variety of media: in public buildings, on coinage, in literature and other materials. From the Republican period onwards the material manifestation of divine ideology was generated not only by Roman leaders, but also by their supporters and detractors. The discourse of divine support was not static, but shifted and changed according to context. For example, Sulla underscored his connection with Venus while dealing with the Greek-speaking East, but emphasised his connection to Fortuna in interactions that took place in the West.[48] Similar phenomena occur under the Severans, but the period also saw development and innovation. This will be discussed more fully in the following chapters.

Writing Severan history: Cassius Dio, Herodian and the *Historia Augusta*

There are three main ancient historical accounts of the Severan period, though a large number of other literary works were produced during the dynasty.[49] Two historical works were produced by Greek authors: Cassius Dio and Herodian. The other main textual source is the biographies of the Severan emperors contained within the *Historia Augusta*. All three of these texts are interdependent: it is evident that Herodian was reliant on Dio for at

[44] Dio 68.1.2; Alföldi 1999: 44–5; Carradice 1998: 112; Scott 1936: 167. [45] D'Ambra 1993.
[46] Ramage 1989: 649. [47] Hekster 2002: 103–11. [48] Santangelo 2007b: 204–7.
[49] On the literary output of the Severan dynasty see Sidebottom 2007: 52–82.

least some of his account, and the *Historia Augusta* knew of Herodian's work, going so far as to cite the author by name.[50] The precise relationship between all these works, however, remains controversial, subject to the ebb and flow of *Quellenforschung*.

Dio's *Roman History* for the Severan period survives in epitome, except for a small section covering the period AD 217/18. Dio himself tells us that he initially wrote about the omens that accompanied Severus' rise to power, then a history of Severus' civil wars and only later turned to writing a complete Roman history.[51] Dio writes that it was a divine spirit appearing to him in a dream which commanded he expand his modest work into a larger history.[52] In what year Dio made this decision is not known, but it is likely to have been after the death of Severus in AD 211.[53] The large majority of Dio's history on the Severan period was probably written under Severus Alexander.[54]

A senator from Nicaea in Bithynia, Dio was consul twice during his career, the second time holding the office with the emperor Severus Alexander.[55] It is at this high point of his own life that he ends his work.[56] It is clear that some of his earlier work on the omens of Severus' rule (*omina imperii*) is present within his account of Severus' reign. Selections from this laudatory pamphlet sit somewhat uncomfortably with Dio's overall narrative of this period (though, of course, it is difficult to discern the precise tone of Dio from an epitome).[57] Dio records the signs that indicated Severus' rise to power (75.3.1–3), but also records actions of Severus that were not to his liking (75.2.1–6). The idea of duplicity is present throughout the epitome of Dio's account of Severus. The author records that all pretended to support the emperor in spite of their real feelings (76.8.5). Presumably Dio must count himself among this number, since he wrote a laudatory pamphlet but later included several negative assessments of Severus in his *History*.

50 On the level of Herodian's dependence on Dio see Bowersock 1975: 229–36; Icks 2008a: 143; Kolb 1972; Kolb 1995: 179–91; Roos 1915: 191–202; Rubin 1980: 85–92; Scheithauer 1990: 335–6; Sidebottom 1998: 2781–92; Sidebottom 2007: 78–91; and Zimmermann 1999b. For the dependence of the *Historia Augusta* on Herodian see Barnes 1970: 30; Bertrand-Dagenbach 1990: 136; Ferrero 1999: 191–216; and Kolb 1976: 143–52. Kolb also argued that the *Historia Augusta* knew of Dio, though this is less certain, since the author never mentions Dio directly as a source. For criticism of Kolb see Barnes 1975: 368–73; Bowersock 1975: 229–36; Rubin 1980: 90–130.

51 Dio 73.23.1; Millar 1964: 29.

52 Dio 73.23.2. Modern discussions of Dio's history are numerous. See in particular Aalders 1986: 282–304; Barnes 1984: 240–54; Hammond 1932: 88–102; Millar 1964; Millar 2004: 17–40; Moscovich 2004: 356–68; Rubin 1980; Schmidt 1997: 2591–649; and Ameling 1997: 2482–96.

53 Barnes 1984: 252.

54 Barnes 1984: 240–54; Millar 2004: 31; Moscovich 2004: 356.

55 Dio 80.2.1; Barnes 1984: 253.

56 Bowersock 1985: 711.

57 Barnes 1984: 253.

Further duplicity is found in the text concerning Severus' praetorian prefect Plautianus. Dio states that Plautianus knew the secrets of the entire empire although no one knew his (76.14.4–5, 76.15.1–2), and that during the trial of Constans Severus confirmed that no harm would come to Plautianus although he would be dead within the year (76.16.2–4). Antoninus uses duplicity to destroy Plautianus (77.3.1–4), and then finally begins to plot against Severus (77.14.1–7). In spite of this, the summary of the reign preserved at the end of Dio's account of Severus is positive.[58]

By contrast, Dio's epitome presents an unashamedly hostile vision of Caracalla.[59] The difference between outward presentation and private thought continues as a theme: Antoninus and Geta pretend to love each other, but in reality plot against each other (78.1.4), Caracalla pretends to support his tutor Clio while plotting his death (78.4.2–5.1), and the emperor sends people to unhealthy climates, ostensibly to honour them, but actually causing their deaths (78.11.6–7). Caracalla tricks foreign kings (78.12.1–2), claims to be pious while causing bloodshed (78.16.1), and destroys the population of Alexandria in spite of professing affection for them (78.22.1). Dio flags this theme at several points throughout his account: he notes that Caracalla learnt the great penalty that is incurred when one practises deceit upon friends (78.12.2), and later observes that liars and deceivers are never believed, even if they occasionally tell the truth (78.16.8).

Dio was absent from Rome during the majority of Elagabalus' rule, having been sent by Macrinus to be curator of Pergamum and Smyrna in AD 218.[60] As a result, his account of Elagabalus contains a series of anecdotes grouped by subject to demonstrate to the reader the character faults of the emperor.[61] Dio was also out of Rome during the reign of Severus Alexander, under whose rule his history ends.[62] He provides a potted summary of events up until the Persian War, and the epitome of his work ends with Dio recording his decision to return to his home in Bithynia.

Little is known about the life and career of the other major historian of this period, Herodian. His own work informs us that he lived outside Rome and had 'some part in the imperial service'.[63] Current consensus places the historian in Western Asia Minor, but there is little evidence to make this

[58] Dio 77.17.1–4; Millar 1964: 139. [59] Millar 1964: 138, 151. [60] Millar 1964: 120.
[61] Millar 1964: 169. [62] Dio 80.1.1–3.
[63] Hdn. 1.2.5, 2.11.8. As with Dio, scholarship on Herodian is extensive, though much of it focuses on his sources rather than on the work itself. See in particular Alföldi 1971: 204–33; Alföldy 1974: 89–112; Càssola 1968; de Blois 2003: 148–56; Marasco 1998: 2837–927; Polley 2003: 203–8; Sidebottom 1997: 271–6; Sidebottom 1998: 2775–836; Sidebottom 2007: 74–81; Whittaker in the introduction to the Loeb translation; Widmer 1967; and Zimmermann 1999a: 119–43.

hypothesis conclusive.[64] The date when Herodian wrote his work is ultimately unknown. His history begins with the reign of Marcus Aurelius and ends with Gordian III, a period that Herodian describes as covering his own lifetime.[65] Since it was not common practice to write a history of the current emperor, and Herodian does not present a favourable view of the Gordians, or of young emperors in general, scholars have placed the work after the reign of Gordian III, with suggestions ranging from the reign of Philip to that of Decius.[66] Traditionally, scholars have taken Herodian's claim to be describing events in his own lifetime at face value. But it is clear that Herodian's description of Commodus' participation in gladiatorial games is derived from Dio's account, and this brings Herodian's claim to be a contemporary of this event into question.[67] Sidebottom used this fact to suggest that Herodian may not have been completely honest about his claim to have seen the games and suggested that the work might even have been composed after the reign of Decius, perhaps under Gallienus.[68] Herodian's fictive description of the plan of Caracalla and Geta to divide the empire (4.3.5–6), the earliest mention of such an idea, echoes the territorial divisions of Valerian and Gallienus and suggests a date after AD 254.[69] Whatever the date of composition, the mistakes and inconsistencies within the text suggest that Herodian's history remained unrevised and unfinished.[70]

The reliance of Herodian on Dio for the account of Commodus' gladiatorial games places his value as an independent source in doubt. Zimmermann has resuscitated the thesis of Kolb, who argued that Dio formed the main source (the *Hauptquelle*) of Herodian's account.[71] There is no denying that Herodian knew of Dio's *History*: Herodian's criticism of authors who 'have made the life of Severus the theme of their entire work, have given detailed treatments of the stages of his march, his speeches at each city, the frequent manifestations that were interpreted as signs of divine providence', and 'the topography of each place' can be read as a sly reference to Dio and his work.[72] And yet this does not automatically mean that Herodian derived the majority of his information from Dio: quite often he presents details not in the Bithynian's work, and when Dio runs out after

64 de Blois 2003: 148; Zimmermann 1999b: 303.

65 Hdn. 1.2.5, 2.15.7, 1.1.3; Alföldi 1971: 204.

66 A date under Philip: Rubin 1980: 87 and Whittaker (in the LCL translation) xv-xix. For Decius: Alföldi 1971: 215–19 and Zimmermann 1999b: 287. A date between AD 238 and 253 is suggested by Polley 2003: 203–8.

67 Kolb 1972: 25; Zimmermann 1999b: 129–34, 285.

68 Sidebottom 1997: 271–6; Sidebottom 2007: 79.

69 Alföldi 1971: 219; Sidebottom 1997: 275.

70 Sidebottom 1998: 2813.

71 Zimmermann 1999b.

72 Hdn. 2.15.6; Sidebottom 1998: 2781.

the reign of Severus Alexander the quality and style of Herodian's history down to Gordian III does not change.[73] Herodian often presents an alternative (and occasionally more reliable) image than his Bithynian counterpart.[74] For example, he is the only one to give a description of the Emesene god Elagabal, and to give the original names of Elagabalus and Severus Alexander – Bassianus and Alexianus.[75] One might argue that Herodian used sections of Dio that have not been preserved in the epitome, but for the later Severan emperors Dio is preserved in the original: Herodian must have had another source for the original names of the last two Severan rulers. Herodian mentions other sources in his work, notably artwork.[76] Although Zimmermann dismissed many of Herodian's descriptions of paintings and sculpture as invention or exaggeration, Sidebottom points out that we cannot apply to Herodian the same extreme criticism that characterises the *Quellenforschung* debate surrounding the *Historia Augusta*.[77] Unlike the *Historia Augusta*, there are strict limits to Herodian's inventions. As a source his work is, as characterised by Sidebottom, 'true enough'.[78]

More so than Dio, Herodian presents his history within a set interpretative framework. The focus of the work is on the benefits of *paideia* (education) in creating virtue or *arete* within a ruler. For Herodian education and Greek culture (*paideia*) forms the basis of good rule.[79] Marcus Aurelius is introduced at the beginning of the work as the embodiment of good rule through possession of *paideia*, a model against which all succeeding emperors are judged.[80] By making *paideia* the criterion for a good ruler, Herodian instils a sense of control in his Greek-speaking audience: *paideia*, after all, is the prerogative and possession of the Greek élite.[81] Herodian's framework does not rule out the influence of a ruler's character completely, but explores the beneficial qualities of *paideia* on imperial rule. Older, more experienced emperors are presented as possessing greater virtue than younger, less experienced rulers.[82]

The biographies contained in the *Historia Augusta* come more than a century after Dio and Herodian, and are written in Latin, not Greek. The problems associated with the *Historia Augusta* are well known: though purporting to be the work of six different authors, it is evident the

73 Sidebottom 1998: 2787–8.

74 Bowersock 1975: 229–36; Icks 2008a: 143; Scheithauer 1990: 343; Sidebottom 1998: 2788.

75 Hdn. 5.3.3–6; Bowersock 1975: 234; Sidebottom 1998: 2787.

76 Rubin 1975a: 428 suggests Herodian used the arch of Severus for his account of Severus' siege of Hatra. See the discussion in Sidebottom 1998: 2786.

77 Zimmermann 1999b: 309; Sidebottom 1998: 2786–7.

78 Sidebottom 1998: 2821.

79 Zimmermann 1999b: 21; Sidebottom 1998: 2804–5.

80 de Blois 1998: 3402; Sidebottom 1998: 2805; Zimmermann 1999b: 22.

81 Sidebottom 1998: 2825.

82 Sidebottom 2007: 81.

biographies are all written by the same individual. Fact and fiction are interwoven throughout the accounts, and often the lives function more as a commentary on the author's fourth-century context than as a dependable historical account.[83] Anecdotes and literary playfulness targeted at his contemporary audience form a large part of the work and, in the case of the later Severan emperors, arguably outweigh the historical accuracy of the account. Nonetheless, some truth is preserved amongst the fiction, particularly in the lives of Septimius Severus and Caracalla.[84] For the biographies of Elagabalus and Severus Alexander, however, it is clear that the author was commenting on his own contemporary context.

Interpreting Severan coinage

It is difficult to gauge the size of the audiences that read Dio, Herodian and the *Historia Augusta*. At the very least, their narratives would be confined to the literate segments of Roman society. Visual media, however, such as coins, paintings and other monuments, could be seen and understood by non-literate segments of society, forming 'a non-verbal, truly public discourse'.[85] In Roman society, where extensive literacy was limited to a select minority, the world of images formed an important communicative tool.[86] Important to this visual discourse was the coinage struck in the emperor's name, which was used as a medium to express the imperial ideology that supported the régime. As an official statement of the imperial government, coins and the images they displayed can be interpreted in a variety of ways and allow the historian to uncover shifting imperial ideologies.

The selection of coin types

It is generally believed that the emperor (or one of his advisors) had some degree of control over his numismatic image, and that coin types formed a

[83] Seminal modern studies on the *Historia Augusta* include Barnes 1978; Baynes 1926; and Syme 1971.

[84] Syme 1971: 55–9. For studies assessing the *Historia Augusta*'s life of Septimius Severus see Alföldy 1960: 145–64; Birley 1994: 19–42; Frend 1975: 470–80; Jacques 1992: 119–44. For Caracalla see: Alföldy 1996: 9–36; Meckler 1994; Meckler 1999: 39–46; Meckler 2005: 221–31; Penella 1980: 382–4. For Elagabalus: Alföldy 1976b: 11–21; Barnes 1970: 13–43; Mader 2005: 131–72; Optendrenk 1969; Sommer 2004: 95–110; Syme 1972: 275–91; Turcan 1988: 38–52. For Severus Alexander: Barnes 1972: 53–74; Bertrand-Dagenbach 1990; Birley 1991: 345–6; Blázquez 1990: 25–36; Chauvot 1994: 285–91; Ferrero 1999: 191–216; Straub 1970.

[85] Schmitz 1999: 90. [86] Gregory 1994: 83.

means of visualising and communicating the ideology of the princeps.[87] Levick proposed an alternative model: that the mint was responsible for the selection of types and that designs were chosen to please the emperor, not targeted at the wider population.[88] If this were the case, the motifs of virtue, military prowess and religious support were not a form of pre-industrial 'propaganda', but a visual panegyric. The position of moneyer in the imperial period was an appointment made by the emperor, usually given to men of promise who went on to have distinguished careers.[89] Thus, similar to Pliny's *Panegyricus*, the *monetales*, at the beginning of consular careers, may have engaged in a narrative of praise using the media at their disposal.[90] However, one might also suggest that the emperor consciously selected men who were well aware of his public image and would be sensitive to the production of suitable types.[91] Ultimately, however, there is no way to determine what influence the *monetales* or other mint officials had in the selection of coin types under the principate.[92] In many senses the debate is irrelevant, since it is obvious that the designs were flattering to the emperor and subject to his approval.[93]

Textual evidence confirms that Romans believed the emperor was responsible for his own coin types, and that coinage formed an official statement. The anonymous author of the fourth- or fifth-century work the *De rebus bellicis* even offers advice on coin types, appending illustrations of designs to his work.[94] Suetonius makes mention of Augustus' Capricorn type and a coin showing Nero playing the lyre, indicating that ancient authors did take an interest in what graced their ruler's coinage.[95] Dio makes reference to the images on the coins of Julius Caesar and Brutus.[96] Eusebius states that Constantine ordered a coin type showing him praying.[97] Julian is criticised for issuing coins showing a sacrificial bull.[98]

87 Metcalf 2006: 42; Sutherland 1986: 89–93; Wolters 1999: 292.

88 Levick 1982: 104–16; Levick 1999: 41–60.

89 Birley 1953: 202; Buttrey 1972b: 108 (who suggests that Vespasian himself may have held the position); Hamilton 1969: 188; Pink 1946: 121. For examples of the careers of imperial *monetales* see *AE* 1914, 130; *AE* 1969/70, 169; *CIL* 2.4510; *CIL* 3.6812; *CIL* 5.1812; *CIL* 5.4347; *CIL* 6.1339; *CIL* 6.1365; *CIL* 6.1368; *CIL* 6.1422; *CIL* 6.31740; *CIL* 6.32412; *CIL* 6.41145; *CIL* 6.41192; *CIL* 10.3724; *CIL* 10.3850; *CIL* 11.3002; *CIL* 14.2501; *CIL* 14.3599.

90 Saller 1982: 69–71. 91 Cheung 1998: 59. 92 Pink 1946: 125; Wallace-Hadrill 1986: 79.

93 Metcalf 2006: 42. 94 *De rebus bellicis* 3.4. 95 Suet. *Aug.* 94.12, *Ner.* 25.2–3.

96 Dio 47.25.3, 44.4.4.

97 Euseb. *Vit. Const.* 15.1. The statement has generally been tied to the portrait type of Constantine with eyes looking upwards 'towards heaven' (Longtin 2000: 9, 13). This may have been Eusebius' interpretation of the image, but a portrait with eyes looking upward also recalled the portrait of Alexander the Great.

98 Sozom. *Hist. eccl.* 5.19; Socrates *Hist. eccl.* 3.17, with further examples and discussion provided by Ando 2000: 216; Duncan-Jones 2005: 462–3; Price 1979: 278; and Wolters 1999: 292.

A coin carried the emperor's portrait, and consequently it formed an official statement. If a coin type was not to the emperor's liking, it would undoubtedly have ceased to be struck, or may even have been recalled. However, one imagines that such an occurrence would be a rare event: the selection of individual moneyers by the princeps, in conjunction with their desire to use this position for career advancement, doubtless resulted in a system in which the numismatic image of the emperor was carefully considered. The coins of the Severan emperors in particular display new and creative imagery, suggesting that coin types were closely linked to the imperial person. The radical transformation of the numismatic image of the emperor from one Severan to the next (explored in the following chapters) demonstrates this connection convincingly, underlining the importance of numismatics to any understanding of the public image of the princeps in this period.

There was an extremely close association between the emperor and his coinage. Epictetus stated that he would accept a coin of Trajan, but not one of Nero 'because it is rotten'.[99] Epictetus may have been punning on the fact that χαρακτήρ could refer to both a person's character and the die of a coin, but the statement must reflect at some level an association between a coin and the ruler responsible for it. Analysis of the coin finds in Pompeii suggests that Epictetus' statement may have had some basis in the market place. A bar excavated in *insula* 1.8 contained some 1,300 bronze coins; less than 1 per cent of them bore Nero's effigy, though Tiberius and Claudius had substantial representation.[100] Nero's reform of the coinage may have contributed to his poor representation in the archaeological record (he reduced the weight and silver content of the currency). But whether from financial or moral considerations, Epictetus' statement may have held true in the ancient world: Nero's coinage, like his character, was 'rotten'.

Other evidence attests to the connection between the princeps and the coinage in his name. The coinage of Caligula and Geta was reportedly recalled after their *damnatio*, and Dio reports that under Caracalla it was a crime to carry a coin with the emperor's image into a brothel.[101] Talmudic texts after the Bar Kokhba revolt reveal that coins showing the bust of Hadrian were no longer used.[102] The connection seems to have been

[99] Arr. *Epict. diss.* 4.5.16–17; Wallace-Hadrill 1986: 66–87. [100] Duncan-Jones 2003: 174.

[101] Dio 60.22.3, 78.12.6, 78.16.5; Philostr. *VA* 1.15. See also Dio 78.14.4, where Caracalla's debasement of the coinage is connected with the emperor's character. An emperor who had suffered *damnatio* often had his coinage defaced or countermarked (Howgego 1985: 5–6; Kindler 1980: 3–7). On this 'charismatic' aspect of coinage see Wolters 1999: 316–17.

[102] Wolters 1999: 317.

taken to an extreme in late antique Egypt, where people were judging the worth of a coin by the size of the imperial portrait on it, prompting the emperor to issue a law that all solidi (gold coins) were worth the same amount.[103]

The diverse range of types seen under each emperor, and the existence of types confined to or favoured by individual emperors, strongly suggests that if the princeps himself did not play a role in the selection of types, someone very familiar with the ideals of the régime did. The emperor was probably involved in coin design or influenced it, though he may not have chosen every type that issued from the mint.[104] Here the appointment of the *monetales* by the emperor himself may have been important. Similarly, one would not expect that the emperor had a role in the minutiae of the decoration and design of an arch or any other imperial monument. Indeed, different emperors may have had different levels of involvement in their numismatic iconography. Buttrey argues that Vespasian, for example, may originally have held the position of moneyer, and that his antiquarian interest in old coinage may have been the motivating force behind the resuscitation of old coin types during his reign.[105] Just as Hadrian reportedly wanted to design the temple of Venus and Rome himself, so too different emperors may have had wanted closer than usual involvement in their coinage, while others may have entrusted the process to a close advisor.[106]

The literary evidence illustrates that coins functioned as a visual medium of the regime and that the populace held emperors responsible for any imagery placed upon them. Romans interpreted their coins as statements of the emperor and imperial intent.[107] Crawford has suggested that the relative silence of ancient sources on coins and their designs suggests we ourselves should not take them too seriously as historical sources.[108] The list of textual references given above undermines this statement. Coinage does appear in ancient texts, and the use of coinage in invented histories like the *Historia Augusta*, for example, demonstrates the idea that coinage was considered a fitting source from which to write about an emperor and his rule.[109] The discussion of coinage within ancient textual evidence should be viewed alongside ancient discussions of inscriptions and monumental architecture.[110] These do not form the focus of many ancient works, but all remained an

[103] *Cod. Theod.* 9.22.1 with discussion by Lendon 1990: 115 and Manders 2008: 16.
[104] Crawford 1983: 59; Ehrhardt 1984: 41–54; Sutherland 1986: 85–93.
[105] Buttrey 1972b: 89–109. [106] On Hadrian see Dio 79.4.3–6 and Ridley 1989: 551–66.
[107] Wallace-Hadrill 1981b; Wolters 1999: 292. [108] Crawford 1983: 47–64.
[109] On coinage in the *Historia Augusta* see Tomlin 1980: 255–69.
[110] Cheung 1998: 61; Hedlund 2008: 30.

important output of the imperial regime, offering an insight into the history and ideology of the period. The effort expended on the design and execution of a changing series of coin types from the Republican period onward would hardly have continued unless coins were used and viewed as a monument of publicity.[111]

Viewing coin types

Since Jones' provocative suggestion that coin images were no more persuasive than modern-day postage stamps, the significance of numismatic imagery has been the subject of debate.[112] When one considers that the coinage of each Severan emperor formed only a portion of the currency already in circulation (archaeological evidence suggests that Severan coinage entered a pool of currency dating back to the first century AD), the potential of a coin to communicate in any meaningful way with the inhabitants of the empire becomes uncertain. We may be guilty of viewing the ancient world with a modern perspective that anticipates a media saturation only possible with recent technologies; the little that coinage could do in terms of communication may have been deemed significant in the Roman world. The issuing authority would not have expected the impact possible with modern media, and given the absence of other direct forms of contact with the emperor, the population may have been more alert to new coin types than we are today. The ancient literary evidence cited above demonstrates that some attention was paid to numismatic iconography.

Noreña's recent work on Vespasian's Temple of Peace has demonstrated the connection of coinage with other imperial monuments, highlighting their importance as a part of the broader visual language of Rome.[113] In a society where a large proportion of the population was illiterate, images served to communicate ideologies.[114] Ancient authors themselves emphasised the power of images, and our increasing understanding of the role of visual culture in the ancient world underlines the importance of considering all imagery, however physically small.[115]

There are several approaches to the interpretation of coinage in the Roman Empire, and each has a part to play in the reconstruction of imperial

[111] Morstein-Marx 2004: 82–92 provides a good analysis of the role of coinage within the wider monumental framework of the Republican period.

[112] Jones 1956: 13–33; Duncan-Jones 2005: 459–71; Newman 1990: 33–67

[113] Noreña 2003: 25–43. [114] Hölscher 2004; Zanker 1988.

[115] Noticeably Hor. *Ars* 180–2. See Freedberg 1989: 50; and Gregory 1994: 80–99 for a discussion, and Eastmond 2003: 73–85 for the importance of images in Byzantium.

ideology. It is possible to examine the imagery of a coin in isolation, to view a coin in the context of other types struck with it (as part of an emission), and to consider an emperor's coinage in its entirety. The combined image provided by the totality of an emperor's coinage would give an overall impression, however general, to the population. But significance also lies in the very act of joining the emperor's portrait to a particular image. At some level a conscious decision was made to bind the emperor's image to the concept of Pax, for example, or Virtus. The resulting coin was a monument of the emperor, knowledge and memory of which lasted well beyond his lifetime.[116] These alternative but complementary perspectives can each provide valuable information.

A quantitative perspective on Roman coinage

Viewing an emperor's coinage as a whole can be achieved through a quantitative analysis utilising surviving coin hoards. A hoard consists of coins deposited together at a discrete period in time. Modern scholarship has begun to exploit the enormous potential of coin hoards for the understanding of the Roman economy and, more recently, for the understanding of coin types.[117] It is the latter application that is of interest here; different coin types were struck in different quantities, contributing in different ways to the emperor's overall numismatic image. Current coin catalogues, such as *Roman Imperial Coinage*, do not adequately spell out how common a coin was in antiquity. This is because the catalogues incorporate evidence from large public and private collections that focus on the collection of rare types, distorting our perception of how common these coins actually were.[118] Understanding the relative frequency of a particular image is important in gauging the type's purpose and communicative potential. An image that was joined with the emperor's portrait for a single occasion and presented to a particular audience had a very different function to imagery that was repeatedly connected with the emperor and formed a substantial part of the new currency in circulation.

[116] Buttrey 1972b: 96–108 and Cheung 1998:56–8, who suggests we view coins as 'monuments in miniature'.

[117] Coin hoards for the economy: Duncan-Jones 1993: 139–52; Duncan-Jones 1994; Duncan-Jones 2001: 75–89; Duncan-Jones 2002: 342–5; Howgego 1993: 119–236; Reece 2003: 283–8. Coin hoards for understanding coin types: Bruun 1991: 65–83; Carradice 1998: 96–112; Carson 1983: 66–7; Christiansen 1988: 15; Hekster and Manders 2006: 135–44; Kemmers 2006; Noreña 2001: 146–68; Noreña 2003: 29–30.

[118] Metcalf 1999: 3; Noreña 2001: 148.

There may be several reasons behind the fact that different coin types were struck in different quantities. Different amounts of coinage were produced each year. Consequently a type selected in a year in which the output of coinage was great would be struck in larger numbers than a type selected when output was small. In acknowledgement of this, this work provides wherever possible an estimation of coin types in relation to other coins struck in the same year. Given that not all Severan coinage has been dated to a specific year, however, this was not possible for all coin types.

Workshops (*officinae*) within the mint were also likely identified by different reverse types, which acted as a control mark on the currency. Each workshop struck a different reverse type, making it easy to identify who was responsible for each coin.[119] Generally, Roman coinage had two categories: 'substantive' coinage, which was struck in large numbers, and 'commemorative' coinage, minted in much smaller numbers and usually struck in conjunction with a specific event (for instance an emperor's *vota* or *decennalia*). The latter rarely appear in coin hoards.[120]

Ideally, quantitative numismatic studies should be performed through die analysis. This entails an analysis of how many dies were used to make each issue, from which one can estimate the total amount of coinage struck. The large volume of Roman coinage, however, makes this undertaking impractical, if not impossible.[121] It is still uncertain how many coins each die could create, whereas coin hoards provide a concrete, though relative, figure.[122] The method is basic, but generally reliable.[123] Studies of the composition of coin hoards have illustrated that in many ways they reflect the pool of currency in circulation at a particular time. Since coins were not normally hoarded on the basis of type, hoards can provide some idea of the degree to which different coin images were present in a particular area and time period.[124]

Noreña's examination of the emperor's virtues highlights how coin hoards might be used to gain new insights into Roman numismatic iconography.[125] Roman imperial coinage is one of the few artefacts from the ancient world to have survived in sufficient numbers for a quantitative

119 Carson 1956: 227–39. 120 Carson 1983: 67. 121 Carson 1956: 228.

122 Buttrey 1993: 335–51; Buttrey 1994: 341–52; and de Callataÿ 1995: 289–311.

123 Metcalf 2006: 42.

124 Studies have shown that the distinction between 'savings' hoards (accumulated over a long period of time) and 'emergency' hoards (an assemblage of coinage withdrawn straight from circulation) is not a valid one, since the average lifetime of a single worker (in which he would have accumulated his savings) is not long enough for there to be a significant distinction between one pool of circulation and another (Reece 1987: 61). See also Duncan-Jones 1994: 67.

125 Noreña 2001: 146–68.

analysis. A study using hoards should be able to supply a relative (not, it must be emphasised, absolute) quantity of different types. There may be many different motivations behind the collection and deposit of a coin hoard, but the underlying instinct is one of economic benefit: the money will be protected and/or potentially worth more at a later date. As Noreña notes, some coins may have been kept as mementos or have formed ancient coin collections, but such instances are easy to identify and will not impact a wider analysis drawing upon a large sample of hoard remains.

Any quantitative study of Roman coinage has to address the problem of attrition.[126] Every coin at some stage fell out of circulation, at a rate determined by value, metal content and innumerable other factors. The *terminus post quem* of the hoards used in an analysis is thus vital: one should not look in a fourth century hoard to gauge an idea of circulation in the first or second centuries. This study incorporates hoards dated from the beginning of the Severan period until AD 270. Hoards with a *terminus post quem* after the Severan dynasty were included, since an emperor's coinage could take several decades to reach a peak in circulation.[127] Bland and Abdy's analysis of Severan coin hoards suggests that the process could take up to twenty or thirty years in Britain.[128] Given this fact, and in the interests of gathering the maximum amount of data possible, hoards abandoned up to thirty-five years after the Severan period were included.

This study has attempted to overcome some of the problems posed by the process of attrition by discussing a coin's frequency in relation to other coins struck in the same mint in the same year. Coins struck in the same year and in the same mint (thus with an approximately similar metal content) should undergo attrition at a similar rate regardless of type.

Ideally, any hoard study should take into account gold, silver and *aes* (bronze) denominations, but the nature of the Roman economy and the finds that survive from the Severan period make this task extremely difficult.[129] Hoards of gold from this period are extremely rare, and many of those that do exist have been published poorly, if at all.[130] The few published hoards that contain Severan gold coins possess them in small numbers (for example the Rennes hoard only contains twenty-two coins from the Severan

[126] Buttrey 1993: 337–8, 345–7. [127] Bolin 1958: 55; Duncan-Jones 1994: 106.
[128] Bland and Abdy 2002: 25. [129] Carson 1983: 66.
[130] For example, the Karnak hoard (Kunisz 1983: 163). See Bland and Abdy 2002: 20; Bolin 1958: 250; Carson 1983: 66; and Duncan-Jones 1994: 70 on the rarity of gold hoards from the Severan period.

dynasty).[131] These circumstances mean that Severan gold does not survive in sufficient bulk for a general quantitative analysis of types.

Similarly, an *aes* or lower denomination hoard analysis poses numerous problems for the Severan dynasty. Cities in the Roman East were allowed to strike their own *aes* denominations displaying local civic imagery. *Aes* coinage struck in Rome generally only circulated in the West of the empire. This in itself is not an insurmountable obstacle; one might explore the different quantities of *aes* coin types that circulated in the West. However, *aes* hoards from the third century contain very little Severan material.[132] An example of this can be seen in the hoard of Plaisans (Drôme), which was found in the interior of a Gallo-Roman villa that suffered a fire in the second half of the third century. The hoard contained 3,266 *aes* coins struck before AD 192 (95.6% of the hoard), and only 149 coins struck after AD 192 (4.4%).[133] This is comparable to other hoards found in France and the west continent, as well as in Britain.[134] Buttrey has suggested that *aes* coins of the second century continued to function as small change in these areas; fresh coin was not being supplied from Rome.[135] This would have had the unintentional effect of connecting the Severan dynasty to its Antonine predecessors, something that would not have been unwelcome to Severus.

Aes hoards within Italy also present a problem. The composition of third-century *aes* hoards in Italy varies greatly according to region.[136] Severan coins are also dramatically weighted towards Severus Alexander. In the Caminada hoard (*terminus post quem* AD 249) 114 coins of the total 586 were Severan, but 91 of these were from the reign of Severus Alexander.[137] Similarly in the Martellago hoard (*terminus post quem* AD 253), 113 of the total 497 coins are Severan, but 86 of these are from the reign of Severus Alexander.[138] The Biassono hoard (*terminus post quem* AD 225) contains 184 Severan coins in its total of 2,239, but here too there is a distinct bias towards Severus Alexander.[139]

It seems that *aes* issues of the Severans were struck in small numbers, though production may have increased under Severus Alexander (at least, there are substantially more *aes* coins of Severus Alexander in surviving hoards than any other Severan emperor). The reasons behind this are likely to be complex. Some have connected the small numbers of gold and *aes* coinage with the debasement of silver under Septimius Severus, though this

[131] Gentilhomme 1943: 29–43. [132] Buttrey 1972a: 45–55.
[133] Amandry and Hollard 1997: 22.
[134] Bland and Abdy 2002: 21; Buttrey 1972a: 49–50; Walker 1988: 282. [135] Buttrey 1972a: 49.
[136] Buttrey 1972a: 50. [137] No. 13/1 (1) in *RMRVe* II.2. [138] No. 8/2 in *RMRVe* VI/3.
[139] Ermanno and Arslan 1995.

theory has its critics.[140] Production may have increased again under Severus Alexander because of a shortage of small change. We may note here that Severus Alexander claimed to be a 'restorer' (*restitutor*) of the coinage, a title only struck on *aes* types.[141] Though one may be able to collect enough information on Severus Alexander's *aes* coinage for an analysis, the relative paucity of *aes* hoards from this period, their strong geographical diversity and their distinct bias towards the end of the Severan period means that *aes* coinage is not looked at quantitatively in this study.

Coin types and Roman memory

How are we to interpret coin imagery that is not very abundant? The absence or near absence of 'commemorative' types in hoards, and the relative paucity of gold and *aes* coinage in this period means that these types could not have functioned as a large-scale communicative medium. However, a long-term view of Roman imperial coinage shows that these issues, though smaller in quantity, were no less important in significance.

It has long been recognised that the Roman mint re-struck old types from decades or even centuries past.[142] As mentioned above, the emperor Vespasian struck numerous pre-Flavian types, particularly types of Augustus. Buttrey has analysed this phenomenon and has pointed out that the care with which the earlier types were copied suggests that what was being celebrated were the older coins themselves.[143] Coinage struck during the civil wars of AD 68–69 referenced types of Augustus and the Republic.[144] Roman Republican types were also reissued under Trajan, and Marcus Aurelius reissued a legionary denarius type of Mark Antony.[145] As Buttrey has demonstrated, the types re-struck under Trajan included coins of great rarity, pieces that would not have been in the memory of any living person.[146] The piece of Marcus Aurelius is remarkable not only for the time gap between the two issues, but also for the fact that Antony was Augustus' defeated rival. Perhaps one of the most extraordinary cases of 'restitution' coinage occurs under Constantius II. A medallion issued in the name of the emperor in AD 357 and a late antique contorniate both show the abduction

140 Walker 1988: 300, with criticism by Buttrey 1972a: 54–5, who suggests instead local authorities may have lost interest in importing small denominations from Rome.

141 Mattingly, Sydenham et al. 1938: vi; *RIC* IV.2 *Severus Alexander* 589. Coarelli 1987: 444 suggests the type might refer to restoration works done on the mint itself.

142 Komnick 2001.

143 Buttrey 1972b: 101.

144 Wallace-Hadrill 1981a: 34.

145 *RIC* II *Trajan* 765–814 (Republican types), 815–36 (early imperial types); Dio 68.15.3; Seelentag 2004: 410–84; *RIC* III *Marcus Aurelius* 443, a restitution of Crawford 544/19.

146 Buttrey 1972b: 103.

of the Sabine women, the precise image that had been engraved on a medallion of Pius over two hundred years earlier.[147] The Pius medallion, by its very nature, would not have been in wide circulation (medallions were presented as gifts, not as currency). The sum of the evidence here suggests that there was a memory or archive of coin types in Rome.[148]

This is also suggested in the ancient literary evidence. Suetonius records that Augustus gave old and foreign coins as gifts.[149] How did Dio know of Caesar's coins, or the coin type struck by Brutus, when both had long ceased to circulate by his lifetime?[150] He must have viewed an example of the coin or its design, or learnt about it through another source. At the very least, Dio illustrates that knowledge of coin types lasted well beyond their circulation life and were considered a source of evidence that could be consulted and included within a history. Crawford suggested that Dio's knowledge (and Suetonius' knowledge of the coin types of Augustus and Nero) might have derived from a literary source: a chronicle of Brutus, or the memoirs of Augustus or an associate.[151] This suggests that coin types were worthy of mention in historical records, that they were viewed, recorded and interpreted as statements of a particular individual.

What precise form this memory or archive of coin types took is unknown. Knowledge may have been based on antique coin collections, a collection of old dies and/or coins, written records or receipts, a 'type' book or the personal experience of the mint workers. Perhaps most attractive is the idea that old dies were preserved within the mint. Within each obverse die was etched an image of the reigning emperor, an image which was revered and imbued with power. Various instances are recorded in antiquity of people escaping arrest because they held an image of the emperor, or of people being convicted for treason for carrying an image of the emperor into a lavatory or a brothel.[152] Within the context of these tales, it is hard to imagine that dies bearing the emperor's image were melted down or

[147] Holden 2008: 121–42.

[148] This may even have existed as early as the Republican period. Crawford 369–71 (82–80 BC) use the same types and dies as Crawford 263–5 (127 BC); the moneyers in both instances were of the same *gens*. The dies were likely preserved somehow (perhaps amongst the family heirlooms and monuments) and were reused (Crawford 1974: 752). See also Meadows and Williams 2001: 27–49.

[149] Suet. *Aug.* 75: 'Saturnalibus, et si quando alias libuisset, modo munera dividebat, vestem et aurum et argentum, modo nummos omnis notae, etiam veteres regios ac peregrinos.'

[150] The hoard analysis conducted for this work did not uncover any instances of these coins, though Mark Antony's legionary denarii were present.

[151] Crawford 1983: 52.

[152] Tac. *Ann.* 3.36.1; Suet. *Tib.* 58, Philostr. *VA* 1.15, with further examples and discussion in Wolters 1999: 310–12.

destroyed after use. Regardless of the precise mechanism by which this record was achieved, the phenomenon of restitution coinage throughout the entire imperial period indicates that knowledge of coin types was preserved, and not just types that formed the most frequent issues in circulation. Rare 'commemorative' types entered into Roman memory as well.

Cheung suggested that, just as a triumphal arch was intended as much for posterity as for contemporaries, so too coins functioned as monuments of the emperor long after his death.[153] Viewing coins as 'monuments in miniature', Cheung suggested that legends were not intended for the edification of contemporaries, but to ensure that the type remained understandable for later generations.[154] This may be going a little far; the legend on the coin more likely served to identify and define images for a contemporary audience. Identification for posterity may have been an unintended bonus.

The connection between monumentality, memory and coin types has significant implications for how we are to view the images and legends that graced Roman currency. A coin type was not just a tool of communication aimed at the Roman public, but something that was archived for later generations long after it had ceased to circulate. Thus in some senses the full catalogue of coin types that appeared under each emperor might be viewed as a narrative or history of the period, one that could be recalled or accessed at will. Though some types may have been struck in greater numbers than others, each formed a part of the record of a particular reign. That the Roman mint continued to mark events such as *vota*, an emperor's *decennalia* and other religious festivals on imperial coinage struck in very small quantities suggests that the design and striking of a coin might have functioned as an important record of events. Like some inscriptions, the very act of recording, rather than the potential to be seen and understood by an audience, may have been what was significant.[155] This idea is explored more fully in the following chapter.

By employing these approaches to the numismatic evidence we can begin to utilise coin evidence to its full potential. Viewing coinage as a whole, in conjunction with other materials (archaeological remains, inscriptions and literary evidence), means we can survey imperial imagery at a broader level. The potential of numismatics for this relatively new approach to ancient Rome has yet to be fully realised.[156] The design and execution of every coin type had a symbolism and significance in the construction of the emperor's image. But a broader perspective also allows us to see how imperial imagery

[153] Cheung 1998: 57. [154] Cheung 1998: 58; followed by Meadows and Williams 2001: 27–49.
[155] Beard 1985: 138–9. [156] Hedlund 2008: 21–5; Kemmers 2006: 197; Wolters 2003: 201.

could function as a coherent system with semantic conventions and multiple messages.[157] For the Severans the contribution of numismatics is particularly important given the paucity and problems of other forms of evidence.

We now turn to an exploration of the divine support claimed by the Severan dynasty. By tracing the changing divine ideologies employed by each member of the dynasty, the vitality of the imperial image in this period is revealed. A close analysis of the divine support invoked by the Severan emperors demonstrates that in each case specific contexts have importance, but the phenomena we see in this period can be connected to the broader tradition of divine support that had characterised Rome since the Republic.

[157] Hölscher 2004; Kemmers 2006: 197.

3 | Septimius Severus, Liber Pater and Hercules

> The late revenge of the Semites on Graeco-Roman culture, whose shackles they had silently borne through the centuries, erupts with demonic force during the reign of Septimius Severus. The triumph of the new Hannibal is embodied in the worship of his wife Julia Domna as Virgo Caelestis, the city-goddess of ancient Carthage.[1]

Von Domaszewski's assessment of the impact of Severus' rule on Roman culture embodies the modern characterisation of the emperor as an 'outsider'.[2] A closer examination of the reign of Septimius Severus, however, reveals a delicate balance between tradition and innovation in his imperial ideology.[3] In constructing and implementing the dynastic, political and religious basis for a new dynasty, Severus and his advisors drew upon his Lepcitanian heritage, but also utilised precedents established by Augustus and the Antonines.[4] The result was a complex and multifaceted ideology, communicated through monuments, rituals and other public ceremonies. This ideology was interpreted in turn by local cities and individuals, who created their own monuments and rituals to express their relationship with the emperor. The final result is a collection of material that presents varied images of Severus as a ruler.

Though born in Lepcis Magna, Severus undoubtedly had a very 'Roman' upbringing and followed a very 'Roman' career path.[5] Neither Cassius Dio nor the sophist Philostratus (who were both probably in the company of the emperor at some stage) characterise Severus as an 'African'. Herodian only mentions in passing that Severus was from Libya.[6]

[1] von Domaszewski 1909: 148.

[2] See also Aitken 2004: 267–84; Hall 2004: 137; Palmer 1978: 1085–6; Platnauer 1965: 141–4; and Swain 1999: 159–60.

[3] Potter 2004: 100–1; Potter 2008: 206–7.

[4] On the use of Augustus as a model: Cooley 2007: 385–400; Desnier 1993: 584–620; and Gorrie 2007: 1–17. On the use of Trajan: Desnier 1997: 191–3. On the traditional 'Jovian Theology of Power': Fears 1977: 258–62. Dynastic links: Lusnia 1995: 119–39; Lusnia 2004: 517–44; and Lusnia 2006b: 196–9.

[5] Barnes 1967: 87–107; Haywood 1940: 175–85; Haywood 1962: 786–90.

[6] Hdn. 2.9.2. Though originally used to denote the Greek colonial area of Cyrenaica, Libya could also denote a much larger area, even the whole of Africa (Reynolds 1996: 855–6).

A more significant portrayal of the emperor as 'African' can be found in the *Historia Augusta*. The author names Severus' *patria* as Lepcis Magna and intersperses the *Vita* with anecdotes to highlight the emperor's foreign origin. For example, Severus was allegedly embarrassed at his sister's poor Latin, and is even said to have had an 'African' accent.[7] At the very end of the *Vita* the author notes that Severus constructed the Septizodium (a large nymphaeum at the foot of the Palatine Hill) with the aim that it should 'strike the eyes of those who came to Rome from Africa'.[8] That the *Historia Augusta* includes this information, and not Dio or Herodian, may be because of the work's reliance on a Latin source, or may simply reflect invention or gossip.[9] Those who emphasise the 'Africanity' of the emperor, like von Domaszewski above, pursue an idea not appreciably present in the surviving literary evidence.

At the death of Pertinax in AD 193, Severus was the commander of the Pannonian legions. By AD 197, he would be in control of the Roman Empire. This extraordinary rise to power needed legitimatisation, and Severus went to considerable lengths to demonstrate that his position was not only won by military force, but that his rise to power reflected the will of the gods. Particular focus was given to the deities Liber Pater and Hercules in these ideologies. These gods were the tutelary deities of Lepcis Magna, but under Severus were employed in conjunction with a broad array of imagery. The result was a complex image of imperial power that could be interpreted on many different levels. Severus was able to meld his own particular brand of divine support with the wider infrastructure that formed the basis of the principate. The Romans had a clear idea of what an emperor 'looked like', and any aspirant to the throne had to style himself accordingly.

'African' deities and civil war (AD 193–197)

If one believes the ancient evidence, Septimius Severus was born to rule. Divine portents played a significant role in his ideology, reflected in both the ancient literary evidence and the monuments erected by Severus throughout

[7] *SHA Sev* 1.1–1.2, 2.4–2.6, 15.7, 18.3. Remarkably, around the time the *Historia Augusta* was composed, Libyans had gained a reputation for their excellent Latin (Lydus *Mag.* 73=251.4 in the edition of Bandy 1983). The story of the accent may thus have been present in an earlier source, also suggested by the description of Severus as an African in Aurelius Victor (*caes.* 20) and in Eutropius (8.18).

[8] *SHA Sev* 24.3.

[9] Barnes 1967: 96 suggests it is preserved slander.

Rome.[10] Herodian notes these omens were recorded by Severus himself in his autobiography and were commemorated with statues erected by the emperor.[11] One of the better-known portents is Severus' dream, in which Pertinax is thrown from his horse only for the animal to pick up Severus instead. Both Dio and Herodian recount this tale; both authors were likely dependant on Severus' autobiography, which was probably published in AD 197/8 as a justification of the civil wars.[12] Herodian records that the portent was monumentalised by a bronze statue, and the Severan arch in the forum was pointedly constructed on the spot where the two riders crossed over.[13]

Dio's pamphlet on the dreams and omens that foreshadowed Severus' rule reflects the centrality of divine omens and portents to the ideology of the period, which Dio capitalised on to win favour. Dio records that Severus sent him a long and complimentary letter upon reading his work.[14] Herodian states that Severus believed he was called to rule 'by divine providence', that the prodigies indicated divine favour.[15] Severus also styled himself as the avenger of the emperor Pertinax, who had been killed by the soldiers in Rome and replaced by Didius Julianus.[16] These justifications of power (the omens, the divine support, and vengeance for Pertinax) would later expand to include dynastic connections to the Antonines and would culminate in the establishment of the Severan dynasty, when Severus' son Caracalla would be named co-emperor.

Avenging Pertinax and the 'Saeculum Frugiferum'

When Pertinax was killed in AD 193, there was no ready successor to the throne.[17] Four contenders emerged: Clodius Albinus (a commander in Britain), Septimius Severus in Pannonia, Pescennius Niger in the East and

[10] Dio 75.3.1; Hdn. 2.9.3–7; *SHA Sev.* 1.6–10; Rubin 1971: 83–112. [11] Hdn. 2.9.4.

[12] Dio 75.3.3, Hdn. 2.9.5–6; Chausson 1995a: 183–98.

[13] Hdn. 2.9.6; Bloch 1943: 31–2; Lusnia 1998: 96–103. Zimmermann 1999b: 309 argues that Herodian's knowledge of the city of Rome was faulty, and in the absence of other evidence confirming that a statue of Severus existed in the forum we should dismiss Herodian here. However, the absence of a bronze sculpture from antiquity should not automatically lead us to dismiss its existence. What may be an equestrian statue of Severus is shown on coinage from AD 201 (*RIC* IV.1 *Septimius Severus* 169). Lusnia suggests that the statue may have stood in the middle of the forum, where the equestrian statue of Domitian once was: here the Severan pavement of the forum leaves the base available for reuse, suggesting that this may have once supported a Severan statue (Lusnia 1998: 97).

[14] Dio 73.23.1–5; Rubin 1971: 88. [15] Hdn. 2.9.7. [16] Dio 74.10.1–3; Hdn. 2.5.3–9.

[17] Birley 1988: 95.

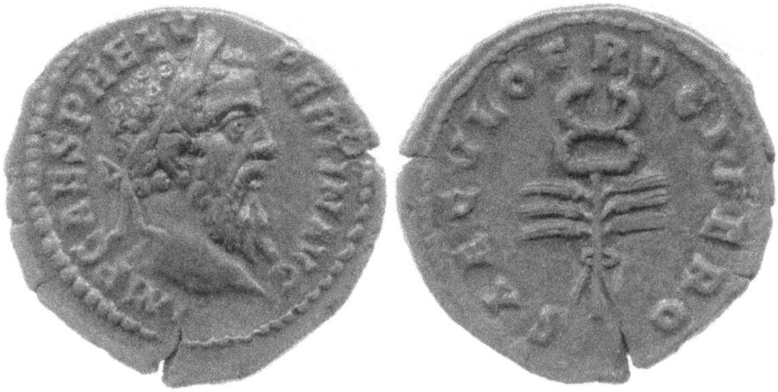

Figure 2: Denarius of Pertinax displaying a *caduceus* with corn ears, with the legend SAECVLO FRVGIFERO.

Didius Julianus, who was reportedly declared emperor in Rome after a bidding war for the throne.[18] Severus secured the support of Albinus as his Caesar and then moved against Julianus in Rome.

The imperial capital was taken and Julianus defeated. The coin issues that followed reflect Severus' claim to be the successor and avenger of Pertinax.[19] Severus' dream had connected him to the slain emperor, and Severus proceeded to deify Pertinax and adopt his name.[20] Dio devotes a substantial portion of his history to detailing the *consecratio* or deification ceremony of Pertinax; this in turn may have inspired Herodian's own digression on Severus' *consecratio*, which he introduces with characteristic irony.[21] Severus also styled himself as the continuator of Pertinax's *Saeculum Frugiferum*, the 'fertile age'.

Under Pertinax, coin types were released with the legend SAECVLO FRVGIFERO, accompanied by the image of a *caduceus* with six corn ears attached to it (Figure 2).[22] The meaning of the type is straightforward: the beginning of a fertile age after the demise of Commodus. The legend and its iconography disappear under Julianus but re-emerge when Severus comes to power. The legend SAECVLO FRVGIFERO reappears on a coin of Albinus with some modification to the imagery: a radiate, half-draped figure now holds the *caduceus* (still with corn ears attached), as well as a trident

[18] Dio 74.11.3. [19] Dio 74.17.3; Hdn. 2.9.8; *SHA Sev.* 5.5.

[20] *RIC* IV.1 *Septimius Severus* 24A–24B (deification issues of Pertinax); Dio 75.4.1–75.5.6; Hdn. 2.10.9.

[21] Dio 75.4.1–5.5; Hdn. 4.2.1–11. Herodian begins his digression by noting that 'it is normal Roman practice to deify emperors who die leaving behind them children as their successors'. On Herodian's use of irony see Sidebottom 1998: 2809.

[22] *RIC* IV.1 *Pertinax* 12.

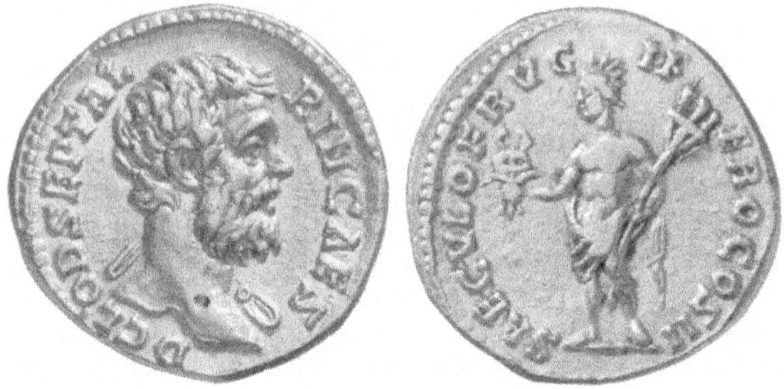

Figure 3: Aureus of Clodius Albinus with a radiate figure carrying a *caduceus* and trident and the legend SAECVLO FRVGIFERO COS II.

(Figure 3).[23] This type also appears on coins struck for Septimius.[24] The common legend and imagery illustrate a knowledge of, and conscious connection to, Pertinax's earlier coin. Albinus and Severus would bring forth the fertile age promised by the dead emperor. This is compelling evidence for the significance attached to coin imagery in this period: though the message may also have been present in other monuments, Pertinax had only released a single coin type advertising the *saeculum frugiferum* and yet its iconography was remembered and consciously redeployed. The legend does not appear on the coinage of Severus' rival Pescennius Niger, though he also promised an age of prosperity (SAECVLI FELICITAS) from his mint at Antioch.[25]

A variant of the SAECVLO FRVGIFERO type on Albinus' coinage shows a bearded god wearing a fez-like headpiece and a robe, seated left on a throne flanked by two sphinxes (Figure 4).[26] The iconography is that of the Hadrumentine deity Baal Hammon.[27] Albinus likely originated from Hadrumentum.[28] The image of Baal Hammon on Roman coinage is highly unusual and calls for explanation. Gagé believed the image and legend were an 'African' interpretation of the new age (identifying *frugifer* as a specifically 'African' word).[29] Barnes, in an article downplaying the 'African'

[23] *RIC* IV.1 *Albinus* 8–9, 56. [24] *RIC* IV.1 *Septimius Severus* 19, 655.

[25] *RIC* IV.1 *Niger* 73–4. Reference might have been made to Pertinax's death with the type of Mars Ultor (the avenger) (Buttrey 1992: xii). Alföldy 1976a: 1–10 suggests Niger may have been proclaiming the beginning of a new Golden Age.

[26] *RIC* IV.1 *Albinus* 10. The type also appears on medallions struck for Albinus. See Gnecchi 1912: (vol. 2) 73 no. 4.

[27] Birley 1969: 265; Xella 1991: 126. [28] *SHA Albinus* 1.3; Birley 1988: 98.

[29] Gagé 1934: 66–8. The word does not have specifically 'African' connotations (it is used by Roman authors to signify 'fruit-bearing'), though it was a common epithet for deities in North Africa (Cadotte 2003: 187–200).

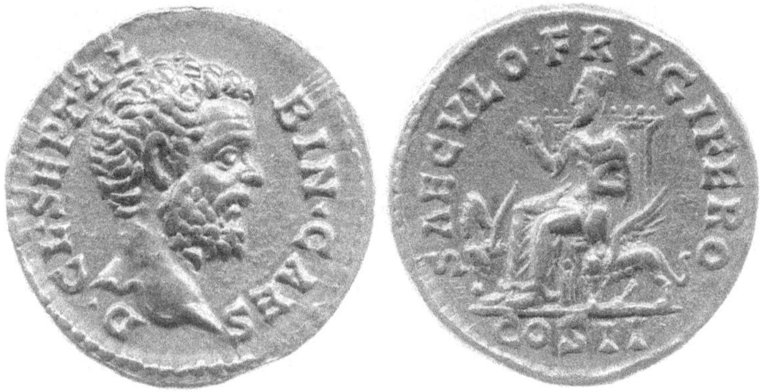

Figure 4: Aureus of Clodius Albinus with Baal Hammon and the legend SAECVLO FRVGIFERO COS II.

connections of Severus, suggested the type was an innovation on a Latin phrase, *saeculo frugifero*.[30] Birley believed that both the legend and image referred to a Hadrumentine god named Saeculum Frugiferum.[31] Alföldi suggested that Saeculum Frugiferum was the African interpretation of the Alexandrian divinity Aion Plutonios.[32] Desnier subsequently opposed this suggestion and asserted that the slogan SAECVLO FRVGIFERO referred to the return of a fertile age, and that the coin types celebrated the divinities who presided over the new abundance.[33] Lichtenberger noted that the phrase was both a political slogan and the surname of the god from Hadrumentum.[34]

The variety of interpretations underlines the unusual nature of the representation. Desnier's hypothesis is the most attractive: it seems that a variety of images were employed to visualise the new and abundant age. The legend is adopted from the reign of Pertinax, so we need not see any overwhelmingly African connotations. Nonetheless, there was a decision to portray a deity well outside traditional Roman iconography. One imagines that this would not have been done without the permission or directive of the emperor or his Caesar. Herodian comments that Severus gave permission to the mint of Rome to strike coins for Albinus.[35] The statement

[30] Barnes 1967: 104. [31] Birley 1969: 265–6; Birley 1971: 169; Birley 1988: 112.

[32] Alföldi 1977: 1–30; Cadotte 2003: 196; Mattingly and Sydenham 1936: 41–2. Codotte's collection of evidence from Roman Africa shows that *frugifer* was an epithet that could be given to different deities, as well as acting as a deity in its own right.

[33] Desnier 1994: 753–4. [34] Lichtenberger 2011: 104.

[35] Hdn. 2.15.5. Although Herodian may have included the anecdote to illustrate that Severus had accepted Albinus as a partner in the empire, the decision to use this specific example alludes to the importance of coinage as an expression of the emperor's wishes.

demonstrates the ancient view that there was communication between the mint and the princeps, and that coinage was the privilege of the emperor and his co-ruler. Albinus, and his particular brand of divine support, would bring abundance to the empire in a new age of fertility.

Only one specimen of Albinus' Baal Hammon type survives to the modern day, preserved in the British Museum. Struck in gold, probably in very small numbers, it is evident that the imagery was not intended for wide circulation. The appearance of the Baal Hammon type on medals also suggests a targeted audience.[36]

Medallions differed from ordinary coinage in several ways, not least because they probably formed a gift given directly by the emperor himself. Consequently, they can be very closely connected with the person of the princeps. Most medallions were probably given out during New Year's Day celebrations, as indicated by the fact that some examples carry the wish for a lucky and happy year (*S P Q R AN(num) F(austum) F(elicem)*).[37] Medallions might also have served as gifts on other occasions (for instance imperial marriages, births and deaths), but this is uncertain.[38] The variety of subject matter displayed on medallions led Toynbee to conclude that they were distributed on a variety of occasions, yet it is just as likely that the medallions given on New Year's Day celebrated all the events of a previous year.[39] The survival of medallions of Commodus dating to *after* the emperor's death illustrate that these medals could be prepared in advance (in this instance, the death of the emperor meant that the medals were probably never distributed).[40]

The relatively small number of surviving specimens and the archaeological contexts of medallions suggest that they were given to select groups, probably to those in high civil or military office.[41] They were evidently

[36] Gnecchi 1912: (vol. 2) 73 no. 4. Gnecchi knew of three examples.

[37] For example Gnecchi 1912: (vol. 2) 14 no. 44 (from the reign of Antoninus Pius); Toynbee 1944b: 40. See Alföldi 1938–1941: 312–41 and Boon 1958: 237–40 on the similar practice of cake distribution at festivals. For the presentation of coins by the emperor at festivals, particularly on New Year's Day, see Ov. *Fast.* 1.218–30; Mart. 8.33.11–12; Suet. *Aug.* 57, *Tib.* 34, *Calig.* 42; Auson. *Ep.* 13; Symmachus *Relat.* 7; Bellinger 1958: 127; Clay 1976: 253–65; Grant 1957: 167–74; Toynbee 1944a: 73–121; and Toynbee 1944b: 27–44.

[38] Clay 1976: 254–62; Toynbee 1944a: 73–121.

[39] For example, medallions recording a military victory of Marcus Aurelius were not struck until the following year, probably because the medallions were only struck for the New Year festivities (Clay 1976: 256).

[40] Toynbee 1944b: 39. The coins are dated by Commodus' tribunician power. Though the memory of Commodus was resuscitated under Severus, these pieces show Commodus as a living ruler (in possession of tribunician power) rather than as a deified one, and thus must have been prepared while he was still alive.

[41] Toynbee 1944a: 112–13.

treasured: medallions from the second century have been found in tombs of the third and fourth centuries, suggesting that they had became heirlooms.[42] *Aes* medallions, with which we are concerned here, were distinguished by their fine design and heavy weight. The weight of medallions bore no relation to the metrological systems in use, suggesting they were not meant to circulate as currency.[43]

The presence of Baal Hammon on this imperial gift would have underlined the deity's connection to Albinus and Severus in the minds of the recipients. Though these medallions were not created in large numbers, and did not enter wider circulation, they were created with a specific audience in mind, and the targeted message would have been received upon the presentation of the gift. The message contained in the medallion achieved its purpose, regardless of later use or context.

Consequently, despite the small number of surviving specimens, the introduction of the imagery of Baal Hammon to the Roman mint is significant. The broader message of a new age had been borrowed from Pertinax, but Hadrumetine imagery was introduced to signify the role of Albinus (and his divine support), in the new reign of abundance. This integration of the 'provincial' into the wider rhetoric of Rome would become a feature of Severus' reign, and those of his successors.

Sharples' study of Albinus' other SAECVLO FRVGIFERO type (the composite deity with *caduceus* and trident) uncovered eight examples, including two in hoards.[44] Severus' SAECVLO FRVGIFERO silver type had three examples in the hoard analysis: one in the large Shapwick Villa hoard in Britain, one in the Rustschuk hoard (Bulgaria) and one example in the Reka-Devnia hoard (Bulgaria). Like Pertinax's type, these were not large issues, but their significance lies in the acquisition and personalisation of a previous emperor's ideology.

The defeat of Pescennius Niger and Severus' eastern mints

Severus entered Rome in AD 193 and then turned his attention to his remaining rival, Pescennius Niger. During his campaign against Niger Severus again adopted the imagery of another, this time his competitor. Niger's coinage included types of Spes, Fides, Ceres, Felicitas, Fortuna and Moneta. All of these types also appear on Severus' coinage: even the legends

[42] Molinari 2002: 203–17; Toynbee 1944a: 121. [43] Clay 1976: 253–4. [44] Sharples 1981: 18.

are identical.[45] To understand this phenomenon more fully, we must locate the mints of Severus as he travelled east.

In the *Roman Imperial Coinage* catalogue, Mattingly attributed Niger's coins to the mint at Antioch. For Severus, he identified three different 'styles' of coinage, which he assigned to four different mints: Rome, Alexandria, Emesa (since this was the homeland of Domna) and Laodicea ad Mare.[46] The last was chosen instead of Antioch since Severus had punished the city for supporting Niger.[47] Mattingly supposed that as a consequence, the mint in Antioch was closed. Close analysis of Niger's coinage now suggests that he not only struck coins at Antioch, but at Caesarea in Cappadocia and at Alexandria.[48]

Recent studies on the 'eastern' coinage of Septimius Severus have also advanced Mattingly's original attributions. Both Butcher and Buttrey have pointed to the marked similarities between Niger's coinage and Severus' eastern types and concluded that Severus took over Niger's Antioch mint.[49] Not only is there a continuity of types between the two rulers, but the style of the lettering is also very similar, suggesting that the same mint workers cut dies for Niger, and then for Severus (the coins of Niger and Severus are both characterised by a 'hook' on the letter F).[50] The most probable conclusion is that Niger's mint at Caesarea was closed after his defeat, and that Severus took over Niger's mints at Antioch and Alexandria.[51] This hypothesis also fits well with the metallurgical analysis of Severan denarii, which suggests two different mints for Severus' eastern types.[52]

Since it is likely that Severus took over Niger's mints, Buttrey has questioned the extent to which Severus' eastern coin types can be seen as a conscious programme. Did the mint workers simply continue to strike the same images, with little thought given to the change of emperor? The question is an important one: in at least one instance Severus is accidentally given Niger's reverse legend.[53] However, a new type (*liberalitas*) was introduced for Severus, and Niger's IVSTITIA AVGVSTI types (which had

45 Bickford-Smith 1994/5: 58. 46 Mattingly 1932: 177–98. See also Pink 1933: 21.

47 Downey 1937: 141–56; Kushnir-Stein 2000: 149–54; Thiel 2005: 103–18; and Ziegler 1978: 493–514.

48 van Heesch 1978: 57–72, developed by Bland, Burnett et al. 1987: 65–83. See also Buttrey 1992: iv–xxi, xix; McAlee 2007: 260; and Metcalf 1996b: 255–6. For the relationship between the Roman mint and that at Caesarea in Cappadocia see Metcalf 1996a: 83–90.

49 Butcher 2004: 98–108; Buttrey 1992: xx. 50 Buttrey 1992: xx.

51 Bland, Burnett et al. 1987: 70. 52 Gitler and Ponting 2003.

53 Instead of VICTOR SEVER AVG, the reverse legend reads VICTOR IVST AVG (*BMCRE* V *Septimius Severus* 338 (pl. 15.9), 398 (pl. 17.8); Buttrey 1992: xxi). IVSTVS was a title bestowed on Niger. Here presumably is an obvious mint error, and future study of the number of examples and dies of this piece may shed some light on whether this error was caught at the mint, and what actions (if any) might have resulted.

obvious associations with Niger's title 'the Just'), and SALVS AVGVSTI types were abandoned. The abandonment of the *salus* type, Buttrey observed, is difficult to understand.[54] Both the *iustitia* and *salus* types, however, have been tied to the mint at Caesarea; their cessation might then reflect little more than the closure of the mint after Niger's defeat.[55] Moreover, the introduction of the *liberalitas* type illustrates the ability of the Antioch mint to adapt if directed from above or motivated from within. It is thus possible that the mint consciously and intentionally continued to strike Niger's imagery for Severus, creating a deliberate assimilation of Niger's reverse types. Through this absorption Severus could negate Niger's public image.

Dio records that Vitellius kept Otho's coin types in circulation even after the latter's defeat in the civil war of AD 69.[56] Cheung believes this is significant, since a destruction of Otho's coins would have been tantamount to a comprehensive *damnatio memoriae* of a principate that left no other monument except a tomb at Bedriacum.[57] Severus was more ruthless. By assuming for himself the imagery of Niger's only 'monuments', his actions were equivalent to a *damnatio*. Given the large number of dies known for Niger's coinage and the very small number of surviving specimens, it is likely that much of Niger's coinage was recalled and re-struck in the name of Severus.[58] It was visual obliteration, and Severus absorbed the imagery and ideology of his rival. The continuation of Niger's types thus had a very different tone to the reuse of themes from the reign of Pertinax.

Hercules and Liber Pater in civil war ideology

The initial encounter with Niger by Severus' army at Nicaea in December AD 193 resulted in victory, and Pescennius withdrew to Antioch.[59] It was after this victory (for which Severus received the title *imperator* for the second and third times) that the coin type showing Liber Pater and Hercules was released, with the legend DIS AVSPICIB(us) (Figure 1). Severus' divine sanction was displayed in an explicit manner. This was the first time the gods Liber Pater and Hercules had been portrayed together on Roman coinage, a clear reference to their close association within the city of Lepcis Magna. The legend, *dis auspicib[us]*, was also new.[60]

Within Lepcis Magna, Liber Pater and Hercules were hellenised versions of the Phoenician gods *Mlk-strt* and *Sdrp'*.[61] Both were 'romanised' by the

[54] Buttrey 1992: xxii. [55] Bland, Burnett et al. 1987: 67 n.7. [56] Dio 65.6.1.
[57] Cheung 1998: 57. [58] Buttrey 1992: xxii. [59] Birley 1988: 110.
[60] Lichtenberger 2007: 45.
[61] Lipinski 1993: 41–50. By the Severan period it is likely that little trace of the original Phoenician cult remained, making any suggestion that Severus 'romanised' the deities misleading (Lichtenberger 2007: 38; Mundle 1957: 86; Rubin 1971: 9).

Severan period, but retained elements of their earlier Phoenician and Punic heritage.[62] Coinage issued by Lepcis from the first century BC displays images of Hercules and Liber Pater, as well as the Tyche of the city.[63] Epigraphic evidence attests to the importance of the two gods within the local cultural life of the city as *di patrii*.[64] The close portrayal of the two deities together on Roman imperial coinage had Lepcitanian overtones: Severus was using his *patria* in civil war ideology.

The *dis auspicib* type was released in gold in early AD 194, then in both gold and silver later in the year.[65] The silver type is absent from the hoards analysed. One might then question the significance of the issue: it would not have formed an overwhelming proportion of the emperor's numismatic imagery in this period, or after. However, the meaning of the iconography may not lie in quantity, but in chronology. Liber Pater and Hercules appear on Severus' coinage *before* Jupiter, who was traditionally associated with assumption to the throne.[66] Jupiter only appears on Severus' next emission, shown handing a globe to the emperor.[67] The god does not appear on Severus' *aes* coinage until AD 195/6, more than a year after the Lepcitanian deities.[68] That the Roman mint joined the image of the emperor with Liber Pater and Hercules before Jupiter reflects contemporary perceptions of who was responsible for the Severus' military success.

Another type was released concurrently with the *dis auspicib* image, showing Liber Pater with *thyrsus* and a leopard. The reverse legend read LIBERO PATRI, and the type was struck at the Roman mint until AD 198 (Figure 5).[69] The type only appears on silver and gold coinage, not *aes*. A similar image had appeared on cistophoric tetradrachms under Hadrian (intended for circulation within Asia Minor), but this was the first time the image and the legend had been placed on imperial coinage struck in Rome. Liber Pater was connected in the Roman world with Dionysus/Bacchus, conqueror of the East.[70] Considering that the war against Niger took place in the East, and was followed with a war against Parthia, the Lepcitanian Liber Pater articulated Severus' achievements within a thoroughly 'Roman' context. Having a particularly close connection to the deity through his Lepcitanian heritage, Severus could expect the support of Liber Pater/Bacchus, a god with very 'Roman' significance.

62 Lichtenberger 2007: 29–38; Lichtenberger 2011: 34.
63 Jenkins 1973–4: 29–35; Vanni 1990: 33–73. 64 *IRT* 289, 275, 287–8, 294–6, 298.
65 *RIC* IV.1 *Septimius Severus* 25, 31. 66 Fears 1981: 3–141.
67 *RIC* IV.1 *Septimius Severus* 34–5. 68 *RIC* IV.1 *Septimius Severus* 704.
69 *RIC* IV.1 *Septimius Severus* 32, 44, 99, 112. 70 Bruhl 1953: 13–14.

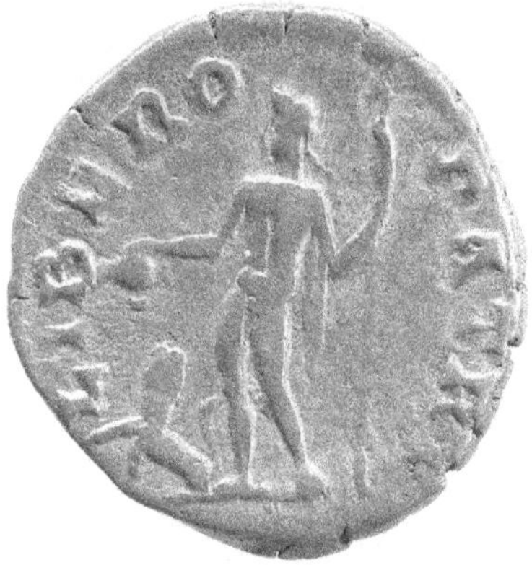

Figure 5: Denarius (reverse) of Septimius Severus with Liber Pater and the legend LIBERO PATRI.

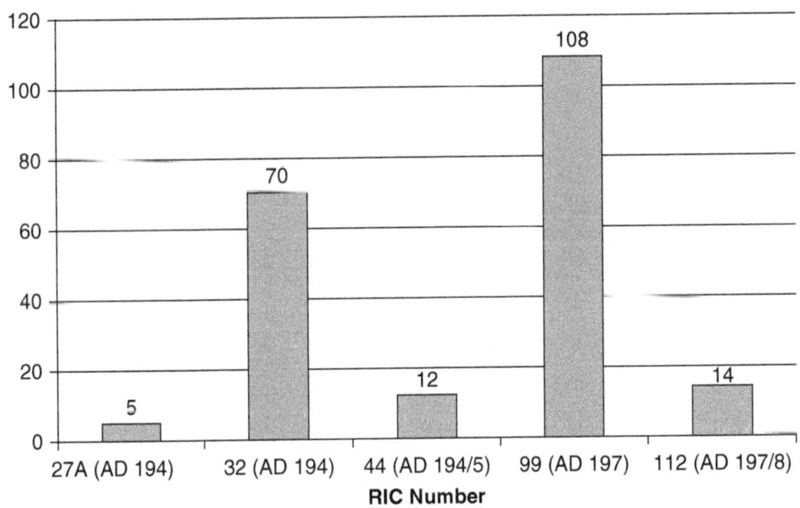

Figure 6: Silver Liber Pater types of Severus (AD 194–198) as represented in hoards.

This divine support was combined with other ideologies that communicated the inevitability of a Severan victory. Literary evidence preserves the omens surrounding Niger's defeat that may have been included by Severus in his autobiography.[71] That Hercules and Liber Pater were only part of a wider ideology is revealed in the coin hoard evidence. Within the hoard sample, a significant number of Liber Pater types struck in AD 194 were uncovered (Figure 6). We can contextualise these raw numbers by comparing the Liber Pater types with other coin types known to have been struck in

[71] Dio 75.8.2.

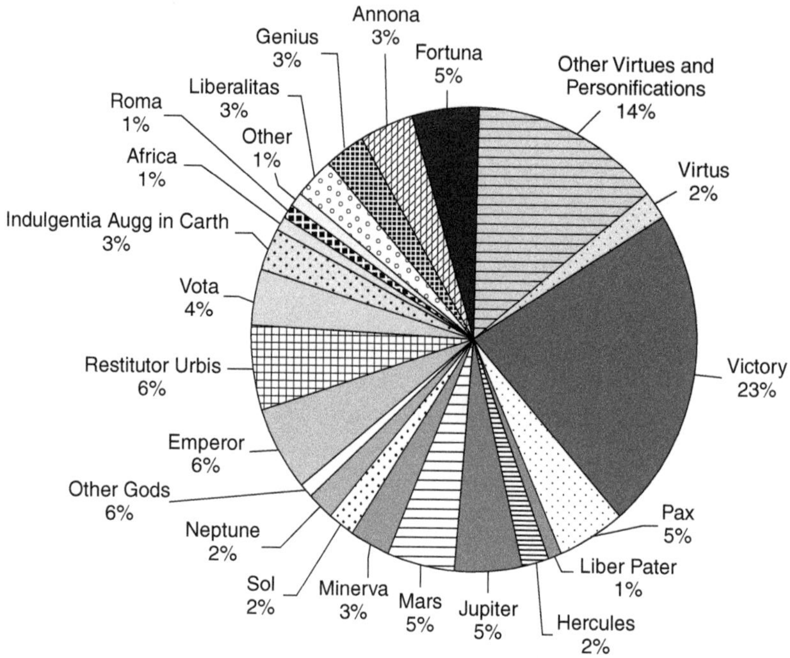

Figure 7: Reverse silver types of Septimius Severus as represented in hoards (n = 15,100).

AD 194. This suggests that the two Liber types (*RIC* IV.1 *Septimius Severus* 27A, 32) constituted approximately 33 per cent of the silver coins of Severus that we can securely date to that year. The type increases in quantity again in AD 197, the year Severus defeated Albinus.

When we examine all of Severus' denarii in the hoard sample, however, it is evident that the Liber Pater types only constituted 1 per cent of the emperor's total silver coinage (Figure 7). The association of the god with the emperor would thus not have been overwhelming from a broader, long-term perspective. The types clearly formed a focus for a discrete period, and for a particular historical context. By contrast, the great majority of Severus' silver types emphasised the emperor's victories and military might. This was communicated through traditional Roman iconography: Victory, the emperor's *virtus*, trophies and captives. A substantial number of personifications also graced the emperor's coinage (Figure 7). Images of victory, virtues, personifications and *pax* make up more than half of Severus' reverse types. In this sense Severus' public image was that of a military emperor, and it is not surprising that some of his coinage recalls the emperor Trajan.[72] However, the new iconography of Liber Pater and Hercules introduced to

[72] Desnier 1997: 191–3. One coin type shows Severus on a horse with the legend S P Q R OPTIMO PRINCIPI (*RIC* IV.1 *Septimius Severus* 169, 415), an obvious reference to Trajan.

Roman coinage, and connected to Severus by his portrait on the other side of the coin, reflect a contemporary association. A conscious decision was made to expand the repertoire of the mint, and the divine associations of the emperor. This highlights the close connection between the emperor and his coinage discussed in the Introduction.

The *dis auspicib* type displaying Liber Pater and Hercules also appears in medallic form.[73] Released in AD 195, this medallion likely referred to Severus' victory over Niger the year before. Other medallions that can be securely dated to AD 195 also have military themes, including the *fides* of the army and the image of Victory.[74] As discussed above, medallions were closely connected to the person of the emperor, and the presence of Liber Pater and Hercules within this context is a significant statement about their association with Severus' military success.

Hercules Defensor and the war against Albinus

After the final defeat of Niger and a Parthian campaign, Severus was proclaimed *imperator* for the eighth time. After settling matters in the East, he returned to Rome in AD 196. It was apparent that Severus intended to break with Albinus, who was stationed in Lugdunum. Caracalla was made Caesar, indicating that Severus' biological son, and not Albinus, was to inherit the throne.[75] Herodian's account implies that he went straight from one civil war to another, though, as Birley observes, Severus could not have acted that quickly.[76] In AD 196/7, around the time Severus broke with Albinus, another new coin type was introduced at the Roman mint. This time Hercules is portrayed alone, with bow and lion-skin, accompanied by the legend HERCVLI DEFENS (Figure 8).[77] This epithet is traditionally interpreted as an abbreviation of *defensor*, and thus we might see here a representation of Hercules as a defender or protector. Just as Bacchus/Liber Pater was traditionally associated with conquests in the East, Hercules was believed to have brought civilisation to the West.[78] Once again there is a multi-layered

[73] Gnecchi 1912: (vol. 2) 73 no. 4; Grueber and Poole 1874: no. 2.

[74] Gnecchi 1912: (vol. 2) 75 no. 16, 23–5. [75] Heil 2006: 55–85.

[76] Hdn. 3.5.1; Birley 1988: 121. The accounts of the civil wars in Dio and Herodian are complex and problematic. Herodian's account in particular has chronological problems (Kolb 1972: 70–7; Zimmermann 1999b: 173–201).

[77] *RIC* IV.1 *Septimius Severus* 79, 97, 111, 488. Hercules *defensor* is known from inscriptions: *AE* 1993, 1338 (Apulum); *AE* 1999, 24 (Rome); *CIL* 6.308 (Rome); *CIL* 6.309 (Rome); *CIL* 6.333 (Rome).

[78] Desnier 1994: 760.

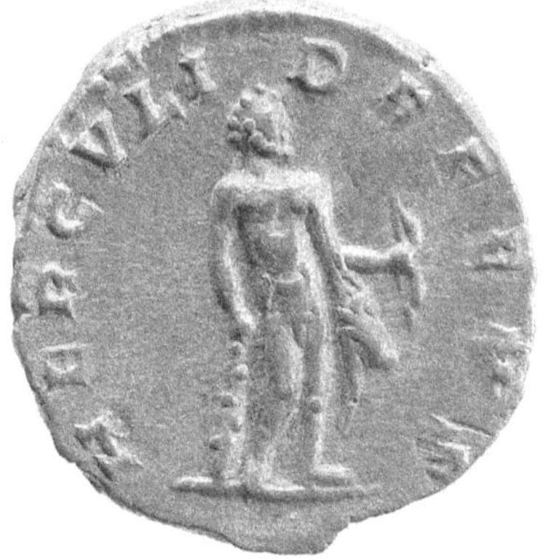

Figure 8: Denarius (reverse) of Septimius Severus displaying Hercules with bow and club and the legend HERCVLI DEFENS.

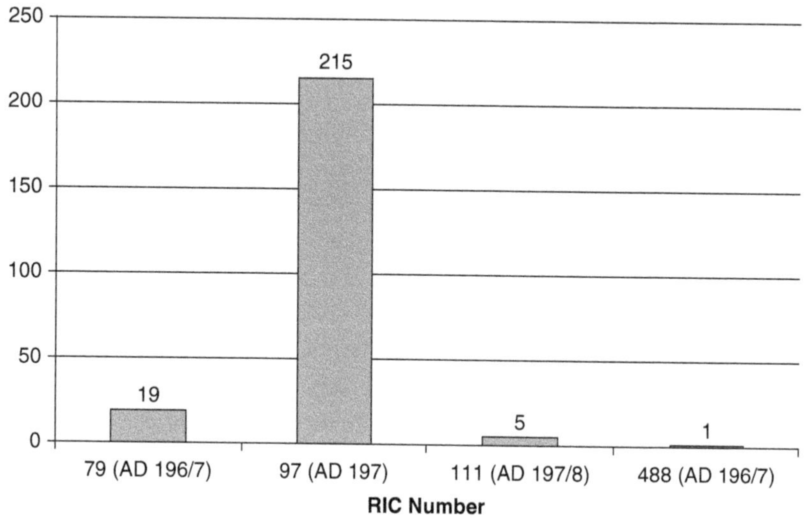

Figure 9: Silver Hercules types of Severus (AD 196–198) as represented in hoards.

meaning within the Severan image: Hercules was simultaneously a patron deity of Lepcis Magna and closely connected with the West of the empire. Roman and Lepcitanian implications were simultaneously apparent in this particular part of the ideology employed in the war against Albinus.

Hoard analysis reveals that this type reached a peak in production in AD 197 (Figure 9).[79] The type itself was only struck from AD 196 to 198,

[79] The near absence of the eastern type of Hercules *defensor* (*RIC* IV.1 *Septimius Severus* 488) may reflect the fact that it is only differentiated from *RIC* IV.1 *Septimius Severus* 97 on the basis of style. Those without specific training in Severan numismatics may not have been able to differentiate between the two identical types.

suggesting that it had a specific context: the war against Albinus.[80] Hercules' epithet *defensor* was likely connected to the propaganda that formed part of Severus' campaign. Herodian may preserve some of this. He records that Severus did not immediately break with his Caesar, but sought a pretext: Albinus had become a threat to Rome.[81] *Defensor* highlights the idea that Albinus was a menace, and the epithet was apt for the god who would guide Severus to victory.[82] Whether by coincidence or design, the two deities whom Severus could lay special claim to could, in turn, represent Severus' conquest of the East and of the West within a recognisable Roman ideology. In AD 197, after Albinus was defeated at Lugdunum, Severus could claim to have reconquered the Roman world, marked by another peak in the production of the Liber Pater type (Figure 6).

Hercules and the Antonine adoption

In going to war against Albinus, Severus had to contend with his rival's impressive lineage.[83] This was doubtless a contributing factor in Severus' decision to adopt himself into the Antonine dynasty as the son of Marcus Aurelius and brother of Commodus.[84] Adoption into the Antonine dynasty provided Severus with much-needed legitimacy, but one imagines that the deification of the unpopular Commodus must have been a delicate affair. A glimpse of the reaction to the Antonine adoption is provided by an anecdote preserved in Dio. Upon hearing of the adoption Auspex (a man famous for his humour) proceeded to congratulate Severus on having found a father.[85]

The deification of Commodus and Severus' adoption into the Antonine dynasty lent yet another layer of significance to the Herculean imagery in the conflict against Albinus. At the end of his reign Commodus had become closely associated with (and assimilated to) Hercules, appearing on Roman coinage in AD 192 wearing a lion-skin headdress.[86] Dio records that Commodus gave himself the name of Hercules, and reverse legends on Commodus' coinage read HERCVLI ROMANO AVG.[87] Commodus is also portrayed as Hercules in statuary, perhaps most notably in the bust found in

[80] Hekster 2002: 188. [81] Hdn. 3.5.3.

[82] Part of the propaganda might also have been picked up by the author of the *Historia Augusta*, who records that Albinus caused the civil war by revolting in Gaul (*SHA Sev.* 10.2).

[83] Dio 76.6.2; Hdn. 2.15.1, 3.5.2; *SHA Albinus* 1.3–4.

[84] Dio 76.7.4; SHA *Sev.* 11.8; Cooley 2007: 385–6. [85] Dio 77.9.4.

[86] *RIC* III *Commodus* 247, 250–4, 616, 629, 634, 637–40, 643–5; Alföldi 1999: 54–6; Hekster 2002: 104–6; Palagia 1986: 147.

[87] Dio 73.15.2.

the *horti Lamiani* and now in display in the Capitoline Museum in Rome.[88] In aligning himself with Hercules Commodus was continuing a tradition that had become popular since the time of Alexander the Great, but might also have been referencing the large Hercules cult in Lanuvium, the city of his birth.[89] Like Severus' use of the god, the Herculean support of Commodus probably had differing levels of association, referencing both his *patria* and wider Hellenistic and Roman ideology. Severus' association with Hercules recalled that of his adopted brother, underlining the connection between Septimius and the dynasty he was claiming as his own. A statue of the weary Hercules with a head of Commodus attached to it was uncovered in the 'stadium' or *hippodromus Palatii* in the imperial complex on the Palatine.[90] It is now in the Palazzo Pitti in Florence. That this statue should have been found in the area, along with Severan period decorations, suggests that it might have been displayed in the Severan 'stadium' area, perhaps as a monument to Severus' adopted brother.[91]

The connection between Severus and Commodus was made even more explicit in AD 202, on a medallion showing Severus with a lion-skin headdress.[92] The image has obvious parallels with Commodus. Severus was also shown with a lion-skin on select coin issues, though in these instances the skin rests around the emperor's shoulder.[93] The medallion, with a specific (and presumably receptive) audience in mind, was able to take the imagery further. By being shown with a lion-skin Severus recalled both Commodus and his patron deity.[94] That this portrait of Severus was influenced by a Commodian prototype is apparent when one considers Severus' other portraits. Severus' beard recalls those of the Antonine emperors, particularly Marcus Aurelius, Severus' adopted father.[95] Severus' very features were designed to underline his connections with the preceding dynasty.

The reception of these divine and dynastic claims is evident in the Rennes patera, found in a hoard in that city in France in 1774.[96] The centre of the gold patera contains a dining scene with Hercules and Dionysus, symbolising the contest between strength and wine. The scene is framed by sixteen aurei all with their obverse sides on display, portraying portraits ranging from Hadrian to Julia Domna. Both the central scene and the outer ring of

88 Hekster 2002: 121–2. 89 Hekster 2002: 108. 90 Lusnia 1998: 207–8.
91 Lusnia 1998: 208.
92 Gnecchi 1912: (vol. 3) 39 no. 1, pl. 152 no. 6; Hekster 2002: 192; McCann 1968: 56.
93 *BMCRE* V *Septimius Severus* 192–192a, pl. 31; McCann 1968: 56. 94 Vermeule 1977: 292.
95 Baharal 1989: 579.
96 Vermeule 1975: 12; Bibliothèque Nationale (Paris) Department of Coins, Medals and Antiquities, Chabouillet no. 2537.

portraits strongly suggest that this piece was constructed in the Severan period, though it was not buried in the hoard until sometime during the reign of Aurelian. The image of Hercules and Dionysus echoes the divine claims of Severus, and the selection of the outer portraits recalls the Severan adoption into the Antonine dynasty. By interspersing the portraits of Severus, Caracalla, Domna and Geta with the portraits of Hadrian, Antoninus Pius, Marcus Aurelius, Faustina the Elder and Faustina the Younger, the piece communicates the idea of one unified Antonine dynasty. The overall impression from the piece is that of a sophisticated private interpretation of imperial ideology, and one that made poignant use of coinage.

Although this work has focused on the numismatic representations of Hercules and his connection to Severus, it is evident that coinage formed merely one medium through which the emperor's divine support was communicated. A lead seal of Severus in the British Museum carries the portrait of the emperor on one side and a portrait of Hercules on the other.[97] A terracotta tile coming from the imperial estates of Severus is stamped with an image of Hercules leaning on a club.[98] These examples hint at the fact that the ideology seen on Severus' coinage would also have been carried on other media, although these other pieces have not survived in the same numbers as their numismatic counterparts.

The reception of imperial ideology: the *equites singulares Augusti*

A series of inscriptions set up by the *equites singulares Augusti* may also reflect recognition within Rome of the rôle claimed for Hercules in the war against Albinus. The *equites singulares* were mounted imperial bodyguards who acted as the cavalry arm of the Praetorian Guard and followed the emperor on campaign. Severus increased their number and built a new complex for them on the Caelian Hill.[99] On the 8 June AD 197 three of the *equites* erected an inscription in Rome celebrating the return of the unit, most likely from the campaign against Albinus in Gaul.[100] The inscription was dedicated to Hercules *Invictus* and to the other gods and goddesses for the health (*pro salute*) of the imperial family. Similar dedications were made to Hercules *Invictus* by the *equites* in AD 200, AD 202 and sometime before AD 205.[101] Given the proximity of these troops to the emperor, these dedications may reflect a conscious incorporation of imperial ideology

[97] BM 1907, 0503.3. [98] BM 1926, 0324.131. [99] Lusnia 1998: 51–7; Speidel 1994b: 59.
[100] *CIL* 6.224; Birley 1988: 128. [101] *CIL* 6.226; *CIL* 6.227; Speidel 1994a: 77–83, nos. 55–7, 59.

into a more 'private' religious sphere. A broader examination of the religious life of this group as it is preserved in the epigraphic record reveals a tendency to sacrifice to a large variety of gods, both Roman and provincial, including Hercules.[102] Dedications to Hercules *Invictus*, though, only appear under Septimius, underpinning the idea it was connected to the emperor's religious programme. The epithet *Invictus* ('the unconquerable') has decidedly military overtones, which complement the association of the deity with Severus' campaigns. That there were a number of dedications, set up over a number of years, suggests the continued connection of Hercules 'the invincible' with the person of Severus in the minds of the *equites singulares*.

In his examination of the *equites singulares*, Speidel noted the discovery of a large statue of Bacchus of very fine workmanship in the barracks on the Caelian Hill.[103] Since Bacchus is not otherwise known in the religious life of the *equites*, he suggested that the statue's presence might be connected to the reign of Septimius Severus.[104] Considering Severus was responsible for the construction of these barracks, this is very plausible. Both Liber Pater and Hercules might have been incorporated into the cultic activities of the *equites*, a reflection of the close connection between these individuals and the person of the emperor. The *equites* could have appropriated Severus' ideology to underscore their own high status as cavalry members of the imperial bodyguard.

After the civil wars, Severus spent a brief period in Rome before embarking on a second Parthian war, then journeying to Egypt. He would be absent from Rome for five years.[105] He returned to the city as a military victor, having been in power for ten years. The presence of the princeps in the capital was marked by a series of celebrations, notably the emperor's *decennalia* and the saecular games. These games would form an arena through which Severus could proclaim his divine support, the eternity of the Severan dynasty, and the benefits of his rule for the empire.

Sacra saecularia: the celebration of the saecular games (AD 204)

Herodian describes the celebration of the saecular games under Severus in AD 204.[106] The author's claim to have been an eyewitness of the event

[102] Speidel 1994a: 30–2.

[103] Frothingtham Jr 1886: 222. Lanciani believed the statue originally stood on one of the 43 marble pedestals found in a hall.

[104] Speidel 1994b: 140. [105] Birley 1988: 129. [106] Hdn. 3.8.10.

should be treated with caution: it is precisely when Herodian claims to be an eyewitness that his text becomes closest to what is preserved of Dio.[107] His dependence on Dio's account of the games of Commodus has already been discussed, and he also appears to be dependent on Dio for his 'eyewitness' description of the walls of Byzantium.[108] For the description of the saecular games Herodian may have been using a section of Dio not preserved in the epitome, or he may have transplanted information from the celebration of the games in AD 248.[109]

Dio's description of the games may also be preserved, but his account may have been obscured by the fact his work survives in epitome. In what is widely believed to be a description of Severus' *decennalia* Dio describes an awe-inspiring spectacle:

> The entire receptacle in the amphitheatre had been constructed so as to resemble a boat in shape, and was capable of receiving or discharging four hundred beasts at once; and then, as it suddenly fell apart, there came rushing forth bears, lionesses, panthers, lions, ostriches, wild asses, bisons (this is a kind of cattle foreign in species and appearance) so that seven hundred beasts in all, both wild and domesticated, at one and the same time were seen running about and were slaughtered. For to correspond to the duration of the festival, which lasted seven days, the number of animals was also seven times one hundred.[110]

Carlson pointed out that what Dio describes is similar to the Severan *acta*, an inscription that details the celebration of the Severan saecular games in AD 204.[111] In addition to the solemn celebrations, Severus held additional games or *ludos honorarios*.[112] The *acta* record that the imperial generosity extended to a hunt of 700 wild animals, including lions, lionesses, leopards, bears, bisons, wild donkeys and ostriches.[113] The number and type of animals match Dio's account so closely that the quote above might be a remnant of his description of the saecular games. Both Dio and the *acta* also echo coin types struck for Severus and Caracalla showing a ship surrounded by animals (including an ostrich and a lion) and *quadrigae*, with the legend LAETITIA TEMPORVM (Figure 10).[114] The legend on the coin echoes the *acta*, which also proclaim the 'joy of the times'.[115]

107 Sidebottom 1997: 273 n.15. 108 Hdn. 3.1.6–7; Dio 75.10.1–6; Kolb 1972: 70–7.
109 Sidebottom 1997: 273 n.15. 110 Dio 77.1.4–5. 111 Carlson 1969: 20–1.
112 Pighi 1965: 161, V.44. On the *ludi sollemnes* and *ludi honoraria* see Erkell 1969: 168.
113 Pighi 1965: 161, V.43: *munificen[tia] nostra leones lea[e] leopardi ursi bison(t)es onagri str [uthiones] centeni erunt.*
114 *RIC* IV.1 *Septimius Severus* 274; *RIC* IV.1 *Caracalla* 133, 157; *RIC* IV.1 *Geta* 43.
115 Pighi 1965: 143, I.26: *[cum XVuiri s. f.] c. c. u. u. pro temporum laetitia et felicitate sanctissimorum.*

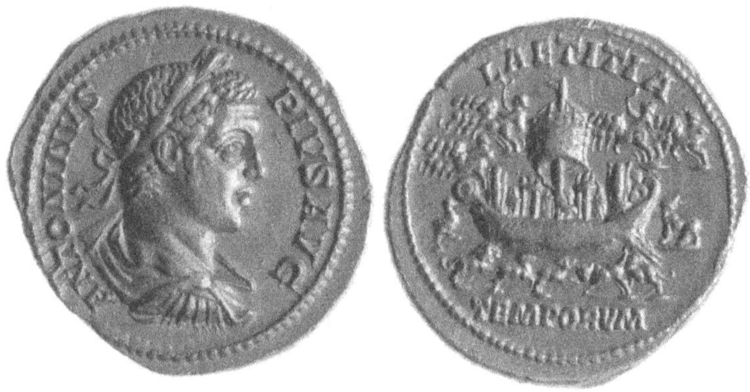

Figure 10: Aureus of Caracalla with a ship surrounded by animals and *quadrigae* and the legend LAETITIA TEMPORVM.

Races with *quadrigae* formed part of the Severan celebrations, and this may have been what prompted the die engravers to include chariot racers on the coin type. Carlson postulated that pages may be missing from the epitome of Dio, so that his description of the *decennalia* and the saecular games have become conflated. In view of the evidence, this is a distinct possibility.

In the epitome of Dio this section comes after the description of Severus' *decennalia* in AD 202, where Dio emphasises the extravagance of the emperor, and before the eruption of Vesuvius (which is believed to have occurred in AD 203).[116] If Xiphilinus preserves the order of Dio's original text (if not the full narrative), then Dio may never have intended this description of the ship and seven hundred animals to form part of his account of the games of AD 204. Dio may have transplanted details of the saecular games to Severus' *decennalia* in order to underscore the extravagance of the emperor. In this Dio may have been inspired by the *acta*, or perhaps by the coin displaying the ship and animals.

While in the Republican period the saecular games were held in times of disaster, under Augustus the celebration was altered to celebrate the success of the princeps and to herald the beginning of a new era.[117] This reinvention is important in understanding how the religious proclivities of an emperor could impact and influence the celebration. During the reign of Severus, his tutelary deities would have a role in the games, but one that was not without precedent.

[116] Dio 77.1.1–3. [117] Davis 2001: 114; Taylor 1934: 101–20.

Saecular games in the imperial period

Saecular games were customarily held at the beginning of each new *saeculum*, defined by the Sibylline oracle as a period of 110 years, though the games themselves were held more frequently than this.[118] There appear to have been two dating systems for celebrating the games during the principate.[119] The emperor Claudius held a celebration in AD 47, evidently calculating the *saeculum* from Rome's founding (AD 47 equates to the 800th anniversary of the founding of Rome). This dating system may have also been followed by Antoninus Pius (AD 147, 900th anniversary) and by Philip (AD 248, 1000th anniversary). Other celebrations followed a different dating system, based on the Republican festival: Augustus (17 BC), Domitian (AD 88) and Severus (AD 204). The games held on the Augustan reckoning have strong similarities in terms of the material produced, and significant differences to those games celebrated according to the Claudian dating. While Augustus, Domitian and Severus all struck coins showing the celebrations and sacrifices, Claudius and Antoninus Pius struck no coins at all, and Philip's series displayed a variety of animals.[120]

Here we are concerned with the games celebrated on the Augustan reckoning. Zosimus provides the best literary description of the saecular games and their history.[121] He records that once it was decided that the games should be held, heralds were sent out inviting people to a spectacle that they had never seen before and would never see again.[122] Citizens brought gifts of agricultural produce to the temples and would receive materials from the *quindecemviri sacris faciundis* (the priesthood responsible for the games) to purify their homes. The *ludi* would then be celebrated, with six sacrifices constituting the main part of a celebration that lasted for three days. Night sacrifices were performed for the *Moerae* (Fates), *Ilithyiae* (associated with childbirth) and Terra Mater, and day sacrifices were held for Jupiter, Juno, Apollo and

118 Taylor 1934: 103. 119 Pighi 1965 remains the best collection of saecular games material.

120 Though Pius' 'commemorative' coin types have often been associated with the saecular games, these coin types might be better connected with the construction of the temple to Venus and Rome, since they continue Hadrianic imagery, and are chronologically connected to the temple (they end in AD 144, when the temple was probably completed), rather than the date of the saecular games in AD 148.

121 Zos. 2.1.

122 The games were only held once in a man's lifetime. It was this tradition that allegedly provoked mirth in relation to Claudius' celebration of the games, since when the herald invited people to games 'which no one had seen before or would ever see again' some of the audience had in fact seen the games before and some of the actors had even appeared in the previous celebrations (Suet. *Claud.* 5.2).

Diana.[123] Pageants were performed and games held in honour of Apollo and Diana.[124] On the second day the matrons of Rome would sacrifice and sing to Juno on the Capitoline and on the third day twenty-seven boys and twenty-seven girls would sing hymns and paeans 'by which the cities subject to the Romans are kept safe'.[125] The final comment by Zosimus reflects the idea that the performance of these games every *saeculum* ensured the continuation of Roman power. Preserved *acta* from the games note the rituals and sacrifices are performed in order that the *imperium* and *maiestas* of the Roman people might continue.[126] For Zosimus, the failure of Constantine to celebrate the games in AD 313 was one of the reasons the 'empire gradually collapsed and was imperceptibly barbarised'.[127]

Contextualising divine ideology in the saecular games

The presence of Liber Pater and Hercules in Severus' celebration of the games has long been recognised.[128] Their presence has been seen as a product of the emperor's provincial background.[129] A closer examination of the history of the saecular games, however, illustrates that Severus' inclusion of his patron gods had precedent in both the reigns of Augustus and Domitian, underscoring the flexibility of Roman religious ritual.

Augustus' transformation of Rome included the transformation of the saecular games to reflect his own ideology. Part of this process was a new focus on Apollo, the god with whom Augustus most closely associated his success.[130] Apollo has a significant place in Horace's *Carmen Saeculare* (the hymn sung during the games), he was given new sacrifices in the saecular festival and overlooked the celebrations from his new temple on the Palatine. That this emphasis had more to do with Augustus' own programme than archaic religious ritual is evident from other aspects of the games. The weight

[123] Zos. 2.5; Sobocinski 2006: 584. [124] Zos. 2.5. [125] Zos. 2.5.

[126] The formula that accompanied each sacrifice in the Severan games is the same, and is preserved in the *acta*: *uti tu imperium maiestatemque p. R. Q. duelli domique auxis utique semper Latinus obtemperassit.* See Pighi 1965: 156, IV.7 (Juno Regina), 162–3 V.49 (Terra Mater), 164 V.56 (Apollo).

[127] Zos. 2.7; Ridley 1982: xi, xiii. Zosimus' account was apparently influenced by the 'Augustan' dating of the games: no mention is made of Philip's celebration.

[128] Carlson 1971–2a: 9–11; Carlson 1971–2b: 27–9; Cooley 2007: 392; Desnier 1994: 764; Gagé 1934: 65–9; Gorrie 2002: 475–9; Hekster 2002: 192–3; Mundle 1957: 147–75; Rubin 1976/7: 155–6; Tocchi 1956: 3–20; Traversari 1956: 21–30.

[129] Carlson 1971–2a: 9–11; Daguet-Gagey 2000: 382.

[130] The god had been present in Republican celebrations of the games (Taylor 1934: 106), but received unprecedented emphasis under Augustus (Barker 1996: 439; Davis 2001: 114–27; Haight 1918: 341–66).

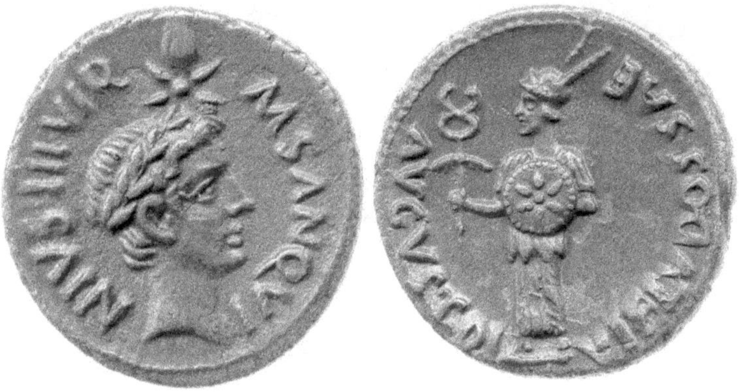

Figure 11: Denarius of the moneyer M. Sanquinius with the head of Caesar on the reverse and saecular herald on the obverse. The reverse legend reads AVGVST DIVI F LVDOS SAEC.

given to matrimony and children in the celebration was reflective of Augustus' marriage legislation, as was the fact that the games were tied closely to the deification of Julius Caesar.[131] The comet that appeared at Caesar's funeral was interpreted as a sign of the new *saeculum* and the *sidus Iulium* was incorporated into the iconography of the celebration.[132] Several coins were released to mark the games, one of which depicted the saecular herald with the comet on his shield (Figure 11).[133]

The comet is also present on the reverse of the coin, above a head probably to be identified as Julius Caesar. This is combined with the obverse legend AVGVST(VS) DIVI F LVDOS SAEC to reinforce the connection of the new *saeculum* with Augustus' divine father.[134] It is evident that the celebration of the saecular games, closely entwined with the continuing success of Rome's empire, also became closely connected to the reigning princeps. Given the power of the emperor to influence Rome's fate, this connection is not surprising. The ideology of the emperor was granted a place in the ritual, shaping it in a way not possible under the Republic.

In Domitian's celebration Minerva was given visual prominence.[135] Coin types reflect the strong association of Domitian's patron deity with the celebration of the games, continuing the Augustan precedent. Literary evidence mentions the Domitianic games briefly, and no inscriptional *acta* survive.[136] The main evidence for the presence of Minerva is thus numismatic. Two coin types of Domitian show the head of either Roma or Minerva on the shield of a *ludio* or participant

[131] Davis 2001: 116. [132] Taylor 1934: 118. [133] *RIC* I^2 *Augustus* 340.
[134] Sobocinski 2006: 589. [135] Dio 77.1.2; Scott 1936: 166–86. [136] Suet. *Dom.* 4.3.

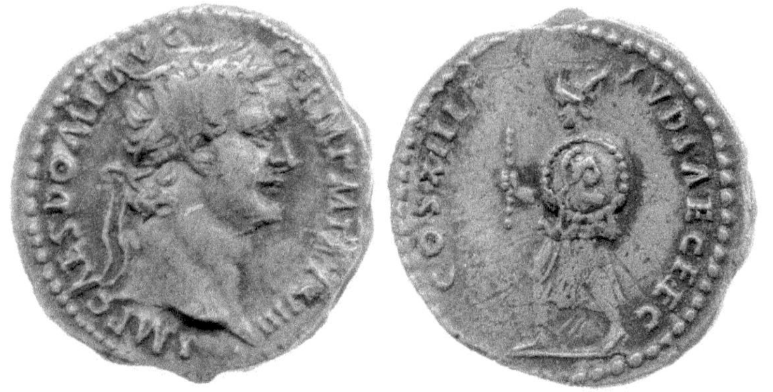

Figure 12: Denarius of Domitian displaying a saecular *ludio* holding a shield decorated with the head of Minerva and the legend COS XIIII LVD SAEC FEC.

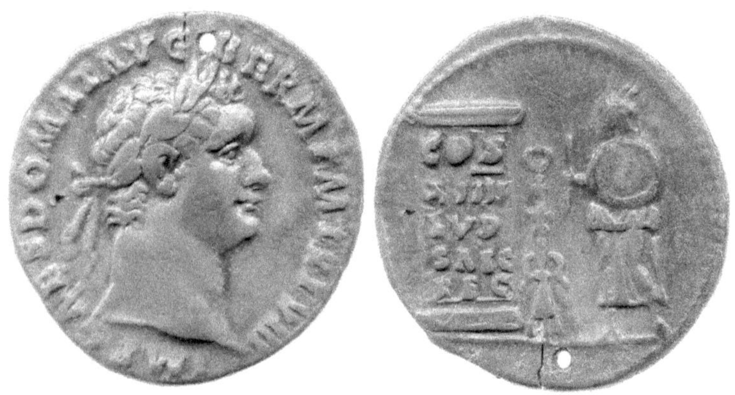

Figure 13: Denarius of Domitian with a *ludio*, candelabrum and *cippus* inscribed COS XIIII LVD SAEC DEC.

in the games (Figures 12–13).[137] Minerva is the most likely interpretation given what we know of Domitian's penchant for the goddess.[138] Her presence here may be symbolic on the part of the die engraver, but it may also reflect the actual dress of the *ludiones* under Domitian.

Domitian appears to have changed the emphasis of the saecular games from Apollo to Minerva, just as Septimius would similarly introduce Liber Pater and Hercules. The saecular games, although tied to ancient ritual, offered opportunity for innovation and change. This may have been because

[137] Sobocinski 2006: 587.

[138] The emperor's coin types have an unparalleled emphasis on the goddess (Mattingly and Sydenham 1926: 151).

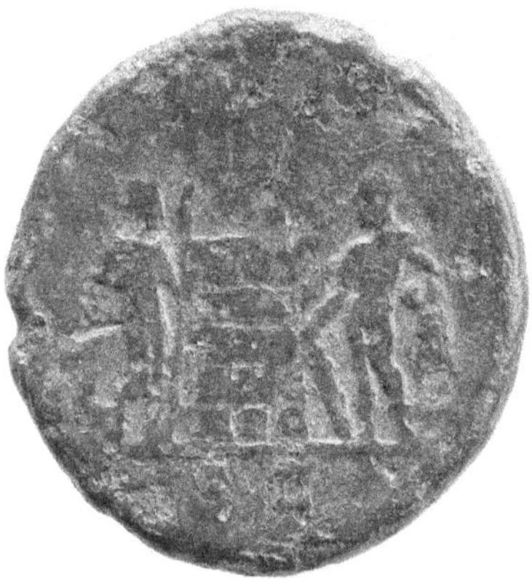

Figure 14: As of Caracalla displaying Liber Pater and Hercules with a *cippus* between them inscribed COS LVD SAEC FEC.

the games were held so rarely (every 100 years or so), that there was no one living who could remember previous celebrations or their precedents. Davis speculates this meant that the ritual was open to reshaping and manipulation in a way more frequently held rituals were not.[139] On the other hand, modern analysis of other Roman rituals suggests that they were not as strict and archaic as previously thought.[140] Alterations in the celebration of the saecular games are equivalent to the modifications and variation found within other Roman religious rites. A balance existed between archaic ritual and the more flexible elements that reflected the contemporary religious ideology of the emperor in power. The introduction of Liber Pater and Hercules to the celebrations was done in the context of this delicate balance.

The Severan saecular celebration and Liber Pater and Hercules

In AD 204 a coin type was released showing the *cippus* onto which the saecular *acta* were inscribed, flanked by Hercules and Liber Pater (Figure 14).[141] This was more conspicuous than Domitian's allusion to Minerva on the shield of the *ludio*, or Augustus' reference to *divus Iulius*. The two gods also appear on coinage without the *cippus*, accompanied by the legend COS III LVDOS SAECVL FEC (Figure 15).[142] The hoard sample indicates that denarii displaying the latter type were not struck in large numbers. Only five examples were uncovered for Severus (*RIC* IV.1 *Severus* 257),

[139] Davis 2001: 113.

[140] Beard 1985: 114–62; Wiseman 2008: 18–23. The polymorphism of Roman religion might also have enabled emperors to change the focus of religious ceremonies. See King 2003: 295 for a discussion.

[141] *RIC* IV.1 *Caracalla* 420.

[142] *RIC* IV.1 *Septimius Severus* 257, 763B, 764A, 765; *RIC Caracalla* IV.1 74, 421.

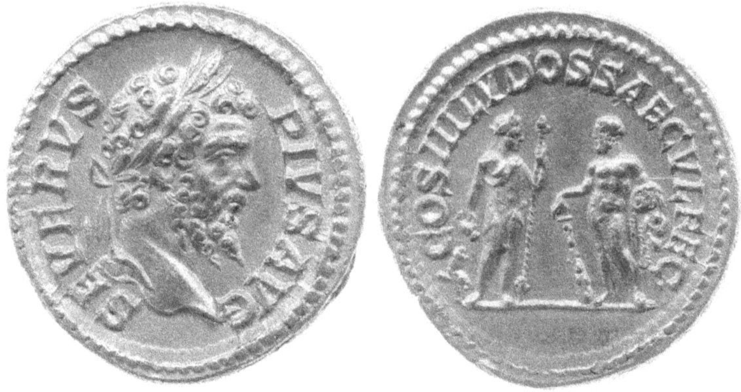

Figure 15: Aureus of Septimius Severus with Liber Pater and Hercules and the legend COS III LVDOS SAECVL FEC.

and only four instances for Caracalla (*RIC* IV.1 *Caracalla* 74), constituting less than 1 per cent of each emperor's total coinage. Another silver saecular games type showing a sacrifice with the legend SACRA SAECVLARIA (*RIC* IV.1 *Severus* 293A) had only two occurrences. One might consequently classify these coins as 'commemorative' pieces, struck to mark the celebration. Though only a small issue, these types have a remarkable geographic spread, present in hoards in modern-day Britain, Germany, Bulgaria and Turkey.[143]

Several other coin issues were released showing scenes from the celebration of the games. Different members of the imperial family were portrayed sacrificing in front of a temple, often accompanied by Tiber, a flute player and a harpist.[144] The legend on these coins reads SACRA SAECVLARIA, and the type is struck on all three metals issued from the mint. Liber Pater and Hercules are absent from these types, which led Mundle to conclude that the legend *sacra saecularia* ('saecular sacrifice') was joined to images relating to the sacrifices and rituals of the games, while the legend *ludos saeculares fecit* ('produced the saecular games') accompanied the imagery of Severus' patron deities, Liber Pater and Hercules.[145] Mundle believed that this division of legends was intentional and that Severus used different phrases to clearly differentiate between the required ritual sacrifices and his patron deities, who were honoured in other, acceptable ways throughout the celebration.

143 Analysis of these very small issues may yield greater insight into the operation of the Roman economy. That this small issue travelled so far suggests an integrated economy, where currency (or silver at least) circulated widely.

144 *RIC* IV.1 *Septimius Severus* 293, 816; *RIC* IV.1 *Caracalla* 462; *RIC* IV.1 *Geta* 132, 137–8.

145 Mundle 1957: 166.

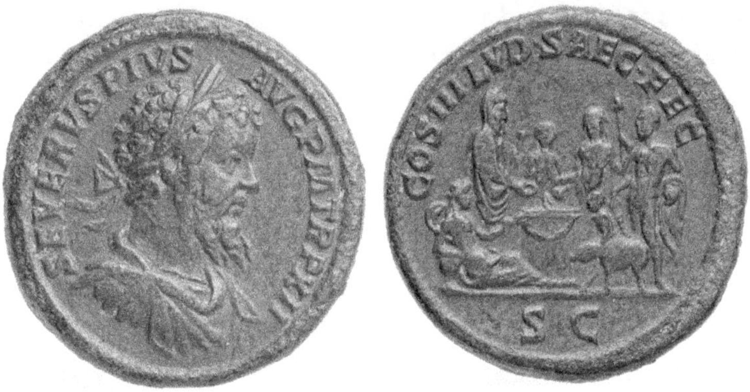

Figure 16: Sestertius of Septimius Severus displaying a sacrificial scene with the emperor, Liber Pater, Hercules, flute player, *victimarius*, pig and Tellus, with the legend COS III LVD SAEC FEC S C.

Mundle's thesis is attractive and suggests that Severus was careful in modifying the celebrations. One coin issue, however, undermines the idea of a careful and deliberate separation of Liber Pater and Hercules from archaic ritual. The type, issued in bronze, shows Liber Pater and Hercules at a scene of sacrifice. Severus (or, alternatively, Caracalla) is shown sacrificing over an altar with Hercules and Bacchus facing him. An attendant with a pig is portrayed approaching the altar, with a personification, likely Tellus, reclining to the left (Figure 16).[146] The presence of the pig suggests that what is represented on the coin was the sacrifice of the pregnant black sow to the earth.[147] Mundle suggested that if Hercules and Liber Pater were also being offered sacrifice, another victim would be present.[148] The suggestion does not consider the limited space of a coin; often scenes were abbreviated for practical reasons. There is thus the distinct possibility that Liber Pater and Hercules also received, or were associated with, the sacrifices of the games. In Tarentum, where the sacrifice of the sow took place, Severan reliefs were found showing scenes from the story of Alcestis and Hercules.[149] The reliefs are extremely fragmentary, so that any explanation remains hypothetical. La Rocca thought that the frieze once formed part of a fence around a monument of the *ludi saeculares*.[150] A large monument bearing scenes from the games and myths from Severus' patron deities, near the area in which the saecular sacrifice took place, remains hypothetical but is certainly possible considering the iconography of this coin.

[146] *RIC* IV.1 *Septimius Severus* 761; *RIC* IV.1 *Caracalla* 418. [147] Zos. 2.6.
[148] Mundle 1957: 173. [149] Romanelli 1931: 313–45; Gorrie 2002: 475.
[150] Gorrie 2002: 476; La Rocca 1984; Lusnia 1998: 164–6.

The Severan *carmen saeculare* also suggests the continuation of Augustan and Domitianic tradition. The *carmen saeculare* was sung during the celebration of the games, part of the Latin paeans mentioned by Zosimus.[151] The best-preserved *carmen* is that composed by Horace for the games of Augustus, in which Apollo featured significantly.[152] The Severan song is preserved in a fragmentary inscription.[153] From what remains, the word Bacchus can be discerned (a god synonymous with Liber Pater).[154] Diehls believed that the mention of these gods in the *carmen saeculare* was an indication that they received sacrifice during the games.[155] The coin showing Hercules and Liber Pater at the sacrifice of the sow (Figure 16) argues in favour of Diehl's interpretation.

The coin type was also directly borrowed from Domitian.[156] As part of the saecular games series of AD 88 Domitian struck a sestertius type showing the emperor sacrificing to Tellus, with an attendant leading a pig to an altar, with two musicians in attendance. The legend on the Domitianic piece is positioned in the same way as the Severan specimen (at the top left and in the exergue), and the composition of the scene is similar. The only difference between the two is that Hercules and Liber Pater have replaced the Domitianic harpist. Since the Severan mint was working from an earlier prototype, the decision to alter the image to include Hercules and Liber Pater must have been a conscious one. Even if Severus did not directly include these gods in the ritual sacrifices, their visual association with the sacrifice nonetheless illustrates that the boundary between innovation and ritual was not clear-cut. As discussed above, personal religious ideology could be incorporated into the celebration of the saecular games. Since the time of Augustus this was just as traditional as the rites themselves. The presence of Liber Pater and Hercules in Severus' celebration cannot be seen as the result of the emperor's provincial background, or as a corruption of a traditional Roman festival.

Saecular coinage, memory and ritual

The close similarities between the saecular games types of Augustus, Domitian and Severus encourage us to look at this coinage from another perspective. In addition to the similarities in type design discussed above,

[151] Zos. 2.6. [152] Barker 1996: 434–46; Davis 2001: 111–27; Putnam 2000.
[153] Pighi 1965: 165.
[154] *rae auratis fundere campia Bacchum pa[...........]imitum coga* (AE 1932, 70; Pighi 1965: 165 V.67).
[155] Diehl 1932, against which Mundle 1957: 162–75. [156] *RIC* II² *Domitian* 614.

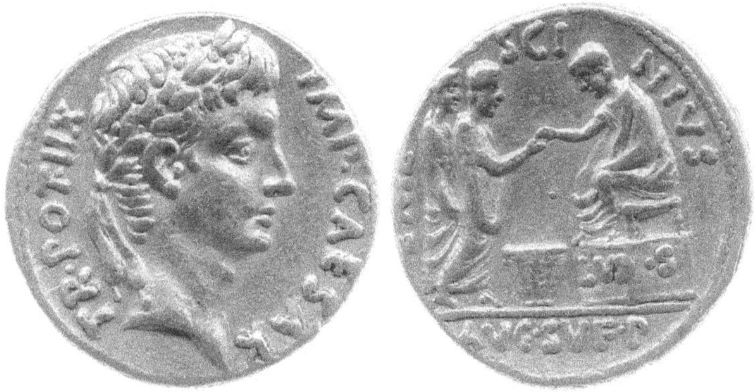

Figure 17: Aureus of Augustus showing the distribution of *suffimenta*.

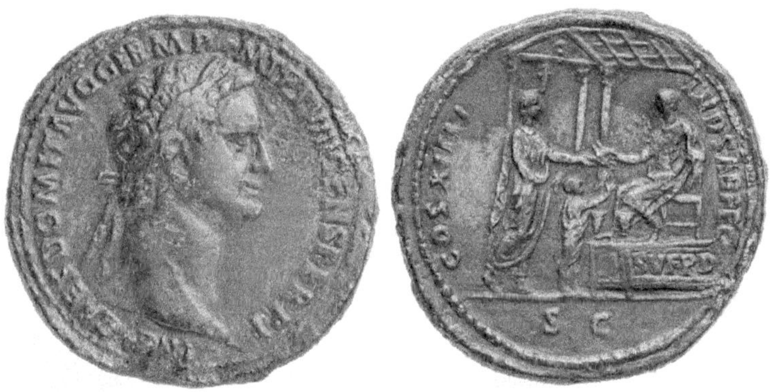

Figure 18: Sestertius of Domitian showing the distribution of *suffimenta*.

Augustus, Domitian and Severus all released coinage showing a *cippus*, on which the final *acta* of the games were inscribed by decree of the senate.[157] Since the coin types and the *acta* of Augustus, Domitian and Severus were over one hundred years apart, any similarities in language or imagery are remarkable. All three emperors likely also released a coin type showing the distribution of *suffimenta*, i.e. materials for purification (Figures 17–19).

This has not been widely recognised, since Severus' type bears the legend FELICITAS SAECVLI.[158] The image has usually been identified as a *liberalitas* distribution. But the legend of Severus' coin, and the similarities to the depiction of the *suffimenta* ceremony on coins of Augustus and

[157] *RIC* I^2 *Augustus* 138–9, 354–8; *RIC* II^2 *Domitian* 600–5; *RIC* IV.1 *Septimius Severus* 764A; *RIC* IV.1 *Caracalla* 420.

[158] *RIC* IV.1 *Septimius Severus* 263.

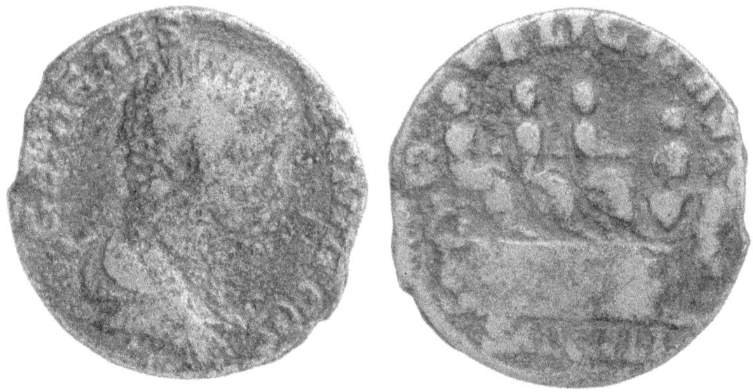

Figure 19: Aes coin of Geta showing the distribution of *suffimenta*.

Domitian suggest otherwise, and we should not be surprised that Severus, having two legends on his saecular games coinage, would employ a third. The iconography of the coin has similarities to the *liberalitas* type, but there are also significant differences. Severus' *liberalitas* types are characterised by the presence of Liberalitas herself, holding an account board and *cornucopiae.*[159] That figure is absent on this issue, as well as the usual legend, LIBERALITAS. The figure behind the urn is best understood as an attendant at the *suffimenta*, one of the priests, or perhaps even Julia Domna. Liberalitas types also typically show the recipient with arms outstretched in front of a ladder; these features are absent from Severus' FELICITAS SAECVLI type. Instead an urn is shown in front of the emperors (something not present on Liberalitas types) and a togate citizen is portrayed taking something directly from the hand of the emperor. All of these factors suggest an identification of the scene as a distribution of *suffimenta*. The *suffimenta* types of Augustus and Domitian both show urns, and also portray togate citizens taking materials directly from the hand of the emperor. The Severan *suffimenta* motif was adapted to include Severus' sons (whom the *acta* record taking an active part in the ritual) and the legend FELICITAS SAECVLI was perhaps introduced as an allusion to Pertinax's promised age of abundance.

Domitian and Severus employ identical legends on their coinage (COS LVD SAEC FEC), the formula only changing to express the different number of consulships each emperor had held. Domitian's saecular coinage incorporated the *candelabrum* present on Augustus' types and continued many other aspects of the Augustan saecular iconography. Sobocinski

[159] For example, *RIC* IV.1 *Septimius Severus* 278–9.

provides an excellent overview of these similarities and their obvious Augustan influence.[160] The connections even extend to the depiction of the emperor's divine support. Under Augustus the *sidus Iulium* is shown on the shield of the herald, while under Domitian Minerva is shown on the shield of a *ludio*.

Sobocinski postulated that the Domitianic mint officials used Augustan coins or dies as one source of their design. A similar phenomenon must have occurred under Severus; Domitianic dies or coins were used as *exempla* to create new pieces. The Severan *acta* echoed the language of former celebrations, and similarly the coins drew upon earlier imagery.[161] Unlike the saecular games coinage of Severus, Domitian's types appear to have been struck in fairly large numbers.[162] In spite of this it is unlikely that Domitianic coins in circulation would have served as inspiration for the mint some 110 years later.[163] One must then posit an alternative source. The phenomenon of 'restitution coinage' (types that had long fallen out of circulation being revived) suggests that a record of coin types was kept in Rome. A record or archive would have allowed the mint workers to recreate and modify types that had been created before they had been born. The original Republican mint was located in the forum near the Tabularium, where official records were kept.[164] It is thus not improbable that Roman coinage could also have functioned as a record or had associations with records and archives.

If the dies or designs for the saecular coins were kept on record, coin types not only served as a decoration of the currency, but as a visual record of the emperor's performance of his religious duty. In the same way that the *acta* of the games were inscribed on a *cippus* (with particular attention paid to the fact that the prescribed ceremonies were performed), coinage may also have functioned as a record of the celebration. The fact that Domitian went to great lengths to portray each and every saecular sacrifice on his coinage argues in favour of this hypothesis.

160 Sobocinski 2006: 586.

161 The Augustan *acta* preserves a formula similar to that found on its Severan counterpart: *uti imperium maiestatemque p. R. Quiritium duelli domique auxitis, utique semper Latinus obtemperassit* (Pighi 1965: 94, 114).

162 The quantitative analysis (using museum pieces and coin hoards) provided by the second edition of *RIC* II illustrates that many of Domitian's saecular pieces were common, including the model for the Severan sestertius, *RIC* II^2 *Domitian* 614.

163 Some of the *aes* hoards from the Severan period suggest that Domitianic coinage was still in use, for example the Caminada hoard (*RMRVe* II.2 no. 13.1), Bassano hoard (*RMRVe* IV.2 no. 2/16 (1)) and Martellago hoard (*RMRVe* VI.3 no. 8.2).

164 Meadows and Williams 2001: 27–49.

Domitian's coinage formed a visual narrative: each of the major events of the games is portrayed, with the entire series recording the sequence of the celebration.[165] The ability of the viewer to read and understand this narrative is dubious. As Scheid observed, one would have needed a good knowledge of each ritual, and a copy of *each* of Domitian's saecular coins to be able to fully decipher the significance of each type.[166] Without viewing all the coins together, it is difficult to differentiate one sacrifice from another. Scheid believed that the coins, in this sense, were a reflection of the actual ritual: the priests and magistrates charged with the execution of the rites (and thus with front row seats at each occasion) would have been able to understand or 'read' more than someone from a lower class, or who lived outside Rome.[167] As a consequence, coinage reflected the hierarchy of power and knowledge. Domitian's coin types, and the saecular types of Augustus and Severus, make a great deal more sense if viewed together. One set of the coins (or the dies) may have been stored together as a record of religious duty discharged.

Just as the preserved Severan *acta* show an earlier influence or 'archaising' elements, the coin types emphasised continuity with the past, with similar motifs being employed and redeployed to signify the appropriate completion of the festival. The ability of the average Roman citizen to read the saecular *acta* is questionable; Scheid acknowledges that anyone who may have wanted to read the *acta* in Rome would have required a ladder and a lamp.[168] The act of inscribing the details of the games probably formed part of the religious ritual itself, serving to record that the deed had been performed. Consequently, the inscription was not really intended for a broad audience. Beard has illustrated this concept for the Arval *acta*; here the principal reason for inscribing the rites was not as a record for consultation, but as a symbolic part of the religious process.[169] It is clear from the repeated representation of the *cippus* on saecular games coinage that this act of epigraphy became an important part of the ritual itself. Similarly, the design and striking of saecular games coinage may have functioned as an important record of the occasion, regardless of who may or may not have been able to 'read' these pieces.

This is not to discount the potential of these coins to act as a means of communication, but simply to suggest that communication may not have been the main function of these particular types. The striking of coins may have become as much a part of the ritual as the inscribing of the *acta*. The

[165] Sobocinski 2006: 582. [166] Scheid 1998b: 13–35. [167] Scheid 1998b: 33.
[168] Scheid 1998b: 14. [169] Beard 1985: 114.

fact that the same or similar iconography could be resuscitated after a period of more than 100 years (on more than one occasion) suggests that these coins functioned as a record of the event. The iconography on these coins might be interpreted as a record of the games that was intended to survive just as long as the *acta*. The presence of Liber Pater and Hercules on these types then takes on an added significance. That the coin types show change alongside continuity reflects the potential for innovation inherent within the celebration itself.

Unlike Domitian, the Severan mint did not release a type to mark every ritual of the games. Severus' coinage focused on a handful of rituals: the *suffimenta*, the offering to the *Ilithyiae*, the sacrifice to *Terra Mater* and another sacrifice, probably that to Apollo and Diana on the Palatine.[170] We might see the 'abbreviation' of the ritual narrative as a product of Severus' third century context. Hedlund observes that coinage of the later third century ceases to form 'narrative sequences'; rather, single images could function symbolically to represent the whole.[171] From this perspective we can begin to understand the transformation of Domitian's narrative sequence of images into Severus' more select types; the phenomenon is representative of the developments in visual culture from the first to third centuries AD.

Travelling ideology: Quintus Aiacius Modestus in Petra

The official epigraphic and visual output of the régime served to record and communicate the celebration of the games. But the ideologies surrounding the celebration also travelled throughout the empire by less official routes. A glimpse of this is provided by the epigraphic activity of Quintus Aiacius Modestus. As governor of Arabia under Severus, Modestus erected a series of altars in the temple of the Dousarēs in Petra. An altar was erected to Hercules, one to Liber Pater, one to Apollo, one was probably erected

170 The presence of Tiber on one type (*RIC* IV.1 *Septimius Severus* 293, 816; *RIC* IV.1 *Caracalla* 462) identifies the scene as the sacrifice to the *Ilithyiae*, which took place in Tarentum at a riverside altar. This was a bloodless sacrifice, and the absence of any victim on this type confirms the identification. A pregnant sow was sacrificed to Terra Mater, and the presence of a pig on some of the types (*RIC* IV.1 *Caracalla* 418) argues for identifying the scene with this ritual. The last type portrays Septimius and Caracalla sacrificing before a distyle temple (*RIC* IV.1 *Septimius Severus* 826; *RIC* IV.1 *Geta* 132). What ritual is represented here is difficult to identify, but the absence of a victim or any personification argues in favour of identifying the scene with the sacrifice of cakes to Apollo and Diana that took place on the Palatine. For a comparison with Domitianic coinage see Sobocinski 2006: 585.

171 Hedlund 2008: 88.

to Diana, one to Pax and one to *Spes Temperantia*.[172] All the altars were set up for the health (*pro salute*) of Severus and the imperial family. Modestus describes himself as *vir clarissimus*, consul designate, legate and as a *XVvir s(acris) f(aciundus)*.[173] Christol recognised the significance of the last title: it was the priesthood responsible for the celebration of the saecular games, and the altars were all erected to deities closely associated with Severus' celebration.[174] The role of Liber Pater and Hercules has been discussed in detail above, and the Severan *acta* reveal that Apollo and Diana retained a prominent rôle. Christol suggested that Pax and Spes Temperantia were the promised conditions brought by the new *saeculum*; the concepts certainly fit with the conclusion of Severus' wars and the establishment of a dynasty.[175] Modestus may have been in Rome in his capacity as a *quindecemvir sacris faciundis* during the celebration of the games before becoming governor of Arabia for AD 205–208. He would thus have possessed an intimate knowledge of the Severan celebration and its associated ideology, which he brought with him to one of the furthest outposts of the empire.

The preserved saecular *acta* mention an Aiacius Modestus on several occasions.[176] His altars in Petra can be connected with the Severan games, and his own rôle as priest on the occasion of their celebration. The monuments underline his own personal connection with the emperor and his high status. Aiacius Modestus serves as an excellent example of how ideology could travel through the empire via the movement of people, and uncovers another potential means by which Severus' divine support could be communicated.

Though the surviving evidence does not allow us to conclude that any other *quindecemviri* adopted the ideology and imagery of the saecular games in a way similar to Modestus, an intaglio preserved in the Martin-von-Wagner-Museum illustrates that other individuals did commemorate the event. The intaglio reproduces the image of the ship surrounded by animals represented on Severus' coinage (Figure 10), and described by Dio.[177] Lichtenberger argued that the similarities between the intaglio and the coin might indicate the involvement of the imperial house in its production.[178] Severan gems found in England, also inspired by coin designs, suggest that there was a close connection between gem production and the

[172] Parr and Starcky 1962: 13–20; Starcky and Bennett 1968: 41–66.

[173] Starcky and Bennett 1968: 43

[174] Christol 1971: 124–40; Lichtenberger 2007: 69–70; Lichtenberger 2011: 69.

[175] Christol 1971: 125. [176] Pighi 1965: 146 II.11 and 13, 157 IV.8, 159 V.31.9, 171 VIII.4.

[177] Zwierlein-Diehl 1986: 275 no. 842; Lichtenberger 2007: 23–4. [178] Lichtenberger 2007: 24.

presence of the imperial family.[179] Alternatively, the owner of our piece may, like Modestus, have had a significant role in the saecular celebrations, and consequently may have wished to communicate this by adopting the imagery of the games on a personal ornament.[180] Whether created on private or imperial initiative, the piece attests to the adoption of the imagery of the saecular games by individuals, and the potential for this process to carry imperial ideology and imagery to the wider empire.

Similar to the Augustan celebrations, the Severan games took place against a backdrop of imperial buildings intimately connected with the emperor. The restored temple of Vesta, the triumphal arch of Severus in the forum, as well as the Septizodium would have overlooked many of the rituals.[181] A colossal temple to Liber Pater and Hercules may also have towered over proceedings. If we can place this temple inside Rome it would have formed a dominant backdrop to Severus' saecular celebration, and to the city itself.

The temple to Liber Pater and Hercules

He [Severus] also spent a great deal uselessly in repairing other buildings and in constructing new ones; for instance, he built a temple of huge size to Dionysus and Hercules.[182]

Dio's assessment here neglects to mention that much of Severus' building activity was necessary after a fire destroyed sections of the city under Commodus.[183] (Though, of course, this did not stop Severus from capitalising on the necessity.) Dio's comment remains the only explicit evidence we possess that Severus constructed a temple to Liber Pater and Hercules. The identity and location of this temple have been the subject of fierce debate, one that may never be resolved.

The problem lies in the fact that no conclusive archaeological evidence has yet been found to identify a temple to Liber Pater and Hercules in Rome, let alone one 'of huge size'. Consequently, the suggestion has arisen that Dio is referring to a temple constructed in Lepcis Magna.[184] Remains of a Severan period temple within the new Severan forum in Lepcis lend some credibility to this theory, though it is not known specifically to

179 Henig 1986: 378–9; Marsden and Henig 2002: 419–20; Worden 2001: 343–55.
180 Walters 1926: lvii. 181 Gorrie 2002: 461–81. 182 Dio 77.16.3.
183 Daguet-Gagey 2004: 184; Gorrie 2007: 1–17; Lusnia 1998: 30–1.
184 Birley 1988: 151; Hasebroek 1921: 149–50; Mattingly 1994: 121.

which deity/deities the temple was dedicated.[185] But would Dio have known of a temple constructed in North Africa? In the main he relied on his own personal experience to construct his history of the Severan period, supplemented by the accounts of friends and acquaintances.[186] Would Dio's knowledge have extended to Severus' activities in Africa?[187] He makes no mention of the granting of Italian status (*ius Italicum*) to Carthage, Utica and Lepcis Magna, or the imperial construction activities in Lepcis Magna, though admittedly his work only survives in epitome. That Dio would mention a temple constructed in the city of Lepcis, however, remains unlikely.[188] Rather, Dio's reference to the temple to Liber and Hercules is made in the context of a wider statement about Severus' building projects inside Rome itself. This suggests that the temple was built in Rome, where Dio himself could witness the emperor's extravagance.

The theory that Severus' temple to Liber Pater and Hercules was located in Rome has gradually gained support. Santangeli Valenziani has identified it with the colossal temple on the Quirinal Hill.[189] Only fragments now remain of this structure, which would have dwarfed the surrounding buildings and would have been one of the most prominent landmarks in Rome from its position high on the Quirinal. A section of the temple remained preserved until the seventeenth century, when it was removed with the permission of Pope Urban VIII.[190] None of the surviving fragments (now located in the gardens of the Palazzo Colonna and its environs) provide clues as to the temple's original identity. The decoration of the surviving fragments merely suggests a Severan date. As a result, the remains have been connected with Aurelian's temple of Sol, Caracalla's temple to Sarapis, the temple to Liber Pater and Hercules and, most recently, Taylor has suggested that the site is to be identified as a temple to Sarapis built by Hadrian and renovated in the Severan period.[191]

There is little evidence to support the view that the temple was dedicated to Sol, particularly since literary evidence places this temple in a different

185 Ward-Perkins 1993: 31 only suggests that 'it was associated in some way with the cult of the ruling family'.

186 Millar 1964: 121; Moscovich 2004: 356–7.

187 Moscovich 2004: 360–8 suggests that one of Dio's sources was Philostratus, particularly for Dio's account of the campaign in Britain.

188 Lichtenberger 2007: 39.

189 Santangeli Valenziani 1991: 7–16; Lichtenberger 2011: 38–40.

190 The temple contained the statues of the Dioscuri that remain to this day on the Quirinal Hill, and the river gods that are now in the Piazza del Campidoglio. Columns from the temple may have been reused by Maxentius in his basilica (Taylor 2004: 223–66). On the reuse of the marble from the temple see Picozzi and Valeriani 1999: 54.

191 Taylor 2004: 234–66.

locale.[192] The identification of a temple to Sarapis has been attractive because a handful of inscriptions to the god have been found in the area. *CIL* 6.570 (found in the church of Sant'Agata dei Goti, and probably reburied after it was recorded) mentions a temple to Sarapis constructed by a Marcus Aurelius Antoninus.[193] The problems associated with this inscription will be examined in the next chapter, but only a tenuous link can be forged between this modest plaque and the enormous temple that once stood on the Quirinal Hill.[194] Moreover, the find spot of this plaque is sufficiently distant from the Palazzo Colonna that one may doubt whether it originated from that area.[195] Other Sarapic inscriptions in the area are also far enough from the Quirinal, and close enough to Sant'Agata dei Goti, to raise doubts as to whether they can be connected with the Quirinal complex, or whether we might be better served looking for another location for the temple to Sarapis.[196] Amongst the ruins in the area of the Palazzo Colonna was found a small statue of a crocodile, made of red granite.[197] Again, a small statue of a crocodile is not conclusive evidence for a temple to Sarapis.

Taylor's attribution of the temple to the reign of Hadrian depends on drawings done by the Renaissance architect Palladio, who witnessed the excavation of part of the temple during the preparations for the construction of the Villa Colonna. Palladio's initial sketches and final drawings often had numerous differences between them (and indeed this is the case here) so it is impossible to know whether he faithfully reproduced the temple in question. Close analysis of the architect's works illustrates that often his representations of ruins reflected his own conceptions of how Roman architecture should have functioned rather than what actually survived.[198] Admittedly what is sketched has structural similarities to Hadrian's pantheon, but this should not be viewed as conclusive evidence that the building was constructed at his direction.

Taylor believed further confirmation of a Hadrianic temple to Sarapis could be found on one of the emperor's sestertii, which shows a temple with 12 columns accompanied by the legend S C.[199] The image has usually been identified as a representation of the Hadrianic temple to Venus and Rome. Taylor pointed to the absence of an identifying legend (VENERI FELICI or

[192] Taylor 2004: 236. [193] Hülsen 1894: 394–5. [194] Lusnia 1998: 184.

[195] Lusnia 1998: 183.

[196] Hülsen 1894: 394–5. In 1879 an inscription was found in the foundation of the Palazzo Capranica del Grillo, and another inscription was found in a palace near the Piazetta delle tre Cannelle.

[197] Picozzi and Valeriani 1999: 60. [198] Boucher 2000: 296–311.

[199] *BMCRE* III *Hadrian* 1490; Strack 1937: 660; Taylor 2004: 255.

ROMAE AETERNAE), and to the presence of free-standing columns on either side of the temple (a feature not present on other representations of the temple to Venus and Rome). Taylor concluded that these features meant that the coin showed a Hadrianic temple to Sarapis, providing confirmation that such a construction existed.

This perspective does not allow for the varying and creative representations of imperial buildings on Roman coinage: features could be added or taken away by different engravers. (Indeed, coins could even represent buildings that were never actually constructed).[200] A coin does not provide a photographic reproduction of an ancient structure, but an interpretation of it.[201] The fact that this particular image differs slightly from other portrayals of the temple of Venus and Rome does not automatically mean it depicts another building entirely. In fact, both this image and other representations of the temple to Venus and Rome show a decastyle structure, arguing in favour of the traditional interpretation that both images show the same temple. The difference in representation on Taylor's sestertius (dated to *c.* AD 132) may reflect the fact that the final construction of the temple had not yet taken shape. Construction on the temple to Venus and Rome was probably not begun until AD 125/6 and only completed in the reign of Antoninus Pius.[202] The representation of the temple in AD 132 may thus have incorporated features that were planned (the columns to either side of the temple), but which did not make it into the actual structure (explaining their absence on later types). A similar phenomenon occurs under Augustus, where the differing portrayals of the temple of Mars Ultor on coinage probably reflect architectural changes that occurred as it underwent construction.[203] That there may have been a change in the architecture of the Temple of Venus and Rome is certainly hinted at in the literary evidence: Dio records that Hadrian and the architect Apollodorus had a disagreement over the design, which the emperor insisted on doing himself.[204]

The design work on the surviving carved marble of the colossal temple suggests artists of the Severan period: the surviving pilaster capital closely resembles that on the Severan propylon of the *Porticus Octaviae*, while the band of acanthus-leaf masks on the decorated architrave is similar to that found on the arch of Severus in the Roman forum and the *Porta Argentariorum*.[205] This is what prompted Taylor to suggest a Severan

[200] Fishwick 1984: 263–70. [201] Burnett 1999: 137–64.
[202] Boatwright 1987: 121; Ridley 1989: 559; Snijder 1940: 6; Strack 1937: 69.
[203] Rich 1998: 83–5. [204] Dio 69.4.3–6; Ridley 1989: 551–66.
[205] Lusnia 1998: 181; Taylor 2004: 237.

renovation. However these remains may also indicate a Severan date for the entire construction.[206] As these pieces are our only surviving evidence, they remain the most reliable way to date the temple. But even with a Severan date the problem of identification remains: was the temple consecrated to Liber Pater and Hercules under Septimius, or was it constructed in honour of Sarapis under Caracalla? Medieval and later sources retain the idea that a temple to Bacchus and another deity was located on the Quirinal, though the accounts are somewhat confused.[207]

While the remains of the colossal temple were sketched before their destruction, the surviving drawings offer no clue as to the identity of the building, beyond confirming the Severan period decoration and the temple's impressive size.[208] Taylor estimated that the height of the temple would have exceeded the temple of Venus and Rome and even perhaps the temple of Jupiter Capitolinus, with its precinct covering an estimated 17,000 cubic metres.[209] Such a structure might well have prompted Dio to employ the adjective ὑπερμεγέθη.[210] Ultimately, one cannot conclusively identify the temple as that of Liber Pater and Hercules, but the circumstantial evidence makes this identification just as likely, if not more likely, than a temple to Sarapis. The fact that a temple to Liber Pater and Hercules is not mentioned in the Regionary Catalogues does not present a major problem: these works were written later, and were by no means complete.[211] Indeed the very size of the temple may have meant that it fell into ruin faster than its neighbours.

If we can identify the colossal temple on the Quirinal with Severus' temple to Liber Pater and Hercules, Septimius' patron deities would have had a profound effect on the landscape of Rome. The temple would have been one of the largest in the city (if not the largest), acting as a visible declaration of Septimius' favour with the gods. It would have been located near the temple to Salus on the Quirinal and would have loomed over the

206 Lichtenberger 2007: 40 also argues from the remains that a Hadrianic date, or one under Aurelian, is unlikely.

207 Lusnia 1998: 186–7. The medieval works *Mirabilia* and *Graphia* refer to a *templum Saturni et Bachi*. The Codex Escurialensis contains an illustration of a statue of Hercules, described as found, in Monte Cavallo in the chapel of Hercules (Hülsen, Michaelis et al. 1906: 106–7, fol. 37). Monte Cavallo was the name given to the Quirinal after the statues of the Dioscuri that remained there.

208 A convenient reproduction of these images is to be found in Taylor 2004: 223–66.

209 Taylor 2004: 223.

210 Dio 77.16.3. Santangeli Valenziani argues that this is the only Severan period structure that could have provoked the adjective (Santangeli Valenziani 1991: 15).

211 Lichtenberger 2007: 41; Lusnia 1998: 192.

eastern part of the Campus Martius. The religious support and protection of the emperor would have been visible to all.

Lusnia observes that further evidence for an enormous construction under Severus can be found in the quarries at Dokimeion.[212] Extremely large column drums with quarry inscriptions from AD 206 have been uncovered, and may be linked to the construction of the colossal temple on the Quirinal.[213] Coin types from the period AD 205–207 also suggest that the gods Hercules and Liber were transferred into the religious space of Rome in this period. These types, and others, all with spectacular designs, warrant further consideration.

Severan imagery AD 205–207

In the period AD 205–207 a series of coins displaying images of Liber Pater/ Bacchus and Hercules were released with intricate designs. No coin was struck showing the temple to Liber Pater and Hercules (but then again no explicit coins mark the completion of a Sarapeum by either Caracalla or Hadrian). But these types hint at a visual language associated with the presence of the Lepcitanian pair in the religious landscape of Rome.

Two of these coin types were struck for Caracalla. One showed Hercules with Potitius and Pinarius (Figure 20), mythical figures from Rome's early history who were entrusted with the cult of the god. The other displayed

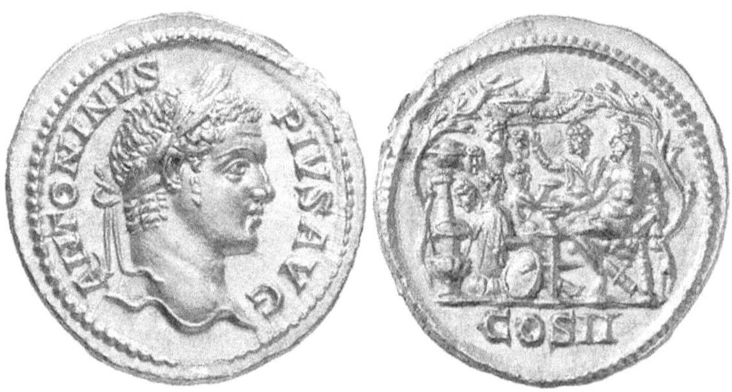

Figure 20: Aureus of Caracalla displaying Hercules dining with Potitius and Pinarius and the legend COS II.

[212] Lusnia 1998: 191.

[213] The size of the drums is appropriate for the colossal temple and matches the upper diameter of a column of a drawing made of the structure (Lusnia 1998: 192).

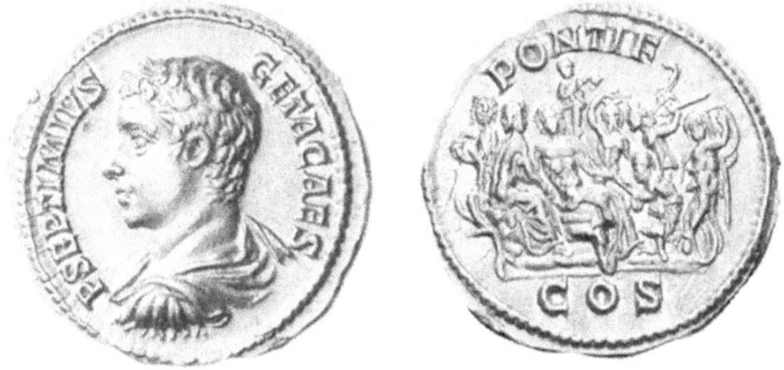

Figure 21: Aureus of Geta displaying the marriage of Bacchus and Ariadne and the legend PONTIF COS.

Bacchus/Liber Pater with a team of four leopards and dates to AD 206. Hurter noticed an obverse die link between the Hercules coin and two others, one showing Eshmun/Aesculapius and the other showing Jupiter Sospitator.[214] The former dates to AD 207, and thus provides an approximate date for the Hercules type, which Hurter believed was AD 206. A parallel issue was struck for Geta, showing Bacchus and Ariadne (Figure 21).[215] The intricate detail of this type suggests that it was struck contemporaneously with the Hercules piece of Caracalla. The selected myths show Severus' patron deities in a very Roman context; in fact, the Hercules piece is derived from an earlier medallion of Antoninus Pius.[216] The celebration of the myths surrounding these deities through the use of spectacular numismatic pieces may hint at the construction of a temple to the two in the city of Rome.

Further die links confirm that these pieces date to the period AD 205–207. The Liber/Bacchus *quadriga* coin of Caracalla (AD 206) has an obverse die link with a coin depicting Mars (AD 205), which in turn links to an aureus of Caracalla showing the temple of *Roma Aeterna*. The reverse of this last coin was also struck with an obverse of Septimius. This Septimius obverse was combined with a reverse die showing the emperor being crowned by Victory with the legend PACATOR ORBIS COS III P P, and a type of Severus on horseback, dated to AD 205.[217] The intricate connections

[214] Hurter 1980: 40–1. [215] *RIC* IV.1 *Geta* 33.

[216] Gnecchi 1912: (vol. 2) no. 81, pl. 54.3; Lichtenberger 2007: 58.

[217] Classical Numismatic Group, Triton VI (14 January 2003) 939 with discussion (not listed in *RIC*) and Numismatica Ars Classica Auction 25 (25 June 2003) 508 (Calicò 2509).

between dies here (of both Severus and Caracalla) reveal the operations of the Roman mint in this period; it may be that a single workshop or *officina* was producing aurei, resulting in a complex series of die connections.

Damsky believed these types were connected with other unusual aurei of Severus from the same period.[218] One showed the stadium of Domitian and has an obverse die link suggesting it was produced between 10 December AD 205 and 9 December AD 206.[219] Another aureus showed Jupiter seated between Hercules and Liber Pater.[220] The type is known from a single example, said to come from India. It is worn, but there appears to be an obverse die link to Severus' pieces mentioned above, showing the emperor on a horse, and as *pacator orbis* (pacifier of the world).[221] It is then clearly connected to this wider series of aurei.

The image of Jupiter between Hercules and Liber Pater recalls the well-known type of the Capitoline Triad. Jupiter is usually shown seated between Minerva and Juno.[222] In fact, the Capitoline Triad also appears on Severus' coinage, on a silver piece dated to AD 206.[223] We might view this piece as a counterpart to the aureus displaying Jupiter, Hercules and Liber, with which it is contemporary. By adapting the established iconography of the Capitoline Triad, the mint may have been highlighting the place Liber and Hercules had within the city, housed in their spectacular new temple. Jupiter, who was closely aligned with the person of the emperor,[224] is shown with the deities most closely associated with him and the princeps: Juno and Minerva on a silver piece, and then Liber Pater and Hercules on a gold issue. Damsky was probably correct to connect these coins to the completion of the temple of Liber and Hercules in the period AD 206/7.[225] The two gods are displayed in an elaborate fashion on the aurei mentioned above, while the stadium aureus commemorated the celebrations held in conjunction with the ceremony of dedication, in a period that also saw the

[218] Damsky 1990: 87–8. [219] Damsky 1990: 80.

[220] Hill 1982: 159–60; Lichtenberger 2011: 55. A relief in Carrara also shows Jupiter between Hercules and Liber Pater, a possible reference to Severan imperial ideology. See Lichtenberger 2011:55, 82.

[221] Classical Numismatic Group, Triton VI (14 January 2003) 939 and Numismatica Ars Classica Auction 25 (25 June 2003) 508.

[222] For example, Gnecchi 1912: (vol. 2) 16 no. 66 (Antoninus Pius); Gnecchi 1912: (vol. 2) 43 no. 6 (Marcus Aurelius).

[223] Numismatica Ars Classica Auction 41 (20 November 2007) 116, not in *RIC*.

[224] A third coin type should also be mentioned here, showing the emperor facing forward, flanked by Caracalla and Geta, who are seated (*RIC* IV.1 *Geta* 42, 65; *RIC* IV.1 *Caracalla* 106). This is another play on the Capitoline Triad type.

[225] Damsky 1990: 89.

110th anniversary of Antonine rule.[226] The year AD 207 also saw the fifteenth anniversary (*quindecennalia*) of Severus' rule, and the tenth anniversary (*decennalia*) of Caracalla.

In the period AD 200–202, sestertii of Geta were released showing Liber Pater and Hercules accompanied by the legend DI PATRII.[227] The type also appears on coins of Severus and Caracalla in the year AD 204.[228] No examples of the denarius type were found in the hoard analysis. The reverse legend DI PATRII is remarkable: the same description of the gods is found in an inscription in Lepcis Magna.[229] A *deus patrius* was the protecting god of a place, similar to a *genius loci*.[230] Barnes suggested the type was initially released in the name of Geta to commemorate the commencement of a temple to Liber Pater and Hercules, and then struck again when the temple was dedicated.[231] The legend DI PATRII thus referred to the transformation of these deities from the protecting gods of Lepcis to the protecting gods of Rome and the empire. Barnes' theory is attractive, but it is hard to see how the colossal temple to Liber and Hercules could have been constructed in only two years. A better explanation may be that the DI PATRII coins marked the beginning of construction of the temple, the moment in which these gods became the *di patrii* of Rome, and that the other, elaborate types discussed above were released in conjunction with the temple's on-going construction. If these coins mark the beginning of the temple's construction, the gods would now have had a physical presence in the Roman landscape, highlighted by their prominence in the celebration of the new *saeculum*. That these extraordinary aurei were struck alongside military types (Severus as *pacator orbis*, Severus on horseback) highlights the association of these gods with Severus' military success, as well as Severus' public image as a military emperor.

Historical contexts of Severan aurei and imperial donatives

Both Dio and Herodian agree that Severus was particularly lavish in his celebration of games and in his gifts of money to the Roman people. Dio

226 Damsky 1990: 188. Hill's suggestion that these were 'commemorative' pieces to mark the anniversary of the saecular games (Hill 1964: 173) is refuted by Damsky 1990: 82.

227 *RIC* IV.1 *Geta* 112, 117.

228 *RIC* IV.1 *Septimius Severus* 762; *RIC* IV.1 *Caracalla* 76, 422.

229 *IRT* 289.

230 Mundle 1957: 90.

231 Barnes 1967: 104. Noreña 2003: 40 observes that the completion of Vespasian's Temple of Peace was not commemorated on coinage through representation of the temple, but with the idea and personification of Pax. A similar phenomenon may be occurring here: the construction of a temple to Liber Pater and Hercules may have been communicated by the presence of these deities on coinage, and need not have entailed the numismatic representation of the structure itself.

records that for his *decennalia* Severus presented to those on the grain dole and to the Praetorian Guard ten gold pieces, one for every year of his reign.[232] Dio observes that no other emperor had given so much to the populace at once and estimates the total spent as two hundred million sesterces. He comments that Severus gave spectacles to celebrate his return to Rome, for his *decennalia* and for his victories.[233] Herodian also records Severus' generosity in dispensing money and describes the shows given on several occasions.[234] The suggestion of Damsky, that there may have been games to mark the opening of the temple of Liber Pater and Hercules, or on the occasion of Severus' sixtieth birthday, or to mark the 110th anniversary of Antonine rule, would be in keeping with what we know of Severan spectacles.[235]

Indeed, it is possible that these intricate gold pieces formed part of a *donativum*. Dio's description of Severus' *decennalia* suggests that the practice of distributing gold was possible, though perhaps Dio here is taking liberties in order to depict the emperor as extravagant. Dio takes pains to mention that Severus gave gold pieces (χρυσοῦς), not merely an amount. Either Dio chooses the word to highlight to his audience the outrageousness of Severus' actions, or his text may reflect that fact that this donative, at least, was given in aurei.[236] Indeed, if we believe the extravagant amount distributed upon Severus' *decennalia* (almost a quarter of the annual revenue of the empire),[237] gold pieces would be the most economic and efficient method of distribution. The mint would have found it difficult to strike and transport that amount in *aes* denominations, or even in silver. If it were given in *aes*, one would imagine we would possess a substantially larger amount of Severan *aes* coinage than currently survives. And if the donative of AD 202 were given in any other denomination, the significance of ten pieces equating to the ten years of Severus' reign would be lost.[238]

In addition, recent work on the Roman economy suggests that *donativa* could be given in gold, the easiest and most economical denomination to transport and distribute.[239] The recent analysis of coin finds from Pompeii illustrates that *aes*, silver and gold coins circulated together, are suggestive of the rôle gold played in society.[240] These findings force us to rethink the

232 Dio 77.1.1. 233 Dio 77.1.3. 234 Hdn. 2.14.5, 3.6.8, 3.8.4–5, 3.8.9, 3.9.2.
235 Damsky 1990: 89. 236 Chastagnol 1984: 114–20; Lusnia 1998: 85. 237 Millar 1991: 156.
238 Millar 1991: 156.
239 Duncan Jones 1994. 82, Hedlund 2008: 38; Lo Cascio 2008: 160–73; Millar 1991: 143–59; Wolters 2001: 579–88.
240 Andreau 2008: 208–25; Duncan-Jones 2003: 161–80; Lo Cascio 2008: 161–2; Wolters 2003: 191.

notion that the imagery on gold coinage was only seen by the élite.[241] But if gold did form a donative metal for Severus or other emperors, one must imagine that even if the initial recipient were plebeian, the gold pieces would quickly have entered into circulation and come into the hands of the wealthier segment of the population.

The extraordinary range of gold pieces discussed above may thus have served as *donativa* given by Severus (or on his behalf). The fact that the production of *aes* medallions slows in Severus' reign makes the theory that these gold coins were presentation pieces even more attractive.[242] The aurei formed an important medium through which the incorporation of Liber Pater and Hercules into the city of Rome could be communicated to select groups.

The *di patrii* and the journey to Africa

Another interpretation of the *di patrii* coin type is that it refers to an imperial journey to Africa, and to Lepcis Magna.[243] Hasebroek believed the type commemorated an imperial visit to Lepcis Magna in AD 203, the legend DI PATRII referring to the position of the deities in Severus' home city. In reality, the date of Septimius' visit to Africa is uncertain, and our speculations are dependent entirely on circumstantial evidence.

The possibility that Severus visited Africa is also hinted at in Philostratus. In recounting the life of Apollonius of Athens (a rhetor under Septimius Severus)[244] Philostratus details the rivalry between Apollonius and another rhetor named Heraclides.

> Heraclides spread a false report about Apollonius that he was to set out forthwith to Libya, when the Emperor was staying there and was gathering about him the talented from all parts, and he said to Apollonius: 'It is a good time for you to read the speech *Against Leptines*'. 'Nay for you rather', reported Apollonius, 'for indeed it was also written on behalf of exemptions.'[245]

Philostratus' work does not provide any framework for dating Severus' stay in Libya: the lives he recounts are not presented chronologically, but as a collection of anecdotes. Philostratus composed the work late in his life while at Athens, well after the reign of Severus (the *Lives* are dedicated to

241 Hekster 2003: 20–35. 242 Damsky 1990: 103.

243 Bober 1943: 7; Hasebroek 1921: 135; Mundle 1957: 90. 244 Kotula 1985: 152.

245 Philostr. *VS* 2.20.2 (= #601). The interpretation of Wright (LCL p. 257) that 'Libya' here must refer to Egypt has no foundation.

Gordian). Thus the date of the work also provides no hint as to when this imperial visit occurred.[246] Immediately preceding the section quoted above Philostratus describes Apollonius' embassy to the emperor Severus in Rome, which resulted in Heraclides losing his privilege of exemption from liturgies.[247] It was this that provoked Heraclides to spread the false rumour. The mention of Demosthenes' famous speech *Against Leptines* is a fitting work to allude to (it called for the repeal of a law which denied anyone exemption from liturgies), but it may also have functioned in a secondary sense, as a pun on Septimius' native city of Lepcis (also known as Leptis).

The visit of Septimius to Africa (and thus Lepcis) has generally been dated to AD 203/4 on the basis of coins alluding to the emperor's *indulgentia* towards Carthage.[248] The series displays the goddess Dea Caelestis on a lion, with water springing from a rock, accompanied by the legend INDVLGENTIA AVGG IN CARTH (Figure 22). The type appears on *aes* types in AD 203.[249] The silver and gold types are undated, but are presumably contemporary with this period. The number of examples found in the hoard analysis suggests it constituted a major issue, forming approximately 3 per cent of all Severus' silver coinage (Figures 7, 23).

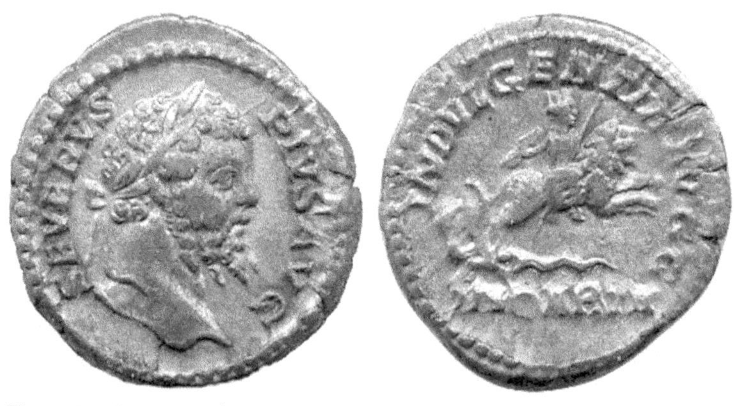

Figure 22: Denarius of Septimius Severus with Dea Caelestis on a lion and the legend INDVLGENTIA AVGG IN CARTH.

[246] Anderson 1986: 7.

[247] Philostr. *VS* 2.20 (= #601). Kotula 1985: 152 places Apollonius in Rome in AD 197.

[248] *RIC* IV.1 *Septimius Severus* 193, 266–67B, 759–59A; *RIC* IV.1 *Caracalla* 130–1, 415(a–d), 418A, 471; *RIC* IV.1 *Severus for Julia Domna* 594; Babelon 1903: 159–60; Pera 1979: 107. On connecting this series to an imperial visit to the region see Barton 1977/8: 60 (who suggests AD 202/3); Birley 1988: 146; Haywood 1940: 177; Mundle 1957: 90; and Ward-Perkins 1951: 227.

[249] *RIC* IV.1 *Septimius Severus* 759–60.

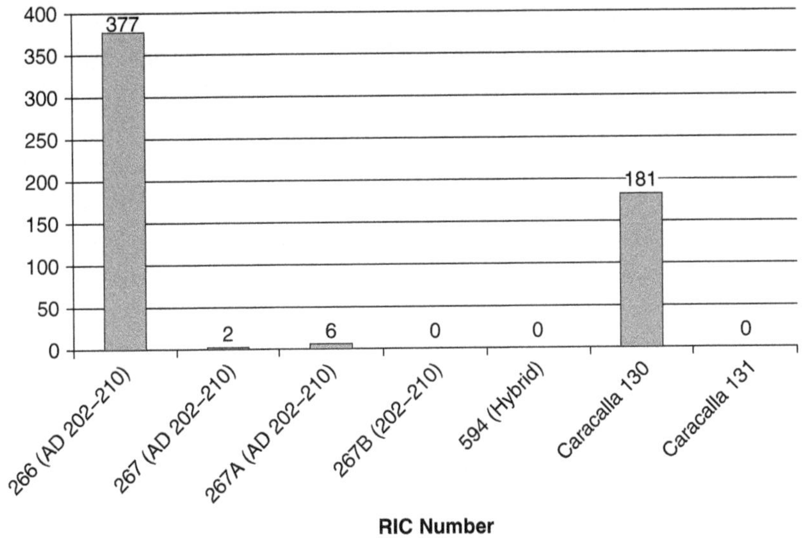

Figure 23: Silver *Indulgentia Augg* in Carth types of Severus and Caracalla (AD 202–210) as represented in hoards.

The precise action this coin type commemorates remains unknown. Babelon believed it marked the emperor's removal of the tax on the aqueduct at Carthage.[250] Pera, noting the existence of a parallel type with the legend INDVLGENTIA AVGG IN ITALIAM and an image of *Italia*, suggested that both issues referred to Severus' generous distribution of olive oil.[251] The *Historia Augusta* records that Severus introduced a largess of olive oil to the populace, and that after his death there was an excess of olive oil in Rome and Italy.[252] Lepcis and other cities in North Africa may have donated the oil to Rome for the *annona* in gratitude for *ius Italicum*.[253] Rives believed the issue commemorated the granting of *ius Italicum* to the cities of Carthage, Utica and Lepcis Magna.[254]

The wealth of theories related to the INDVLGENTIA AVGG IN CARTH series reflects the ambiguity of the reference. The coin communicates the

[250] Babelon 1903: 157–74.

[251] Pera 1979: 103–26. The parallel issue, *Indulgentia Augg in Italiam* (*RIC* IV.1 *Septimius Severus* 268; *RIC* IV.1 *Caracalla* 132), had only a single occurrence in the hoard analysis, in the Shapwick Villa hoard in Britain. Pera also suggested the *Indulgentia Augg in Carth* coin type may have marked Severus' decision to grant Carthage Pythian games. Tertullian (*Scorp.* 6.2) records Carthage had the right to host the games, but does not mention which emperor bestowed the honour. A third-century inscription from Heraclea also mentions the celebration of Pythian games in Carthage (*IGRR* 1.802).

[252] *SHA Sev.* 23.2, *Sev. Alex.* 22.2; Lusnia 1998: 37.

[253] Haywood 1941: 246–56; Wilson 2007: 306–7.

[254] Ulpian *Digest* 50.158.11; Rives 1995: 70.

emperor's *indulgentia* rather specifying a particular action or event. Dea Caelestis functions as visual shorthand for the city of Carthage, just as Italia is represented on the parallel issue. Both are beneficiaries of the emperor's munificence.

The prominence of this coin type in Severus' numismatic imagery has also fuelled the idea that Domna was publicly associated with Dea Caelestis. For von Domaszewski, the increased prominence of Dea Caelestis under Septimius was the beginning of the corruption of Roman religion by non-Roman forces, illustrated by the quote at the beginning of this chapter.[255] von Domaszewski relied on an inscription found in Carvoran in Britain for his theory, but the inscription in question does not mention the empress and von Domaszewski's interpretation has since been convincingly refuted.[256] The Carvoran inscription, and two others that explicitly connect Domna and Caelestis, were all erected on private initiative.[257] This is not enough to suggest any wholesale importation of the cult of Dea Caelestis as part of a wider 'orientalisation' of religion by Septimius. Private conceptualisation of the imperial family was very different to imperial actions or ideology. Indeed, the number of inscriptions mentioning Dea Caelestis in connection with the imperial family is small and for the most part found in Africa, where the epigraphic presence of the goddess is to be expected.[258]

The idea that we can use these coin types to date the imperial visit to Africa is also problematic. The emperor did not have to be present in a city to grant it a petition or a privilege. Other evidence suggests a later date for the Severan visit to Africa.[259] The arch erected in Lepcis to honour the imperial family shows Caracalla and Geta in a style similar to their coin portraits from AD 207. The portraits on the arch bear little resemblance to the younger portraits of AD 203/204, seen on coins and on the arch of the *argentarii*.[260] This in itself is not positive evidence for the dating of the African trip, since it is not known when the arch was completed. The *quadrifons* may have been constructed before the imperial visit, or

255 The theory has recently been resurrected by Clauss 2001: 161–8. See also Marsden 1997: 5; McCann 1968: 57; Mikocki 1995: 70; and Turcan 1978: 996–1084.

256 *RIB* 1791; Levick 2007: 133–4; Mundle 1961: 228–37.

257 *CIL* 13.6671 (heavily restored) with discussion by Mundle 1961 and Clauss 2001: 174. Also *AE* 1957, 123 where Clauss rightly points out that the assimilation with Dea Caelestis was a result of the text being changed because of the *damnatio memoriae* of Plautilla (Clauss 2001: 166). This cannot be used as evidence for any 'official' assimilation of Domna to Caelestis.

258 *AE* 1998, 1538 (reign of Caracalla, Carthage); *AE* 1991, 1687 (reign of Elagabalus, Numidia); *AE* 1915, 80 (reign of Septimius Severus, Thala).

259 Hannestad 1988: 272; McCann 1968: 76; Säflund 1968: 119–34.

260 Cordovana 2007: 418; Säflund 1968: 120.

afterwards as a commemoration of the event, if it represented an actual historical occurrence.[261]

However, a close examination of the reliefs of the arch in Lepcis reveals other details that assist in dating the structure. Geta is present (indicating a date before AD 212), but the notoriously influential praetorian prefect Plautianus is not.[262] This is strong evidence for dating the arch after AD 205, when Plautianus fell from power.[263] By contrast, the arch of the *argentarii* in Rome (erected in AD 204) named Plautianus and his daughter Plautilla in the inscription and depicted them in relief alongside the imperial family.[264] Dio casts the prefect as an individual who wanted the power of an emperor, whose greediness and misdemeanours were ultimately a reflection on the rule of Severus, who deferred to Plautianus on all things.[265] In this characterisation Dio writes that Plautianus had more statues and images than any other non-imperial citizen, erected both in Rome and abroad by individuals, communities and even the Senate.[266] Even if this might be deemed an exaggeration on the part of Dio, Plautianus was consul designate in AD 204, was connected to the imperial family through the marriage of his daughter to Caracalla, and was also a native of Lepcis. His absence from the reliefs of the arch in Lepcis is significant. If the decoration of the arch dates after AD 205, then the visit to Africa may have taken place after this date as well. The absence of the praetorian prefect and the lack of alterations suggesting he had been tactfully erased, is telling evidence.

Epigraphic evidence does little to clarify matters. Inscriptions mentioning Severus in Lepcis begin in AD 196/7 (*IRT* 387). Inscriptions specifically mentioning the emperor's *indulgentia* appear from AD 202 (*IRT* 393). Barton's exploration of the inscriptional material at Lepcis has suggested that the majority of the dedications to the imperial family probably coincided with an imperial visit to the city, but a large quantity of the inscriptions do not have secure dates.[267]

Birley linked Severus' visit to Africa with the creation of the province of Numidia.[268] The earliest evidence for this is AD 208: Subatianus Proculus is the first dated legate of Numidia.[269] This would suggest that Severus

261 The suggestion that the arch was erected after Septimius' death (Strong 1972/3: 28) has little to recommend it. Ward-Perkins suggested it may have been put up to greet the emperor on his African tour (Ward-Perkins 1951: 227), but it could just as plausibly have been erected afterwards as a commemoration of the visit.

262 The prefect's connection with the imperial family was recognised within Lepcis, reflected in the surviving epigraphic evidence (e.g. *AE* 1988, 1099).

263 On Plautianus' fall see Dio 77.3.1 and Hdn. 3.2.3.

264 Elsner 2005: 94; Haynes and Hirst 1939: 22.

265 Dio 76.14.1–15.1.

266 Dio 76.14.7.

267 Barton 1977: 10.

268 Birley 1988: 147.

269 *ILS* 9488; Birley 1988: 251 n. 3.

travelled to Africa in AD 207 (a date that correlates with the sculptural evidence on the Lepcitanian *quadrifons*). Indeed, the only epigraphic evidence in support of a date of AD 204 is found in Lambaesis, an inscription dedicated to Septimius Severus in AD 203 by the *familia rationis castrensis*.[270] The presence of imperial staff in an area, however, does not automatically equate to the presence of the imperial family. Hasebroek originally dated Severus' visit to Africa using a large quantity of inscriptional material, but not one of these inscriptions directly mentions the presence of the emperor in the area.[271] A reference to the reigning emperor in an inscription erected during his reign is hardly surprising and cannot be interpreted as an indication that the emperor was in the region.

An inscription found in the temple of Jupiter Dolichenus in Lepcis Magna records the return of the emperor to his city (*urbem suam*).[272] The date is given as 11 April, but no year is provided.[273] While some have seen this as a votive dedication in honour of Severus' return to Lepcis, *urbem suam* could equally refer to the city of Rome. The 11 April was also Severus' birthday, and the inscription was thus probably erected in connection to the festivities of this occasion, not his arrival in Rome or Lepcis.

The epigraphic, sculptural and numismatic evidence all suggest a date of AD 207 for Severus' journey. In this year coins struck at the Roman mint displayed Africa, a type that had not been seen since AD 194.[274] Using the information gathered from the hoard analysis, it is apparent that Africa constituted a large proportion of the silver emissions of that year, along with a continued emphasis on Severus' military success (Figure 24). A galley type was also struck in AD 207, which may reflect imperial travel (though this type was absent from the hoards).[275]

Säflund noted that the imagery employed by the Roman mint in this year (Victory, trophies, Severus as military victor) was akin to that employed on the *quadrifons* at Lepcis.[276] Coins were struck showing Jupiter trampling the giants, a parallel to the scenes of the gigantomachy that grace the Severan temple in Lepcis.[277] Indeed, the coin type recalls medallions of Antoninus Pius and Marcus Aurelius.[278] In the Roman imagination, predominantly in Latin literature, Africa was remote and foreign, and was often associated with the gigantomachy, particularly through the snakes for which the

[270] *CIL* 8.2702, 8.18250. Severus is listed as *trib. potest* XI. [271] Hasebroek 1921: 134.
[272] *IRT* 292.
[273] Kotula 1985: 158 suggests the inscription referred to Severus' arrival in Rome in AD 202, after the Parthian War.
[274] *RIC* IV.1 *Septimius Severus* 207–207A. [275] *RIC* IV.1 *Septimius Severus* 215, 774.
[276] Säflund 1968: 124. [277] *RIC* IV.1 *Septimius Severus* 204. [278] Maderna 2005: 66.

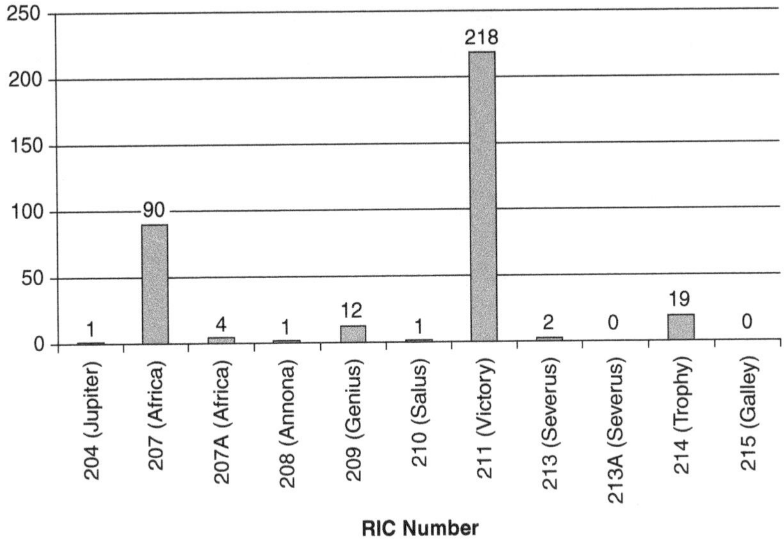

Figure 24: Severus' reverse silver types of AD 207, as represented in hoards.

continent was notorious.[279] Hercules and Bacchus/Dionysus both had a role in the gigantomachy myth: Hercules killed Alcyoneus and Dionysus slew Eurytus with his *thyrsus*. The threat believed to be posed by Africa was often expressed through a gigantomachy topos, seen in Lucan's *De bello civili* and Silius' *Punica*.[280] Considering that the conquest and civilisation of Africa had long been conceptualised in terms developed from the myth, the use of gigantomachy imagery here may allude to Severus' own encounter with 'untamed Africa', or may symbolically reflect his position as the civiliser of the known world. The topos of a gigantomachy highlighted the role of the emperor as a timeless defender against external threats, and signified the order brought to the world by imperial rule.[281]

A gold coin type of this year shows the statue of Aesculapius/Eshmun between two snakes in a temple.[282] Babelon identified the image as a specifically Carthaginian representation of the deity.[283] The two snakes were an attribute of the god Eshmun, who was aligned with Aesculapius in

279 Bassett 1955: 1–20; Leigh 2000: 95–109. 280 Asso 2002: 57–72; Fantham 1992: 98.

281 Maderna 2005: 73.

282 *RIC* IV.1 *Septimius Severus* 205. The type was also struck in AD 207 for Geta (*RIC* IV.1 *Geta* 129) and Caracalla (*RIC* IV.1 *Caracalla* 99).

283 *RIC* IV.1 *Septimius Severus* 77, 205; *RIC* IV.1 *Caracalla* 99; *RIC* IV.1 *Geta* 129; Babelon 1903: 169.

this period and who possessed a famous temple at Carthage.[284] Though there is no numismatic representation of the Aesculapius at Carthage, coins struck by the city of Berytus indicate that the Phoenician Eshmun was portrayed with two snakes.[285] Severus' coin might thus refer to an imperial visit to Carthage towards the end of AD 207. The city had already been represented on Severus' coinage through the goddess Dea Caelestis, perhaps on this occasion it was represented by its other famous cult.

The evidence for placing the visit of Severus to Africa in AD 207 is certainly circumstantial, but the accumulation of the evidence here makes this a more favourable option than AD 203. Kotula suggested that a visit may have been planned in the period AD 202–204, but obligations in Rome delayed the journey until much later.[286] This may have been the case, or the visit may have always been planned for *c.* AD 207.

Negotiating the imperial image in Lepcis Magna

If Severus visited Africa in AD 207, then he almost certainly visited Lepcis Magna. During his reign the city underwent an extraordinary building program: a new forum, basilica, temple and nymphaeum were constructed, as well as an artificial harbour with lighthouse, warehouses and temples.[287] This display of imperial munificence, in conjunction with the grant of *ius Italicum* and Severus' Lepcitanian heritage, all undoubtedly persuaded the inhabitants of the town to adopt the title *Lepcitani Septimiani.*[288]

The decoration of the arch and the basilica in Lepcis Magna offer an insight into how Severus' divine ideology was interpreted and visualised within the city. It is evident that the visual representation of the emperor and his family in Lepcis was unique, and reflected the fact that the city publicly associated itself with his success. Imperial ideology was adapted at a local level to communicate the relationship of the city to the ruling power.

The Severan *quadrifons*

At the intersection of the two main streets in Lepcis Magna stood a *quadrifons* or arch that was probably erected by the city's inhabitants

[284] On the iconography of Eshmun see Will 1988: 23–4. On the temple of Aesculapius at Carthage see Strabo 17.3.14 and App. *Pun.* 130, who describes the temple as one of the richest and most renowned in the city.

[285] *BMC Phoenicia* (Berytus) 215. [286] Kotula 1985: 151–65.

[287] Ward-Perkins 1993: 1. Procopius (*De aedificis* 6.4.5) writes that Severus left a palace in Lepcis 'as a memorial of his good fortune'.

[288] *IRT* 283, 393, 410.

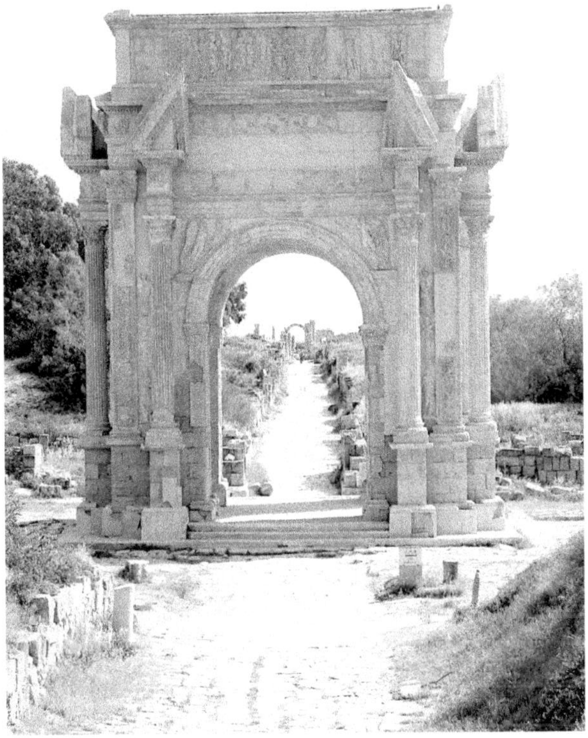

Figure 25: The Severan *quadrifons* at Lepcis Magna.

(Figure 25).[289] Di Vita suggests that the arch had stood in the area since the time of Trajan, and that it was later decorated with marble panels during the Severan period.[290] Miniscule fragments of what may have been the dedicatory inscription have been pieced together, but these reveal little except the words DIVO and DIVAE.[291] The decoration of the arch sets out to connect Severus and his imperial power with the city of Lepcis, a theme that supports the idea that the monument was erected by local citizenry. The arch focused on Severus' military victories, the imperial family and the emperor's connection to Lepcis, which in turn could claim some reflected part of the emperor's glory.[292] The reliefs show, amongst other imagery, the emperor and his family in a variety of ceremonial contexts.[293]

289 Bartoccini 1932: 32–152; Townsend 1938: 524; Ward-Perkins 1951: 226; Wilson 2007: 297.

290 Di Vita 1975: 3–26; Di Vita 1977: 135–43; Fähnd Rich 2005: 32.

291 Di Vita 1975: 3–26; Ioppolo 1968: 83–92. 292 Newby 2007: 209–11.

293 For a detailed description of the reliefs see Bartoccini 1932: 32–152; Bober 1943; Hannestad 1988: 272; and Mundle 1957.

Though the citizens of Lepcis likely erected the arch, the size of the monument (and the surrounding building programme by the emperor in the city) suggests that Severus would have been represented within an accepted visual language.[294] Though the initiative and expense was born by the civic élite, one must allow for the possibility that the citizens consulted Severus while constructing the arch, and that its design reflected the way Severus wished to be portrayed inside the city. This process is suggested by the surviving correspondence of Pliny with the emperor Trajan, in which the governor was anxious to keep the emperor informed of all local building projects. If this correspondence is typical, then Severus must at least have known of the construction of the arch reliefs. The arch allowed the citizens of Lepcis to highlight their own personal connection with the emperor and his munificence, but this representation was undoubtedly couched in terms acceptable to the emperor.

The 'triumphal' relief

Four friezes, each about 1.72m high, were placed along the top of the four facades of the arch.[295] Facing Oea to the west was a relief measuring 6.355m in length, depicting the imperial family in procession (Figure 26).[296] The surviving fragments suggest that one slab is missing from either end of the frieze.[297] Septimius, Caracalla and Geta are depicted frontally in a chariot, being led by an individual wearing a medallion around his neck. This figure is perhaps the *gens Septimiana*.[298] Decorating the chariot are Hercules and Liber Pater, shown on either side of the Tyche of Lepcis. Hercules is crowning the goddess. On the left side of the frieze behind the chariot are four horsemen, two of whom bear *vexilla*, wearing togas. In front of the *gens Septimiana*, on the right hand side of the relief, are two bearded figures clothed in tunics and mantles and three pairs of porters who carry a *ferculum* with Parthian prisoners. In front of these is a guard with two more Parthian prisoners. Along the relief, behind the main scene, is a row of spectators and a lighthouse in the background. Another slab with a trophy and Victory probably completed the frieze.[299]

294 Mayer 2010: 130 suggests that the different imperial representations created by different groups may in fact reflect the differing way the emperor represented himself to different sections of the populace.

295 Bober 1943: 33. On the possible significance of the placement of these reliefs (the 'triumphal' scene faced Oea, the sacrificial scene faced the old forum and the city temples) see Fähnd Rich 2005: 29–45.

296 The descriptions of the reliefs of the arch are in the main drawn from Bober 1943.

297 Bober 1943: 34. 298 Townsend 1938: 515. 299 Bober 1943: 36.

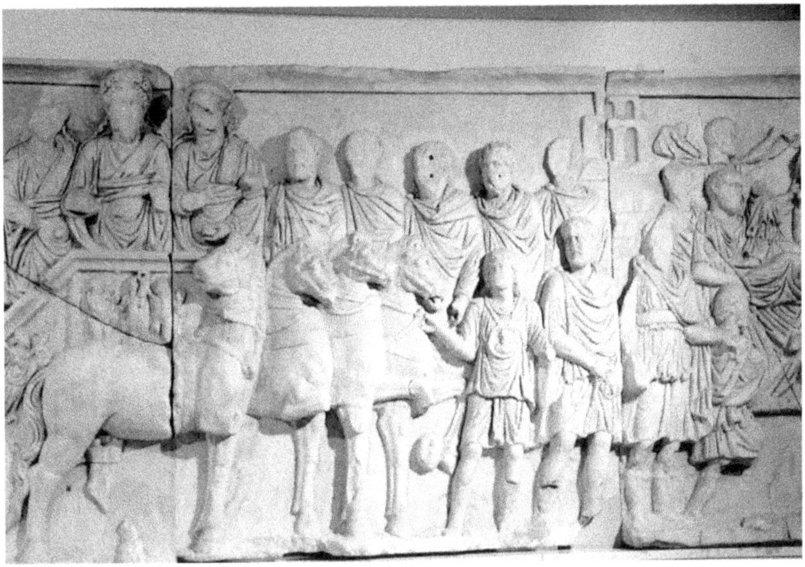

Figure 26: Central section of the 'triumphal' relief from the Severan *quadrifons* at Lepcis Magna.

Townsend believed the presence of Liber and Hercules in the chariot and the depiction of the lighthouse meant that the relief represented a triumphal procession that had taken place in Lepcis after Septimius' eastern victories.[300] Townsend suggested the depiction of the lighthouse signified the harbour at Lepcis, so as to place the entire scene within the city. This explanation dated the arch to AD 203/4, after the conclusion of the Parthian War. As discussed above, this date is problematic on several fronts. Moreover, the likelihood that Septimius would have held a triumphal procession in Lepcis in AD 204 or at any other time is minimal. If Septimius had decided to break with tradition and had held a triumph outside the city of Rome, this fundamental change surely would not have gone unmentioned by the authors of the period.[301]

The Parthian war of Severus was complete by AD 198 and in AD 202, Severus travelled from the East to Rome where Herodian records the victorious emperor was received by the Roman people.[302] The spoils of the war are displayed in relief on the arch of Septimius Severus in the Roman forum.[303] It is worth noting that nowhere on the arch in Rome is Severus shown in a triumphal procession; rather, the spoils of war are paraded from the personification of Parthia to the goddess Roma. The

300 Townsend 1938: 517. 301 Bandinelli, Caffarelli et al. 1966: 47. 302 Hdn. 3.10.1.
303 Brilliant 1967: 137.

barbarians also submit before Roma, not Severus. Brilliant believed this impersonal representation matched the character of the inscription on the arch: *ob rem publicam restitutam imperium populi Romani propagatum.*[304] But the abstract nature of the representation might be interpreted in a different light if we are to believe the author of the *Historia Augusta*, who wrote that Severus could not hold a triumph because of his lifelong struggle with gout.[305] Dio and Herodian also note that Severus suffered from this disease.[306] The Roman arch may thus represent a politic manner of presenting a victory for which a triumph was never held. Whether this is truth or rumour is impossible to tell; one may only observe that neither Dio nor Herodian give a detailed description of a Severan triumph. The absence of a triumphal procession featuring the emperor from the arch in the forum may merely reflect the fact that the arch was created by the Senate, who subscribed to the idea that the emperor was a leader among equals.[307] Whatever the cause, the triumphal scene on the arch at Lepcis is markedly different to that represented on its counterpart in Rome.

There are problems with identifying the Lepcitanian scene as a triumphal procession. The mounted, togate riders shown behind the imperial *quadriga* are accompanied by military standards, excluding their identification as magistrates or senators.[308] These civic officials are instead depicted at the front of the procession. Strocka noted that this depiction was inconsistent with the right of *albata decursio* given to the high officers of the empire; that is, the right to walk or ride behind the emperor in a triumphal procession.

Bandinelli suggested the relief depicts a triumphal procession or *reditus* of the emperor on his way to Rome.[309] He observed that in Roman art a lighthouse almost always indicates Ostia or Alexandria, and that the scene at Lepcis might represent Severus' triumphal return to Rome through the port at Ostia. This theory is also called into question by the existence of the mounted riders behind the chariot. Moreover, triumphal processions and the ceremony of *reditus* never took place in the city of Ostia, only in Rome.[310]

Bandinelli's suggestion would mean that the artists in Lepcis were reliant on imperial imagery issuing out of the capital. The other reliefs on the Lepcitanian arch do have some similarities to the arch in the Roman forum: Lusnia noted parallels between the military scenes on each arch and suggested these sculptured reliefs likely derive from imperial paintings.[311]

[304] Brilliant 1967: 146. [305] *SHA Sev.* 16.6, 18.9; Aur. Vict. *caes* 20; Strocka 1972: 169.
[306] Dio 77.16.1; Hdn. 2.15.4, 3.14.2, 3.15.2. [307] This is the suggestion of Mayer 2010: 127–30.
[308] Strocka 1972: 166. [309] Bandinelli, Caffarelli et al. 1966: 47. [310] Strocka 1972: 166.
[311] Lusnia 2006a: 272–99.

Herodian mentions the existence of such media, recording that after his eastern victories Septimius sent a report to the senate, and ordered that his battles and victories be painted and displayed.[312]

An image of triumph probably did circulate in the provinces, perhaps through the paintings mentioned by Herodian, and this imagery may have been transferred into the designs of local currency. Nicopolis in Moesia Inferior struck several types alluding to Severus' military victories, including one showing a triumphal procession of the emperor.[313] Septimius and Caracalla are shown in a triumphal *quadriga* with a trophy in the background. Virtus leads the procession carrying a *vexillum*. A similar coin was struck for Caracalla, and the same magistrate at Nicopolis released coin types showing Hercules, and others displaying Liber Pater.[314]

The same scene, complete with trophy in the background and Virtus with *vexillum*, also appears on a coin of Mytilene in Lesbos.[315] The similarities here are likely due to the fact that the provinces were influenced by Roman imperial imagery.[316] The scene was ultimately derived from earlier imagery of the Antonine period: a nearly identical image appears on medals of Aurelius and Verus commemorating a Parthian victory.[317] Given Severus' adoption into the Antonines, the continuation of Antonine imagery of Parthian victory is significant and likely conscious. It again underlines the continuity with the previous dynasty.

Provincial artists took Severan imperial imagery and interpreted it according to their medium and culture.[318] The visual depiction of a scene of triumph is particularly interesting given that Severus may never have held

312 Hdn. 3.9.12. 313 CNG Mail Bid Sale 61 (25 September 2002) 101.

314 Varbanov 2431; Mouchmov 933. The same type was reused under Macrinus, see H.D. Rauch GmbH, Mail Bid Sale 9 (23 September 2005) 337. Hercules: Varbanov 1234 (Hercules and the Cretan bull); Varbanov 2067 ('Farnese' Hercules); Mouchmov 1010 (Nemean lion). Liber Pater: Mionnet Supp. II 375; Varbanov 2432. For a full and detailed listing of the variations, see Mouchmov. The magistrate, Aurelius Gallus, also struck coins showing Victory (Gorny & Mosch Münzhandlung, Auction 156 (5 March 2007) 1677), the emperor mounted and spearing a boar (Gorny & Mosch Münzhandlung, Auction 156 (5 March 2007) 1678), the emperor mounted riding over a Parthian (Münzen & Medaillen Deutschland GmbH, Auction 16 (19 May 2005) 367), and an altar between two military standards (Münzen & Medaillen Deutschland GmbH, Auction 16 (19 May 2005) 366).

315 *BMC Lesbos* (Mytilene) 212–13.

316 Given the geographical distance between Mytilene and Nicopolis ad Istrum, the similarity in the imagery here may be more than the product of travelling die engravers.

317 Gnecchi 1912: (vol. 2) 47 nos. 17–19.

318 Provincial images of Severus' war and 'triumph' include *BMC Galatia* (Tavium) 21–2 (emperor in *quadriga*); *BMC Lydia* (Bogis) 25 (Severus mounted, hurling a javelin at Parthians); *BMC Mysia* (Cyzicus) 247 (the emperor crowning a trophy with a river god beneath); *SNG Levante* (Tarsus) 1027 (emperor in *quadriga* holding Nike); Numismatik Lanz München, Auction 109 (27 May 2002) 571 (Pautalia in Thrace, Severus with military trophy and Parthian captives).

one. The imperial coinage never shows Severus as a *triumphator* (or, if it did, no specimens survive).[319] It thus appears that the imagery of triumph need not have reflected an actual event; an image of triumph may have been included amongst the paintings detailing Septimius' eastern victories because of its symbolic value, or perhaps because the artist(s) assumed one would be forthcoming.

The artists in Lepcis may also have drawn on a common imperial iconography in their design of the arch reliefs; the sculpture need not reflect a ceremony of triumph in Lepcis itself, or even in Rome. Strocka argued that the representation of the emperor on the Lepcitanian arch was allegorical, a symbol of the eternity of imperial victory in which Lepcis Magna claimed a share by visually juxtaposing specifically local scenes and deities.[320] This is the best avenue of interpretation. The similarities to the iconography of a Roman triumphal procession, in conjunction with the peculiar additions and changes that are inconsistent with a Roman triumph (the lighthouse, the riders), suggest that the relief is a provincial interpretation of a Roman triumph.

Lepcis Magna would not have been ignorant of Severan imagery; the emperor had artisans in the city constructing several monuments that reflected wider imperial ideology. This is intimated by the remains of the Severan temple, located in the new Lepcitanian forum and built at the directive of the emperor.[321] The fragmented reliefs that survive from this temple show scenes from the gigantomachy.[322] The presence of imagery associated with this myth on the coinage of Severus has been discussed above.[323] The artisans who created the reliefs on the Lepcitanian arch (who were not local)[324] were undoubtedly familiar with the iconographic repertoire of the imperial house.

If the 'triumphal' relief drew inspiration from imperial artwork, we can begin to understand why it has similarities to the representation of a triumphal procession. It is a Lepcitanian interpretation of a triumph, not a reflection of an historical occurrence. The lighthouse was given to Lepcis as part of the Severan building programme. Its very presence advertises the imperial favour towards the city, and the city's close connection to the emperor and his military glory. Likewise, the representation of Liber and Hercules on the chariot is likely to be simultaneously a reflection of Severus' patronage of these deities, and a conscious attempt by the Lepcitanians to

319 By contrast, several types of Caracalla show him as *triumphator* in a *quadriga*, both under Severus and during his sole reign: *RIC* IV.1 *Caracalla* 77, 87, 103–4, 210, 499, 506.

320 Strocka 1972: 147–72.

321 Ward-Perkins 1993: 31–53.

322 Squarciapino 1974: 7.

323 *RIC* IV.1 *Septimius Severus* 204 (AD 207); Gnecchi 1912: (vol. 1) 45 no. 1.

324 Kleiner 1992: 343; Walda and Walker 1984: 81–95; Ward-Perkins 1951: 228.

advertise their particular connection to the imperial person. As Strocka has concluded, the additions to the relief were not merely superfluous trimmings, but a manifestation of Lepcis Magna within the fame and glory of Severus.[325]

The *dextrarum iunctio* relief

The top south side of the Lepcitanian arch displayed a scene of *dextrarum iunctio* between Severus and Caracalla (Figure 27).[326] Septimius and Caracalla grasp right hands in front of a third figure whose face was originally missing, and who has been restored as Geta. To the left of the scene stands Julia Domna and Virtus holding a sword and *vexilla*. Behind Domna, Minerva is represented with a spear and shield. The Tyche of Lepcis, Hercules and Liber Pater stand behind Septimius and Caracalla.[327] To the right are military figures with Mars in the background. These balance the five togate civilians to the very left of the relief.[328] The scene is one of unity and harmony, emphasising the *concordia* within the imperial family.

Multiple interpretations of this relief have been put forward. Bartoccini thought the scene celebrated the proclamation of Geta as *princeps*

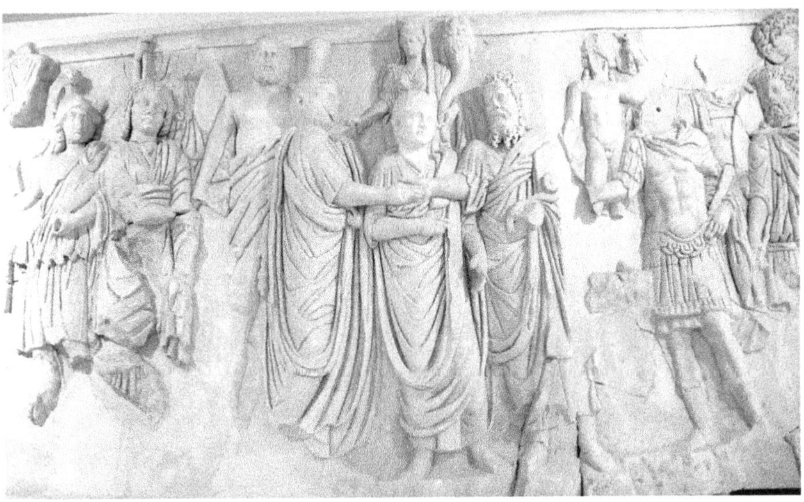

Figure 27: Central section of the '*dextrarum iunctio*' relief from the Severan *quadrifons* at Lepcis Magna.

325 Strocka 1972: 166. 326 Bober 1943: 39.

327 Traditionally, the female figure behind the imperial family has been interpreted as Concordia, but Strocka correctly points out that the mural crown of the figure makes Tyche a much more probable identification (Strocka 1972: 167).

328 Bober 1943: 39–41.

iuventutis. Bober believed it was somehow related to the African garrisons, perhaps an honorary command given to Caracalla.[329] Rubin suggested that the scene reflected Septimius' introduction of his sons into the forum of Lepcis and the bestowal of the *toga virilis* on Geta in the city.[330] Townsend suggested that the image was allegorical, symbolising the *concordia* within the imperial house.[331] This is the most likely interpretation. Once again the citizens of the city utilised sculptural relief to emphasise their connection to the emperor and his successors. Liber Pater and Hercules functioned as the guarantors of *concordia* within the *domus divina*, ensuring the continuation of the imperial house. This ideology is also seen on imperial numismatic imagery: a coin type struck in Rome shows Caracalla and Geta shaking hands, one being crowned by Hercules, the other by Liber Pater (Figure 28).[332] The coin type was released sometime around AD 210.

The artistic motif of *dextrarum iunctio* is employed on the Lepcitanian arch to symbolise imperial harmony. The addition of Liber and Hercules echoes imperial ideology as well as communicating Lepcis' own particular connection to the imperial *concordia*. The artists who created this scene may have been influenced by imperial imagery, but the scene is ultimately

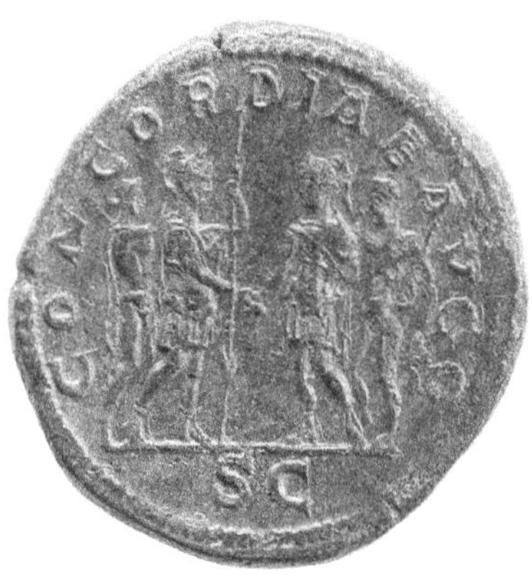

Figure 28: Sestertius (reverse) of Caracalla showing Caracalla and Geta clasping hands, one being crowned by Hercules and the other by Liber Pater. The reverse legend reads CONCORDIAE AVGG S C.

[329] Bober 1943: 43. Bober's interpretation here and elsewhere was based on the *Historia Augusta*'s account of a victory over the African tribes (*SHA*, *Sev.* 18.3).

[330] Rubin 1971: 374; Rubin 1976/7: 169. Cordovana 2007: 421 also argues in favour of the scene commemorating an actual event.

[331] Townsend 1938: 519.

[332] *RIC* IV.1 *Caracalla* 459, 508, 537; *RIC* IV.1 *Geta* 155, 184. Mistakenly identified by Mattingly as Hercules and Apollo, and Victory and Apollo.

provincial, a specifically Lepcitanian interpretation. Though a demonstration of the harmony of the imperial family may have taken place in Lepcis, this scene probably does not represent a historical event. Rather, it is an interpretation of imperial imagery that reflects an interaction with the ideology of Severus' principate.

This interpretation gains strength when one examines other provincial imagery. The *concordia* between the imperial family, particularly between Geta and Caracalla, was a popular theme on provincial coinage.[333] By adopting this imagery and ideology at a local level, individual cities could contribute their own perspective to the wider imperial image. Of particular interest here is an obvious variation of the official *concordia* coin struck in Rome, pictured above. On a coin of Mytilene, Caracalla and Geta are shown in military dress shaking right hands. Instead of being crowned by Liber Pater and Hercules, as on the Roman coin, Caracalla is crowned by Nike and Geta by the Tyche of Mytilene, who sits behind him.[334] In this case the imperial iconography is adjusted in order to connect the city of Mytilene to the imperial power. We should see the adaptation of imperial iconography in Lepcis Magna in a similar vein.

The 'sacrifice' relief

The third relief on the outer frieze of the arch, on the opposite side to the *dextrarum iunctio* relief, shows Domna sacrificing over an altar (Figure 29). To Domna's right stand a flute player and Roma, who holds a globe in her

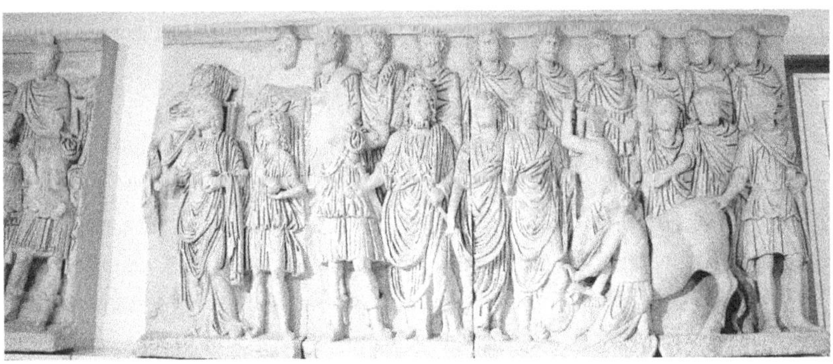

Figure 29: Right section of the 'sacrificial' relief from the Severan *quadrifons* at Lepcis Magna.

333 Examples include *BMC Pisidia* (Antioch) 51, *BMC Thrace* (Bizya) 5, *BMC Thrace* (Byzantium) 75, *BMC Thrace* (Perinthus) 49, and *BMC Lesbos* (Mytilene) 208.

334 *BMC Lesbos* (Mytilene) 216.

extended right hand. After Roma is Severus, who is crowned and holding a thunderbolt (?) and sceptre. Bober believed the two figures between Severus and the sacrificial bull may have been the *duoviri* of Lepcis.[335] Above Domna is an enthroned figure, perhaps Juno. Behind the scene is a row of spectators. Bober's desire to equate these with the famous philosophers who gathered at Lepcis (according to the account of Philostratus mentioned above) is fanciful.[336] On the left side (not reproduced here) are military personnel and more spectators, as well as another sacrificial bull. Since the main section of the frieze is lost, we cannot know to whom the sacrifice was made. Bober suggested that it was for the patron divinities of Lepcis Magna, Hercules and Liber Pater.[337] There is nothing to argue for or against such a conclusion; there is simply not enough evidence. What is significant is the extremely close identification of the emperor and empress with Jupiter and Juno (Severus with a thunderbolt, Juno behind Domna), reflecting the conceptualisation of imperial power within the city.

The fourth frieze is extremely damaged, but it is likely that it too showed an interpretation of a triumphal procession.[338] Surviving fragments show mounted riders similar to those shown on the other 'triumphal' relief, and one fragment shows Domna adjacent to a victory palm.[339] Other fragments display military trophies, and a goddess.[340]

The inner reliefs

We now turn to the reliefs placed on the inner faces of the four piers that formed the *quadrifons*. One of the better preserved shows Severus and Domna in the guise of the Capitoline Triad (Figure 30). The emperor and empress are shown as Jupiter and Juno, with Minerva and an owl to the right and the Tyche of Lepcis and an eagle on the left.

Traditionally it has been thought that this representation of Severus suggested an imperial alignment with Sarapis (through the use of 'corkscrew curls' in the emperor's beard).[341] This theory has little to recommend it. There is no evidence apart from a similarity in hairstyle to suggest that Septimius Severus consciously aligned himself with Sarapis.[342] Any message conveyed by the emperor's portraits had to be clear and easily recognised.

335 Bober 1943: 46. 336 Bober 1943: 48. 337 Bober 1943: 47. 338 Bober 1943: 48.

339 BSR photographic archives, Ward Perkins Collection, WP[PHP]-LibG16–059b.

340 BSR photographic archives, Ward Perkins Collection, WP[PHP]-LibG16–060b and WP[PHP]-LibG16–060d.

341 Bonanno 1976: 147; L'Orange 1982: 82; McCann 1968: 53.

342 Baharal 1989: 566–80; Baharal 1996: 84–91; Lichtenberger 2007: 116; Raeder 1992: 175–96.

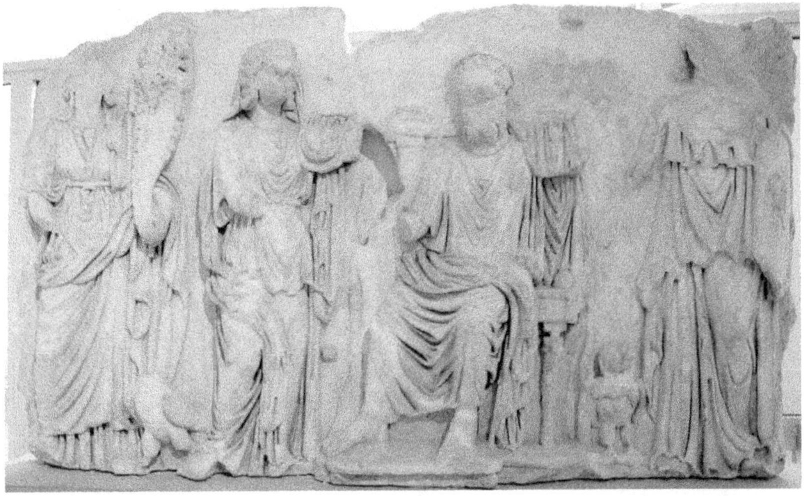

Figure 30: 'Capitoline Triad' relief from the Severan *quadrifons* at Lepcis Magna.

A slight similarity in hairstyle (and Baharal illustrates that the hairstyle of emperor and god are by no means identical) is not sufficient to connect Septimius to Sarapis, particularly considering that the same hairstyle is also common to Jupiter, and that similar styles graced the portraits of Marcus Aurelius, Lucius Verus, Commodus, Pescennius Niger and Albinus.[343] A better interpretation of Septimius' coiffure is that it was another way by which Severus sought to connect himself to the Antonine dynasty. The presence of Minerva and the eagle in this relief, as well as Severus' seated position, point towards an identification of the emperor with Jupiter.[344] As ruler of Rome, the emperor is akin to the ruler of the heavens, Jupiter.

Another section of the inner relief, probably located opposite the relief discussed above, displayed a pantheon of deities: Apollo and Diana, Venus and Mars, the city goddess and a companion, Dionysius, and perhaps Mercury and Virtus.[345] Other fragments suggest that Luna, Vesta, Minerva and Sol may also have been represented.[346]

One interior relief shows a scene of sacrifice (Figure 31). The upper section of this relief portrays Severus and Caracalla, along with another togate figure (probably Geta); the emperors have their heads covered for the sacrifice. To the right of Caracalla is a statue of Silvanus on a pedestal. Between Caracalla and Severus stands a facing Hercules. The remains of a

[343] Baharal 1989: 568–79.

[344] Baharal 1989: 567–9; Mundle 1957: 126–30; Raeder 1992: 175–96.

[345] Bober 1943: 9–11.

[346] Bober 1943: 12–13.

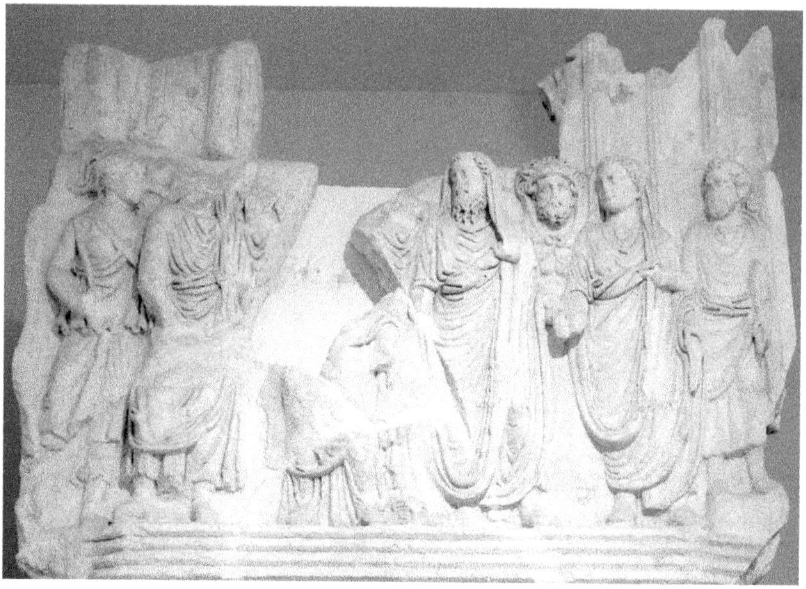

Figure 31: Top section of the inner sacrifice relief from the Severan *quadrifons* at Lepcis Magna.

female figure can be seen behind Severus, most likely Domna.[347] Severus takes Caracalla's hand in his, and his right hand (now broken away) stretches out towards Domna in a similar gesture. On the left of the relief, behind Geta, is a figure with long, curly hair, likely Liber Pater.[348] To the left of Geta is an image of Roma or Virtus. A classical temple forms the backdrop to the scene. The lower section of the relief (not reproduced here) displays the sacrificial victim. Flanking an altar are two bulls led by *victimarii* and accompanied by a man in a short tunic. In the background stand nine spectators, all wearing togas. These are likely representations of the citizens or magistrates of Lepcis Magna.[349]

Mundle believed that the two scenes represented a sacrifice that had taken place while the imperial family were in the city, probably in the Forum Vetus.[350] This explanation is certainly possible. The Forum Vetus possessed three temples: one to Liber Pater, one to Rome and Augustus and a third temple probably dedicated to Hercules.[351] The representation of these deities could thus serve to contextualise the sacrifice. The covered heads

[347] Mundle 1957: 123.

[348] Bober 1943: 21. Mundle points out that this figure is extremely similar to that portrayed on the Bacchus pilasters in the Severan basilica and on coins issued by Lepcis Magna (Mundle 1957: 124).

[349] Bober 1943: 22. [350] Mundle 1957: 125. [351] Di Vita, Di Vita-Evrard et al. 1999: 75.

of the emperor and his sons signify that the imperial family is a participant in, not a recipient of, the sacrifice. The chief gods of Lepcis are represented on the relief: Silvanus, Hercules, Liber Pater, Tyche and Roma/Virtus. The civic statues of these deities are most likely reproduced in the relief, indicated by the pedestal underneath Silvanus. Above all, the scene communicates the devotion of the imperial family to the tutelary deities of Lepcis. The symbolic nature of the other representations suggests that this image too may be idealised. Whether the imagery recalled an historical occasion or not is almost immaterial, the image conveyed the piety of the imperial family towards the gods of the polis.

Bartoccini believed the relief was connected with the army, and that the reliefs depicted a sacrifice to Silvanus, the protector of the army in Africa.[352] Bober suggested that the presence of what seem to be military officials and the personification of Virtus meant that the scene was related to the Lambaesis garrison.[353] The presence of Liber and Hercules, as well as the location of the relief inside the city of Lepcis, suggest that it is better understood as a display of the *pietas* of the emperor towards the city. Similar, though abbreviated, representations are seen on provincial coinage in this period: the emperor is shown sacrificing to a civic deity to communicate the connection of the emperor to a city, his patronage and, at times, his actual presence.[354]

Other fragmentary inner reliefs from the arch allude to the cult of Hercules and Liber Pater. Mundle believed one scene might have represented the Lepcitanian cult of these two deities (Figure 32).[355] Hercules is portrayed on a small base, naked with a lion-skin over his left shoulder and arm. To the left of him is a table with three people around it (who are much smaller than Hercules). In the background is a door. Below is a headless figure whose pose suggests Liber Pater with a *thyrsus*. Bober observed that the table was supported by lions' heads and legs and was framed by crossed elephant tusks.[356] At the right are two small busts (which are damaged, but Bober believed bore some resemblance to Severus and Domna) in a frame, as well as a small arch and crossed elephant tusks. Bober concluded that this was a local scene of sacrifice, noting that offerings of ivory were given to Liber in this area (the god may have acted as a patron of ivory merchants).[357]

352 Bober 1943: 24. 353 Bober 1943: 24.

354 On a temple in Esna/Latonpolis (Egypt), the Severan family are shown (in pharaonic guise) sacrificing to the city gods of Latonpolis, Chnum, Nebtu and Heka. The scene was executed around the time the family visited Egypt (Hein 1991: 282).

355 Bartoccini 1932: 89; Mundle 1957: 131. 356 Bober 1943: 29.

357 Aurigemma 1940: 67–86; Bober 1943: 30; *IRT* 295.

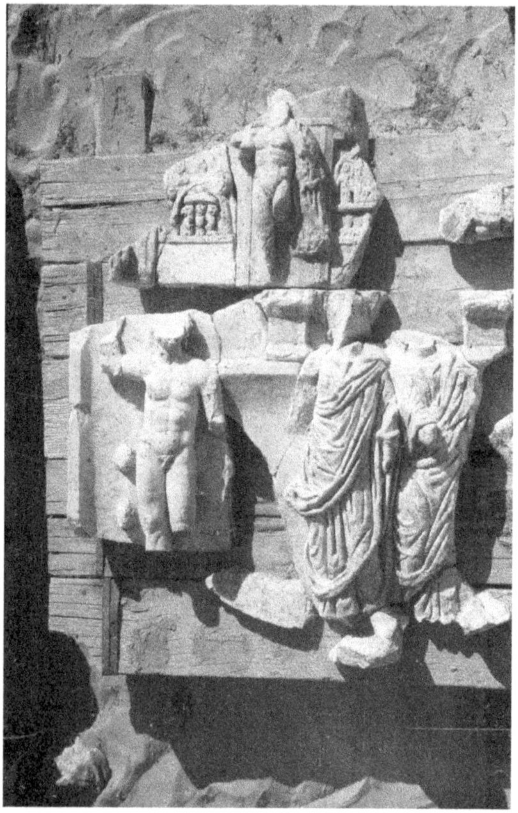

Figure 32: Inner relief from the Severan *quadrifons* possibly displaying Lepcitanian cultic activity.

Interior and exterior reliefs also depicted images of a siege and military trophies.[358] The details of these reliefs are not the focus of this work, but it is likely that they represent scenes from Severus' Parthian War and not a local military campaign, as Townsend believed.[359]

Interpreting the sculpture of the Severan *quadrifons*

The decoration of the Severan arch in Lepcis represents a local interpretation of wider imperial ideology. Provincial cities constantly engaged in declarations of status, a discourse that focused on civic titles and imperial benefactions. Lepcis Magna found itself in a unique position. Not only was it the *patria* of the emperor, it had been gifted with *ius Italicum* and an enormous imperial building programme. Denied the numismatic mode of

[358] Bober 1943: 24. [359] Bober 1943: 26–7.

expression available to their eastern counterparts (only cities in the East of the empire had the privilege of striking their own coinage in this period), the citizens of Lepcis monumentalised their close connection to the emperor through a medium popular in Roman North Africa: the *quadrifons*.[360] This monument could communicate to citizens and to visitors the special status of Lepcis under Severus. Imperial imagery was combined with local ideology and interpreted at a local level, resulting in an almost creole representation of the imperial family and their achievements.[361] Severus' military exploits, his close connection with the divine, and the *felicitas* and *concordia* of the imperial house are all commemorated. The city's close connection to all these areas is expressed through the addition of the Tyche of Lepcis, Liber Pater and Hercules to the reliefs. The latter two gods were also part of imperial ideology, and so their presence has a dual significance. That no other city in this period reproduces this particular type of sculptural iconography (though provincial building programmes were abundant, particularly in Africa)[362] illustrates Lepcis' unique position in this period, and the fact that Liber and Hercules are used as markers for the city.

Only a handful of inscriptions link Septimius Severus to his tutelary deities outside Africa, where their worship is to be expected.[363] Modestus and the *equites singulares*, both examples discussed above, were individuals closely connected with the emperor and could be expected to possess some knowledge of Severus' ideology. No other inscriptions outside Lepcis name Liber Pater and Hercules together in connection with the emperor. Since, numismatically at least, the bulk of the surviving imperial imagery refers to military success and the benefits this brings, this situation is not surprising. The military image of Severus is reproduced more frequently in the provinces, reflecting the official emphasis issuing out of Rome. The absence of Liber and Hercules elsewhere underscores the fact that their presence in the sculpture of Lepcis was largely a result of their role in local culture.

360 There is an abundance of honorific arches throughout North Africa, particularly from the Severan period (Wilson 2007: 307). See Cotton and Eck 1997: 11–20 for an honorific arch for Severus in Jerusalem.

361 On the validity of this term for the Roman provinces in the empire see Webster 2001: 209–25.

362 Wilson 2007: 307–26. Cyrene, for instance, set up a relief for Severus, but it has no reference to Liber or Hercules, and portrays the emperor in a military context (Bonanno 1976: 156–8; Bonnano 1976–7: 19–20; Lusnia 2006a: 288; Strong 1972/3: 27–35). On building programmes of Severus in the East see Malalas 12.20–3.

363 One inscription in Lepcis Magna connects Liber Pater with the *lares* of the Severan family (*IRT* 295).

The Severan forum and basilica

Many of the other buildings in Lepcis constructed in this period were built at the initiative of the emperor. Of interest to our discussion is the Severan forum, which was begun under Severus but not completed until the reign of Caracalla in AD 216.[364] The structure consisted of a central open space, surrounded by porticoes, with a temple at the south-west end. North-east of the forum was a basilica with four carved pilasters at each end (Figure 33).[365] At the south-east end of the basilica two outer pilasters supported the entablature; these were decorated with a heavy medallion scroll acanthus featuring rosettes, flowers, beasts and other animals.[366] An inner pair of pilasters was carved with images portraying the myths of Hercules, showing the hero's twelve labours and other stories.[367] At the top of the inner left pilaster is an image of Minerva, or perhaps Roma.[368] At the top of the inner right pilaster is an image of Victory carrying a palm.[369] The image of Victory also sits atop the right side of one of the acanthus scroll pilasters, which supports the entablature on the right-hand side of the basilica.

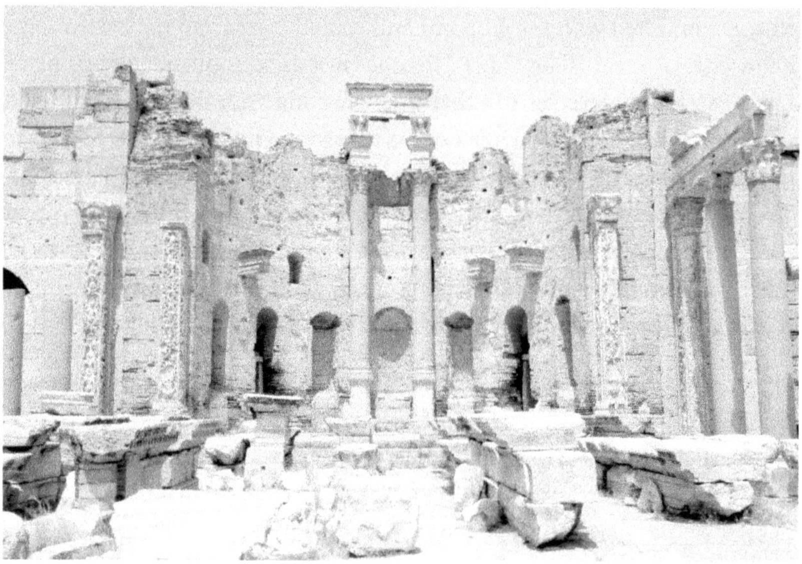

Figure 33: The Severan basilica in Lepcis Magna.

[364] *IRT* 428; Ward-Perkins 1993: 55. [365] Ward-Perkins 1948: 73.
[366] Ward-Perkins 1948: 73. [367] Squarciapino 1974: 108. [368] Squarciapino 1974: 101.
[369] Squarciapino 1974: 111.

The pilasters at the north-west end of the basilica mirror this organisation, but the inner pilasters focus on the myths of Liber Pater/Bacchus. The outer pair of pilasters is decorated with acanthus scroll medallions, with the left-most pilaster displaying an image of a Medusa head at the top.[370] This is no doubt meant to recall the decoration of the adjacent Severan forum, whose porticoes were decorated with a series of Medusa heads. The inner pilasters at this end are not as well preserved as their Herculean counterparts, but enough survives to note that they displayed a variety of myths connected to Liber Pater.[371] The inner left pilaster is decorated with a Victory carved at the top left side.[372]

The decoration of the north-west end of the basilica with images of Liber Pater, and the decoration of the south-east end with myths of Hercules, reflects the central role of these two deities in Lepcis Magna, as well as their association with the emperor. The presence of Victory at each end of the basilica evokes the military achievements of Severus and his sons, conquests that were also proclaimed in the dedicatory inscription that ran along the basilica.[373] The inclusion of Victory on the carved pilasters served to bind Severus' military success with the two deities who formed the focus of the other pilasters: Hercules and Liber Pater. It is perhaps better to see the figure atop the inner left pilaster as Roma, who would thus serve to connect the scenes to the imperial capital, the residence of the emperor.

The identity of the temple placed in the Severan forum remains unknown. It may have been connected with the *gens Septimiana*, which was worshipped in Africa.[374] The surviving sculptural pedestals of the columns of the temple portray scenes of the gigantomachy. Both Liber Pater and Hercules are shown amongst this decoration, a phenomenon that can be explained by their rôle in the myth. One scene (block 15) shows Liber Pater, Hercules and Mercury at a scene of sacrifice.[375] Maderna notes that this is not accidental: Liber and Hercules are represented in this way to communicate their central rôle in Severus' reign.[376] Since the forum was not complete until after Severus' death, the temple may have been connected with the worship of the imperial family.[377] Ward-Perkins, noting that a fragment of the inscription read ONCO, restored this as *concordia* and was tempted to identify the temple with this deity.[378] This is an attractive hypothesis.

[370] Squarciapino 1974: 121. [371] Mundle 1957: 106; Squarciapino 1974: 121.
[372] Squarciapino 1974: 124. [373] Mundle 1957: 114.
[374] Bandinelli, Caffarelli et al. 1966: 93 (who suggest that it was dedicated by Caracalla to his father); Townsend 1938: 524; Ward-Perkins 1993: 31.
[375] Maderna 2005: 68. [376] Maderna 2005: 72. [377] Cordovana 2007: 368.
[378] Cordovana 2007: 375; Ward-Perkins 1948: 65; Ward-Perkins 1993: 31, 53.

In the Severan building programme, the emperor's divine ideology was incorporated into the sculptural decoration, but in the context of Lepcis Magna the deities also had a local importance. The gigantomachy scenes in particular have African relevance, since the myth was associated with conquest and civilisation of the area. Since this was a monument created at the instigation of the emperor, not the local populace, the interplay between the official and the local was complex: scenes of the gigantomachy were also present on official Severan coinage in AD 207, as discussed above. The porticoes of the Severan forum were decorated with Medusa heads, a subject that also appears on Severus' coinage with the legend PROVIDENTIA, on issues likely to have been struck in AD 207.[379] From these examples we might imagine that a dialogue of imagery ran between Rome and Lepcis in this period. The pilasters and sculpture from the basilica and the forum emphasised the emperor's divine support, and his connection to the city and its culture. It would have served as a statement of imperial power to the citizens of Lepcis, and perhaps the surrounding garrisons.

Ironically, the imperial favour bestowed upon Lepcis Magna through this impressive building programme probably had a detrimental effect on the city in the long term. The large amount of construction proved too much for the city's resources and actually sped its decline in the third century.[380] But the example of Lepcis Magna highlights the ways in which provincial cities adapted imperial ideology to promote status. Another excellent example of this is found in the city of Perinthus in Thrace.

Perinthus and the Hercules medallions

The city of Perinthus could also claim a close connection to Septimius Severus. In Severus' campaign against Niger, Perinthus served as Severus' headquarters, while his rival was based in nearby Byzantium. After Niger's defeat Byzantium was stripped of its privileges and handed over to Perinthus.[381] Perinthus was also given a neokorate (a temple of the emperor), the first city in Thrace to receive this honour.[382] Neokorates were a sign of imperial favour, and the number held by a city was frequently

[379] Cordovana 2007: 356; *RIC* IV.1 *Septimius Severus* 205A, 285–6. Though these are undated, a Medusa type struck for Caracalla was uncovered after the publication of the *RIC*, and this is dated to AD 207 (Cordovana 2007: 446–7).

[380] Barton 1977/8: 60; Ward-Perkins 1948: 60.

[381] Birley 1988: 108; Burrell 2004: 236.

[382] Burrell 2004: 236.

deployed in provincial contests of prestige. Perinthus' privileged position lasted for Severus' entire reign. When Geta was raised to the rank of Augustus in AD 209, the city's privileges were also increased, and Caracalla and his brother were included in the local imperial cult, perhaps resulting in a second neokorate for the city.[383] To mark the 'concord' between Caracalla and Geta, Perinthus was granted a festival called the *Philadelphia*, a title that evoked the idea of brotherly affection.[384] This was likely a Pythian festival, based on those celebrated in honour of Apollo at Delphi.[385]

Burrell argued that the extension of the neokorate to Severus' sons so soon after the initial grant showed Perinthus' close connection to the Severan dynasty.[386] Numismatic pieces released by the city in conjunction with the *Philadelphia* highlight this association. The imagery on these coins included the city goddess holding a temple in each hand, the emperor in a *quadriga*, and the neokorate temples, but the overwhelming majority of types portrayed the labours of Hercules.[387] It is clear then that the city's neokorate and the *Philadelphia* were closely connected to the visual language of the Severan dynasty. Perinthus' increased status was linked to Severus' civil war campaigns, which in turn were linked to the support of Hercules. The god was thus closely associated with Perinthus' neokorate, which was granted in recognition of the city's loyalty to Severus.

A significant quantity of Hercules' labours were represented on Perinthus' coinage: the Nemean lion, the hydra, the Cerynean hind, the Erymanthian boar, the Stymphalian birds, the Cretan bull, the horse of Diomedes, the cattle of Geryon, the apples of Hesperides, and the kidnapping of Cerberus.[388] This iconography continued after Severus' death, but not to the same extent. However, two Perinthian coin types struck under Caracalla's sole rule are of note: one showing the emperor as Hercules, and another showing Caracalla receiving apples from Hercules over a flaming altar.[389] The latter seems to be a variation of the traditional image of Jupiter handing the emperor a globe.

The continuing production of medallion-sized pieces showing the labours of Hercules under Caracalla, Elagabalus and Gordian III reflects the continuing claims of Perinthus to be the most eminent city in Thrace.

383 Burrell 2004: 237–9. 384 Burrell 2004: 239. 385 Burrell 2004: 238.

386 Burrell 2004: 239.

387 City Goddess: Varbanov 212–13. Emperor in *quadriga*: Varbanov 250, 252. Two temples: Varbanov 215. Other types included Poseidon (Varbanov 216) and Persephone (Varbanov 217).

388 Varbanov 200–17, 249–65, 327–34. 389 Varbanov 249 and 251.

After Geta's death, the *Philadelphia* disappeared, and the city's position as a pre-eminent metropolis was threatened. Elagabalus granted the city's rival Philippopolis a neokorate. The Perinthians responded by highlighting their role as temple wardens of not one, but two emperors.[390] In communicating this status, the city employed coin types that recalled those released under Severus: not only the temple types, but also scenes from the labours of Hercules.[391] The continuing need by Perinthus to stress its primacy in Thrace explains the continued Herculean imagery after Severus' death.

The arch of Severus in the Roman forum and the arch of the *argentarii*

Two structures in Rome also highlight differing responses to Severan ideology: the arch in the Roman forum, and the monument erected in the Forum Boarium by the *argentarii*. The arch of Septimius Severus in the Roman forum is well studied.[392] It was granted to Severus by the senate in AD 195 and was completed in AD 203.[393] The arch celebrated Severus' eastern victories and was closely connected with Severan propaganda from the beginning of the emperor's reign.

Voted by the senate, the arch in the forum contributed to the Severan ideological dialogue, and assisted in transforming the momentary military victory of Severus into an eternal ideology.[394] The arch would have formed a backdrop to the saecular games, along with other Severan constructions and restorations in the area.[395] Its decoration for the most part focused on Severus' military victories, but there may also have been a small place for the emperor's tutelary deities. On the north-west keystone of the arch there are the fragmentary remains of a nude, muscular figure (Figure 34). This figure has been convincingly identified as Hercules (there appears to be a lion-skin slung over the left arm, and the figure closely corresponds to other Severan representations of the deity).[396] The figure that originally adorned the south-west keystone does not survive, but Brilliant postulated that it might have been Liber Pater.[397] This is an attractive idea, but must ultimately remain a hypothesis in the absence of conclusive evidence. Hercules was traditionally associated with emperors and with military campaigns. The god's presence on the keystone fits in well with the rôle the god played

[390] Burrell 2004: 239–41. [391] Burrell 2004: 239–40. [392] Brilliant 1967.
[393] Brilliant 1967: 92. [394] Hölscher 2006: 27–48 for a discussion of this phenomenon.
[395] Gorrie 2002: 470. [396] Brilliant 1967: 123. [397] Brilliant 1967: 126.

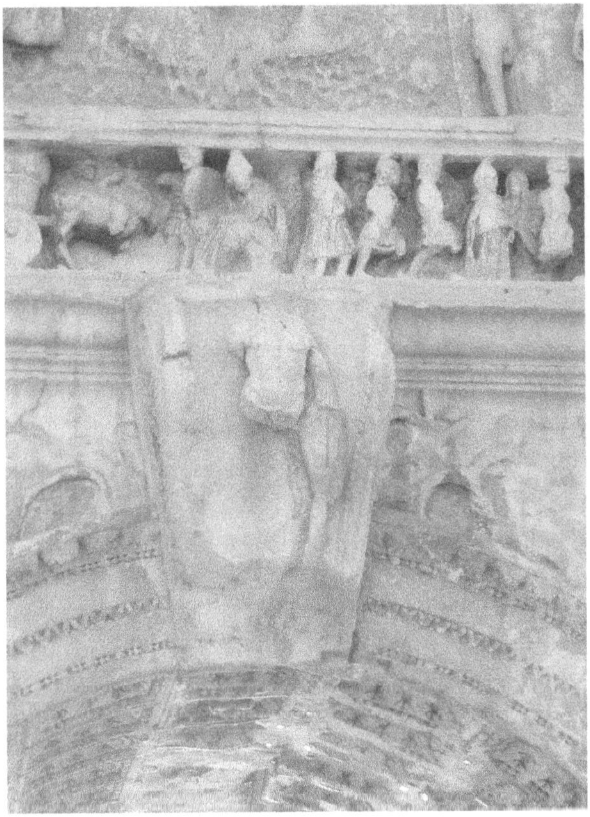

Figure 34: North-west keystone of the Arch of Severus in the Roman forum.

in Severus' rise to power. And yet, the image of Hercules constitutes only a small fraction of the overall design of the arch, which instead focuses on conquest and capture in the East. This matches Severus' numismatic image, which largely portrays him as a military victor.

The other surviving Severan 'arch' in Rome is that erected by the corporation of the *argentarii* and *negotiantes boarii* (the silversmiths, bankers, moneychangers and auctioneers in the Forum Boarium).[398] Commonly labelled an arch, it is more accurately a *portus* or entryway. What structure lay beyond the gate is the subject of debate, but given the lack of decoration on the north side, it may have formed the entryway into the *schola* or meeting-hall of the dedicants.[399] The gate was dedicated in AD 204.[400] The *portus* was probably erected in response to an imperial benefaction

[398] Daguet-Gagey 2005: 499–516; Haynes and Hirst 1939; Lusnia 1998: 167; Madaule 1924: 111–50.

[399] Haynes and Hirst 1939: 12–13. [400] Haynes and Hirst 1939: 8.

and now stands adjacent and partially built into the church of San Giorgio al Velabro.[401] The remaining outer relief on the west pier shows a Parthian captive between two soldiers; below this is a smaller fragmentary relief showing the driving of cattle, an activity traditionally associated with the Forum Boarium.[402] The outer relief on the south-west side of the west pier displays a badly worn togate figure, perhaps a patron of the guild.[403] These scenes are framed by pilasters carved with images of military standards and acanthus scroll-relief. The inner reliefs show the imperial family at sacrifice.[404] On the east pier Domna and Severus are shown with a third figure that has been erased. On the west pier Caracalla is portrayed alongside two erased figures. These spaces were likely once filled with the images of Geta, Plautilla and Plautianus. It is probable that Geta was portrayed alongside Domna and Severus, and Plautilla shown next to her husband Caracalla and her father Plautianus.[405]

Desnier observed that the decoration of the arch highlighted all the bases of Severan power: the army, the connection to the Antonines, and the focus on the regeneration of the imperial capital.[406] Framing the inscription on the entablature of the gate is the figure Hercules and a figure of the Genius of the Roman people, with *cornucopia*, mural crown and high-topped boots.[407] Hercules rests his right hand on a club that is on a rock, and a lion-skin hangs over his left arm (Figure 35). Though the *porta* was constructed by private initiative, its decoration was no doubt composed within the boundaries of the official ideology of the imperial family, particularly in view of its purpose and location.[408] The later alteration of the reliefs to reflect the *damnatio memoriae* of Plautianus, Plautilla and then of Geta highlights this: the arch was not intended to give offence to the imperial family. Mundle argued that the pairing of Hercules and the *Genius Populi Romani* reflected an acknowledgement that Hercules was simultaneously both the protective god of the emperor and of the Roman people.[409] The structure was also not far from the oldest cult statue of Hercules in Rome in the *Ara Maxima*, and the temple of Hercules Victor.[410]

The entire gate was designed to illustrate the relationship between the emperor and the *argentarii/negotiantes boarii*. In this way it functioned in a similar manner to the arch erected by the citizens of Lepcis. The monument

401 Haynes and Hirst 1939: 8–9 suggest that it may have been set up in gratitude for Severus' urban renewal of the area, or perhaps a legal concession.
402 Haynes and Hirst 1939: 27–9, 32. 403 Haynes and Hirst 1939: 27.
404 Elsner 2005: 83–98. 405 Elsner 2005: 94. 406 Desnier 1993: 593; Lusnia 1998: 174.
407 Elsner 2005: 94. 408 Mundle 1957: 176. 409 Mundle 1957: 181. 410 Mundle 1957: 182.

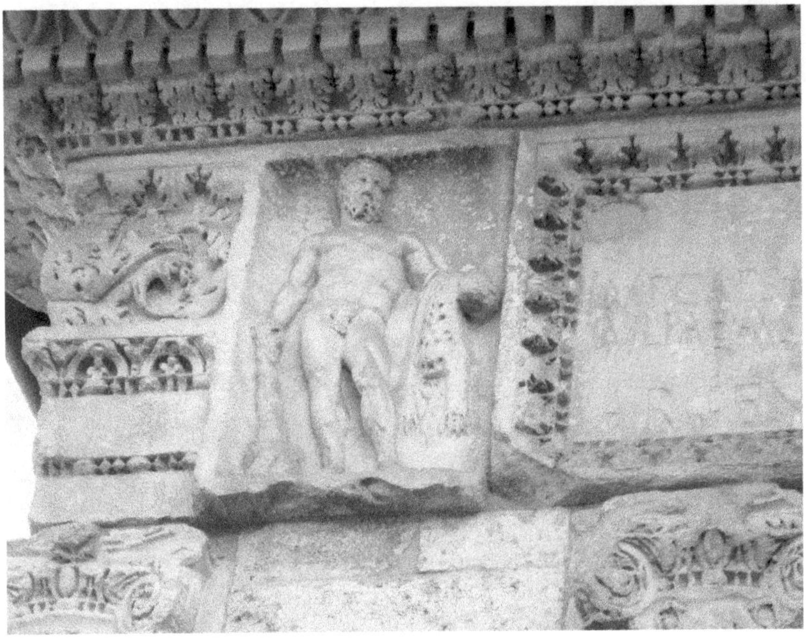

Figure 35: Representation of Hercules on the arch of the *argentarii.*

itself was a marker of the imperial favour enjoyed by the guild, and the decoration was designed to underline this connection with the emperor. Severus' achievements in Parthia were juxtaposed with the cattle traditionally associated with the Forum Boarium, and deities common and important to both (Hercules, and the Genius of the Roman People) were chosen to frame the dedicatory inscription. The *porta argentariorum*, intended both as a monument immortalising imperial benefaction and a visual link between the silversmiths and the imperial family, illustrates that the imperial emphasis on Hercules did not go unnoticed in the city of Rome. The design of the gate reflects the dissemination, reception and interpretation of Severus' claims to power.

Neptune and the British war

Along with gods traditionally associated with the person of the emperor (Minerva, Mars and Jupiter), Neptune has a significant presence on the coinage of Severus, constituting approximately 2 per cent of all his denarii (Figure 7). Neptune, as well as the representation of a Triton, appears on Severus' coinage from AD 209 to 211 and Mattingly rightly concluded that the types must refer to Severus' journey to Britain.[411] Dio records that the emperor decided to travel to Britain in spite of omens that foretold he would die there.[412] The omens proved correct, and Severus died in York in AD 211.

To land in Britain Severus had to cross the channel, and it was presumably this journey that formed the motivation for the introduction of Neptune into the imperial imagery. But Neptune remained on the emperor's coinage after Severus had arrived safely in Britain. It is clear then that the support of the god was considered important throughout the entire British campaign.

Both Dio and Herodian employ a mixture of fact and myth in their accounts of the wars and peoples in Britain.[413] Dio relates that as Severus advanced in his campaign he experienced difficulties, particularly due to the water in the area.[414] By contrast, the indigenous people of Britain are reported to be able to stay in swamps for days, with only their heads poking up above the water.[415] Herodian includes a similar tale, perhaps inspired by Dio's account, observing that barbarians in Britain either swim or run through the swamps.[416] He also records the efforts of the Roman soldiers to cross the waters by way of pontoons, and notes that the tides in Britain meant the area is continually a marshland.[417]

Neptune's prominence in the ideology of the British war was likely due to the fact that troops and supplies had constantly to be ferried across the English Channel.[418] The good graces of Neptune were paramount, and the mint introduced the type to the Severan repertoire either in acknowledgement of the emperor's divine support, or in an attempt to win over the support of the god.

The Neptune types were released in large numbers, forming one of the major reverse types of Severus' denarii in this period (Figure 36). A good proportion of these Neptune types were found in hoards from Britain.[419] This may reflect the channelling of financial resources to this area in support of the military campaign.[420]

The introduction of Neptune into the array of imperial divine support illustrates the flexibility of the emperor's image. Though Severus had closely connected his earlier campaigns with Hercules, Liber Pater and Jupiter, the circumstances of his last campaign needed a different source of support. The

[411] *RIC* IV.1 *Septimius Severus* 228–9, 234, 241, 244; Mattingly and Sydenham 1936: 70.
[412] Dio 77.11.1. [413] Birley 1988: 255–6. [414] Dio 77.13.1. [415] Dio 77.12.4, 77.13.2.
[416] Hdn. 3.14.6, 3.14.10. [417] Hdn. 3.14.5. [418] *RIB* 1143.
[419] If the Reka-Devnia hoard is excluded, then Britain has a greater number of Neptune types than any other geographical area.
[420] Dio (77.11.2) writes that Severus took an enormous amount of money with him.

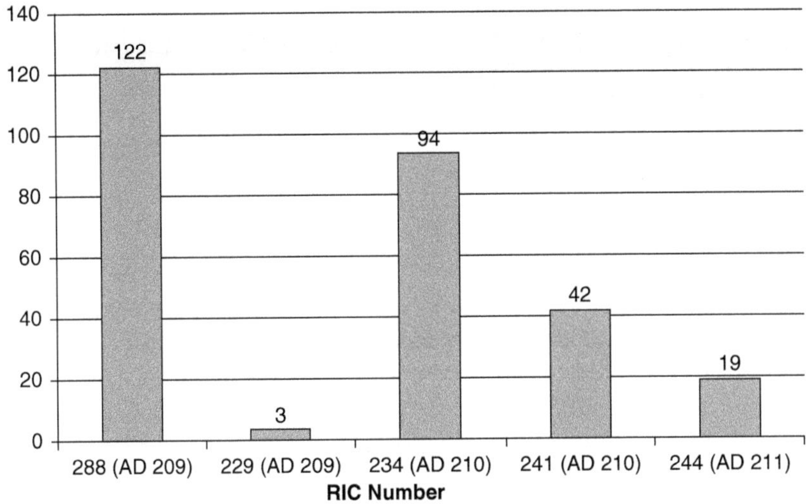

Figure 36: Silver Neptune types of Severus (AD 209–211) as represented in hoards.

official imperial image changed accordingly. In this respect, the image of the emperor in this period was a mixture of tradition and innovation, closely tied to contemporary circumstances. The changing nature of imperial divine ideology is highlighted again with the ascension of Caracalla to the throne.

4 Medical tourism and iconographic dialogues in the reign of Caracalla

> But to Antoninus no one even of the gods gave any response that conduced to healing either his body or his mind, although he paid homage to all the more prominent ones. This showed most clearly that they regarded, not his votive offerings or his sacrifices, but only his purposes and his deeds. He received no help from Apollo Grannus, nor yet from Aesculapius or Sarapis, in spite of his many supplications and his unwearying persistence. For even while abroad he sent to them prayers, sacrifices and votive offerings, and many couriers ran hither and thither every day carrying something of this kind; and he also went to them himself, hoping to prevail by appearing in person, and did all that devotees are wont to do; but he obtained nothing that contributed to his health.
>
> Dio 78.15.5–7

Severus died in York in February AD 211, and was succeeded by his two sons, Caracalla and Geta. The joint rule did not last long: Geta was murdered by his brother in December of the same year.[1] This act of fratricide seems to have influenced Caracalla's entire principate, or at least the construction of it in the ancient world. Dio, Herodian and the *Historia Augusta* all afford the fratricide a significant place in their accounts. Philostratus composed a letter to the emperor chastising him for the murder, saying that he had sacked his own house, though it is highly unlikely he sent such an explosive epistle.[2]

The change in emperor was accompanied by a new ideology that in turn was recorded and communicated by a change in numismatic imagery. Liber Pater and Hercules cease to have a close connection to the person of the emperor, a fact that further underlines their particular connection with Severus. Liber Pater disappears entirely from imperial coinage. Hercules remains a reverse type for only two years.[3] The god likely functioned as a

[1] Barnes 1968: 524.

[2] Philost. *Ep.* 72; Anderson 1986: 4–6, who suggests this is the same Philostratus that composed the *Lives of the Sophists* and *The Life of Apollonius of Tyana*.

[3] *RIC* IV.1 *Caracalla* 192, 206.

point of continuity from the reign of Severus, serving as a link to Caracalla's deified father. Hercules constitutes approximately 6 per cent of Caracalla's coinage in the hoard evidence (Figure 38).

By contrast, Sarapis appears on Caracalla's coinage from AD 212, as does a type of Salus.[4] Neither of these formed coin types of Severus before his death; their appearance signals a shift in the ideology of power. The change in the imperial image is also apparent when one compares the coin types of Caracalla struck during his rule with Severus, and the types struck for him during his sole rule (Figures 37–8). The hoard evidence suggests that while co-regent with his father, Caracalla's silver types had an emphasis on personifications and virtues (26%), Victory (10%) and Virtus (8%), and featured the deities Mars, Minerva and Sol. As sole ruler, Caracalla instead emphasised a variety of gods (Venus, Sol, Jupiter, Mars, Apollo, Aesculapius, Hercules and Sarapis).[5] A comparison of this assembly against

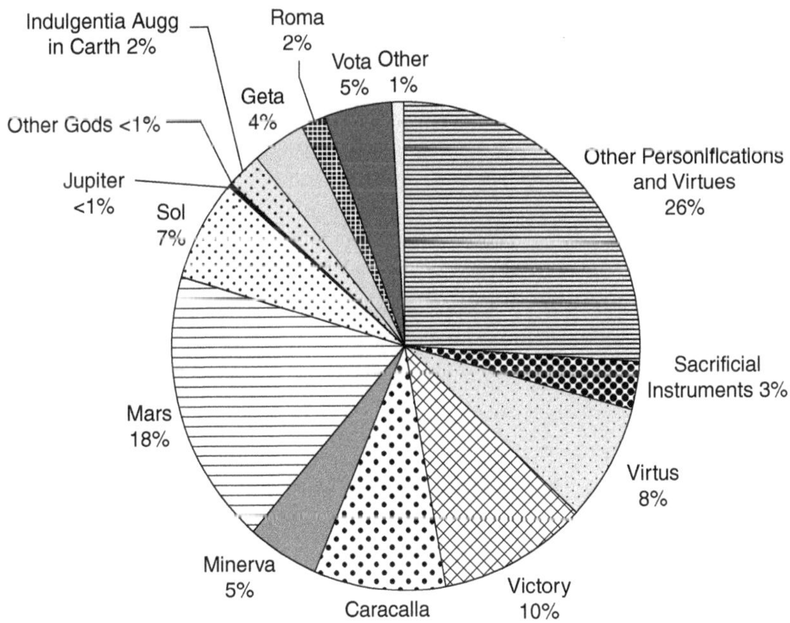

Figure 37: Reverse silver types of Caracalla (joint rule with Severus) as represented in hoards (n = 6,739).

4 *RIC* IV.1 *Caracalla* 193–4, 196.

5 The substantial amount of coinage showing Moneta (7%) prompted the decision to display the type separately from the Virtues/Personifications category. The frequency of this type might reflect the introduction of the *antoninianus* under Caracalla. Fides formed the next largest personification type (4%).

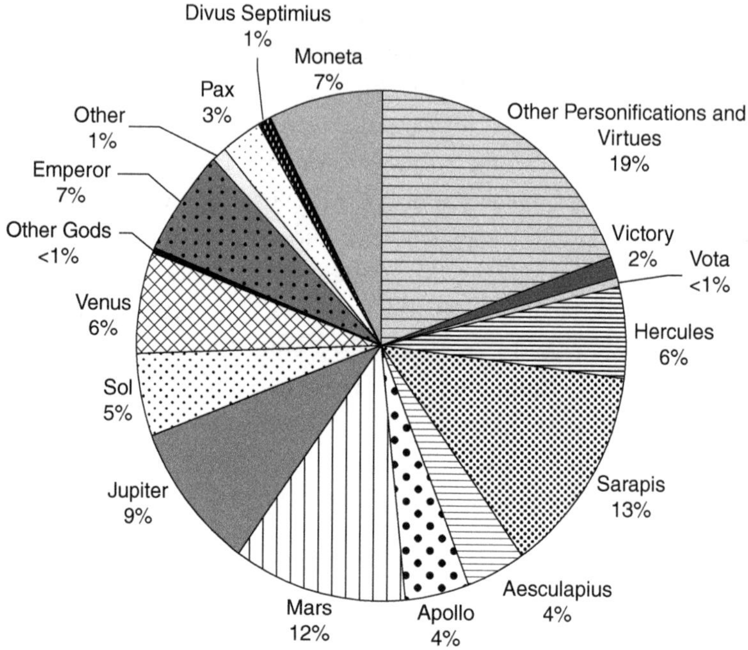

Figure 38: Reverse silver types of Caracalla (sole rule) as represented in hoards (n = 4,893).

Severus' reverse types (Figure 7) highlights the transformation of the imperial image. Both emperors have a similar proportion of coin types communicating personifications and virtues, but there is a significant shift in the quantity of reverse types showing deities. Gods grace approximately 21% of Severus' coinage, but for Caracalla they form 59%. Unlike the marked emphasis on victory seen under Severus (23%), Caracalla's victory types only constitute approximately 2% of his silver coinage. The focus is clearly on divine support instead of military prowess; the public image of the emperor and the justification of his power were reshaped.

An imperial illness? The representation of Caracalla in the ancient literary record

The quantitative analysis of Caracalla's coin types also reveals that a significant amount of coinage was struck showing Apollo, Aesculapius and Sarapis, the three deities mentioned by Cassius Dio in the quote provided at the beginning of the chapter. Dio presents Caracalla's affliction as the result of the murder of Geta; the emperor is haunted by the murder of his brother, and the enchantments of the Alamanni. This, however, would hardly have been the official stance of the imperial palace.[6] Dio describes Caracalla as being ill in both mind and body, with visible and secret ailments.[7] An illness may explain the connection of Caracalla to these three deities, all of whom were known for healing. A similar homage to Apollo, Sarapis and Aesculapius is known from Aelius Aristides, and is preserved in his *Sacred Tales*.

Dio's hostility towards Caracalla is obvious from the outset and we need to treat his report with caution.[8] Millar has established that Dio's account here combines annalistic and biographical techniques. Often disparate information is grouped together to illustrate the emperor's character, rather than for events to be narrated in strictly chronological order.[9] As a result, many of the events included by Dio are anecdotal, a fact only confounded by the nature of the transmission. The epitome of Xiphilinus is fragmentary in this section, and editors have relied on various *excerpta* to reconstruct the text. This naturally results in a somewhat anecdotal account. The *excerpta Vaticana*, one source used by modern editors of Dio, may in fact reflect an expansion of Dio's account rather than a strict epitome.[10] In addition to these difficulties, what we can reconstruct of Dio's history illustrates that his opinion of Caracalla was damning.

In one section Dio observes that Caracalla, descended from three different races, managed to combine all their faults: Gaulish fickleness, cowardice and recklessness, African cruelty and harshness, as well as the craftiness associated with Syrians.[11] Dio highlights these ingrained character flaws throughout his account. The κακία or wickedness of the emperor is introduced to the reader during the execution of Geta: Caracalla murders his brother in front of their mother, an act of unspeakable cruelty.[12] Though Dio's outline of events under Caracalla's reign is for the most part accurate, the motivations he attributes to the emperor are questionable. An example of this is the description of the *constitutio Antoniniana*, the edict granting Roman citizenship to most of the inhabitants of the empire. Caracalla was responsible for the edict, but Dio's sceptical statement that it was done to increase tax revenue is somewhat less believable, since many of the recipients of the decree would not have been overly wealthy.[13] The statement

[6] Dio 78.15.3. [7] Dio 78.15.3. [8] Millar 1964: 150–60. [9] Millar 1962: 124.

[10] Meckler 2005: 223.

[11] Dio 78.6.1a. Caracalla was born in Gaul, and it is evident from this statement that Dio believed ethnicity was affected just as much by a person's place of birth as the origin of their parents.

[12] Dio 78.2.1–6.

[13] Dio 78.9.6; Williams 1979: 73 (though see Millar 1962: 131 for an alternate view). Dio himself admits that 'nominally' Caracalla was honouring the citizens of the Empire (also see Garnsey 2004: 134).

about Caracalla's physical and mental disease occurs towards the end of a long, non-chronological section of Dio's history emphasising the inherent baseness of the emperor's character: his desire for money, his hatred of his dead brother and his murder of soldiers and senators. Caracalla did pay homage to Apollo, Aesculapius and Sarapis, but similarly to the description of the *constitutio Antoniniana*, the motivation Dio attributes to the princeps should be viewed with caution.[14]

Herodian also claimed the emperor was troubled by a guilty conscience.[15] For Herodian, Caracalla is the antithesis of an emperor who rules with *paideia* and *arete*, and instead leads the life of a soldier.[16] Geta, by contrast, is presented as a young emperor, but one safely surrounded by learned counsel.[17] Like other sections of his history, Herodian's account of the reign of Caracalla has sections influenced by Dio's work, but also has points of difference. Overall, though, the portrayal of Caracalla is negative, since the emperor does not conform to Herodian's vision of an ideal ruler. As Sidebottom illustrates, even actions of Caracalla that can be thought positive (for example, winning over the northern barbarians, 4.7.3), are negated by Herodian with an ironic or malicious comment (in this case, that the emperor wore a blonde wig).[18] Herodian states that Caracalla sought treatment in the temple of Aesculapius, and observes that the emperor visited Alexandria to worship the god Sarapis and to honour the memory of Alexander the Great.[19] Both motivations are fitting for a Roman emperor, and imperial illness does not dominate the account to the same extent as Dio's *History*. However, Herodian probably had Dio's account in mind when he composed the Alexandrian segment of his history.[20]

The *Historia Augusta* mentions an imperial illness in the context of a larger description of Caracalla's activities in Gaul: the emperor falls ill after behaving badly towards his subjects.[21] Similarly to Dio, the author here notes that the emperor's illness was a result of his crimes. The crime of fratricide dated back to the very foundations of Rome with the death of Remus at the hands of Romulus. Roman literature (particularly from the Augustan age) highlights an enduring belief that the consequence of Romulus' actions was a curse on his descendants, the Roman people,

[14] Millar 1962: 124; Sillar 2001: 407–23. [15] Hdn. 4.7.1. [16] Sidebottom 1998: 2809.
[17] Hdn 4.3.2–4; Zimmermann 1999b: 206. [18] Sidebottom 1998: 2809. [19] Hdn. 4.8.7.
[20] Kolb 1972: 97–8; Sidebottom 1998: 2782; Whittaker (LCL lxvii–lxviii).
[21] *SHA M. Ant.* 5.3. On the *Historia Augusta*'s life of Caracalla see Barnes 1968: 523. See also Kulikowski 2007: 244–5; Meckler 1994; Meckler 2005: 221–31; Penella 1980: 382–4; and Syme 1971: 118.

compelling them to continue to commit the offence.[22] That this idea was still present under the Severan dynasty is evident in Herodian. In his account of Caracalla's reign Herodian includes a speech discussing self-defence against plots, where he details various other instances of fratricide in the imperial period.[23] With typical Herodianic irony, Caracalla justifies himself by saying that even Marcus Aurelius (Herodian's ideal ruler), killed his brother-in-law.[24] The irony that Caracalla should claim Marcus Aurelius as his model, in a speech written for the emperor by Herodian, alerts us to the fact that the death of Geta formed an ideal topic for a literary trope or a rhetorical digression. Penella has already observed the 'Neronisation' of Caracalla that occurs in the *Historia Augusta*, and it may be that the connection between the two existed in the third century.[25] Given the associations of fratricide in the Roman world, the emperor's public patronage of healing cults may have been reshaped to illustrate the pathos of someone who had committed an unspeakable and yet ultimately historic crime, a literary allusion that tapped into Romans' conceptions surrounding the very beginnings of their city.

The following chapter examines in detail Caracalla's patronage of Apollo, Aesculapius and Sarapis. From a reassessment of the evidence, we are better placed to evaluate Dio's statement and to provide an assessment of Caracalla's religious activities. Dio's statement may be true: Caracalla, physically and mentally ill, may have sought healing from a variety of deities, and this circumstance defined his divine associations. Conversely, like other emperors before him, Caracalla may simply have honoured the local cults of the cities he visited. This was an established tradition that cemented the relationship between emperor and subject and was a ritual often performed as emperors made their way East.[26] Dio, or his contemporaries, may have used the prominent connection of Caracalla to Apollo, Aesculapius and Sarapis to construct an image of an emperor gone mad, an emperor for whom Dio had 'unabashed hatred'.[27]

Caracalla and Apollo

The campaigns in Germany and Apollo Grannus

The first deity mentioned by Dio is Apollo Grannus. There is good evidence that the emperor visited the temple of Apollo Grannus, whose cult centre was located in Faimingen, near Raetia in Germany. Early in Caracalla's sole

[22] Carrubba 1966: 29; Wagenvoort 1956: 169–83. [23] Hdn. 4.5.5–6. [24] Hdn. 4.5.6.
[25] Penella 1980: 382–4. [26] Harl 1987: 52. [27] Millar 1964: 150.

reign (*c.* AD 212–213), the emperor went on campaign against the 'Alamanni'.[28] It was while he was in Germany that Caracalla probably had contact with Apollo Grannus, a deity with strong Celtic roots.[29]

Archaeological excavations at Faimingen have uncovered a sanctuary to Apollo Grannus and Hygeia.[30] The latter's presence suggests the temple was associated with healing. The proximity of Faimingen to the area of Caracalla's Germanic campaigns, in addition to the extraordinary building initiative seen in the sanctuary around this period, make it probable that the emperor visited the sanctuary in *c.* AD 212/13.[31] Milestones dating to AD 212 detail the construction of roads and bridges in the area.[32] These need not have been built while the emperor was present, but Dio mentions that Caracalla undertook a building programme while campaigning against the 'Alamanni', so the emperor may have been in the area when the work took place.[33] The milestones state the distance to *Phoebiana*, a place name with such striking resemblance to the epithet *Phoebus* that Dietz believed it referred to the distance to the sanctuary of Apollo itself.[34] In the absence of any known place in the region called *Phoebiana*, this theory has much to recommend it.

More conclusive evidence for the emperor's presence at the sanctuary of Apollo Grannus in AD 212/13 can be found in an inscription from Ephesus. The text of the inscription details the activities of an ambassador, who represented the city's interests before the emperor on several occasions, journeying to Rome, Britain and upper Germany, to (the sanctuary of) Apollo Grannus and to Sirmium, Nicomedia and Antioch.[35] This seems conclusive evidence of Caracalla's presence at the sanctuary.

The exact motive behind the Caracalla's visit remains ambiguous. Dio emphasises the mental and physical illness of the emperor, interpreting the

[28] Dio 78.13.4; Hdn. 4.7.2; Aur. Vict. *Caes* 21; *RIC* IV.1 *Caracalla* 273; Drinkwater 2007: 43–4. Drinkwater notes the problems associated with the term 'Alamanni' in this period; the name may be a later gloss or interpolation. It is used here for convenience. A temple to the Germanic victory of Caracalla was erected in Dougga, Africa (Brouquier-Reddé 2003: 457–89; Golvin, Khanoussi et al. 2005; Khanoussi 2003: 447–56).

[29] A good discussion of the provincial aspects of the god and its imperial contexts can be found in Woolf 2003: 139–52.

[30] Eingartner, Eschbaumer et al. 1993: 122–36; Weber 1978: 511–21. *SHA M. Ant.* 5.4 mentions the emperor's presence in Raetia.

[31] Weber 1978: 519–20. [32] Dietz 1985: 75–86. [33] Dio 78.13.4.

[34] Dietz 1985: 77, 81; Eingartner, Eschbaumer et al. 1993: 131. For Phoebus as an epithet of Apollo Grannus see *CIL* 13.3635.

[35] *AE* 1971, 455 = *IvE* 3.802. For other possible (fragmentary) evidence of Caracalla at the sanctuary of Apollo Grannus see *CIL* 3.5874; *AE* 1983, 714; *AE* 1983, 716; Eingartner, Eschbaumer et al. 1993: 121–36.

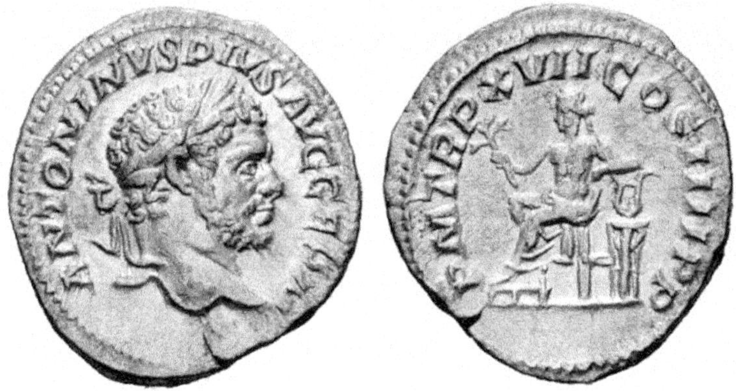

Figure 39: Denarius of Caracalla with Apollo holding a branch and resting his left arm on a lyre, which is on a tripod. The reverse legend reads PMTR P XVII COS IIII P P.

religiosity of the princeps in a sceptical and malicious manner.[36] Alternatively, Caracalla may have visited the temple to garner support amongst the local population, his visit acting as a display of piety and divine sanction. Herodian's account certainly suggests that the emperor set out to make himself agreeable.[37]

Apollo appears on the emperor's coinage in the period AD 214–215. Three different types of iconography were employed: Apollo seated, holding a branch and lyre (Figure 39), Apollo standing with a branch and lyre, and Apollo in a long dress, holding a branch and spear.[38] The second type reappears on imperial coinage again under Trebonianus Gallus with the legend *Apollo Salutari*, highlighting the god's associations with health and healing.[39] The Apollo types make up a significant amount of the silver coinage of AD 214 found in the hoard analysis, equating to about 29 per cent of the types struck that year (Figure 40). The other major types of this year were Jupiter and Caracalla himself.[40]

Apollo types continued to be struck in significant quantities in AD 215, constituting approximately 22 per cent of the silver coinage struck that year in the hoards (Figure 41). The large amount of attention given to divine types in AD 215 (coins were also struck with images of Aesculapius, Diana, Isis, Jupiter, Sarapis and Sol) again stands in contrast to the numismatic iconography of Septimius Severus and highlights the reshaping of the imperial image.

[36] Letta 1989: 279–80. [37] Hdn. 4.7.3–8. [38] *RIC* IV.1 *Caracalla* 238A, 254–5.

[39] *RIC* IV.3 *Trebonianus Gallus* 5, 32, 188. Mattingly connected the type to the plague of AD 251 (Mattingly, Sydenham et al. 1949: 154).

[40] Only types that can be concretely attributed to AD 214–215 were considered in the analysis; other, undated, coins may also have been released in this period. Nonetheless, the Apollo types have a significant presence.

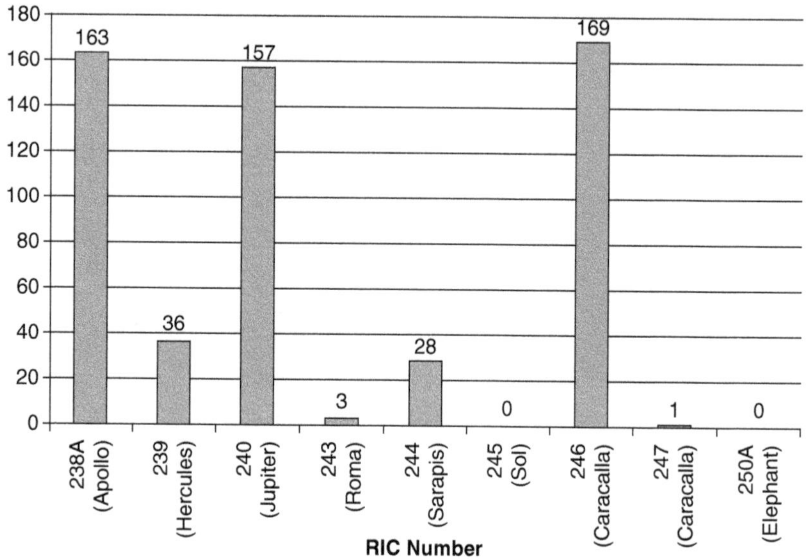

Figure 40: Caracalla's reverse types from AD 214, as represented in hoards.

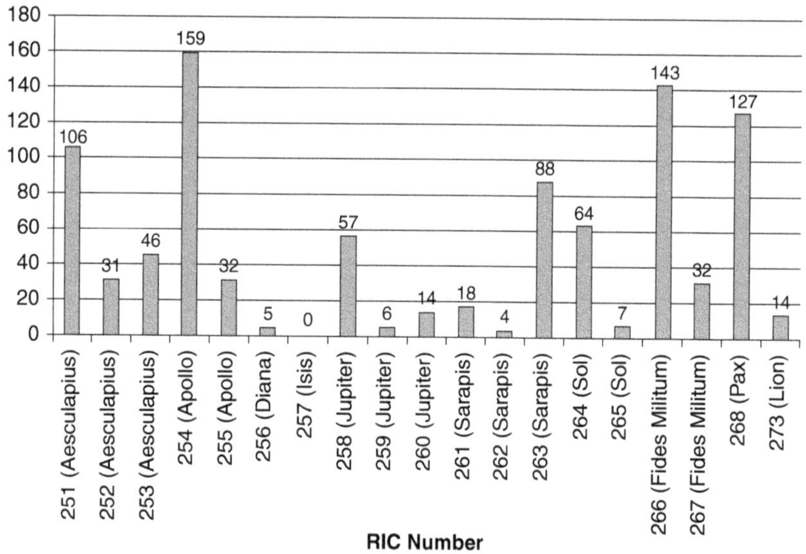

Figure 41: Caracalla's reverse types from AD 215, as represented in hoards.

Can we connect these Apollo types to Caracalla's patronage of Apollo in Germany?[41] Caracalla's victory over the German tribes is communicated on coins as early as AD 213, with the addition of the title *Germanicus* to the

[41] Eingartner, Eschbaumer et al. 1993: 134: 'Ob der neue Reverstyp des Apollo mit Leier auf einer Münzprägung des Caracallas den Apollo Grannus verkörpert, kann nur vermutet werden.'

emperor's titulature.[42] If Caracalla's visit to Apollo Grannus occurred at roughly the same time, one would expect any coins commemorating the event also to be released in this year. Apollo Grannus was most commonly shown standing nude with a *cithara* in one hand and a cloak over one shoulder.[43] This is not the image displayed on the emperor's coins, though this need not mean that we should automatically dismiss Caracalla's visit to Faimingen as the occasion for striking the types. But there may be another explanation for the images, one that is better suited to the chronology of these coins and their iconography.

Dedications 'to the gods and goddesses' and the oracle of Apollo at Claros

An event that better suits the timeframe and iconography of the Apollo types is a possible consultation of the oracle of Apollo at Claros, which was located near the city of Colophon in Ionia. Birley was the first to suggest that Caracalla consulted the deity, connecting the event to a series of identical inscriptions.[44] Though found in different parts of the empire, these dedications all possess the same phrase: *dis deabusque secundum interpretationem oraculi Clari Apollinis* ('To the gods and goddesses, in accordance with the interpretation of the oracle of Apollo at Claros'). Birley argued that only an emperor would have had the power to order the same phrase be inscribed and erected over such a significant geographical area, and by a military cohort, and suggested that the most likely candidate was Caracalla. He believed that along with Apollo Grannus, Caracalla consulted Apollo of Claros in AD 213, since the two were 'manifestly linked by *interpretatio Romana*'.[45] In 1974 Birley knew of only four examples, but more have since come to light. Inscriptions have been found in Gabii, Marruvium and Cosa in Italy, Corinium in Dalmatia, Aïn Riahi (near Cuicul) in Numidia, at Housesteads in Britain, Sarrok (near Nora) in Sardinia, in Volubilis and Banasa in Mauretania, at Puentes de García Rodríguez in Hispania Citerior, and a Greek version of the inscription has been uncovered in the town of Melli in Pisidia.[46] Further examples will no doubt be found.

[42] *RIC* IV.1 *Caracalla* 206–8, 211. An undated coin, but also probably from AD 213 proclaims VICTORIA GERMANICA (*RIC* IV.1 *Caracalla* 237).

[43] Woolf 2003: 146. [44] Birley 1974: 511–13. [45] Birley 1974: 513.

[46] Gabii: *AE* 1986, 119; Cosa: *AE* 2000, 564; Corinium: *CIL* 3.2880; Aïn Riahi: *CIL* 8.8351; Housesteads: *RIB* 1579; Sarrok: *AE* 1929, 156; Volubilis: Euzennat 1976: 63; Banasa: *BCTH* 1946–9: 437 no. 1; Puentes de García Rodríguez: *AE* 1990, 545; Melli: Mitchell 2003: 151. The Greek inscription from Melli reads [θ]εοῖς καὶ θεαῖς ἀπὸ ἐξηγήσεως χρήσμου Ἀπόλλωνος Κλαρίου. See also Oesterheld 2008: 574 no. 24.

Several similarities are apparent beyond the identical formula. No author or agent is mentioned, except for the Housesteads example, which was erected by the *Cohors I Tungrorum*. Almost all the texts are on plaques or blocks intended for public display.[47] The majority of the inscriptions are in Latin; only one Greek example is known to date. There are small differences between the spacing, spelling and wording of each inscription. The example from Spain has a slightly different formula (it uses *ex* instead of *secundum*) and has an addition to the ending (CAD SACE[---]), the significance of which is not clear. The formula *ex interpretatione* is an unusual one for oracular inscriptions, which more regularly read *ex responso oraculi* or *ex oraculo*.[48] The use of the more atypical *ex interpretatione* or *secundum interpretationem* makes the similarities between the inscriptions all the more conspicuous.

The British inscription erected by the *Cohors I Tungrorum* formed the basis of Birley's study. It is the only inscription to possess a possible dating reference outside palaeography (which provides dates ranging from the mid-first century to the mid-third century AD).[49] The *Cohors I Tungrorum* was stationed in Britain from *c.* AD 103; there is evidence for the unit at Vindolanda under the Flavians.[50] They moved to Housesteads (where the inscription was found) under Hadrian, but also served on the Antonine wall.[51] Under Antoninus Pius the unit was at Castlecary, then may have been located at Cramond or Birdoswald.[52] After returning to Housesteads in the early third century, the cohort remained there for a considerable period; the *Notitia Dignitatum* records their presence in the area.[53] The majority of the epigraphic evidence connected to the cohort at Housesteads is likely third century in date,[54] and it is in this period that we should then seek a context for the *dis deabusque* dedication. Worship at the oracle at Claros seems to have declined after the first half of the third century.[55] It is probable then that the inscription was erected prior to AD 250.

The similarities between the inscriptions have led to the suggestion that they all ultimately derive from a written corpus circulating under the name of Apollo at Claros.[56] Nock and Picard had a slightly different proposal: that the verse was part of a 'stock' response given to numerous individuals inquiring at the oracle.[57] The Cynic philosopher Oenomaus wrote of his disgust with the oracle when it provided him with a response that had been given

[47] Jones 2005: 294. [48] Letta 1989: 265. [49] Nock 1929: 126. [50] Birley 1998: 301.
[51] Mann 2002: 188. [52] Birley 1932: 57–8. [53] Jarrett 1994: 48–9. [54] Jarrett 1994: 49.
[55] Parke 1985: 169. [56] Parke 1985: 161. [57] Parke 1985: 161; Picard 1922: 124–5.

to several others.[58] This suggests the practice existed, though it is difficult to know how much faith to put in the writings of a Cynic philosopher who was trying to illustrate the folly of all oracles. The hypothesis of a 'stock' response would be more credible if other similar or identical inscriptions survived.

There are also problems with the idea of a circulating corpus. The geographical expanse of these inscriptions would mean that any hypothetical corpus must have had a wide circulation, encompassing even minor cities. That eleven distinct parties (including a military cohort) would consult it, and then select *only* this response seems unlikely. There is no other epigraphic evidence of identical responses from Apollo at Claros; hence the whole idea of a corpus is dubious. Herrero and Letta have thus returned to Birley's suggestion that a single consultation of the oracle lay behind the inscriptions.[59] Only an emperor is likely to have had the oracle's instructions recorded in so many different quarters, and by a unit of the Roman army.[60]

The Greek example at Melli was found at the top of a rubble-filled cistern in the courtyard of a large house towards the south end of the site (it is not known what the town was called in antiquity).[61] The excavators believed that this was close to its original setting, and the inscription was probably mounted into a wall below a niche that contained a statue of Apollo of Claros.[62] Mitchell thought it unlikely that Caracalla was behind these inscriptions, since none name the emperor. He also noted the unusual wording of the inscriptions, that they were erected according to an *interpretation* of an oracle. Consequently, Mitchell connected the inscriptions to another oracle of Apollo of Claros, preserved within the city walls at Oenoanda. The text contains thoughts about the nature of god, with decidedly henotheistic overtones.[63]

> Born of itself, untaught, without a mother, unshakeable, not contained in a name, known by many names, dwelling in fire, this is god. We, his angels, are a small part of god. To you who ask this question about god, what his essential nature is, he has pronounced that Aether is god, who sees all, on whom you should gaze and pray at dawn, looking towards the sunrise.[64]

Mitchell suggested that this oracle would have provoked consternation, and that worshippers would have sought clarification through an interpretation, provided by the oracle at Claros. He suggested that it is this clarification that

[58] The text is preserved in Eusebius *Praep. Ev.* 5.22.214A. For a discussion see Parke 1985: 143.

[59] Herrero 1989: 357–64; Letta 1989: 265–80; Merkelbach and Stauber 1996: 40.

[60] Birley 1974: 512. [61] Mitchell 2003: 151. [62] Mitchell 2003: 151.

[63] Hall 1978: 263–8; Merkelbach and Stauber 1996: 41–2. [64] Translation from Mitchell 2002: 86.

is preserved in the *dis deabusque* inscriptions, an interpretation 'designed to reconcile increasingly popular monotheism with the concerns of traditional religion'.[65] That none of the inscriptions name an emperor is unusual if they were erected by imperial order, but it is also unlikely that an oracle given to a citizen of Oenoanda would have prompted cities throughout the empire to erect a clarification.

More recently, Jones argued that these inscriptions were connected with the Antonine plague.[66] Here he reiterates the earlier view of Parke, who noticed in his study of the oracle that many eastern cities consulted Apollo of Claros in response to the disease. Parke suggested that a context for the *dis deabusque* dedications might be found in the epidemic brought back by the soldiers of Marcus Aurelius.[67] Jones believed that this was the reason the dedications were incorporated into walls: they possessed a protective force.[68] He observed that six other oracles of Apollo of Claros could be connected with the Antonine plague.[69] Aurelius himself may have been the consultant, or the oracle may have issued an instruction on its own initiative.[70]

The oracle at Claros was certainly associated with healing, but this too could make it a candidate for a consultation by Caracalla. While other Clarian oracular responses to the Antonine plague have similarities, they are by no means identical in the way the *dis deabusque* inscriptions are.[71] Furthermore, the existence of the inscription at Cosa suggests a third century date for the series, well after the Antonine period. The city of Cosa was practically abandoned in the first century AD, and only had a low level of occupation in the second.[72] It then underwent a revival in the early third century, beginning under Caracalla.[73] The forum was restored, Caracalla appointed a senatorial *curator* in the city, and a Mithraeum was constructed, as was a shrine to Liber Pater.[74] A marble head of Hercules was found within this shrine; hence it may have been dedicated to both Liber Pater and Hercules, Severus' patron deities.[75] Dedications by the *res publica Cosanorum* to the emperor begin under Caracalla.[76] The expense and act of erecting the *dis deabusque* inscription would be better situated in the period of the city's revival: the third century, not the second.

[65] Mitchell 2003: 154–5. [66] Jones 2005: 293–301; Jones 2006: 368–9. [67] Parke 1985: 150.
[68] Jones 2005: 299. [69] Jones 2005: 298. [70] Jones 2005: 301. [71] Várhelyi 2001: 16.
[72] Brown 1951: 20; Fentress, Bodel et al. 2003: 63.
[73] Fentress, Bodel et al. 2003: 63–6; Jones 2006: 369. [74] Fentress, Bodel et al. 2003: 63.
[75] Fentress, Bodel et al. 2003: 66.
[76] Fentress, Bodel et al. 2003: 63. There was an extraordinarily small amount of pottery from the second century AD found in the excavations.

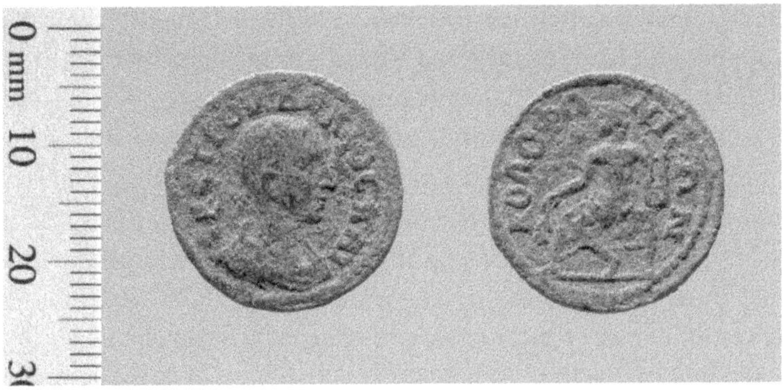

Figure 42: Bronze of Herennius Etruscus from Colophon displaying Apollo seated with branch and lyre.

The oracle of Apollo at Claros and the coinage of Colophon

We thus return to Birley's hypothesis. Birley argued that Caracalla sent an embassy to Clarian Apollo in AD 213 while he was at the sanctuary of Apollo Grannus, since the two gods were linked through *interpretatio Romana*. Further evidence to support the idea that Caracalla consulted Apollo at Claros can be found on the emperor's coinage.

The three types of Apollo minted on imperial coinage under Caracalla have already been outlined. Of these, *RIC* 238A (Figure 39), showing a seated Apollo with branch and lyre, is a type never before seen on imperial coinage.[77] As noted in the previous chapter, the introduction of new iconography at the Roman mint has significance. The iconography of Apollo here bears a striking resemblance to the Apollo depicted on the provincial coins of Colophon. Colophon was the city closest to the oracle at Claros and was responsible for its administration.[78] During the imperial period Colophon minted coins displaying Apollo in a fairly standardised manner: seated, holding a laurel branch and resting his elbow upon a lyre (Figure 42).

In his analysis of the coinage of Colophon, Milne concluded that this Apollo type must have been associated with the oracle at Claros.[79] This is

[77] Hill 1962: 137.

[78] Colophon was 12km from the oracle. For the connection between the city and the oracle see Genière 1992: 204 and Parke 1985: 112.

[79] Milne 1941: 15; Várhelyi 2001: 23. The connection of Colophon to Claros is also evident on a coin of Colophon minted under Trajan, displaying the reverse legend *Artemis Klaria* (Milne 184A–86C) and another struck under Trebonius Gallus (*SNG von Aulock* 2024) showing the seated Apollo in a temple in front of which are thirteen state gods. Von Aulock was convinced the statue was that of the Apollo of Claros.

confirmed by a coin type struck in Colophon for Domitian, displaying the seated Apollo with laurel branch and tripod, accompanied by the legend ΚΟΛΟΦ[ΩΝΙΩΝ] ΚΛΑΡΙC.[80] On this particular example Apollo holds the laurel branch over the tripod, while on Caracalla's imperial coinage the tripod is at the side of the deity. This is a minor difference; an examination of the coinage of Colophon illustrates that the tripod moves even on coins of the city.[81] The tripod was associated with prophecy and reinforces the idea that what is represented here is the Clarian Apollo.[82] The question is whether the Roman mint is consciously alluding to this cult statue.

The analysis of the numismatic representation of Liber Pater and Hercules under Severus has illustrated that the Roman mint was capable of modifying imagery to allude to a particular provincial cult. The iconographic dialogue travelled in both directions. Under Caracalla, 'provincial' iconography was appropriated by the Roman mint in order to allude to the imperial patronage of different cults. Kampmann has shown that the imperial coins of Caracalla depicting Aesculapius were struck with an iconography that recalled the imagery of Aesculapius at Pergamum, and may even have derived directly from the city.[83] A fuller discussion of this is provided below. A similar phenomenon may be occurring here. The cult statue of Apollo from Claros may have been introduced into the iconographic repertoire of the Roman mint to represent the emperor's consultation of the oracle.

The hoard analysis reveals that the Apollo types were prominent on silver coinage in both AD 214 and AD 215 (Figures 40–1). All three of these issues are given the label 'scarce' in the *Roman Imperial Coinage* catalogue. Hoard evidence suggests, however, that *RIC* 238A (seated Apollo holding laurel branch) and *RIC* 254 (standing Apollo with branch and lyre) were struck in substantial numbers and in greater quantities than *RIC* 255 (Apollo with branch and spear). Here we can see the value of hoard analysis: it furnishes a more accurate idea of frequency than the system employed by standard catalogues. Although Apollo was present on Caracalla's coinage for only two years the presence was a significant one; those in receipt of newly struck coins would have been informed of the emperor's association with the deity, a fact perhaps already communicated through other media. The connection would also have been maintained throughout the rest of the emperor's reign and afterwards: Apollo constitutes 4 per cent of all Caracalla's silver issues that survive in hoards (Figure 38).

80 *RPC* II 1052. 81 See Milne 1941: 107 for a listing. 82 Parke 1985: 123.
83 Kampmann 1992/3: 39–48.

Colophon minted very few coins during the imperial period, but had a substantial period of activity under Caracalla. This sudden change in practice might have been a result of the increasing commercial importance of the city, or the declining metal standards of the period.[84] The city might also have been reacting to imperial patronage.[85] After Caracalla, Colophon mints regularly until the cessation of provincial coinage in Ionia under Gallienus.[86] But after Caracalla's reign, the number of coin types being released subsided. For example, Milne's catalogue suggests that only three coin types were released under Severus Alexander.

Milne observed that under Caracalla, Aesculapius occurs on the coins of Colophon for the first and only time, associated with Hygeia and perhaps Telesphoros.[87] The magistrate responsible for this issue, Tiberius Claudius Myron, may also have introduced Sarapis as a reverse type.[88] The choice of deities and their introduction to the repertoire of Colophonic coinage may be coincidental: Sarapis reappears on the coins of Julia Maesa, Maximinus, Gordian III and throughout the rest of the third century. These representations may reflect the cult of the deity in the city, or the popularity of the cult in this period.[89] Alternatively, the appearance of these gods on Colophonic coinage may have been inspired by the association of Apollo, Aesculapius and Sarapis with the princeps.

Dating Caracalla's consultation of the Clarian Apollo

The contexts of the *dis deabusque* inscriptions, the coinage of Caracalla (and perhaps also of Colophon), in addition to Caracalla's known patronage of Apollo as a deity all suggest that Caracalla consulted the oracle of Apollo at Claros. But when would such a consultation have taken place? Birley suggested Caracalla sent an embassy to the oracle in AD 213.[90] Parke proposed that Caracalla might have consulted the oracle while in

[84] Milne 1941: 14 suggested that it indicated a renewal in the commercial importance of the city, reflecting the northward shift of trade routes as the harbour at Ephesus silted up.

[85] Harl 1987: 19 lists the various reasons that might induce a city to begin striking coinage, or to increase coinage output. The presence of soldiers or an imperial retinue in the area is one explanation: the increase in commerce would result in an increased need for small change.

[86] Milne 1941: 106. [87] Milne 1941: no. 202 and p. 17.

[88] Milne 1941: no. 203. Myron also struck a coin in the name of Domna showing Athena Polias on the reverse (Milne 1941: no. 196). Domna was connected to Athena Polias at Athens (Levick 2007: 130; Oliver 1940: 521–30), and this may have inspired the type. Athena Polias was named as an ancestral deity of the city in 307/6 BC, but this is her first appearance on Colophon's civic coinage.

[89] See Milne 1941: nos. 211, 215A–B, 223, 229, 242A, 257, 270, 276.

[90] Birley 1974: 513; Euzennat 1976: 65; Letta 1989.

Pergamum.[91] This is a likely suggestion considering the proximity and connection between these two cult centres, attested by the experience of Aelius Aristides.[92] Aristides was a sophist of the second century who resided in the sanctuary of Aesculapius at Pergamum for a considerable period of time. His experiences are described in *The Sacred Tales*, and include a decision to consult the 'god at Colophon' while he was ill. He sent someone on his behalf and was informed to seek assistance at the Pergamene Aesculapium.[93]

If Claros referred people to the sanctuary of Aesculapius at Pergamum, presumably patrons of the sanctuary at Pergamum could be referred to Claros.[94] Dio and Herodian report that Caracalla sent embassies to various deities and oracles.[95] Imperial coins showing the figure of the Clarian Apollo were released in AD 214, the same year that the emperor released imperial coinage displaying the Pergamene Aesculapius. The combination of this evidence allows for the possibility that while in Pergamum (or in Asia) in late AD 213, Caracalla sent an embassy to the oracle of Apollo at Claros. This consultation may have led in turn to the *dis deabusque* dedications.[96]

The oracle of Apollo at Claros and the *constitutio Antoniniana*

Euzennat and Letta have connected the *dis deabusque* inscriptions not only to Caracalla, but also to the declaration of the *constitutio Antoniniana*.[97] Preserved on a papyrus, and mentioned by Dio and Ulpian, this decree gave citizenship to all free inhabitants of the empire, with the exception of the *dediticii*.[98] Euzennat dated the consultation of the Clarian oracle to the second half of AD 213, and observed that the general *supplicatio* mentioned in the *constitutio Antoniniana* corresponds to the formula preserved in the *dis deabusque* inscriptions.[99] The stated purpose of the Antonine edict was

91 Herrero 1989: 357–64; Parke 1985: 161.
92 For the city of Pergamum consulting the oracle see Graf 2009: 73.
93 Aristid. *Sacred Tales* 3.12; Behr 1968: 243; Parke 1985: 147. 94 Herrero 1989: 361.
95 Dio 78.15.6; Hdn. 4.12.3.
96 Parke has suggested that, instead of ill health, the inquiry might have concerned the Parthian War, or even the prosperity of the empire as a whole (Parke 1985: 161).
97 Euzennat 1976: 63–8; Herrero 1989: 363; Letta 1989: 265–80. On the *constitutio Antoniniana* see Baharal 1994: 531; Benario 1954: 188–96; Bickerman 1926; Buraselis 1989; Garnsey 2004: 133–55; Gilliam 1965: 74–92; Goodfellow 1935; Heichelheim 1940: 10–22; Herrmann 1972: 519–30; Jones 1936: 223–35; Keresztes 1970: 446–59; Millar 1962: 124–31; Oliver 1989: 500; Potter 2004: 139–45; Rubin 1975b: 430–6; Sherman 1928: 33–47; Sherwin-White 1973: 86–98; Visscher 1961: 229–42; Weissert 1963: 239–50; Williams 1979: 67–89; and Wolff 1976, amongst others.
98 Dio 78.9.5–7; Ulpian *Dig.* 1.5.17. 99 Euzennat 1976: 66–7.

to widen the range of people who could pay proper worship to the gods, as a thanksgiving for Caracalla's escape from danger.[100] Euzennat went on to note that if his theory were correct, the surprising silence in contemporary documents surrounding the grant of universal citizenship might be explained: its direct result was the supplication to the gods by all the citizens of the empire, and the erection of the *dis deabusque* inscriptions.[101]

Letta noted the common syncretistic nature of the divinities addressed in both texts. In the *constitutio Antoniniana* the gods are described as 'the immortal gods' (τοῖς θεοῖς τοῖς ἀθανάτοις) while in the inscriptions they are 'the gods and goddesses' (*dis deabusque*).[102] Also common to both texts is the desire of the emperor to involve all the citizens of the empire in a religious action. Letta observed that many of the *dis deabusque* inscriptions were located in communities that were composed of *peregrini* until the grant of universal citizenship.[103] Thus, according to Letta, it was reasonable to suppose that the *supplicatio* announced in the preamble of the *constitutio Antoniniana* formed the basis for the supplications *dis deabusque*.[104] While Euzennat tentatively linked the consultation of the oracle and the promulgation of the edict with Caracalla's German campaigns in AD 213, Letta argued that the consultation of Apollo of Claros and the Antonine constitution rose directly out of Caracalla's need for support after the murder of Geta.[105] The theories of both Euzennat and Letta are thought-provoking, though there is no direct evidence to support their claims. One would imagine that if the *constitutio Antoniniana* were linked to the oracle of Apollo at Claros, the god would be mentioned in the text of the decree. At this point it would be beneficial to re-examine the possible contexts behind the declaration of the *constitutio Antoniniana*.

Despite Dio's claim to the contrary, the official purpose of the *constitutio Antoniniana* was a thanksgiving to the gods in return for the emperor's escape from a particular danger.[106] The danger is not specified. It was an extraordinary decree. Though it might be viewed as a natural conclusion to the increasing number of citizenship grants under the empire, citizenship in this period remained a privilege conferred by the emperor. A mass bestowal was revolutionary.[107]

[100] *P.Giss* 40.3. See Heichelheim 1940: 12. Williams 1979: 67–89 argues that the edict's elaborate and personal style reflects Caracalla's other known decrees.

[101] Euzennat 1976: 68. [102] Letta 1989: 270. [103] Letta 1989: 269. [104] Letta 1989: 272.

[105] Letta 1989: 276.

[106] Dio 78.9.6. The ability of people who were not enfranchised by this time to have a large financial impact on the imperial revenue is questionable.

[107] Garnsey 2004: 135.

In earlier scholarship, the *constitutio* was considered to be so contrary to the character of Caracalla that historians attributed its genesis to Severus, in the belief that it was a natural continuation of the 'provincial' emperor's policies.[108] It is now firmly attributed to Caracalla. Millar suggested a date of AD 214 for the edict.[109] He proposed that the danger mentioned in the preamble was Caracalla's escape from shipwreck while crossing the Hellespont, but argued that its ultimate motive was probably (as Dio suggested) to raise money.[110] Millar's thesis is hypothetical and dependant on a section of the *Historia Augusta*.

> While he [Caracalla] was crossing over from here into Asia the yard-arm of his ship broke, and he ran into great danger of shipwreck, so that, together with his body-guard, he had to climb down into a lifeboat. From this he was taken up into a trireme by the prefect of the fleet and so was rescued.[111]

Millar's use of papyri to trace the spread of the *gentilicum* Aurelius is on firmer ground (the widespread adoption of the name Aurelius is a signifier of people receiving citizenship under the decree), but does nothing more than suggest that the *constitutio* was in effect in Egypt towards the end of AD 214, providing a *terminus ante quem* for the edict.[112]

Gilliam suggested AD 212, or the very beginning of AD 213, as a likely date. Unfortunately the small number of *Aurelii* in AD 212 and AD 213 means that evidence is absent in these crucial years.[113] Rubin connected the edict with Caracalla's Germanic success in AD 213, and Dio's account that Caracalla was rescued from danger by a former charioteer named Pandion.[114] More recently, Baharal has suggested that Caracalla might have been motivated by his adoration of Alexander the Great: the concept of universal harmony presented in Roman accounts of the Macedonian's life may have motivated the emperor to grant universal citizenship.[115] Caracalla, imitating Alexander in numerous other aspects, might also have imitated his hero in this as well. This last hypothesis is attractive, but does not illuminate the danger mentioned in the decree. There remains little evidence to support the claims of Euzennat and Letta.

[108] Sherman 1928: 46–7; Swain 2007: 25; Visscher 1961: 234. [109] Millar 1962: 124–31.

[110] Millar 1962: 130.

[111] *SHA M. Ant.* 5.8. Millar also found support for his theory in Dio's speech of Maecenas (Millar 1962: 129–30), but Barnes 1984: 240–54 has since convincingly argued that Dio wrote most of his history under Severus Alexander, and that the speech of Maecenas most likely reflects conditions under that emperor.

[112] Millar 1962: 129. [113] Gilliam 1965: 74–92. [114] Rubin 1975b: 430–6; Dio 73.13.6.

[115] Baharal 1994: 531; Potter 2004: 144–5.

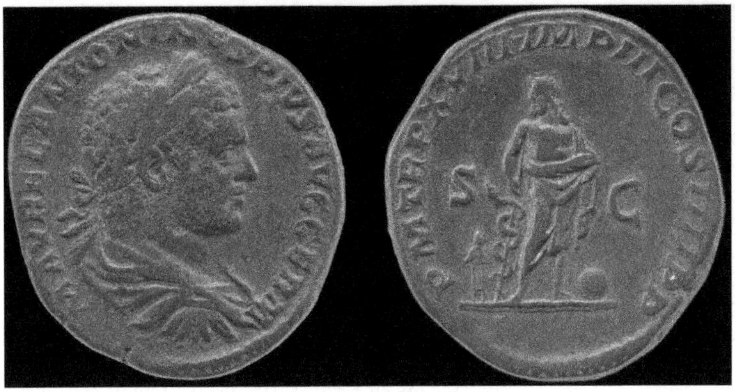

Figure 43: Sestertius of Caracalla displaying Aesculapius with Telesphoros and a globe and the legend P M TR P XVIII IMP III COS IIII P P.

It is clear that Caracalla paid homage to Apollo Grannus in Germany and in all likelihood consulted the oracle of Apollo at Claros. Having considered the evidence that connects Caracalla with Apollo, we move on to the second deity mentioned by Dio, Aesculapius.

Caracalla and the Aesculapium at Pergamum

On his way through Asia Caracalla visited Pergamum, a city famous for its cult of Aesculapius. Dio and Herodian both mention the visit of the emperor to the city, Herodian commenting that the emperor was anxious to have treatment at the shrine.[116] The emperor's experience at the Aesculapium was commemorated on both imperial and provincial coinage.

Crosscurrents: Aesculapius in Rome and on imperial coinage

Aesculapius appears on Caracalla's coinage in the period AD 214–215. The god was portrayed with his characteristic serpent-wreathed wand, accompanied by his son Telesphoros and a globe, with slight variations (Figure 43).[117] An imperial coin type was also released showing Caracalla sacrificing before Aesculapius in front of a temple (Figure 44).[118] Unlike the Apollo types, Aesculapius appeared on all denominations at the Roman mint, first on aurei (AD 214), and then on the other metals (AD 215). The

[116] Hdn. 4.8.3.

[117] *RIC* IV.1 *Caracalla* 238, 251–3, 538a–c, 539, 549a–b, 550a–c, 553a–c, 554a–c.

[118] *RIC* IV.1 *Caracalla* 270a–d.

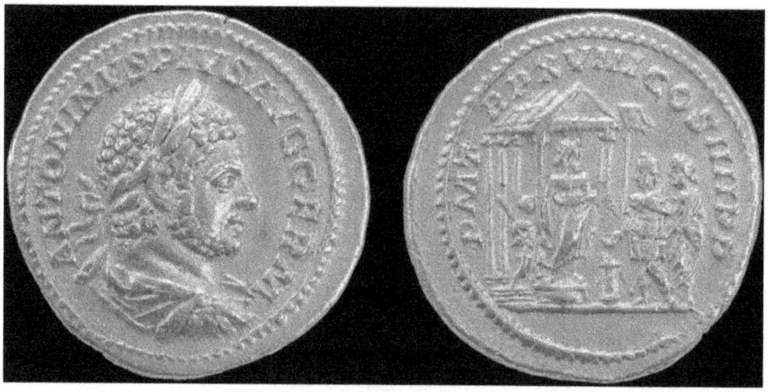

Figure 44: Aureus of Caracalla showing the emperor sacrificing at a temple of Aesculapius accompanied by an attendant. The reverse legend reads P M TR P XVIII COS IIII P P.

short chronological timeframe of these issues is reminiscent of the Apollo types, and suggests that the imagery was a reflection of the emperor's activities in Asia. In the hoard analysis (Figure 41) the types made up about 19 per cent of Caracalla's silver for AD 215.

The globe (or *omphalos*) and Telesphoros had not previously been shown with Aesculapius on coins issuing out of the Roman mint.[119] The god had appeared on coins of previous emperors, but never with these attributes.[120] Kampmann first realised the significance of this, observing that this iconography was commonly associated with Aesculapius at Pergamum.[121]

The appearance of Telesphoros and the *omphalos* on the imperial coinage of Caracalla probably had specific reference to the emperor's experience at Pergamum. Under Hadrian the Roman mint struck types that displayed the emperor greeting cities and provinces as he travelled through the empire.[122] Under Caracalla the representation became more abstract. Provincial gods acted as a marker for the emperor's activities in the provinces, probably because Caracalla himself focused on the worship of these deities. The emperor's patronage of these gods was communicated by the Roman mint

119 Kampmann 1992/3: 42. Kampmann suggests the globe is an *omphalos*, which had a long association with Aesculapius at Pergamum.

120 For example *RIC* IV.1 *Albinus* 2, 57; *RIC* IV.1 *Septimius Severus* 775. See Bernhard 1926: 129–41 for an overview of Aesculapius types of the Roman mint. For Telesphoros see Wroth 1882: 283–300.

121 Kampmann 1992/3: 39–48. A garden attached to the sanctuary in Pergamum contained the oracular serpent of the god and a small cult figure of Telesphoros, the son of Aesculapius and legendary founder of the city. See Behr 1968: 23–40; and Harl 1987: 57. Aelius Aristides also mentions a statue of Telesphoros in the temple of Hygeia (*Sacred Tales* 2.10, 3.23, 4.16).

122 Mattingly and Sydenham 1926: 331–2.

with iconography borrowed from outside the capital. The example of Apollo has already been discussed, and this work will move on to explore the example of the Alexandrian Sarapis. Kampmann suggested that the imperial mint took the iconography directly from Pergamum itself, a process contrary to the traditionally accepted belief that iconography travelled out from Rome to the provinces.[123]

The imperial *aureus* type showing Caracalla sacrificing at a temple of Aesculapius also likely records an activity that took place in Pergamum (Figure 44).[124] The temple of Aesculapius in Rome was located on Tiber Island, which was shaped like a ship's prow. Myth held that the temple was founded in response to plague; the sacred snake of Epidaurus was brought to Rome and disembarked at the site of his future sanctuary.[125] The Epidaurian snake appears on a medallion of Antoninus Pius commemorating the arrival of the cult in the city.[126] A Republican numismatic representation shows the temple with a ship's prow, reflecting the appearance of Tiber Island.[127] None of this iconography is present on the Caracallan piece. When this is considered in conjunction with the fact that the aureus was released concurrently with the types of the Pergamene Aesculapius, at a time when the emperor was in Asia, the identification of the temple as the Pergamene Aesculapium becomes attractive. Though the literary sources suggest Caracalla may have visited the sanctuary for medical purposes, the emperor's presence would also have highlighted his piety towards this important cult centre.[128]

The coin types of Rome had a counterpart in Pergamum itself. Just as the Roman mint communicated the emperor's patronage of Aesculapius, the civic élite of Pergamum seized the opportunity presented by the emperor's presence to underline their connection to the princeps and to advertise the bestowal of imperial favours upon the city. In this manner, they could highlight their status and prestige to the surrounding region.

Celebrating an imperial *adventus*: the civic coinage of Pergamum

The visit of Caracalla to the Aesculapium at Pergamum was commemorated on an extraordinary series of coins released by the city. These

[123] Kampmann 1992/3: 47.
[124] Calabria 1992: 72 n. 17 suggests it is the temple at Rome, but provides no compelling evidence.
[125] Benedum 2001: 187–204; Besnier 1902: 152; Capai 1991: 271–84; Degrassi 1987: 521–7; Hart 2000: 109; Nutton 2004: 159–61; Renberg 2006/7: 87–172; Roesch 1982: 171–9; Ziolkowski 1992: 17.
[126] Grueber and Pooie 1874: 7 no.4; Gnecchi 1912: (vol. 2) 1–3; van Buren 1911: 187–95.
[127] Zehnacker 1964: 739–48, against which Calabria 1992: 65–80.
[128] Harl 1987: 52–61.

communicated Caracalla's patronage of Aesculapius, as well as the bestowal of a third neokorate on the city.[129] Though Smyrna would soon after be granted the honour of a third neokorate by Caracalla, Pergamum could still claim to be the *'first three times neokoros of the Augusti'* and proclaimed itself the 'first city' of Mysia.[130] The grant was a significant coup for the city, and was an official statement of the connection between Caracalla, Pergamum and the sanctuary that made it famous. Coinage formed one of the media by which this imperial honour was monumentalised, and remains the medium best preserved.

The precise date of Caracalla's visit to Pergamum is debated.[131] Dio's account is preserved in a text attributed to Petrus Patricius, in the *Excerpta* compiled on the orders of the Byzantine emperor Constantine VII Porphyrogenitus (in this part of Dio's narrative Xiphilinus is mutilated and Boissevain declared him particularly untrustworthy here). Any chronological context is lost.[132] Herodian places the emperor's visit to Pergamum after his visit to Thrace and before Ilium.[133] Geographically this makes no sense, since if one comes from Thrace, Ilium is reached before Pergamum.[134] If Caracalla were ill, he may have rushed to the shrine, or perhaps he planned to arrive in time for a local festival.[135] Herodian may also be in error here. Caracalla was along the Danube in AD 212/13; hence the visit to Pergamum should be placed sometime between this and his arrival in Nicomedia, which likely occurred before 17 December AD 213 (Dio mentions that Caracalla celebrated the Saturnalia in Nicomedia).[136] A date of late AD 213 seems the most likely. An inscription found in the Aesculapium of Pergamum, along with a veiled head of the emperor, dated to the seventeenth tribunician year of Caracalla (AD 214), describes the emperor as *domino indulgentissimo*, indicating Caracalla had probably already bestowed his benefactions upon the city.[137] The same year marks the beginning of the imperial Aesculapius coin issues. The combination of the evidence suggests a date of late AD 213.

[129] Burrell 2004: 30; Metcalf 1999: 15. The neokorate was likely granted during the emperor's visit to the city.

[130] Burrell 2004: 34; *BMC Mysia* (Pergamum) 318.

[131] Burrell 2004: 30 and Kádár 1986: 31–5 suggest the end of AD 213; Harl 1987: 55 suggests AD 214; and Weisser 2005: 136 gives the year as AD 216.

[132] Dio 78.16.8. The excerpt in question is Petr. Patr. *Exc. Vat.* 147. On the utility of Patricius in reconstructing Dio see Cary (LCL xxii) and Millar 1964: 1.

[133] Hdn. 4.8.3. The *Historia Augusta* does not mention the visit to Pergamum at all.

[134] Levick 1969: 431. [135] On possible festival dates at the Aesculapium see Behr 1968: 32.

[136] Letta 1994: 188–90; Scheid 1998c: 445.

[137] Wiegand 1932: 52 = *AE* 1933, 280; Inan and Rosenbaum 1966: 82, 84.

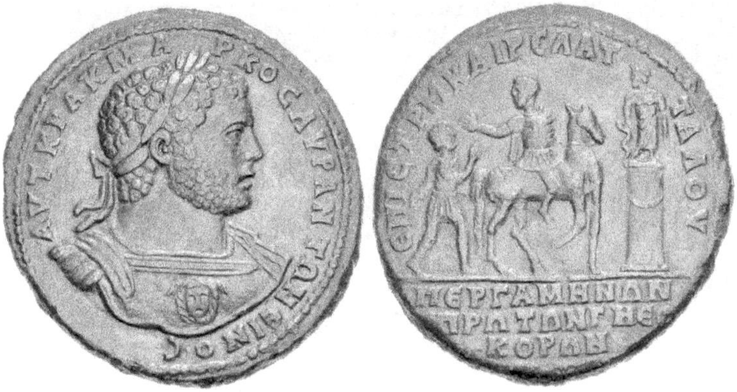

Figure 45: Coin of Caracalla from Pergamum showing the emperor on horseback before a statue of Aesculapius.

Several large provincial bronze coins narrate the emperor's stay at Pergamum. The types are well published and were struck by three separate magistrates: M. Caerelius Attalos, Julius Anthimos and M. Aurelius Alexandros.[138] Each of these *strategoi* held office for a year, meaning the types were released over a period of three years.[139]

The coins of M. Caerelius Attalos are probably the earliest issues referring specifically to Caracalla's visit to Pergamum.[140] Types were released showing the emperor on horseback before a cult statue of Aesculapius on a column (Figure 45),[141] the emperor standing before a hexastyle temple containing a standing statue of Aesculapius[142] and the emperor standing before a temple with a seated statue of Aesculapius.[143] Caracalla and Aesculapius are also shown with an altar between them,[144] and with a *cippus* supporting Telesphoros between them.[145] One issue portrays the emperor raising his right hand towards a serpent-entwined tree, with a small figure of Telesphoros in between (probably an allusion to the oracular serpent in the sanctuary),[146] and another type shows the emperor standing

[138] Burrell 2004: 30–7; Harl 1987: 55; Kádár 1986: 31–5; Weisser 1995: 88; Weisser 2005: 135–42.

[139] Burrell 2004: 30. [140] Burrell 2004: 30.

[141] *SNG von Aulock* 1414, 7514; *SNG France* 2231–3, 2249. See also *BMC Mysia* (Pergamum) 320, *SNG Paris* 2243 (Caracalla on horseback with right arm raised before the Tyche of the city and Aesculapius); *SNG France* 2244 (the emperor on horseback with raised right hand being presented with a statuette of Aesculapius by a citizen).

[142] *BMC Mysia* (Pergamum) 325; *SNG France* 2250–1.

[143] *BMC Mysia* (Pergamum) 324; *SNG France* 2245–7.

[144] *BMC Mysia* (Pergamum) 322; *SNG France* 2239. [145] *SNG France* 2240–1, 2248.

[146] *BMC Mysia* (Pergamum) 326.

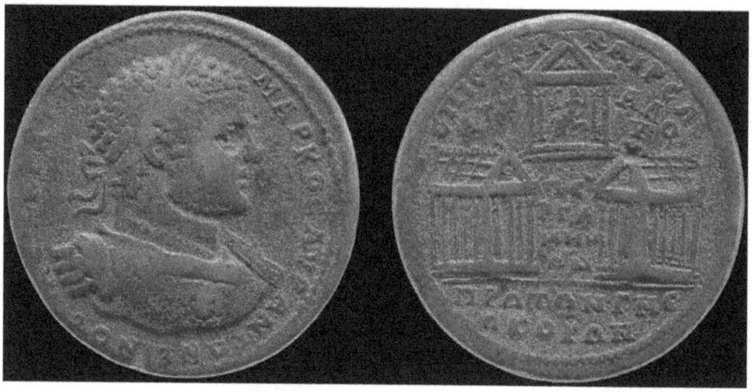

Figure 46: Coin of Pergamum showing the city's three neokorate temples.

with Zeus Nikephoros.[147] Caracalla is also shown on a statue base with a raised right hand between Roma (carrying Victory) and Tyche (?) (carrying a statuette of Aesculapius).[148] The three temples related to the three neokorates of the city also feature on the city's coinage in this period (the other two grants had been bestowed by Augustus and Trajan, Figure 46).[149] Overall, the types provide a visual narrative of Caracalla's stay in the city: his *adventus*, his sacrifice at the two temples to Aesculapius within the sanctuary, his visit to the oracular serpent, and the granting of the third neokorate. Like the saecular games types of Domitian, these coins may have been meant to be viewed together, and to act as a record of the occasion. The types communicate the increased status of the city and the religious devotion of the emperor during his stay at the Aesculapium.[150] The magistrate responsible for the coinage, Attalos, may have played a role in the emperor's visit. Weisser notes that one coin type shows a citizen holding a statuette of Aesculapius, greeting the emperor on horseback in a scene of *adventus*. This depiction is without parallel in Asia Minor, and may represent Attalos himself.[151] In this way the coinage may have communicated both the emperor's patronage and Attalos' eminent position within the city.[152]

147 Gorny & Mosch Giessener Münzhandlung, Auction 169 (12 October 2008) 186.

148 *SNG BN* 2237; Gorny & Mosch Giessener Münzhandlung, Auction 152 (10 October 2006) 1787.

149 *SNG von Aulock* 1411, *SNG France* 2227–9; Burrell 2004: no. 22. See also *BMC Mysia* (Pergamum) 323 (Caracalla and Aesculapius with a bull between them). Other coins show the emperor sacrificing before a temple of Zeus (*SNG France* 2230).

150 Weisser 2005: 137.

151 Weisser 1995: 60.

152 Similar ideas have long been associated with Republican moneyers. See Meadows and Williams 2001: 27–49.

The coins of Anthimos were likely minted later, when Caracalla was involved in the Parthian War (AD 217–218).[153] Though these coins were struck after Caracalla's visit, one of the issues shows the emperor in a scene of *adventus*, hailing a statue of Aesculapius carried by the Tyche of the city.[154] The *adventus* remained a key ceremony in the relationship between emperor and subject in this period: Severus had banished the father of Oppian from Anazarbus because he failed to greet the emperor with the rest of the citizenry during the ceremony.[155] Its importance is highlighted by its frequent appearance on provincial coinage. The image here would have recalled the emperor's visit in AD 214 and highlighted the connection of the city to the princeps. Other types of Anthimos allude to the military success and prowess of the emperor. Caracalla is shown on horseback being crowned by Nike, with a military trophy and two bound prisoners before him,[156] shown jumping over a lion on a horse[157] and sacrificing at an altar between two military *vexilla*.[158] Through this imagery the city could engage in the wider dialogue surrounding the emperor's Parthian campaign. Other types display the titles of the city inside a wreath, the tetrastyle temple of Aesculapius,[159] and mark the celebration of games (*Olympia*) in the city.[160]

The coins of Alexandros are difficult to date with precision.[161] One of the types minted under his magistracy shows the emperor in a tetrastyle temple, likely the temple of the third neokorate.[162] Another issue of Attalos demonstrates that Caracalla shared the neokorate temple with Aesculapius.[163] This coin type shows the three neokorate temples side by side. The middle temple is labelled as the temple of Caracalla, ANT(ΩNEINOΣ), and the other temples are labelled as belonging to Augustus and Trajan (AYΓ and TP).[164] But while the temples of Augustus and Trajan show standing statues of the emperor, Caracalla's neokorate temple contains a statue of the seated Aesculapius holding a snake in his outstretched right hand.[165] Temple-sharing characterised the neokorate at Pergamum: Augustus had shared a temple with the goddess Roma and Trajan with Zeus Philios.[166] Similarly, Caracalla likely shared the temple with Aesculapius, who is shown on the

153 Burrell 2004: 30.

154 *SNG France* 2242–3; Gorny & Mosch Giessener Münzhandlung, Auction 117 (October 2002) 391.

155 Fernando 1992: 235–9. On the ceremony of *adventus* in this period see Benoist 1999: 149–75; and Benoist 2005: 61–101.

156 *SNG France* 2223–5.

157 *SNG France* 2238.

158 *SNG Copenhagen* 499; SNG *France* 2236.

159 *SNG France* 2252.

160 *BMC Mysia* (Pergamum) 318; *SNG France* 2234.

161 Burrell 2004: 30.

162 *SNG France* 2226.

163 Weisser 1995: 90.

164 Burrell 2004: 22; *SNG von Aulock* 7513.

165 Burrell 2004: 24–34.

166 Burrell 2004: 22.

coin instead of the emperor.[167] This would have served as a statement of the connection between the emperor and the deity, one that would be seen again in Alexandria when Caracalla stayed in the Sarapeum.

These provincial bronzes would have operated as 'monuments in miniature', a record of the imperial visit and the grant of the third neokorate. Their importance as a marker of the event is reinforced by the later contexts of similar provincial types. A large bronze coin struck at Pergamum in the names of Caracalla and Geta was found in a catacomb in Rome.[168] A series of provincial protocontorniates was also found at Trier; hence the suggestion that they might have acted as souvenirs.[169] A vessel decorated with provincial bronzes, now in the Boston Museum of Fine Arts and dating to the period AD 200–250, also underscores the potential of these objects to act as mementoes, to function beyond the simply economic sphere.[170] Here the coins were used to decorate a vessel, and the iconography of the different coins was juxtaposed to communicate a connection of provincial culture with Rome.[171] Provincial bronze pieces could have varying contexts and significance; the imagery could possess substantial meaning for the owner.

Both the imperial Roman mint and the provincial mint in Pergamum utilised coinage as a mechanism to record and communicate the emperor's patronage of Aesculapius. Whether this imperial patronage was motivated by ill health is more difficult to uncover. Earlier scholarship mistakenly attributed a poem of thanksgiving to Aesculapius for preservation from a shipwreck to the emperor Caracalla, but this has now been convincingly refuted.[172] Caracalla's acts of devotion towards Aesculapius can be contextualised within the period of the emperor's stay at Pergamum. Considering the strong associations of the Aesculapium with healing, ill health of the emperor remains a good explanation for the imperial presence in the city. But this primary motivation does not automatically discount secondary associations of the visit: the communication of imperial piety towards the provincial deity and the honouring of a major town in the region.

[167] The seated Aesculapius is also shown instead of Caracalla on another issue of Attalos, *SNG von Aulock* 1411.

[168] Vicenzo, Fiocchi et al. 2000: 139–42. A provincial bronze struck under Pius was also found in a catacomb in Rome (Molinari 2002: 214).

[169] Gilles and Weisser 2006/7: 127–36. See also Reusch 1938: 166–71 for Greek provincial types found in Cologne.

[170] MFA Boston 63.2644; Vermeule 1975: 9.

[171] For the significance of the types chosen see Rowan 2010: 5.

[172] Initial attribution: Wiegand 1932: 53–4, with discussions in Millar 1962: 130; Rubin 1971: 177; and Wilhem 1933: 836–59. For refutation see Behr 1968: 52 n. 44; Behr 1981: 425–6; Herzog 1934: 753–69; Letta 1994: 188–90; and Scheid 1998a: 289.

Aesculapius' appearance on the coinage of Caracalla, as well as the coin types of Pergamum, reflects a discrete event, similar to Caracalla's homage to Apollo. The connection of the emperor to these two deities in succession once again highlights the mutability of the imperial image, which changed to reflect contemporary circumstances. Though the connection of the emperor to Apollo and Aesculapius was limited to a specific period, the same cannot be said for the last deity mentioned by Dio, Sarapis. It is clear that Sarapis formed a key supportive deity throughout Caracalla's entire reign.

Caracalla and Sarapis

Caracalla announced the divine support of Sarapis from the outset of his reign. Both Isis and Sarapis had been part of the Roman landscape since the triumviral period, when Mark Antony constructed a temple to both gods in the Campus Martius. The *Iseum et Serapeum* then underwent renovations under Caligula and Domitian.[173] Scattered archaeological fragments also suggest that the sanctuary was renovated during the joint rule of Severus and Caracalla: two inscriptions found in the area of the temple appear to name the two rulers, two papyrus capitals have been tentatively dated to the Severan period and two statues of oceans associated with the temple are dated to *c.* AD 200.[174] Like Apollo and Aesculapius, Sarapis was considered to be a god of healing, particularly at Alexandria.[175]

Immediately upon Caracalla's succession (AD 212), the imperial mint began to strike coins with Sarapis' image, reflecting and communicating the god's central role in the new reign.[176] That Sarapis served as more than a healing deity for Caracalla is evident in the emperor's actions, and the reports of contemporary authors. Dio records that after the death of Geta Caracalla dedicated the murder weapon to Sarapis.[177] If Dio's account is accurate, Sarapis was probably cast as Caracalla's protector from treason and rebellion, and the god was used in the discourse surrounding Geta's fall.[178]

Dio's statement is preserved in Xiphilinus' summary of Caracalla's activities at Alexandria. It is thus probable that this dedication took place in Alexandria. Letta suggested it took place in the Sarapeum in Rome since Sarapis is associated with Caracalla from the very beginning of his sole

[173] Lembke 1994: 65–70. [174] Gatti 1943/4: 157; Lembke 1994: 71; Mancini 1926: 239.
[175] Diog. Laert. 5.76 (Demetrius' sight was restored by Sarapis); Stambaugh 1972: 76.
[176] *RIC* IV.1 *Caracalla* 193–4. [177] Dio 78.23.2–3. [178] Letta 1989: 276; Rubin 1971: 177.

rule.[179] But it is more probable that Caracalla dedicated the sword in the sanctuary in Alexandria. Dio observes that just before Caracalla's death there was a fire in the Sarapeum at Alexandria that did no harm apart from destroying the sword that Caracalla had used to murder his brother.[180] The story has elements of the fantastic, and is obviously included by Dio to illustrate the impiety of the emperor and his disfavour with the gods. But nonetheless the slander could only work if the sword was at Alexandria. The implications of a dedication in Alexandria are worth considering: Caracalla would have had to travel with this symbol of fratricide from Rome through Germany, Thrace, Asia and Antioch. This somewhat macabre turn of events might be understood in the context of the ideology that surrounded Geta's death (that Caracalla escaped from a plot against his life). Herodian records that after Geta's death Caracalla declared that 'he had escaped a great danger and had only just been saved'.[181] Similar justifications are recorded in Dio and the *Historia Augusta*.[182] If the textual evidence preserves any truth about the official story surrounding Geta's death, then Caracalla may have claimed his salvation was aided and supported by Sarapis, and then he may well have dedicated to Sarapis the weapon used to ensure the continuation of his life and his principate.

Caracalla and Sarapis: the coins

There are four forms of Sarapis on Caracalla's coinage. The god is shown with a transverse sceptre and raised hand (Figure 47),[183] holding corn ears[184] and carrying a transverse sceptre and wreath.[185] Another type, previously misidentified by modern scholarship, can be added to this list.

Cohen and subsequent numismatists have thought Caracalla released coins displaying the image of Pluto with Cerberus (Figure 48).[186] Pluto had never before appeared on Roman imperial coinage, and his début under Caracalla would call for explanation.[187] Close examination of this type reveals similarities with Pluto, but an iconography more in keeping with Sarapis. The two deities were closely associated in the Roman world;

[179] Letta 1989: 277. [180] Dio 79.7.3. [181] Hdn. 4.4.3. [182] Dio 78.3.1; *SHA M. Ant.* 2.4.

[183] *RIC* IV.1 *Caracalla* 193–4 (AD 212); 208, 497, 503, 505 (AD 213); 244 (AD 214); 263 (AD 215); 280, 561 (AD 216); 290 (AD 217).

[184] *RIC* IV.1 *Caracalla* 291–2 (AD 217).

[185] *RIC* IV.1 *Caracalla* 289 (AD 217); *BMCRE* V *Caracalla* 187–8 (AD 217).

[186] *RIC* IV.1 *Caracalla* 242.

[187] The god had appeared on provincial coinage, usually in the act of abducting Persephone (e.g. *RPC* I 661, *SNG von Aulock* 6628). Mattingly and Sydenham 1936: 87 admitted 'the point of the Pluto type is not clear'.

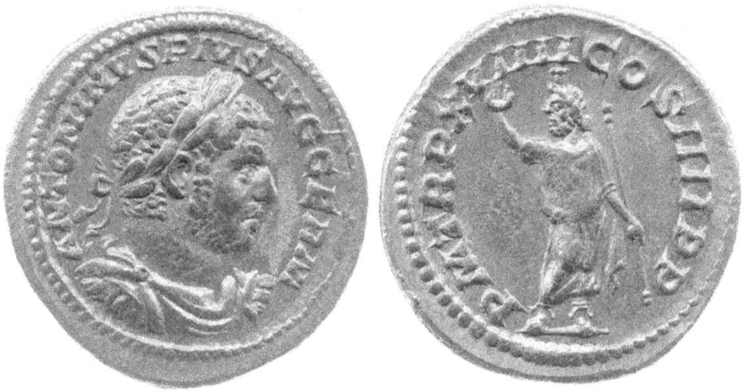

Figure 47: Aureus of Caracalla displaying Sarapis with raised right arm and sceptre with the legend P M TR P XVIIII COS IIII P P.

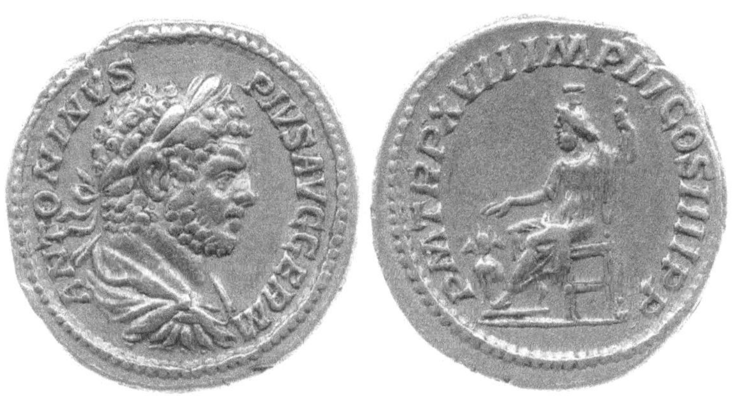

Figure 48: Aureus of Caracalla displaying Sarapis seated with sceptre and Cerberus with the legend P M TR P XVII IMP III COS IIII P P.

consequently their iconography was extremely similar.[188] But from the Hellenistic period onwards the most recognisable image of the Alexandrian Sarapis was as a seated god on a throne with a *calathus* on his head, holding a sceptre in his left hand, and with the three-headed dog Cerberus at his side.[189] This iconography appears on provincial coin types struck in Alexandria.[190] Coin types released under Domitian, probably in connection with the renovations of the *Iseum et Serapeum*, also show Sarapis seated in this manner within his temple (Figure 49).[191] Caracalla's coin type, then, can be identified as a representation of Sarapis.

188 Stambaugh 1972: 27; Plut. *De Is. et Os.* 361D–E.

189 Clerc and Leclant 1994: 666–92; Stambaugh 1972: 14. See also Macrob. *Sat.* 1.20.13–15.

190 *SNG Copenhagen* 642. 191 *RIC* II.1^2*Domitian* 812.

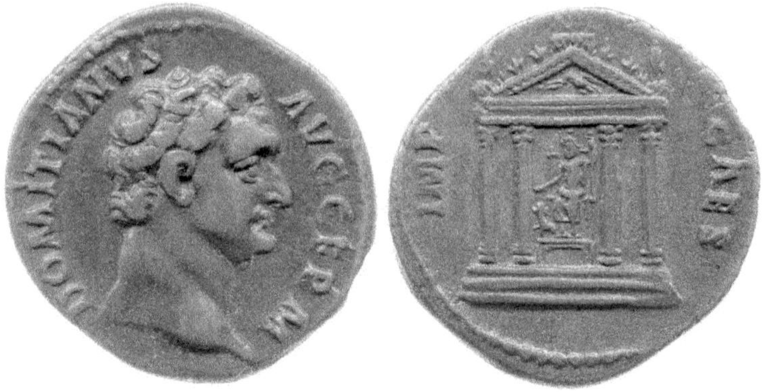

Figure 49: Denarius of Domitian displaying Sarapis seated in a temple with Cerberus and the legend IMP CAES.

Cohen also recorded that Caracalla struck coins showing Pluto with a Minotaur (Cohen 297), providing a line drawing of the type in his publication. The figure is extremely similar to the seated Sarapis type that scholars have identified as 'Pluto', except for the fact that Cerberus' heads are facing front, rather than turning to the right.[192] We should also reinterpret this type as a representation of Sarapis.[193] We can thus add one more type of Sarapis released under Caracalla: the god seated left, extending his right hand towards Cerberus and holding a sceptre (the type is labelled 'Alexandrian' throughout this work).[194] Ancient Romans may have had far less trouble than their modern counterparts in recognising the image.

Commodus had struck coins showing Sarapis as the *conservator* of the emperor, with the god shown standing with a sceptre and raised right hand.[195] This iconography is continued under Caracalla, and is the first type of Sarapis to be struck (AD 212, Figure 47). The reuse of Commodian iconography, where Sarapis was hailed as *conservator Augusti*, underlines a connection to the Antonine dynasty as well as advertising the rôle of Sarapis

[192] This difference may have initially led to the misidentification as a Minotaur.

[193] Cohen's identifications have persisted in the *RIC* and *BMCRE*, as well as the catalogue produced by Calicó (Calicó 2003). *Roman Imperial Coinage* quoted Cohen as their source as well as the publication by Mouchmov of the Reka-Devnia hoard (*RIC* IV.1 *Caracalla* 262). An examination of the plates of Mouchmov's publication shows that once again the coin is identical to the type of the seated Sarapis. That this iconography is better identified as Sarapis has also been suggested by Mennen 2006: 264.

[194] *RIC* IV.1 *Caracalla* 241 (AD 214), 261–2 (AD 215), 279 (AD 216).

[195] *RIC* III *Commodus* 261, 601, 605; Hekster 2002: 110. The image of Sarapis with sceptre and raised right hand first occurs on Alexandrian coins under Domitian, and under Hadrian as a gesture of blessing (Michaelis 1885: 296).

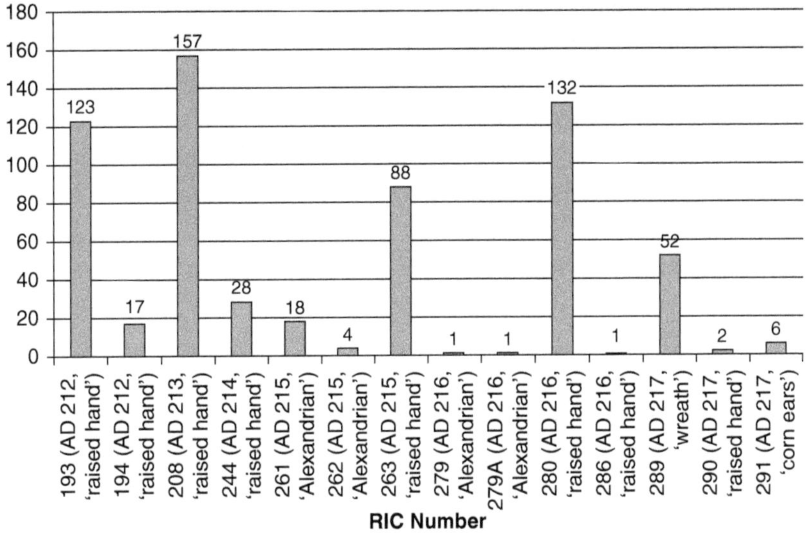

Figure 50: Silver Sarapis types of Caracalla (AD 212–217) as represented in hoards.

in the ideology surrounding Geta's death (Caracalla allegedly killed his brother in order to preserve himself, in which case the god may have been hailed as a *conservator*). The prominent role of Sarapis in this period is evident in the quantitative coin analysis. The Sarapis type constituted approximately 31 per cent of Caracalla's silver types for AD 212, and continued to be prominent in AD 213 (Figure 50). The iconography of a standing Sarapis with raised right hand would periodically reappear throughout the rest of the emperor's reign.

The iconography of Sarapis holding corn ears, and the image of Sarapis carrying a wreath emerges on imperial coinage in AD 217. The motivation behind the iconographic change is difficult to establish (Caracalla was in the East). The types are fairly substantial for AD 217, constituting 27 per cent of the silver types that can be dated to that period (Figure 50). Sarapis crowning Caracalla with a wreath is a known provincial coin type, probably derived from a statue (discussed below). The wreath-carrying Sarapis on the imperial types may have drawn inspiration from this statue.

The seated 'Alexandrian' Sarapis type was relatively infrequent in the hoard analysis. The portrayal of the famous Alexandrian cult statue was likely motivated by the emperor's presence at the Sarapeum in Egypt, similar to the imperial coins minted in conjunction with the emperor's visit to Pergamum. A possible problem with this interpretation is that the Alexandrian Sarapis first appears on Roman coins in AD 214, a year before

Caracalla reached the city.[196] It is not inconceivable, though, that the mint was informed of the emperor's intention to travel to Alexandria. The discovery of the *Antonine Itinerary* illustrates the potential for the Romans to plan the movement of emperors and armies, even if the document does not refer to the emperor Caracalla himself.[197] The mint (perhaps directed by someone on behalf of the emperor) may have tailored its designs to match the emperor's travel plans.

The mint also marked Caracalla's presence in Alexandria through the release of an issue showing Isis presenting two ears of corn to the emperor.[198] The date of the issue is AD 215, the year the emperor was in Alexandria. This does not negate the idea that the seated Sarapis types were also struck in honour of the occasion. The two types together portray the two main cults in Alexandria, which also shared a space in Rome in the Campus Martius. The seated Sarapis type only featured on Caracalla's coinage for a short time (AD 214–216), roughly corresponding to the period when the emperor was in Egypt.

Coinage did not form the only medium through which the divine support of Caracalla was communicated. As with Severus, Caracalla's patron deity would be monumentalised in the imperial capital.

Caracalla and Sarapis in Rome: the temple

An inscription found in the church of Sant' Agata dei Goti in Rome records the construction or restoration of a temple (*aedes*) to the god Sarapis.[199] It was likely reburied after its discovery in the seventeenth century. The inscription was fragmentary, but preserved the name Marcus Aurelius Antoninus, referring to either Caracalla or the emperor Elagabalus. The former is a preferable interpretation given the emperor's strong association with the god. The *Historia Augusta* may also provide incidental, though confused, evidence that Caracalla built or restored a temple to Sarapis. The author observes that the emperor brought the *sacra* of Isis to Rome, 'celebrating her rites with even greater reverence than they had ever been celebrated with before'.[200] Isis was the consort of Sarapis, and the *Historia*

[196] *RIC* IV.1 Caracalla 242, an aureus with the tribunician year listed as XVII. The precise dates of Caracalla's travels are anything but certain, though AD 215 is the most probable date for the emperor's arrival in Alexandria. Whittaker (LCL p. 420) suggests a date of June/September AD 215. The emperor most likely left the city sometime in January/February AD 216.

[197] For a discussion of the Antonine Itinerary see Levick 1969: 439; Reed 1978: 228–54; van Berchem 1973: 123–6; and Whittaker 2004: 71, 81.

[198] *RIC* IV.1 *Caracalla* 257, 544; Mattingly and Sydenham 1936: 88; Rubin 1971: 176.

[199] *CIL* 6.570. [200] *SHA M. Ant.* 9.10–11. For a discussion see Lichtenberger 2007: 119.

Augusta may have conflated the two; the author himself admits to confusion here.[201] Regionary Catalogues mention the existence of a *templum Salutis et Serapis* in *Regio VI*.[202] Two other dedications to Sarapis were also found in the area around the Quirinal and Sant'Agata dei Goti, in the foundations of the Palazzo Capranica del Grillo and near the Piazzetta delle Tre Cannelle.[203] As mentioned in the previous chapter, a crocodile made of Aswan granite was uncovered in the gardens of the Palazzo Colonna, similar to a red granite crocodile uncovered in the vicinity of the *Iseum et Serapeum* in the Campus Martius.[204]

It is probable that there was a temple to Sarapis in the area around the Quirinal Hill, but, as discussed earlier, there are problems in identifying this structure with the colossal temple.[205] The inscription mentioning the dedication or restoration of the temple is too small to have belonged to the colossal temple on the Quirinal Hill. Neither Dio nor Herodian mentions Caracalla constructing a temple to Sarapis, and it is difficult to believe that they could have failed to mention the construction of such a large structure. Rather, there is compelling evidence to identify these remains with Septimius Severus' temple to Liber Pater and Hercules. We might instead look for a temple to Sarapis adjacent to the colossal temple, in an area now occupied by the church of San Silvestro. Ligorio recorded that another fragment of the inscription found in Sant'Agata dei Goti was excavated from the church of San Silvestro, along with some yellow columns, from an area that had the remains of a *cavea* and an apse.[206] Ligorio believed that this was the temple to Sarapis mentioned in the Regionary Catalogues. If he can be trusted, the location of the temple to Sarapis may have been beneath or close to the modern-day church.[207] The state of the evidence as it survives today means that we are reliant on Ligorio for this identification, but the size of the area and the circumstantial evidence makes this a better candidate for a temple to Sarapis than the colossal temple. The size of the area is certainly a better match for the recorded inscription in St Agata dei Goti.

Whether the temple was constructed *de nove* or only restored, the work would have served to underline the association between Caracalla and his

[201] See also Aur. Vict. *Caes* 21. Victor and the *Historia Augusta* may have had a common source here.

[202] Osborne 1983: 220.

[203] Hülsen 1894: 394–5.

[204] Lembke 1994: 239 no. 39; Picozzi and Valeriani 1999: 187.

[205] Beard, North et al. 1998: 254; Osborne 1983: 220.

[206] Pirro Ligorio, *Cod. Taur.*, XV, 156; Santangeli Valenziani 1991: 8. Ligorio also mentions that remains of a Sarapeum beneath San Silvestro in another note preserved in a Paris manuscript (Paris 1123, f. 303).

[207] Santangelo 1941: 170; Santangeli Valenziani 1991: 9.

father, whose temple to Liber and Hercules was very probably in close proximity. It is also worth noting the proximity of the structure to the temple of Salus, who also had a temple on the Quirinal. The healing qualities of Sarapis may have been made even more apparent through this juxtaposition.

The baths of Caracalla

One of the best-known monuments of Caracalla today are the baths constructed in *Regio XII* in Rome. This was one of the largest building projects Rome had ever seen.[208] Brick stamps from the structure suggest that the baths were conceived in AD 211 (perhaps at the accession of Geta and Caracalla), and Jerome suggests the structure was dedicated in AD 216, though it is evident that the complex was not fully completed by this time.[209] The baths were a commanding monument to the emperor's power. It is difficult to know who was responsible for their lavish decoration, though one imagines that the architects designed the structure with a good knowledge of the ideology of Caracalla and his rule. The decoration kept closely to the traditional motifs of *thermae*, but also alluded to the divine support that kept the Severan régime in power.

Only a small portion of the enormous sculptural programme associated with the baths has been preserved to the present day.[210] Many of the sculptures were the victims of limekilns, and, since the baths have been known continuously since antiquity, sculptures could (and were) removed from the site.[211] Nonetheless, the complex still offers the historian a large amount of information. The remains today attest to the decoration of the baths in the last period of use (evidence suggests the complex was still in use under Theoderic), but an analysis of the style and design of the sculptural pieces uncovered in the baths allows us to identify the pieces that were commissioned and installed in the Severan period.[212]

It is in the *frigidarium*, the central room of the complex, where we find the best evidence of traditional *thermae* decoration melded with allusions to the divine sanction of the Severan dynasty. The *frigidarium* was the point at which the two main axes of the complex met, and was a place of social

[208] Delaine 1997: 13; *SHA M. Ant* 9.4. [209] Delaine 1997: 15–16.

[210] On the sculpture of the baths see Delaine 1997: 265–7; Gasparri 1983–4: 133–50; and Marvin 1983: 347–84.

[211] A limekiln was discovered in the west palaestra of the complex, suggesting that many large statues were subjected to this fate (Marvin 1983: 368).

[212] Marvin 1983: 348.

activity.[213] Excavation reports place enormous colossal statues in the Caracallan *frigidarium*, pieces that were rare in size for bathing complexes. The famous Farnese Hercules, showing the hero wearily leaning on his club while holding the apples of the Hesperides behind his back, and the 'Latin' Hercules were placed in the intercolumnar spaces between the *frigidarium* and the room adjoining it to the east. Two other Hercules statues may also have stood in the room.[214] The style of these pieces, and the fact that they were obviously designed to fit into their surrounding spaces, suggests that these colossal statues were commissioned specifically for the baths.[215] They stood amongst other works of sculpture from the Severan period and earlier, including the famous 'Achilles and Troilos' now in the Naples Archaeological Museum.[216] Fragments found beneath the floor of the *frigidarium* (including a hand holding a *syrinx*) and others reported in very early excavations (a larger than life statue holding a cup, and a satyr) might have belonged to another statue group of Dionysus and a satyr.[217] A colossal head of Aesculapius was also found beneath the *frigidarium* and may have belonged to a statue originally placed in the apse of the space between the *frigidarium* and the *natatio* (swimming-pool). Its size (49cm) suggests Aesculapius was the largest sculpture we know of in the Caracallan complex, and Marvin suggests that it might have been balanced by a colossal statue of Hygeia placed in the opposing niche.[218]

The sculptural decoration of the *frigidarium* was reflected and complemented by the use of composite sculptural capitals, which were placed atop the columns of the room. Two of these capitals are of interest to this discussion. One displayed a weary Hercules identical to the Farnese Hercules now preserved in the Naples Archaeological Museum. The three other sides of the capital were decorated with two nymphs and a female figure (either Roma, Venus or Virtus). The other column displayed a sculptured figure of Bacchus, with Mars, Roma and Fortuna on the other three sides.[219] Jenewein suggested that the two columns formed a series of ordered figures: Hercules and Bacchus, Mars and Venus, Roma and

213 Marvin 1983: 378.

214 The Polyclitan Hercules (which likely stood in a niche) and a colossal Hercules crowned with ivy. See Delaine 1997: 266–7, numbers 3 and 27.

215 Marvin 1983: 380–1.

216 Delaine 1997: 266–7 for a full listing. Many of the pieces found in the bath complex are earlier than the Severan period, and Marvin is probably correct in her theory that the cost of commissioning the colossal statue groups meant most of the 108 statue niches in the complex had to be filled by pieces already in existence (Delaine 1997: 380).

217 Marvin 1983: 366.

218 Marvin 1983: 363–4.

219 Jenewein 2008: KMF 1 and 2, 43–5; von Mercklin 1962: 158–60.

Fortuna, and the two nymphs.[220] Though these gods were popular in bathing complexes, the combination of Bacchus and Hercules also recalls the patron deities of Severus, and their pairing here in the centre of the complex may have evoked the divine support behind Severan power. Their juxtaposition on separate but related columns, and perhaps also in two separate sculptures in the room, suggests that the architects were conscious of this secondary association. Similarly, though Aesculapius was suitable for a bathing complex, his colossal statue might also have served to recall Caracalla's patronage of the deity. Several associations may have been at once apparent in this decorative assemblage.

Ionic capitals in the library of the Caracallan complex were decorated with the busts of Sarapis, Isis and Harpocrates. The capitals now decorate the nave colonnades of the church of Santa Maria in Trastevere.[221] It is not known when this outer section of the bath complex was finally completed, but the differences between this section and the main complex suggest it was after Caracalla's death; the capitals themselves suggest a third century date.[222] It is thus difficult to associate the selection of Egyptian themes with Caracalla's connection to Sarapis, unless the design of the library was finalised under his reign, only to be realised after his death.

Caracalla as *philosarapis* and *kosmokrator* in Alexandria

In AD 215 Caracalla arrived in Alexandria. Herodian records that the purpose of the trip was to sacrifice to Sarapis and pay homage to Alexander the Great. It is evident that in this section of his history Herodian is relying on the account of Dio.[223] It is thus unsurprising that both Herodian and Dio mention unrest in the city.[224] Herodian notes that there were many Alexandrian lampoons against Caracalla that 'referred to the destruction of his brother'.[225] Dio writes that Caracalla went to Alexandria since he had heard he was ill spoken of, particularly with regard to the murder of Geta.[226]

[220] Jenewein 2008: 48. [221] Kinney 1986: 379–82; von Mercklin 1962: 123–5.
[222] Delaine 1997: 16.
[223] Kolb 1972: 98; Kolb 1972: 98; Zimmermann 1999b: 207; Zimmermann 1999b: 207.
[224] Whittaker (LCL p. 422–3) believed these civil disturbances were linked to a pro-Geta faction within the city.
[225] Hdn. 4.9.3. The *Acta Heracliti* also attest to civic unrest in the city (Musurillo 1954: 229–32).
[226] Dio 78.22.1.

Caracalla stayed in the Sarapeum while in Alexandria and might have been receiving treatment there.[227] The temple and its surrounding precinct were undergoing a massive rebuilding project after a fire destroyed the earlier structure in AD 181.[228] McKenzie has suggested that the rebuilding of the Sarapeum in AD 202 was connected to the alignment of the Severan dynasty to Egyptian gods.[229] This idea is based on the now outdated notion that Severus aligned himself with Sarapis.[230] The suggestion that Domna was closely aligned with Isis and Caracalla with Horus has also been refuted.[231] That construction on the Sarapeum was still on-going during Caracalla's sole rule is evident from the archaeological remains: the pool in the precinct had a foundation deposit containing coins of Julia Domna and Geta. These deposits have traditionally been interpreted as evidence for the fact that the *piscina* (and the rebuilding of the Sarapeum) was completed under Caracalla's rule.[232] The coins, however, were never fully published, and subsequent conclusions have been based on a preliminary excavation report that was completed before the entire set of coins had been cleaned and examined.[233] One can thus only accept this date with reservations.

Caracalla's decision to stay in the Sarapeum would have created a strong connection between the emperor and the god in the minds of the populace, evident in the epigraphic evidence discussed below. This might also be seen as a precursor to the extremely close connection between Elagabalus and his cultic deity, discussed in the following chapter. While Caracalla stayed in the cult centre of his patron deity, Elagabalus would construct a temple to his tutelary god next to the imperial palace, creating a monumental juxtaposition.

Myth and massacre in Alexandria

Dio, Herodian and the *Historia Augusta* all describe a massacre of the inhabitants of Alexandria that occurred while Caracalla was in the city.[234]

227 Dio 78.23.2. 228 McKenzie, Gibson et al. 2004: 98.

229 McKenzie, Gibson et al. 2004: 98; McKenzie 2007: 196.

230 Baharal 1989: 566–80; Raeder 1992: 175–96. 231 Ghedini 1984: 155; Levick 2007: 126.

232 Handler 1971: 65; McKenzie, Gibson et al. 2004: 98.

233 Rowe 1946: 61–2: 'though some of the coins await cleaning … the coins already cleaned date from the time of Trajan (98–117 A.D.) until that of Julia Domna, wife of Severus (193–211 A.D.), as well as Geta. Therefore if no later ones are discovered, when the balance of these valuable historical objects has been chemically treated, we may assume that the *piscine* dates from about 215 A.D., when Caracalla came to Alexandria.' Obviously the recorded evidence can only provide a *terminus post quem* of *c.* AD 211.

234 Dio 78.22.1–23.2; Hdn. 4.9.6–8; *SHA M. Ant.* 6.2–3.

The accounts of Dio and Herodian differ substantially: Dio describes an indiscriminate bloodbath and the expulsion of foreigners from the city, whereas Herodian describes an imperial 'trap' in which young men were ordered to assemble so that they might form a Macedonian phalanx, only then to be slaughtered 'like animals trapped in a net'. Kolb and Zimmermann believed that here Herodian has transplanted Dio's account of Caracalla's massacre in Germany, in which young men were assembled so they might serve as mercenaries, only to be slaughtered.[235] Sidebottom observes that Herodian often employs formulaic patterns to communicate complicated events more easily to his reader, thus keeping focus on his central theme of *paideia* and its role in good government.[236] The 'trap' is one of these formulaic patterns, which Herodian employs again in his account of Caracalla's encounter with the Parthians.[237]

The *Historia Augusta* may have been reliant on Herodian for the story of a massacre of young men who had been told they were going to be enrolled in the military. But the *Historia Augusta* adds that in this manner the emperor followed the example of Ptolemy Eurgetes.[238] Harker observes that this comparison with Ptolemy VIII 'Physcon' Euergetes likely derived from Alexandrian writers.[239] While in Alexandria Caracalla banished foreigners from the city, and issued an edict expelling the linen weavers, measures likely connected to a riot in December AD 215.[240] Ptolemy VIII had also taken measures against trade in Alexandria and had allegedly executed a rival to the throne.[241] Harker suggests that the narrative of Caracalla's 'massacre' was embellished to produce a more exact comparison between the two rulers.[242] The emperor's slaughter in the gymnasium has overtones of the massacre Euergetes had carried out in the second century BC.[243] The narrative of events and the 'official' documents preserved on papyrus were probably altered to condemn Caracalla.[244] Rather than seeing a massacre, a better interpretation of the surviving evidence is that Caracalla visited Alexandria and probably stayed in the city to celebrate the festival of Sarapis on 25 April. In December of AD 215 riots erupted, which were quashed by Roman troops. Trade guilds and the linen-weavers in particular seem to have been the source of the trouble, and they were expelled from the

235 Dio 78.13.5; Kolb 1972: 103–8; Zimmermann 1999b: 210. 236 Sidebottom 1998: 2816.
237 Hdn. 4.11.4–7. 238 *SHA M. Ant.* 6.2–3. 239 Harker 2008: 137.
240 *P. Giss.* 40 III; *P. Brooklyn Museum* 24; *P. Bon.* 15; *P. Giss. Lit* 6.3; Harker 2008: 133–7; Meckler 1994: 72.
241 *P. Tebt.* 3.700; Diod. Sic. 34.5.14. 242 Harker 2008: 137.
243 Val. Max. 9.2.5; Ath. 4.184; Strabo 17.1.12; Polyb. 34.14; Harker 2008: 137.
244 Harker 2008: 57.

city. The prefect Heraclitus mishandled the riot and was accordingly tried and executed. Harker notes that later authors observe that the executions of the emperor were not unjustified.[245] Beyond this it is difficult to reconstruct the events in Alexandria, but it is worth noting that the *acta* of Heraclitus' trial mention violence against Sarapis.[246] This may have had significance given the particular connection of the emperor to the deity.

Alexandrian coinage under Caracalla

Alexandria did not mark the emperor's visit in the same way Pergamum did on its coinage.[247] Here we should note that the Alexandrian mint legally remained the responsibility of the imperial government.[248] Unlike the cities of the Greek East, the coins minted at Alexandria were never autonomous (not the responsibility of the local élite), and thus had different motivations and contexts.[249] The coinage was probably the responsibility of the *idiologus* or the *dioecetes*; at the very least it was determined by the Roman government and managed in the interests of the emperor.[250] This assists in explaining the differences between the coinage of Alexandria and that of other provincial mints. The lack of types commemorating the imperial visit might also be a reflection of the unrest in the city.

Alexandrian coinage does show the emperor on horseback in a traditional scene of *adventus*, as well as in a *quadriga*.[251] On one type a bust of Sarapis is placed above the chariot.[252] These coins date from AD 212–213, and cannot be connected with the visit of the emperor to the city. Rather, this imagery may have marked the emperor's accession to sole rule; the iconography of *adventus* was adapted to communicate Caracalla's rise to power and his divine support. In the same period a coin type was released showing Sarapis crowning the emperor (Figure 51).[253] This type may have been inspired by a sculpture; scenes of Sarapis crowning the emperor are also known on other provincial coins of the period (discussed below). Caracalla's portrayal with the deity here is perhaps indicative of Caracalla's public affiliation with Sarapis, and the proclamation of divine

245 Harker 2008: 135. 246 *SB* VI 9213; Harker 2008: 136.

247 For a catalogue of coin types struck under Caracalla in Alexandria see Dattari 1901–2; Emmett 2001; Milne 1971; and *BMC Alexandria*.

248 Christiansen 1988: 11. 249 Bland 1996: 113–27; Milne 1971: xvi. 250 Milne 1971: xviii.

251 Emmett 2828–9. 252 Emmett 2830; ANS 1944.100.64236.

253 Classical Numismatic Group, Triton VI (14 January 2003) 603; Milne 1971: no. 2732b var. The same type occurs as a type of Julia Domna (Dattari 1901–2: no. 4040, Emmett 2868).

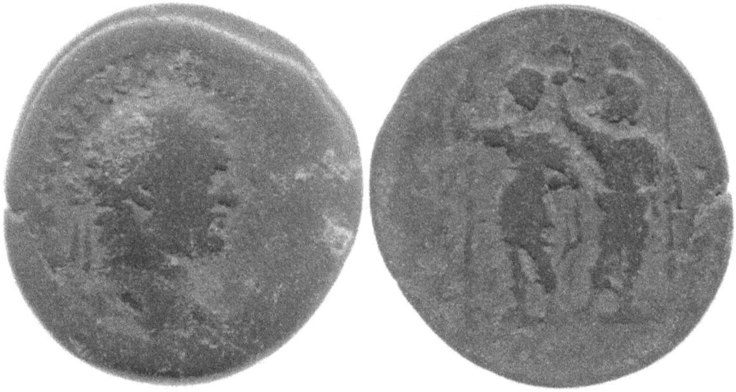

Figure 51: Alexandrian coin showing Sarapis crowning Caracalla with a wreath.

support following the murder of Geta.[254] El-Khachab lists several other types of Caracalla struck in Alexandria, including a coin showing Sarapis handing the emperor a globe, an adaptation of the traditional type of Jupiter handing the emperor a globe.[255] The Alexandrian mint thus reflected the ideology of power issuing out of Rome at the beginning of Caracalla's rule, but was less forthcoming in recording the emperor's visit to the region. One coin type may form the exception to this rule. Dated to AD 214–215 (around the time of Caracalla's visit to the city), this coin type shows the emperor facing the personification of Alexandria over an altar, probably marking the presence of the emperor in the city.[256] But this sole image presents a very different picture to that seen on the provincial coinage of Pergamum, which celebrated the imperial visit on numerous coin types over a period of three years.

Caracalla as *philosarapis*

Though there is little numismatic evidence, it is clear that the Alexandrians recognised the particular connection between the emperor and their major cultic deity. Inscriptions in Alexandria describe Caracalla as *philosarapis*, a title that had not been previously used in connection with a Roman emperor.[257] The title is also preserved in the *Acta Heracliti*, a papyrus found in the cemetery of Hermopolis Magna.[258] The epithet is not known for Caracalla outside Egypt; the Alexandrians probably bestowed it in

[254] Caracalla was not the first emperor to be shown in the company of Sarapis on Alexandrian coinage. Hadrian had been portrayed with Sarapis during his visit to Alexandria (e.g. Milne 1977: no. 1379), and Commodus, who had claimed a special connection with Sarapis, was shown sacrificing to the god (e.g. Dattari 1901–2: no. 3846).

[255] El-Khachab 1961: 127. [256] Emmett 2831. [257] Goddio, Bernand et al. 1998: 131–43.

[258] Acta Heracliti l. 3.

recognition of the emperor's particular devotion to the local cult of Sarapis. In a city where the civic élite did not have control over the design and minting of their own coinage, recognition of imperial favour and benefaction had to be communicated by other means.

The same inscriptions also give Caracalla the title *kosmokrator* (ruler of the world), which is extremely rare in imperial titulature.[259] The epithet is also known for Sarapis, who is described as *kosmokrator* in an inscription discovered in the *pronaeum* of the Mithraeum in the baths of Caracalla in Rome.[260] This dedication was originally to Sarapis, but was later amended to include Mithras.[261] Sarapis as *kosmokrator* was visually represented with a globe; hence the depiction of Sarapis giving a globe to Caracalla (on the coin of Alexandria mentioned above) signifies the sharing of rule, the joint position of *kosmokrator*.[262]

A sculpture preserved in the Mersey Museum in Liverpool, but most likely originating from Egypt, shows the emperor holding a sword in his right hand and the head of a barbarian in his left.[263] The emperor wears a *uraeus* crown, and is clothed in armour with two medallion-like objects that show the head of Sarapis.[264] Here too one can see the particular association between the emperor and Sarapis. The emperor's visit to Egypt was also the probable occasion for the creation of a terracotta bust of the emperor with a *kalathos*.[265]

A statue base from Ephesus shows a wider appreciation of Caracalla's association with Sarapis.[266] The inscription begins with the imperial titulature of Caracalla in the accusative case, followed by the names of those responsible for the dedication.[267] Following this is another dedication to Sarapis, by a Flavius Lucius.[268] In the inscription Caracalla is described as 'master of all the cosmos', a similar title to *kosmokrator*. The text is inscribed on a statue base that probably supported a statue of Sarapis. This would explain the later dedication to the god. The erection of a statue of Sarapis in honour of Caracalla suggests an understanding of the connection between the two, the recognition of imperial ideology in the provinces. Vidmann

259 The only other known use of the title is in an inscription from Arabia, used in the titulature of Lucius Verus and Marcus Aurelius (Goddio, Bernand et al. 1998: 139). For *kosmokrator* as a title of Caracalla see El-Khachab 1961: 124; Hombert 1945: 329; and Vidman 1986: 146.

260 *SIRIS* 389; Fishwick 1987: 342.

261 See the commentary by the editors of the inscription in *SIRIS* and Vidman 1986: 146.

262 Hornbostel 1973: 507–8.

263 Hornbostel 1973: pl. CCXIII 364; Hornbostel 1978: 515–18.

264 Mrav 2000: 87.

265 Hornbostel 1973: pl. CXXXVII 221 (Archäologisches Institut der Karl-Marx-Universität T 286); Hornbostel 1978: 516.

266 *IvE* 1230; *SIRIS* 303.

267 Vidman 1986: 145.

268 Vidman 1986: 145.

concluded from this inscription that Caracalla identified himself with Sarapis.[269] This may go too far. The erection of the statue was an act of private devotion and loyalty, albeit one informed by imperial ideology.

These inscriptions, in Alexandria and elsewhere, reflect an awareness of the special role Sarapis played in Caracalla's principate. Further evidence suggests that provincial cities and private individuals were attuned to the image and ideology of the emperor, and responded accordingly. This is discussed in more detail below.

Responding to the imperial image: Caracalla in Asia and visions of Alexander the Great

The provincial reception and negotiation of imperial imagery has begun to be better understood in modern scholarship. An oft-cited example of this phenomenon is Augustus' emphasis on his birth sign Capricorn, which resulted in many provincial cities incorporating the sign into their coin types.[270] Hadrian's devotion to, and deification of, his lover Antinous was also mirrored in numerous local contexts.[271] Under Caracalla we can also trace local interpretations of the imperial image. But some caution must be exercised. Aesculapius, Sarapis and Apollo all had cultic centres in the provinces; their appearance on a city's coinage is not necessarily a reflection of imperial rhetoric.[272] Consequently this study restricts itself to material that specifically connects the emperor to these deities. Even with this restriction, the evidence is compelling and suggests a wide appreciation of the divine basis of the emperor's rule. The fact that Caracalla spent much of his reign outside Rome meant that many would have had first-hand experience of the emperor. This may have assisted in the dissemination of imperial ideology.

An excellent case study of the influence of imperial ideology in the provinces is provided by Philippopolis in Thrace. Like that of Severus, the public image of Caracalla was multifaceted. Complementing the divine sanction of his régime, Caracalla cultivated an alignment with Alexander the Great.[273] Herodian reports that when Caracalla reached Thrace 'he suddenly

[269] Vidman 1986: 146. [270] Burnett, Amandry et al. 1992: 46.
[271] Harl 1987: 29; Vout 2007. [272] Drexler 1889: 1–234; Magie 1953: 163–87.
[273] Baharal 1994: 524–67; Baharal 1996: 69–72; Castritius 1988: 879–84; Dahmen 2007: 34; Dareggi 1994: 849; Espinosa 1990: 37–51; Gagé 1975: 1–16; Hedlund 2008: 54; Levick 1969: 443–4; Lichtenberger 2011: 42; Salzmann 2001: 173–91; Vagi December 1995: 6–10; Wirth 1975: 39–74.

became Alexander and commemorated him afresh in all sorts of ways', observing with his trademark irony that statues were erected with split faces, one half the portrait of Caracalla and the other half Alexander.[274] Dio also records Caracalla's idolisation of Alexander and notes that he even went so far as to organise a phalanx composed entirely of Macedonians.[275] In his Alexander-imitation the emperor visited Illium and the tomb of Achilles. Both Dio and Herodian record that the emperor sacrificed at the tomb (thus following the example of Alexander).[276] Herodian adds that when his freedman Festus died Caracalla seized the opportunity to have a funeral like that of Patroclus. This imperial patronage of a heroic cult may have inspired Philostratus to compose his *Heroikos*.[277] In his *Life of Apollonius of Tyana*, Philostratus details a trip of Apollonius to the tomb at Illium, probably also inspired by the imperial visit.[278] Particularly compelling here is the fact that Apollonius first visits Pergamum and the sanctuary of Aesculapius before heading to Illium, the precise itinerary given to Caracalla by Dio and Herodian.[279] The city of Illium marked the visit of the princeps by releasing coins showing the emperor, as did the city of Alexandria Troas, which struck types of the emperor being crowned by Nike, and on horseback in a scene of *adventus*.[280]

It is worth observing that Alexander, founder of Alexandria, was also connected with the cult of Sarapis in the Alexander Romance. This connection would have been present in the Severan period, regardless of whether it reflected historical reality.[281] The response to this ideology by Philippopolis in Thrace provides an insight into the historicity of Caracalla's alignment with Alexander, as well as the processes by which provincial cities identified and adapted imperial ideology within local contexts.

[274] Hdn. 4.8.1–2: εὐθὺς Ἀλέξανδρος ἦν.

[275] Dio 78.7.1–4. See also *SHA M. Ant.* 2.2. Baharal 1994: 524–66 notes that this tradition is not carried through into the later epitomes, and suggests that the hostility of Herodian and Dio resulted in an exaggeration of the emperor's devotion. Though Baharal's analysis of the alleged 'Alexander-type' portraits of Caracalla has many illuminating (and ultimately correct) points, her conclusion that Caracalla was privately, rather than publicly, interested in Alexander, is called into question by the decision of Philippopolis to hold the Pythia Alexandreia, discussed in detail below.

[276] Dio 78.16.7; Hdn. 4.8.4–5. Festus' tomb has been identified with Uvecik Tepe, which is seventy-five feet tall (Alcock 2004: 162).

[277] Aitken and Maclean 2004: xx; Jones 2001: 141–9; Maclean and Aitken 2001: xlvi; Rutherford 2009: 237–8, with criticism of the idea by Whitmarsh 2007: 36–7; and Whitmarsh 2009: 207.

[278] Philostr. *VA* 4.11.1–12.1; Grossardt 2009: 75.

[279] Philostr. *VA* 4.11.1; Dio 78.16.7–8; Hdn. 4.8.3–4.

[280] Bellinger 1961: 71 T261, 121 A290 and A 294–7.

[281] Welles 1962: 271–98.

Caracalla as Alexander the Great: the Pythia Alexandreia of Philippopolis

During Caracalla's reign Philippopolis released an extraordinary series of coins commemorating the celebration of the Pythia Alexandreia. The Pythian games were originally a sacred festival held at Delphi every four years, but in the Roman imperial period they were transformed into an honour that could be granted to any city.[282] Permission to stage new Pythian games could only be given by the emperor; the celebration of Philippopolis' festival for the first time must have been a benefaction granted by Caracalla.[283] In this context the title of the games, *Alexandreia*, is of particular interest.

The memory of Alexander the Great was prominent in the Severan period.[284] Cities with a heritage closely connected to Alexander, like Philippopolis, may have capitalised on their historical connections to win new imperial honours.[285] Games in the name of Alexander were held under Severus Alexander and Gordian III in Beroia.[286] The popularity of Alexander's memory is witnessed in the Abukir medallions, a series of gold medallions that commemorated the Hellenistic general. Newell suggested these medallions were intended as a prize for victors at the games in Beroia.[287] Given the value of these pieces (and that they were found in hoards, suggesting a single owner), they may be better interpreted as gifts for the civic or military élite, or for individuals of high status.[288] Some of these medallions show Alexander on the obverse, while others possess the portrait of Caracalla. This suggests an acknowledgement of the fact that the emperor *was* Alexander, and that the two were interchangeable. Dahmen, Vermeule and Dressel date the medallions after Caracalla's reign; if this interpretation is correct, it suggests that the alignment between Caracalla and Alexander continued after the emperor's death.[289]

[282] Weir 2004: 9. This phenomenon was particularly prominent between AD 180 and 260. There were also occasional grants to cities outside Delphi in the Hellenistic period.

[283] Weir 2004: 176.

[284] Niger had aligned himself with Alexander the Great (Dio 75.6.2[a]), and Severus allegedly shut Alexander's tomb when he visited Alexandria (Dio 76.13.2). On the association of other Severan emperors with Alexander see Blázquez 1990: 25–36; Gagé 1975: 1–16; Harl 1987: 40; and Shayegan 2004: 285–315.

[285] Spawforth 2006: 1–26. [286] Gagé 1975: 4.

[287] Dressel 1981: 1–130; Newell 1910: 128–30. Though there was initially doubt over the authenticity of the medallions, they are now accepted as genuine.

[288] This is also the conclusion of Dahmen 2008: 518–19 and Touratsoglou 2008: 487–8.

[289] Dahmen 2008: 521; Dressel 1981: 41; Vermeule 1982: 61–79.

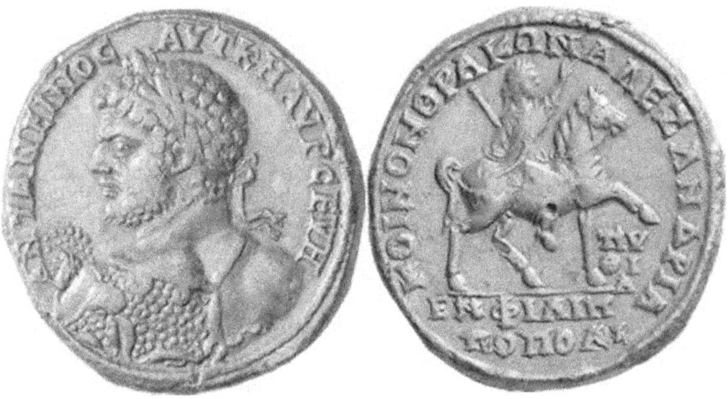

Figure 52: Coin of Philippopolis displaying the emperor in *adventus* and the legend ΚΟΙΝΟΝ ΘΡΑΚΩΝ ΑΛΕΖΑΝΔΡΙΑ ΠΥΘΙΑ ΕΝ ΦΙΛΙΠΠΟΠΟΛΙ.

The games of Philippopolis illustrate how one city adopted the 'Alexander image' of Caracalla for its own benefit. Coins marking the celebration of the games were struck in five different denominations. Harl's assessment of agonistic coinage in the Severan period notes that many issues were struck in conjunction with eastern campaigns, and that games were often timed to coincide with the arrival of the emperor in the city.[290] Pythian games issues of Philippopolis with an image of *adventus* (Figure 52) suggest that this may have been case here, though the *adventus* type could also be employed symbolically.[291] Caracalla traveled through Thrace, and it would be unusual for the emperor to journey through a province without visiting its capital.[292] A coin type showing the emperor paying homage to the cult statue of Apollo Kendrisos (a local cult) while being crowned by Nike (Figure 53), suggests that the emperor may indeed have visited the city.[293] Another type shows the emperor sacrificing over an altar to Apollo Kendrisos, with a sacrificial bull to the left.[294]

As well as constituting a major cult in the city, Apollo was closely associated with the Pythian games: the decision by Philippopolis to portray the emperor sacrificing to Apollo and not other deities thus need not reflect

[290] Harl 1987: 65.

[291] Varbanov 1407. The symbolic use of this type has already been seen at Alexandria. Another example from Ephesus shows Caracalla and Geta on horseback. This type must refer to the bestowal of a third neokorate and cannot signify that the brothers were actually in Asia in AD 211/12 (they were in Britain). See Johnston 1983: 58–76 for a discussion.

[292] Johnston 1983: 58–76; Levick 1969: 426–46.

[293] Varbanov 1402–5; Mouchmov 5335. The medallion displays a specific cult statue of Apollo, often portrayed on a marble column (Kolev 1991: 512).

[294] Varbanov 1552 (O. Gavrailov Collection).

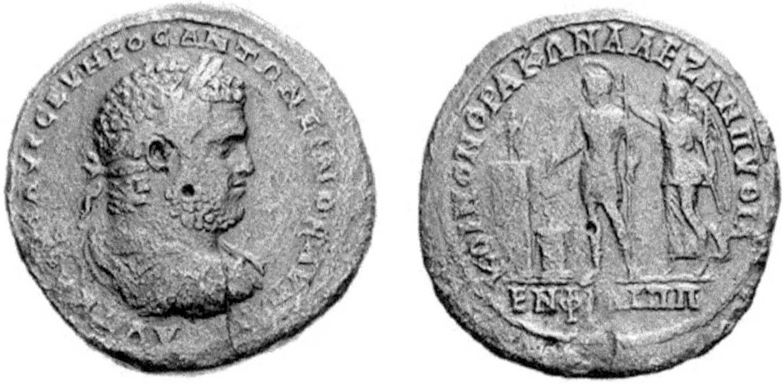

Figure 53: Coin of Philippopolis showing the emperor sacrificing to Apollo Kendrisos while being crowned by Nike with the reverse legend ΚΟΙΝΟΝ ΘΡΑΚΩΝ ΑΛΕΖΑΝ ΠΥΘΙΑ ΕΝ ΦΙΛΙΠΠ.

the emperor's own imperial ideology. Along with Apollo, the Pythian games coinage displayed Aesculapius, Sarapis, Hercules, Hermes, Zeus and Athena, though none of these is portrayed in the company of the emperor.[295] Apollo, Sarapis and Aesculapius all had local cultic centres in the city.[296] Other Pythian Games types show athletes and agonistic urns, and Caracalla as a military victor.[297]

Pythian Games were normally named after a deity or the emperor who had granted the city the privilege. For example, Caesarea Augusta held the *Severeia Pythia*, Laodicea ad Mare held an *Antoninia Pythia*, as did Rome.[298] Aphrodisias held a festival called the *Pythia Valeriana*, while Nicaea called its games the *Valeriana Galliena Dionysia Pythia*.[299] Could Philippopolis have been naming the festival after Caracalla when they selected the name *Alexandreia*? In light of Herodian's comment that

[295] Apollo: Varbanov 1472–3, 1492. Aesculapius: Varbanov 1413, 1431, 1474 (with Hygeia and Telesphoros); Weir 2004: no. 12. Sarapis: Varbanov 1449. Hercules: Varbanov 1435–6, 1464–5, 1481, 1494; Weir 2004: no. 3 and no. 3a; Mouchmov 5365. Hermes: Mionnet supp. II 1578 var.; Varbanov 1447–8, 1454, 1468, 1483; Weir 2004: no. 7. Zeus: Varbanov 1419, 1440, 1450–2, 1455, 1471, 1489–91, 1496; Weber Coll. 2772. Athena: Weir 2004: no.4. Dionysus: Varbanov 1453, 1461–2, 1467. Hera: Varbanov 1463. Helios: Varbanov 1482.

[296] Kolev 1991: 510–25.

[297] Athletes: Varbanov 1395, 1406, 1408–9, 1432–4, 1443–6, 1456–60, 1474–8, 1497–8; Mouchmov 5358; *BMC Thrace* (Philippopolis) 36; *SNG Copenhagen* 780–1; Weir 2004: no. 11. Agonistic Urns: Varbanov 1393–4, 1396, 1399–1401, 1412, 1420, 1423–8, 1437–9, 1441–2, 1469–70, 1485–8; *SNG Fitzwilliam Museum* 1774; *BMC Thrace* (Philippopolis) 37; Weir 2004: no. 6. Caracalla: Varbanov 1392, 1407, 1410, 1417, 1421–2, 1429–30, 1466, 1479–80, 1500; Mouchmov 5334. Legend Within Wreath: Varbanov 1414–16, 1484, 1495; Weir 2004: no. 13. Tyche: Varbanov 1499; Mionnet supp. II 1570.

[298] Robert 1970: 6–27.

[299] Weir 2004: 179–80.

Caracalla suddenly *became* Alexander, this is a possibility. Dio mentions that Caracalla 'actually wrote to the Senate that Alexander had come to life again in the person of the Augustus, that he might live on once more in him, having had such a short life before'.[300] Whether Philippopolis was referring to the emperor or the Macedonian general, or even a happy confusion of the two, cannot be known for sure.

Whether the Pythian Games held any reference to Alexander apart from the name is not known. Roman games outside Delphi were loosely modelled on the original, and enjoyed considerable latitude in deciding which Delphic practices were adopted.[301] In name at least the games were influenced by imperial ideology and illustrate the ideological dialogue between the princeps and his subjects. Philippopolis held another Pythian Games festival under Elagabalus, but this was called the Pythia Kendreiseia, after the epithet of the local cult of Apollo.[302] The Pythia Alexandreia was thus an event specifically connected to the reign of Caracalla.

Recognising divine support: Apollo, Aesculapius, Sarapis and Caracalla in the empire

The coinage of other provincial cities also suggests an awareness of Caracalla's ideology, with coinage being used as a medium to connect local cities with the emperor and the divine basis of his power.[303] A large number of provincial coins show Caracalla in connection with Aesculapius, Apollo or Sarapis. Caracalla's presence in the East, and his particular predilection towards these deities, formed an arena through which local cities could associate themselves with the person of the emperor and participate in imperial ideology. This was not the only sphere of interaction: cities participated in the dialogue of imperial military success by portraying the emperor with captives or military trophies, or the emperor quashing barbarians. Games and other honours also formed an arena for interaction, as explored above. It is the field of divine support, however, that forms the focus of the discussion here.

The coins of Pergamum and Alexandria have already been discussed in detail. Nicaea released coinage showing the emperor in a galley with Sarapis, as well as a coin type showing the emperor being crowned

[300] Dio 78.7.2. [301] Weir 2004: 176. [302] Weir 2004: 189.

[303] For the motivations behind the striking of provincial coinage see Burnett, Amandry et al. 1992: 15; Harl 1987: 19; and Weiss 2005: 62–3.

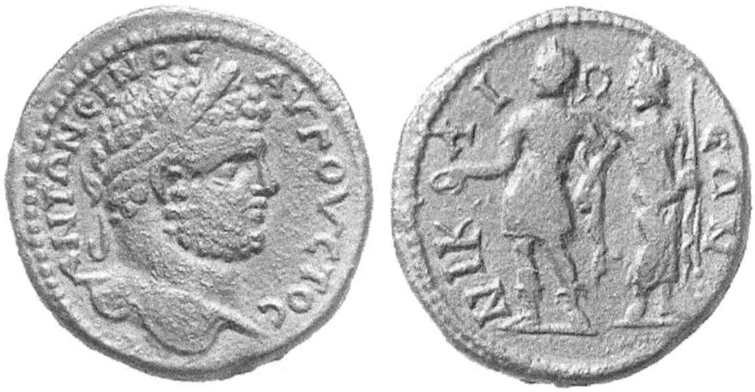

Figure 54: Coin of Nicaea showing Sarapis crowning Caracalla.

by the deity (Figure 54).[304] Nicomedia, Ptolemais (in Palestine) and Alexandria also released a coin type showing Sarapis crowning the emperor.[305] Bosch suggested that the images all drew inspiration from a well-known statue.[306]

In addition to the galley and Sarapis crowning the emperor types, Nicaea struck a type showing Sarapis with his right hand raised and holding a sceptre in his left.[307] Sarapis, as well as Aesculapius and Hygeia, had cults within Nicaea; at least, they had previously appeared on the city's coinage.[308] But the presence of the emperor in the area may have provoked the élite to connect their cults with the imperial person: Caracalla wintered relatively close by at Nicomedia.

Nicaea owed a debt of gratitude to Caracalla. He was responsible for restoring the city to imperial favour after the town lost its privileges for supporting Pescennius Niger.[309] Returning to imperial esteem in *c.* AD 204, Nicaea was granted the right to hold the *Severeia Philadelphia*, a significant coup in the city's on-going rivalry with Nicomedia.[310] Although granted the honour of the games, Nicaea did not regain its former titles, and so was heavily reliant on imagery to project its new status. One coin type of the city displayed Caracalla on the obverse, and on the reverse showed the Tyche

[304] *BMC Bithynia* (Nicaea) 74; Numismatik Lanz München, Auction 125 (20 November 2005) 882; Numismatik Lanz München, Auction 102 (28 May 2001) 761.

[305] The Alexandrian type is discussed above. Nicomedia: *SNG Copenhagen* 571; Johnston 1983: 63. Caracalla built baths at Nicomedia (*ILS* 613, Malalas 11.281; Levick 1969: 429). Ptolemais: Tran 1983: 74, 241 IVC 41; *BMC Phoenicia* (Ptolemais) 33. Unlike Nicomedia and Nicaea this same type appears again at Ptolemais under Severus Alexander (Tran 1983: 242 IVC 44).

[306] Bosch 1935: 288.

[307] *BMC Bithynia* (Nicaea) 72.

[308] For example, *SNG von Aulock* 545, 552.

[309] Burrell 2004: 165. The city was given the title of 'Aurelian Antoninian'.

[310] Weiser 1983: 122.

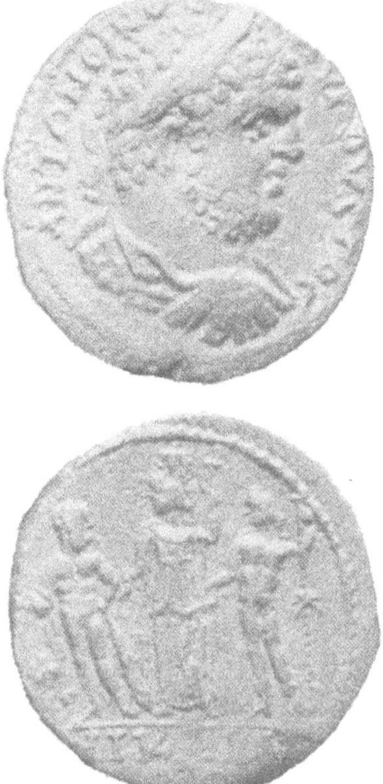

Figure 55: Coin of Nicaea with Tyche standing between Liber Pater and Hercules.

of the city between the gods Liber Pater and Hercules (Figure 55).[311] Dionysus and Hercules had been shown on Nicaea's coinage previously,[312] but the *combination* of the two gods here, as well as their attributes, alludes to Severus' divine ideology (the type was likely struck during Severus' reign). The placement of Tyche in between Liber and Hercules underlines the city's rise to favour, and its connection with the imperial house. The visual communication of status continued throughout Caracalla's sole reign with the types mentioned above. Caracalla's esteem within the city is evident from a coin type showing the emperor in a frontal elephant *quadriga* - an allusion to Alexander the Great.[313]

Sarapis also appears on the coins of Cyzicus, with the emperor shown standing with a raised right hand before a seated figure of the god.[314]

[311] Lindgren Coll. 1, 143. [312] For example *SNG von Aulock* 544, 555, 570.

[313] Gorny & Mosch Giessener Münzhandlung, Auction 118 (15 October 2002) 1720. Ptolemy I Soter had released coinage showing the deified Alexander the Great in an elephant *quadriga* (Svoronos 1904–8: 126; Bosworth 2007: 17–22).

[314] *SNG BN* 778; *SNG von Aulock* 7379.

Caracalla granted the city a second neokorate, and Cyzicus held games in the emperor's honour.[315] The city had a variety of cults, but made a decision to portray the emperor with Sarapis.[316] The tutelary deities of Cyzicus were Demeter and Kore: it is these goddesses who are shown on *homonoia* coinage and pseudo-autonomous issues as a representation of the polis.[317] Kore and Demeter were also shown on neokorate coinage, but not in the company of Caracalla.[318] It is thus likely that the city sought to communicate its particular connection with the imperial person, and his divine ideology, by employing the imagery of Sarapis.

Similarly, the series of coins commemorating the neokorate bestowed upon Laodicea in Phrygia included an issue showing Caracalla between Zeus and Aesculapius.[319] Burrell suggests that the neokorate grant was connected to the city's celebration of Aesculapian games.[320] Coins issued by Laodicea in the local year 88 (probably mid-August AD 215 to mid-August AD 216) advertise the title of neokoria, as well as a festival named the Antonineia, named after the emperor.[321] In the same year coins were struck with a legend referring to a *Pythia Asklepieia*.[322] The visualisation and celebration of Laodicea's neokorate grant was thus in many ways similar to the neokorates of other cultic centres (Aesculapius in Pergamum, Sarapis in Cyzicus). The divine ideology of the emperor was adopted at a local level.

Other cities also connected the emperor to Apollo, Aesculapius and Sarapis. Ancyra held the *Asclepieia Isthmia Pythia* under Caracalla.[323] A public dedication indicates that Caracalla bestowed the honour of these games on the city.[324] Isaura (Cilicia) struck coins showing the emperor accepting a diptych from Apollo;[325] Soli-Pompeiopolis (Cilicia) released a type showing the emperor in the presence of Aesculapius;[326] while Nicaea (Lydia) issued a type showing Caracalla sacrificing before Aesculapius,

315 Burrell 2004: 94; Levick 1969: 430. 316 Drexler 1889: 48.

317 For example *SNG von Aulock* 7339, *SNG France* 602 var., *SNG BN Paris* 596. On the phenomenon of *homonoia* coinage see Butcher 2006: 39–43.

318 Burrell 2004: 94, coin type 7.

319 Gorny & Mosch Giessener Münzhandlung, Auction 147 (7 March 2006) 1843.

320 Burrell 2004: 121. 321 Burrell 2004: 121. 322 Burrell 2004: 121.

323 Harl 1987: 65–6; Weir 2004: 179, 182. 324 Levick 1969: 430.

325 *SNG Delepierre* 49, *SNG von Aulock* 5410–11; *BMC Cilicia* (Isaura) 3–4; Harl 1987: 59; Levick 1969: 435. Admittedly, the youthful bust of Caracalla on the obverse of this coin suggests that it might have been issued while he was co-emperor with Severus.

326 Gorny & Mosch Giessener Münzhandlung, Auction 122 (10–11 March 2003) 1831. The coin is badly worn, but a serpent-entwined staff can clearly be seen, indicating that one of the figures is Aesculapius.

Telesphoros and Hygeia.[327] Hadrianotherai (Mysia) issued a type showing the emperor clasping hands with Aesculapius while being crowned by Tyche.[328] Alexandria Troas struck coinage showing the emperor on a springing horse with raised right hand approaching the statue of Apollo Smintheus.[329] Thyatira (Lydia) struck coins displaying Caracalla on horseback with the city goddess and a statue of Apollo Tyrimnaeus.[330]

The numismatic iconography finds a counterpart in the epigraphic record. Much of this has already been discussed, but a few more examples are worth mentioning here. An inscription in Pannonia records the sacrifice of the *XIII Gemina* to Deus Invictus Sarapis and to Isis Regina for the health and victory of Caracalla and Julia Domna.[331] Other inscriptions from Pannonia also document dedications to *deus invictus Sarapis* for Caracalla and the emperor's divine ideology may have been influential in the cultic activity in this area.[332] Mrav suggests that Caracalla's campaigns in Germany were linked with the god, and that the emperor may have erected a temple to Sarapis in Pannonia. This, he argues, would explain the extremely large Apis bull statue found in the area.[333] The remains of a dedication to Sarapis Invictus on behalf of Caracalla were also found in Rome.[334] An inscription to Caracalla was erected in the temple of the Pythian Apollo in Gortyn.[335] All of these show a conscious connection between emperor and the particular divine support he claimed.

The specific decision by these cities and individuals to connect the emperor to these particular deities suggests an awareness of the imperial patronage of Apollo, Sarapis and Aesculapius. Dio's statement, provided at the beginning of the chapter, also demonstrates knowledge of the emperor's ideology. These provincial numismatic images may have been inspired by imperial coin types, statuary or by the presence of the emperor in the region as he travelled east (for instance, at Pergamum). The imagery often recorded and communicated imperial benefaction, and was thus linked to local demonstrations of status.[336] The adaptation of imperial ideology may

[327] *SNG von Aulock* 2992.

[328] Dr Busso-Peus Nachfolger, Auction 366 (25 October 2000) 584.

[329] *SNG von Aulock* 1472. [330] *BMC Lydia* (Thyatira) 94; Levick 1969: 432.

[331] *AE* 1992, 1412. The inscription records the restoration of a collapsed temple.

[332] *AE* 1962, 40; *SIRIS* 670.

[333] Mrav 2000: 67–97. The Apis bull was linked with Sarapis, since upon death the bull was believed to become Osiris-Apis, a name hellenised to Sarapis (Mrav 2000: 79; Tod 1942: 53–6).

[334] *SIRIS* 499 (erected under Caracalla or Elagabalus); also *SIRIS* 375; and Clauss 2001: 175.

[335] *AE* 1908, 208.

[336] Levick 1969: 427–36. Price 1984: 67 suggests that four of Caracalla's grants of neokoria directly arose from his presence in the cities.

have been performed in the hope of imperial favour, or in recognition of it. Civic élites communicated their privileged position through imagery and language that connected local culture to the princeps and his image. The religious politics of the emperor was a central forum in the negotiations between the emperor and his subjects in the Severan period.

Can we conclusively state that Caracalla was ill? The emperor's patronage of Aesculapius, Sarapis and Apollo may not necessarily prove Dio's statement, but remain powerful circumstantial testimony. These three deities all had associations with healing, and that the emperor should choose to patronise these three deities in particular, and not others, is compelling. Caracalla allegedly intended a similar homage to the temple of Lunus at Carrhae, but was assassinated in AD 217 before this could happen.[337] The religious actions of the emperor may have been motivated by ill health, but would also have served to cement relations between the emperor and provincial cities.[338] The popularity of Caracalla is revealed under his successor. Dio reports that Macrinus took the name Antoninus to assuage the soldiers, and also deified Caracalla.[339] The continuing popularity of Caracalla was one of the factors that assisted Elagabalus in his rise to the throne – he could claim a blood connection.

The material evidence from Caracalla's reign again reflects the multifaceted nature of the imperial image. Though he paid particular homage to Apollo, Aesculapius and Sarapis, the emperor's coinage retained an emphasis on Jupiter, Mars and the personifications traditionally associated with the emperor (Figure 38). One of the most extraordinary things revealed by the hoard analysis is the marked drop in military iconography: victory types only constitute about 2 per cent of the emperor's denarii in the hoard sample. To modern knowledge, Caracalla had no victory arch or monument in Rome. This ancient testimony is in stark contrast to the modern perception of Caracalla as a military man and precursor to the soldier emperors, a theory mainly based on the emperor's short beard and portraiture.[340]

The justification behind Caracalla's rule was heavily reliant on support from the gods; they make up a large percentage of his silver coinage

[337] Hdn. 4.13.3; *SHA M. Ant.* 6.6. Dio merely mentions that the emperor was killed en route from Edessa to Carrhae (Dio 79.5.4). See also Ricci 1982: 179–87.

[338] Harl 1987: 52.

[339] Dio 79.19.2, 79.9.2–3; *SHA Macrinus* 5.9; Hdn. 4.14.5, 5.3.2; Fejfer 1992: 207–19; Gilliam 1969: 284–9.

[340] Hannestad 1988: 284; Meckler 1994: 23; Mennen 2006: 253–7. The idea is also present in the literary accounts, where Caracalla is depicted as being 'one of the soldiers' (Dio 78.13.1–2; Hdn. 4.7.3–7).

(Figure 38). The reason(s) behind the change from Severus (who emphasised military strength) may have been complex, but we can find a precedent in the rule of Commodus. Commodus inherited the throne, and his unpopularity with the senate meant that he was forced to emphasise his divine right to rule.[341] Caracalla found himself in a similar position; inheriting power through his father, he murdered Geta at the beginning of his reign and faced antagonism in the senate. The presentation of Caracalla's strained relations with the senate may be exaggerated, but he nonetheless was in need of a source of support.[342] He found it in the divine, and his patronage of provincial cults formed a large part of his public image. Justification of imperial power through divine sanction would develop even further under Elagabalus, an emperor whose claim to the throne was even more tenuous.

[341] Hekster 2002: 198. [342] Sillar 2001: 407–23.

5 | Elagabalus, *summus sacerdos Elagabali*

After the death of Caracalla in AD 217 the Severan dynasty was interrupted. Caracalla's praetorian prefect Macrinus seized imperial power and appointed his son Diadumenian as Caesar. The break in dynasty did not last long: Macrinus was soon overthrown in favour of Marcus Aurelius Antoninus, later nicknamed Elagabalus.[1] This selection was not entirely by chance: Elagabalus was a young priest in the Syrian city of Emesa, whose grandmother Julia Maesa was the sister of Julia Domna. Elagabalus may have spent some time at the imperial court under Caracalla; his mother Julia Soaemias is mentioned among the equestrian wives in the epigraphic record of the saecular games in AD 204.[2]

Herodian assigns the Severan women a large role in this transfer of power; in his account Elagabalus' grandmother Julia Maesa is instrumental in convincing the soldiers (the *legio III Gallica* stationed at Raphanae) to support Elagabalus as emperor.[3] Dio, on the other hand, speaks of two individuals responsible for Elagabalus' succession: Eutychianus and Gannys, who reportedly worked in conjunction with some freedmen, soldiers, equestrians and the senators of the city of Emesa.[4] In Dio's account the Severan women have a negligible role: Elagabalus is brought into the military camp without the knowledge of his mother or grandmother.[5] The reality may have been somewhere in between, with the imperial women working in conjunction with the army and other individuals. At this stage Elagabalus was only fourteen.[6]

The justification for overthrowing Macrinus in favour of a boy of fourteen was that Elagabalus was the purported son of Caracalla.[7] This claim highlights Caracalla's enduring popularity with the army.[8] The effort put

[1] Given the popularity of this nickname in the modern world, the emperor shall be referred to throughout as Elagabalus, and the god of Emesa as Elagabal.

[2] Arrizabalaga y Prado 2010: 196; Icks 2008a: 45–50. [3] Hdn. 5.3.2–4.

[4] Dio 79.31.3. On the probability that this Eutychianus was P. Valerius Comazon (praetorian prefect in Elagabalus' reign and a commander in Syria at the time of the emperor's rise to power) see Kettenhofen 1979: 29–31.

[5] Dio 79.30.2–34.8. Dio does record that Maesa and Soaemias prevented the army from fleeing during a battle with Macrinus' forces (79.38.4).

[6] Hdn. 5.3.3. [7] Dio 79.31.3, 79.72.2–3; Hdn. 5.3.10–12.

[8] Also suggested in Aur. Vict. *Caes.* 22.

into publicising the claim no doubt reflects the fact that the genealogy was false. Elagabalus was given Caracalla's name (Marcus Aurelius Antoninus), and his portraits were consciously crafted to recall the deceased emperor.[9] Dio records that Elagabalus was dressed in the clothes Caracalla had worn as a child.[10] The text of his history is fragmentary in this section, but Dio hints that those who undertook to destroy Macrinus were also 'partly persuaded by the Sun-god, whom they call Elagabal'.[11] This god would come to play a significant role in the rule of the second Marcus Aurelius Antoninus. The divine support associated with the emperor had changed again.

The reign of Elagabalus (AD 218–222) is unique in the study of the divine ideologies of the Severan emperors. Elagabalus (or his advisors) took the extraordinary step of bringing the cult stone[12] of the Emesene god Elagabal to Rome. As a result, Elagabalus publicly presented himself not only as emperor and *pontifex maximus*, but also as high priest of the Emesene god. He never went to war, as was traditional for a Roman emperor, although Victory types constitute 13 per cent of his silver coinage in the hoard sample (Figure 56). Elagabalus instead relied heavily on dynastic claims and divine support to justify his position as emperor. But his activities were interpreted as religious excess, and Elagabalus was overthrown in AD 222. A *damnatio memoriae* followed, making any reconstruction of the reign difficult.

Damnatio memoriae is a useful modern term for the sanctions enacted against condemned individuals in the Roman world, but the phrase implies that there was a standard procedure. This suggestion has been repudiated in much recent work; the Romans applied a varying range of sanctions against condemned individuals, rather than employing an overarching system of cultural repression.[13] This was certainly the case for Elagabalus: the erasure of the emperor's portrait and titulature on monuments is arbitrary. Active and continual condemnation also played an important role in the *damnatio* process, and was perhaps as important as visual obliteration. In this context numismatic evidence becomes ever

[9] Harl 1981: 163–84; Johnston 1982: 97–147; Turcan 1984: 535–9. [10] Dio 79.33.3.

[11] Dio 79.33.1. For the possibility that the Emesene deity was an oracular god see Commodian, *Instructiones* 18; Baldwin 1989: 338; Frey 1989: 47; and Hajjar 1990: 2257.

[12] Though *baetyl* is the term commonly employed by modern authors in describing the sacred stone of Emesa, there is no evidence to suggest it was known as such in the ancient world. *Baituloi* were a very specific type of stone which possessed demonic powers (they moved, talked or answered questions); the term was not a blanket one to describe all sacred stones (Gaifman 2008: 37–72; Moore 1903: 198–208; Warren 1990: 205). The word may have derived from beth-el, 'house of god' (Moore 1903: 199). Neither Dio nor Herodian describe the Emesene stone as a *baetyl*.

[13] Flower 2006: xix. On the *damnatio memoriae* of Soaemias (Elagabalus' mother) see Varner 2001: 48–9.

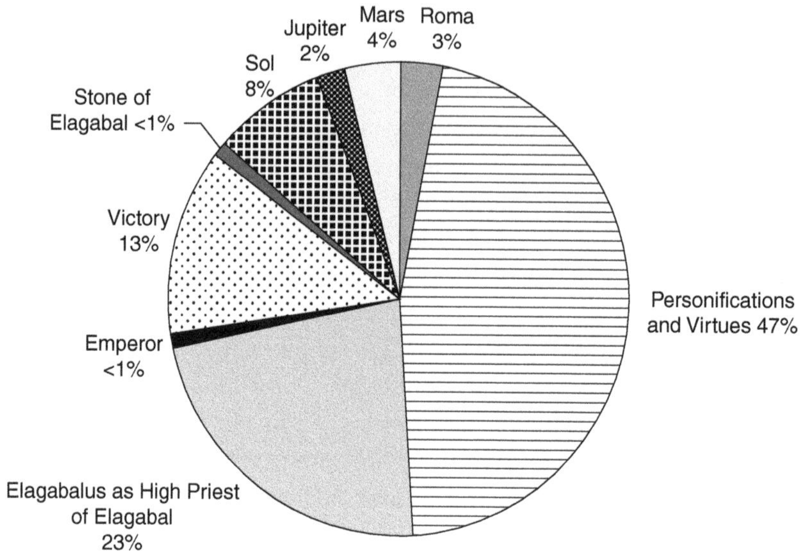

Figure 56: Reverse silver types of Elagabalus as represented in hoards.

more important, since coins were more difficult to destroy than larger monuments. Though there is some evidence for the alteration of coinage struck during Elagabalus' reign (the mutilation of the emperor's portrait, and perhaps even the destruction of certain types), the numismatic evidence remains the most complete record of his rule.

Elagabalus was not the first Severan ruler subjected to *damnatio*, but the process varied in scope. The *damnatio* suffered by Caracalla's brother Geta was widespread and almost exhaustive; as Flower comments, it is hard to imagine that the erasure of the emperor's portrait and titulature was not the result of official initiative.[14] Severus' prefect Plautianus and Caracalla's short-lived wife Plautilla also underwent drastic mutilation in the material record, memorial sanctions which can be seen today on the *portus* of the *argentarii* in Rome.[15] *Damnatio memoriae* was also enacted against Didius Julianus, Pescennius Niger, Clodius Albinus, Macrinus, Diadumenian, and Elagabalus' mother Julia Soaemias.[16] With the exception of Plautianus, these sanctions accompanied the accession of a new emperor and can interpreted as a part of the legitimising process.[17] It is worth observing that a reversal of the *damnatio* could also be employed for dynastic legitimation, as seen in Severus'

[14] Flower 2000: 65; Varner 2004: 198. On the *damnatio* of Geta in Egypt see Hein 1991: 263–98.

[15] Varner 2001: 80–3. [16] Varner 2004: 156.

[17] Plautilla's *damnatio* took place after Caracalla's accession to sole rule in AD 211/12 (Varner 2004: 164).

reversal of Commodus' *damnatio* and his subsequent deification of the previously condemned emperor.

Despite the *damnatio memoriae*, Elagabalus proves an excellent case study for examining the role of the divine in imperial ideology, and the reception of this ideology in the wider empire. Since the god Elagabal's iconography was largely foreign to the Roman world, it is relatively unproblematic to trace the influence of the cult over the four years of Elagabalus' reign. Unlike the earlier Graeco-Roman deities favoured by the Severans (who had numerous cultic centres in the provinces), the cult of Elagabal can be more firmly tied to imperial influence.

The reign of Elagabalus underscores the fact that Roman emperors had to meet the expectations of their subjects. Though the imperial image could vary somewhat, a Roman emperor still essentially had to look and act like a princeps. This tension (between the potential vitality of the imperial image and the expectations of the emperor's subjects) comes to a head under Elagabalus, who deviated from the established norms to such an extent that he was overthrown.

Cultural misunderstanding and tyrannical topos: Elagabalus in ancient and modern literature

Early modern studies of Elagabalus took their cues from the ancient literary evidence, and assessed the reign from a moral viewpoint. More recently research has moved beyond Dio's 'hysterical diatribe'[18] to a more sophisticated understanding of the eastern cultural practices that motivated this emperor.[19] Though a welcome change in attitude, this perspective often neglects the literary motifs deliberately deployed in the ancient accounts.[20] Most recently, Arrizabalaga y Prado has employed a hypercritical approach to the textual evidence with stark results.[21] But while Arrizabalaga y Prado's assessment of the truth of the textual evidence was an overdue reminder to take any ancient account of Elagabalus with a proverbial grain of salt, we might be better served by attempting to understand *why* Elagabalus is presented so poorly in the surviving texts.

[18] Barnes 1970: 31. Barnes goes on to note that not even the *Historia Augusta* could have surpassed Dio's account.

[19] E.g. Frey 1989; Icks 2006: 169–78; Kaizer 2005: 189–90; Pietrzykowski 1986: 1806–25; and Turcan 1997.

[20] For example Frey rightly places the emperor within his eastern context, but remains at times too literal by neglecting the topoi employed in the literary evidence (Frey 1989).

[21] Arrizabalaga y Prado 2010: 55.

While some of the tales contained within the ancient literary tradition might be traced back to Emesene cultic practices, a substantial portion of these accounts also employ common literary motifs to characterise Elagabalus as a tyrant, and more specifically, an oriental tyrant.[22] By not differentiating cultural invention from cultural misunderstanding we run the risk of misrepresenting Elagabalus' reign. Dio's presentation of Elagabalus' sexually deviant behaviour (his circumcision, taking young boys as lovers, defiling a Vestal Virgin) has, for example, strong parallels with Suetonius' presentation of Nero (who also reportedly seduced married women, defiled a Vestal and had sex with young boys, going so far as to castrate one).[23] Indeed, the seduction of young boys, adultery, self-prostitution and acting as a passive partner in homosexual relationships had an established place in Roman invective.[24] Elagabalus did marry a Vestal Virgin, so there is an underlying element of truth to Dio's account, but he presents this truth within the established literary boundaries associated with Roman tyrants. Dio's Elagabalus and Suetonius' Nero possess other parallels: both authors detail the number of murders committed by each emperor and the numerous wives of each.[25] The accounts are not entirely invented. Epigraphic and numismatic evidence, for example, confirms that Elagabalus took a series of wives. But the presentation of Elagabalus, similar to other emperors who had suffered *damnatio*, conforms to certain topoi that correlate with Roman ideas of tyranny.

Just as the emperor's portraiture was mutilated or refashioned after death, so too the literary image of the emperor was transformed. Since favourable accounts of the emperor's reign could not be destroyed as easily as portraiture or large monuments, hostile traditions were probably encouraged as a counter to the positive literature already in circulation.[26] The *Historia Augusta* hints at this phenomenon while describing Elagabalus' treatment of Macrinus and Diadumenian. The *Historia Augusta* records that Elagabalus allegedly forced writers to include unspeakable details in their accounts of the period.[27] The author goes on to note that some of the stories associated with Elagabalus defy belief and may have been 'fabricated by those who wished to vilify Elagabalus in order to curry favour with

22 Alföldy 1976b: 11–21; Icks 2008a: 132–58; Icks 2008b: 476–88; Mader 2005: 131–72; Sommer 2004: 95–110.

23 Suet. *Ner.* 28–9. Self-castration in Rome was a mitigated penalty for criminals (Coleman 1990: 61), something that Dio may have been playing on when he recorded that Elagabalus wished to cut off his genitals (Dio 80.11.1).

24 Barton 1994: 53–4.

25 Dio 80.3.3–9.4; Suet. *Ner.* 33–5.

26 See Ramage 1989: 650 and Varner 2004: 8 on this phenomenon under Domitian.

27 *SHA Heliogab.* 8.4–5.

Alexander'.[28] Whether the *Historia Augusta*'s account is factual here or not, these statements acknowledge the idea that at times negative traditions were actively encouraged by the ruling power.

Just as we cannot use the heavily mutilated portraiture of Elagabalus to reconstruct his physiognomy, we cannot take the posthumously mutilated literary image of the emperor as a reflection of historical fact. Slander and fiction are interwoven with reality; the whole is a testimony to the conscious and continuing damnation of the emperor long after his death. *Damnatio* was not merely an act of obliteration, but involved continuing acts of denigration. The preserved ancient accounts of Elagabalus' reign reflect this.

Herodian provides a more reliable account of Elagabalus' reign than Dio.[29] The superiority of Herodian's account might be attributed to the fact that Dio was in Asia during this period and thus had little first-hand experience of events in Rome.[30] Dio's account of Elagabalus' reign is little more than a collection of anecdotes, a problem perhaps compounded by the fact that the history is preserved through epitome. Some events are absent from the history (for instance the procession of the sacred stone Elagabal from one temple to another in Rome), while other events that Dio narrates seem to be entirely fictive (for instance the emperor's request that doctors fashion him a vagina).[31]

Close examination of Dio's history of Elagabalus' reign reveals a mixture of reliable evidence and literary exaggeration, a combination reflected in the structure of the account. Dio rarely gives Elagabalus his official name (Marcus Aurelius Antoninus) but instead employs a series of derogatory labels: 'Pseudoantoninus', the 'Assyrian', 'Sardanapalus' and 'Tiberinus' (the last reportedly created after the emperor's body was thrown into the Tiber).[32] These names are introduced to the reader at the beginning of Dio's account, setting the mood for the rest of the book. Despite this, the initial sections of Dio's account seem to be based on historical fact, or, at the very least, correlate with other evidence. The emperor's journey to Antioch (80.1.1), his contact with the senate (80.2.1) and his sojourn in Nicomedia (80.3.1–2) all read like a reasonable historical account. Elagabalus' position as consul (80.8.2) is confirmed by epigraphic and numismatic evidence, as are his numerous marriages (80.9).[33] Dio then goes on to mention the

[28] *SHA Heliogab.* 30.8. [29] Bowersock 1975: 229–36.
[30] Arrizabalaga y Prado 2010: 32; Millar 1964: 168. [31] Dio 80.16.7.
[32] Dio 80.1.1. The Assyrian was another name for Sardanapalus (Trapp 1997: 126 n.4).
[33] Elagabalus' marriages are discussed below. On Elagabalus as consul see *AE* 1996, 1247 (consul); *AE* 2001, 938 (twice consul); *AE* 2001, 2165 (three times consul); *AE* 2000, 1203 (four times consul).

'irregularities' surrounding the god Elagabal and the god's marriage (80.11), which reads like a misunderstood account of the emperor's eastern cultic practices rather than pure invention.

Dio's account then changes dramatically.[34] The emperor 'Sardanapalus' is characterised as sexually licentious and perverse. He is presented as effeminate, going so far as to desire a sex change.[35] This portrayal is effected through anecdote, with Dio detailing the emperor's nocturnal activities at brothels (80.13.2–3), his participation in chariot races (80.14.2), his infatuation with a Carian slave Hierocles (80.15.1) and a Smyrnian named Zoticus (80.16.1). This method of treatment continues until Elagabalus' death (80.17.2).

No comparable section can be found in Herodian, who never refers to the emperor as Sardanapalus. Dio's choice of name here is significant: Sardanapalus was the legendary last king of Assyria, who lived in luxury with his harem and female attendants.[36] The ancient vision of this final, effeminate king of Persia was dependant on Ctesias' *Persica*. Ctesias' account is now lost, but glimpses of his creation are preserved by other authors.[37] Athenaeus, contemporary with the Severan period, makes specific mention of Ctesias in his description of Sardanapalus:

> … he [Arbaces] saw the king with his face covered with white lead and bejewelled like a woman, combing purple wool in the company of his concubines and sitting among them with knees uplifted, his eyebrows blackened, wearing a woman's dress and having his beard shaved close and his face rubbed with pumice…[38]

Athenaeus might also have included a discussion of Sardanapalus in his work *On the Kings of Syria*.[39] The quote above would be recognisable to readers of Dio, who records that Elagabalus worked with wool and painted his eyes with white lead and alkanet (80.14.4). It is no coincidence that Dio, the only ancient author to give Elagabalus the name 'Sardanapalus', should take pains to emphasise the emperor's effeminacy and sexual deviation. These characteristics place Elagabalus outside the traditional values of the Roman élite and categorises the emperor as a tyrant.[40]

Dio's choice of Sardanapalus was probably not by chance: tales of the Persian king were traditionally employed as a commentary upon contemporary

34 From 80.13.1. 35 Dio 80.16.7. 36 Ahmed 1968: 43; Streck 1916: 386.

37 Sardanapalus is not mentioned in Photius' summary of Ctesias' work.

38 Ath. *Deip.* 528f.; also Diod. Sic. 2.24.1. For the date of Athenaeus see Braund 2000: 517 and Whitmarsh 2007: 29. On Athenaeus' vision of oriental 'female-kings' see Gambato 2000: 227–30.

39 Ath. *Deip.* 5.211 = *FGrH* 166 F 1, with discussion in Braund 2000: 514–22.

40 Icks 2008a: 138; Sommer 2004: 100–1.

political situations.[41] Dio Chrysostom had used the figure in his discussion of kingship and tyranny, noting that Sardanapalus had become a byword for the latter.[42] The Christian author Clement of Alexandria observed that Sardanapalus embodied the fourth type of kingship, one that only followed desires.[43] The Assyrian king was symbolic of luxury, wealth and hedonism in many works.[44] He was also frequently contrasted with Alexander the Great.[45] As discussed in the previous chapter, Caracalla styled himself as a new Alexander, and Dio might have been playing on the existing Alexander and Sardanapalus dichotomy in his history of Caracalla and Elagabalus. His use of the character of Sardanapalus is selective; the emphasis is on the effeminacy and 'eastern' character of the emperor, not on luxury and indulgence.

It is likely that in this latter section Dio relied upon slander that was associated with Elagabalus after his death. Severus Alexander's coup in AD 222 required the justification of a new régime, and this focused on the faults of his predecessor. This justification through denigration is also apparent from documentary evidence. A horoscope found at Oxyrhynchus from the late third century describes Elagabalus as a κόρυφος or 'catamite', while another giving planetary tables describes the emperor as 'unholy little Antoninus'.[46] Philostratus records that the sophist Aelian composed an 'indictment of Gynnis' targeted at Elagabalus after the emperor had been deposed.[47] Gynnis meant a 'womanish man', a title that recalls Dio's vision of an effeminate emperor.

Herodian may have been aware of this diatribe against the emperor, though unlike Dio, he chooses to explain the emperor's stranger activities by casting them as a product of Emesene culture. This fits well with Herodian's overall theme: Elagabalus is an emperor who embodies a foreign *paideia*, which he attempts to instil in his cousin Severus Alexander.[48] Herodian spends a great deal of time providing background information on Emesa for his readers, and explains the perceived effeminacy of

41 For an analysis of this phenomenon in Cicero see Schneider 2000: 119–27.

42 Dio Chrys. *Or.* 62.5.

43 Clem. Al. *Strom.* 1.24.159.1–2. Sardanapalus is also mentioned at 2.20.118.6.1.

44 Aristid. *Or.* 2.240, 34.61; Dio Chrys *Or.* 64.5.10; Lucian *Iupp. confutatus* 16.19, *Iupp. trag.* 48.18, *Charon* 23.8, *Men.* 18.9, *Rhetorum prae.* 11.8, *Syr. D.* 40.9, *Dial. mort.* 3.1.7, 3.2.12, 6.2.6, 6.2.11, 6.6.9; Maximus of Tyre *Or.* 2.9, 4.9, 7.7 (with discussion in Trapp 1997: 65 n. 22), 14.2, 15.8, 29.1, 32.3, 32.9; Justin *Apol.* 2.7.3.8; Ath. *Deip.* 294e, 335f, 336f, 412d, 528f; Alciphron *Ep.* 3.16.1.3; Them. *Or.* 26 (331); Julian *Ep.* 82.126.

45 Lenfant 2001: 54–5.

46 *P.Oxy.* XLVI 3298–9. The title 'catamite' may also have been present in other papyri (Rea 1968: 60, 62 n.2). See also Lukaszewicz 1992: 43–6 who suggests 'virgin-rapist' as an alternative interpretation of this unusual Greek word.

47 Philostr. *V S* 625.

48 Sidebottom 1998: 2810.

Elagabalus in these terms. Herodian notes that Elagabalus' clothing was barbarous and, to the Roman mind, more appropriate for a woman, so the emperor decided to send a portrait ahead of him to Rome. This way, when he finally arrived in the city the inhabitants would find nothing strange in his appearance (5.5.5–6). Herodian does mention the emperor's use of make-up (5.6.10, 5.8.1), and the promotion of actors and charioteers (5.7.7), but these characteristics are certainly not developed to the same extent as in Dio's account.

In his account of Elagabalus, more than anywhere else, Herodian displays his independence from Dio. Herodian is the only surviving author to provide a description of the sacred stone, the temple of Emesa and the procession of Elagabal between the two temples in Rome.[49] These fit with Herodian's tendency to include numerous religious digressions within his work, and serve to highlight to his readers the foreign nature of the emperor's *paideia*. Some have seen Herodian's religious digressions as a reflection of the religious milieu in which Herodian wrote, but it is worth noting that the author himself justifies these digressions (particularly on cultic practices in the city of Rome) 'in view of the lack of knowledge about this among some Greeks'.[50] Sidebottom argues that here Herodian is playing a game with his élite Greek audience: by explaining various obvious and well-known facts the readers can indulge themselves in the pretence that the Roman Empire is a foreign monarchy of which they know very little.[51]

Herodian differs from Dio in the prominence he gives the imperial women in Elagabalus' reign, particularly Julia Maesa. For Herodian, Maesa was the power behind the throne.[52] Maesa is introduced to the reader before Elagabalus.[53] Maesa and a circle of advisors manage the imperial affairs (5.5.1), it is Maesa who pressures Elagabalus to conform to Roman dress (5.5.5), and it is she who convinces the emperor to adopt Severus Alexander as his successor (5.7.1). Maesa also checks any attempts against the young Caesar's life (5.8.3), and eventually survives Elagabalus' assassination to influence the reign of Severus Alexander (5.8.10). The rôle of Maesa, and later of Mamaea during the rule of Severus Alexander, brings an intriguing tension into the history. Herodian assigns both Mamaea and Maesa a significant role in attempting to instil in Elagabalus and Severus

[49] See the sections beginning from Hdn. 5.3.4 and 5.6.6.

[50] Hdn. 1.11.1. For interpretations of these religious digressions see Whittaker LCL xix; Alföldi 1971: 215–18 and Zimmermann 1999b: 232.

[51] Sidebottom 1998: 2823–4. [52] Kettenhofen 1979: 23–8. [53] Hdn. 5.3.2.

Alexander a sense of Greek *paideia*, and yet the actions of Mamaea presented by Herodian indicate that she herself did not possess this quality. Thus, as Sidebottom illustrates, Alexander's *paideia* is undermined by the very person who was trying to instil it.[54]

Herodian's Elagabalus embodies the foreign, which he juxtaposes against a more traditional concept of *paideia*, a dichotomy embodied in the struggle between Elagabalus and Maesa over Severus Alexander's education.[55] While Elagabalus desired his young cousin to join him 'in his own pursuits of leaping and dancing, and to share the priesthood by wearing the same dress and following the same practices', Maesa removed him from the emperor's influence and trained Severus Alexander 'in the exercise of self-control, introducing him to the wrestling schools and manly exercises, and gave him both a Latin and a Greek education'.[56]

It is worth observing here that there was no great increase in the 'visibility' of the imperial women in this period. Maesa and Soaemias continue the numismatic and epigraphic precedent established by their predecessors.[57] The hoard sample suggests that 18% of the silver coinage of this period was struck for Julia Maesa. This is approximately the same proportion of silver coinage that was struck for Domna under Severus (17%), for Domna under Caracalla's sole rule (16%), and for Mamaea during Severus Alexander's reign (17%).[58] The similarity in ratio across the Severan dynasty suggests that the Roman mint struck a set proportion of coinage for the empresses, perhaps assigning them a workshop within the mint.[59] The possible influence (or not) of these women is thus unlikely to be reflected in the numismatic evidence. If the mint employed a standard ratio, it would not reflect any variation in the power of different imperial women. The divergence between official media and the literary evidence of this period is also apparent when one compares the ancient accounts of licentiousness with the significant quantity of Elagabalus' coinage that

54 Sidebottom 1998: 2811.

55 Sidebottom 1998: 2810; Sommer 2004: 110, though Sommer's decision to connect this with the Sassanian invasions is less certain.

56 Hdn. 5.7.5.

57 Benario 1959: 9–14; Kettenhofen 1979: 75–173; Kosmetatou 2002: 398–414. It is apparent that from the Antonine period imperial women became visually more prominent, but this was as a result of their associations with the idea of dynasty, rather than an increase in power. See Baharal 2000: 318–27; Duncan-Jones 2006: 223–8; Keltanen 2002: 105–46 and Rowan in press.

58 For more on the coinage of the Severan women see Rowan 2011: 241–73.

59 Duncan-Jones 2006: 223 suggests that there was a new production template at the Roman mint from the reign of Hadrian, resulting in an increased amount of coinage being struck in the name of the empresses.

proclaimed the benefits of the régime: personifications and virtues constitute 47% of the emperor's coinage (Figure 56).[60]

The youth of Elagabalus and his successor Severus Alexander makes one question the degree of control held by the *consilium principis* or advisory council in the later Severan period.[61] Whether the imperial women had a central rôle in the governing process, as suggested by Herodian, is very difficult to establish since the mechanisms of imperial representation did not reflect the true governing forces behind a particular emperor. One must wonder whether the *consilium* supported the worship of the god Elagabal, and whether the god's introduction to Rome was part of a planned decision to fundamentally alter the basis of Roman imperial power, rather than the whim of a 'tyrannical' emperor.[62]

Much of the work on the life of Elagabalus in the *Historia Augusta* has been concerned with the reliability of the account, though recently scholars have begun to look at the work from a different perspective.[63] The *Vita* possesses a blend of the topoi present in both Herodian and Dio. The first part of the life is generally considered more historical than the rest, and may have been based on the account of Marius Maximus.[64] The account then falls into anecdote, manipulated to present the last of the Antonine emperors as a despot.[65]

While many of Elagabalus' religious activities in the *Historia Augusta* are de-contextualised to serve in the literary construction of a tyrant, the *Vita* may also have been used as a commentary on the religious politics of the fourth century.[66] The *Historia Augusta* notes that as soon as Elagabalus entered Rome

> he established Elagabal as a god on the Palatine Hill close to the imperial palace; and he built him a temple, to which he desired to transfer the emblem of the Great Mother, the fire of Vesta, the Palladium, the shields of the Salii, and all that the Romans held sacred, purposing that no god might be worshipped at Rome save only Elagabalus. He declared, furthermore, that the religions of the Jews and Samaritans

[60] Of these virtues and personifications Fides was the most abundant, constituting 9% of the emperor's silver coinage in the hoard sample. Libertas types constituted 8%, Providentia 6%, Salus 5%, Abundantia 4%, and Liberalitas 4%. Other types of lesser frequency included Fortuna, Pax, Annona and Hilaritas.

[61] Crook 1955: 86 refuses to discuss the rôle of the imperial council under Macrinus and Elagabalus 'not for lack of evidence ... but because in the serious business of governing the Empire it is a mere lacuna'. This is indicative of the continued biases that have shaped modern studies of Elagabalus' reign.

[62] Arrizabalaga y Prado 2010: 261.

[63] For example Hönn 1911 and Optendrenk 1969. For more recent work see Mader 2005: 131–72.

[64] Barnes 1970: 30–1; Barnes 1972: 53–74; Barnes 1978: 57.

[65] Mader 2005: 131.

[66] Mader 2005: 136.

and the rites of the Christians must also be transferred to this place, in order that the priesthood of Elagabalus might include the mysteries of every form of worship.[67]

The overtones of monotheism here, combined with the fact that the *Vita* contains an epilogue addressed to the emperor Constantine, has led some to postulate that more than the actions of Elagabalus are represented.[68] The author has utilised the *Vita Heliogabali* to comment in a veiled manner upon the emperor Constantine's policies.[69]

Many of the nicknames present in Dio are repeated in the *Historia Augusta*.[70] The nickname 'Pseudo-Antoninus' is also reflected in the erasure of Elagabalus' titulature. In many acts of epigraphic *damnatio memoriae* only the name 'Antoninus' is erased (leaving simply *Marcus Aurelius*), suggesting that there is some truth to the *Historia Augusta*'s claim that the name Antoninus was erased from public records by order of the senate.[71] Indeed, the selective destruction of this single word, across a wide geographical area and in both Greek and Latin, suggests that much of the rhetoric damning the emperor after his death was connected with the idea that he was considered unworthy to bear the Antonine name.

The cult of Elagabal in the provinces

After defeating Macrinus in AD 218, Elagabalus and the imperial retinue remained for a period at Antioch before making their way overland to Rome.[72] The journey lasted over a year: Macrinus was defeated in June AD 218 and Elagabalus arrived at Rome sometime in the second half of AD 219.[73] The imperial retinue included the sacred stone Elagabal.[74] Though

[67] *SHA Heliogab*. 3.4. [68] *SHA Heliogab*. 34.1.

[69] Icks 2008a: 156; Ruggini 1991: 123–46; Turcan 1988: 38–52; Turcan 1997: 150–9; Zinsli 2005: 117–38.

[70] *SHA Heliogab*. 27.5, 1.5.

[71] *AE* 2001, 1915; *AE* 1999, 1529; *AE* 1996, 1247; *AE* 1986, 684; *AE* 1985, 976; *AE* 1981, 1910; *AE* 1973, 412; *AE* 1967, 653; *AE* 1966, 262; *AE* 1948, 212; *AE* 1911, 139; *AE* 1911, 138; *AE* 1889, 150.

[72] Dio 80.1.1, 80.3.2.

[73] *CIL* 6.31162, found in Rome, was dedicated on 29 September *ob reditum domini nostri*. Eutropius records that the emperor arrived in Rome in July AD 219 (Eutr. 8.22), also suggested by *RIC* IV.2 *Elagabalus* 35–6. Frey 1989: 76 and Thirion 1968 date this coin issue to the second half of AD 219.

[74] Robert 1964: 80. The representation of the Emesene god on coins struck early in Elagabalus' reign, in addition to Herodian's discussion of the god's worship at Nicomedia, attest to the fact that the cult statue accompanied the new emperor. Though the cultic stone must then have been absent from Emesa during Elagabalus' reign, the city's provincial coins persist in showing the stone inside the local civic temple (e.g. *BMC Syria* (Emesa) 17).

there was a tradition in Rome of importing foreign cults, no other Severan emperor is known to have transported the cult statue of his patron deity to the city. Under Elagabalus not only was the cult statue removed from its provincial location, it was conveyed in a ceremonial procession through the empire.

After leaving Antioch, Elagabalus travelled to Bithynia and spent the winter at Nicomedia before travelling through Thrace, Moesia and Pannonia to Italy.[75] The precise route taken by Elagabalus is difficult to determine. The most recent proposal is that the emperor travelled from Antioch to Alexandria Iskenderun, then through Hierapolis-Castabala, Flaviopolis, Anazarbus, Mopsus, Adana, Tarsus, Faustinopolis, Tyana, Taurus, Archelais, Ancyra, Juliopolis, and Prusias ad Hypium to Nicomedia.[76] From Nicomedia it is postulated that the emperor travelled through Hadrianopolis, Serdica, Mysia, Pannonia, Aquileia, Padua, Bologna (?) and Arezzo (?) to Rome.[77] This route has largely been reconstructed through numismatic and epigraphic evidence referring to the emperor or his god. However, mention of the emperor (or his tutelary deity) in an inscription or on a coin does not necessarily equate with the presence of the princeps in the area.[78] Taking the representation of the god Elagabal on provincial coinage as an indication of the route of the emperor is fraught with problems. The emperor was a frequent subject of local coinage and art, whether he was present in the vicinity or not. We should apply a similar caution to the sacred stone of Emesa. The precise route of the emperor, then, remains unknown.

The god Elagabal on imperial coinage

Imperial coins released at the beginning of Elagabalus' reign (AD 218–219) show the sacred stone of Emesa in a *quadriga* (Figure 57).[79] Though Mattingly and Thirion attributed these coins to a mint in Antioch, they may have been struck at Nicomedia, or by a mint that travelled with the emperor as he made his way to Rome.[80] Although this image of the Emesene stone has a strong association with the reign of Elagabalus today, the type proves rare in the archaeological record (Figure 56). Only thirteen examples showing the Emesene stone were found in the hoards, a tiny fraction of the

[75] Dio 80.3.1; Hdn 5.5.3. [76] Arrizabalaga y Prado 2010: 122; Arrizabalaga y Prado 2003: 85.
[77] Turcan 1997: 89–95. [78] Arrizabalaga y Prado 2003: 63. [79] *RIC* IV.2 *Elagabalus* 194–7.
[80] Original attribution to Antioch: Mattingly, Sydenham et al. 1938: 26; Pink 1934: 13; Thirion 1968: 14. Nicomedia or a travelling mint: Butcher 1988: 68–9; Mattingly 1950: ccxli–ccxlii; McAlee 2007: 287.

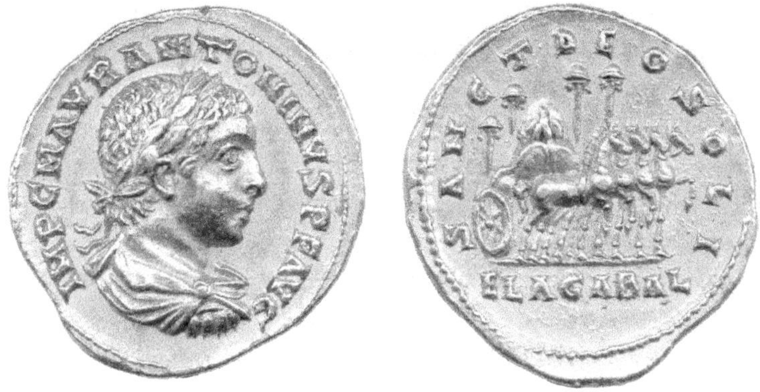

Figure 57: Aureus of Elagabalus with the sacred Emesene stone in a *quadriga* and the legend SANCT DEO SOLI ELAGABAL.

8,582 silver coins struck for Elagabalus in the sample.[81] This is surprising, and one must wonder whether coins showing the sacred stone of Emesa were recalled and melted down as part of the wider *damnatio memoriae* after Elagabalus' death.[82] This *damnatio* took the unprecedented step of including the emperor's tutelary god. Dio records that the god was banished from Rome.[83] Epigraphic evidence reveals that the god's name was erased from inscriptions along with the name of the emperor.[84] Given the close alignment between the emperor and his deity (resulting in the nickname Elagabalus), an associated *damnatio* of the god becomes understandable.

That the archaeological record may not reflect the original number of coins struck showing the Emesene stone is suggested by the relatively large number of surviving dies. Unfortunately, many hoard publications do not provide images of every coin, so one cannot study the dies of those specimens found within the hoard sample. However, an idea of the number of dies used for the issue can be gauged by examining examples in museums and on the market. A sample of sixty reveals thirty-seven individual dies (Appendix 2). This high ratio of dies to known specimens suggests that many more coins may have been struck than now survive. Buttrey has observed that Pescennius Niger's coinage has a survival rate of less than two pieces per die, and concluded that this was because Severus had melted

[81] This included one example of *RIC* IV.2 *Elagabalus* 65, two specimens of RIC IV.2 *Elagabalus* 144 (both from the Reka-Devnia hoard), six of *RIC* IV.2 *Elagabalus* 195, and four of *RIC* IV.2 *Elagabalus* 197 (all four from the Reka-Devnia hoard).

[82] On the destruction of an emperor's coinage see Dio 60.22.3, 78.12.6. [83] Dio 79.21.2.

[84] Examples of *damnatio* targeting the god of Emesa include *AE* 2001, 938 (Assisi, Italy); *AE* 2001, 2165 (Moesia Inferior); *AE* 1985, 976 (Altaua, Mauretania Caesarinis); *AE* 1997, 160 (Rome).

down many of Niger's pieces.[85] A similar situation might obtain for the coins of Elagabalus showing the Emesene stone on a *quadriga*.

The original quantity of the *quadriga* coinage thus becomes difficult to estimate. From what little evidence survives, however, a few conclusions can be drawn. The coins were probably struck to mark the procession of the emperor and his god to Rome. Local Emesene coinage never showed the sacred stone on a *quadriga*. The usurper Uranius Antoninus struck the type after Elagabalus' reign, but he was clearly imitating Roman types.[86] The creation of the new iconography showing the stone in a *quadriga* thus probably reflects an actual historical occurrence: the transfer of the stone to Rome. The unusually long reverse legend on these types (SANCT DEO SOLI ELAGABAL) was likely the result of a need to identify this otherwise foreign iconography to its audience.

The iconography of Elagabal in the provinces

The stone on the *quadriga* type also appears on provincial coinage.[87] As mentioned above, the emergence of the Emesene stone as a provincial coin type has been interpreted as an indication of the processional route taken by the emperor and his god to Rome.[88] However, a closer examination of these coins illustrates that this interpretation can no longer hold.

Aelia Capitolina struck types showing Elagabalus on the obverse, with a frontal *quadriga* on the reverse bearing the Emesene cultic stone (Figure 58).[89] This type was also struck with an obverse bearing the busts of both Elagabalus and his Caesar Severus Alexander. The stone of Emesa may also have been shown between two legionary standards.[90] Alexandria released coinage showing the stone in a frontal *quadriga*, striking the type in the name of Elagabalus, and for Aquilia Severa.[91] Anazarbus in Cilicia minted a slight variation on this type, showing the horses of the *quadriga*

[85] Buttrey 1992: xxii

[86] Baldus 1971: pl. VII no. 12, pl. XIII no. 69. The imitation of other imperial coin types (for instance, Philip's saecular games series, Baldus 1971: pl. VIII no. 13), suggests that it is unlikely that Uranius was influenced by local iconography, though the decision to show the Roman type of the Emesene god was probably intentional.

[87] Icks 2009: 111–20. [88] Arrizabalaga y Prado 2003: 59–100; Robert 1964: 80.

[89] Meshorer 1989: 133a-d, 143–143a; *BMC Judea* (Aelia Capitolina) 85–90; *SNG ANS* 625.

[90] Kadman 1956: 51 no. 152. This type is only known from a single specimen in the collection of Sainte Anne in Jerusalem. The same coin is mentioned in Meshorer 144, who identified it as an eagle between two standards (Meshorer 1989: 47). However Meshorer's explanation fails to account for the conical object seen behind the eagle on this particular coin. The poor condition of the example prohibits absolute identification, but Kadman's identification is preferable.

[91] *BMC Alexandria* 1520; ANS 1944.100.64317, 1944.100.64371; Emmett 2923, 3012.

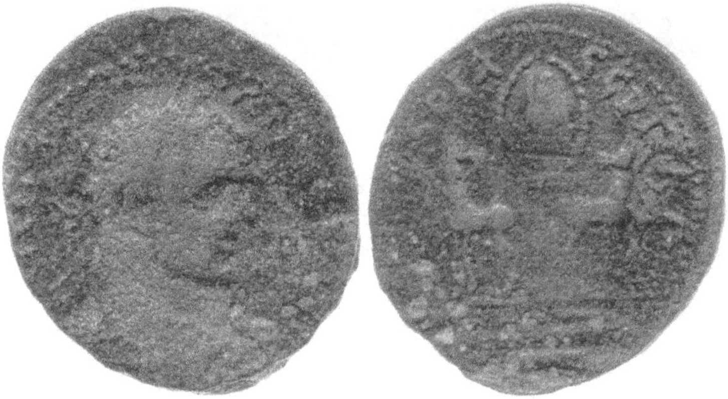

Figure 58: Coin of Aelia Capitolina showing the Emesene stone in a *quadriga*.

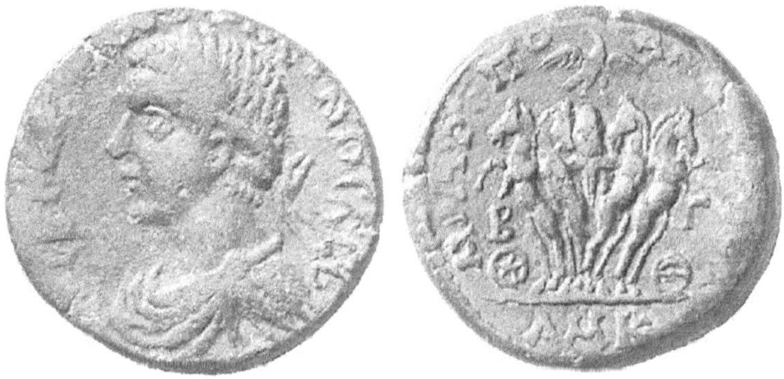

Figure 59: Coin of Anazarbus showing the Emesene stone in a *quadriga*.

rearing upwards, and the eagle above the sacred stone instead of decorating the front of it (Figure 59).[92] An almost identical image is found on coinage of Hierapolis-Castabala.[93] Juliopolis in Bithynia represented the stone and *quadriga* in profile, on a coin type struck in the name of Elagabalus' wife Julia Paula.[94] Laodicea ad Mare released a frontal *quadriga* type.[95] Neapolis in Samaria merged the sacred stone and *quadriga* with a local icon, Mount Gerizim (Figure 60).[96]

The provincial coins display almost identical images, but the dates of the issues vary, and vary in such a way that they cannot be connected with the journey of the emperor to Rome. The type of Juliopolis, struck in the name of Julia Paula, must be dated after AD 219 (the year when the marriage between Julia Paula and Elagabalus took place).[97] The coins of Alexandria

[92] Ziegler 1993: 393–4. [93] Robert 1964: 79, no. 41. [94] Price 1971: 127 no. 11.
[95] Hecht 1968: 35 no. 25; ANS 1944.100.66478. [96] *BMC Palestine* (Neapolis) 101–2.
[97] Price 1971: 127.

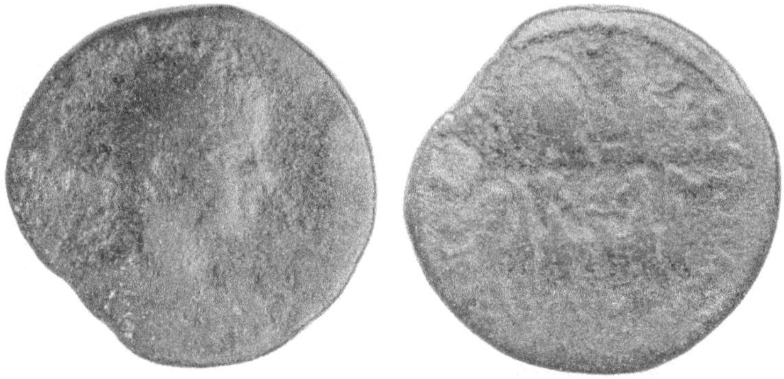

Figure 60: Coin of Neapolis showing the Emesene stone in a *quadriga* and Mt. Gerizim.

date to AD 221, indicated by the local dating system employed on the coinage as well as the fact that the type was struck for Aquilia Severa.[98] The coins of Aelia Capitolina must date from AD 221 or early 222, since they show the portrait of Severus Alexander, who was made Caesar on 26 June AD 221.[99] On those coins that remain the portrait of Elagabalus is mature, not the boyish image seen on earlier imperial coins (though the poor preservation of some of the specimens makes any definitive statement difficult). The dates of these coins indicate that they probably do not mark the procession of the god Elagabal to Rome in AD 218. Indeed, given the presence of the image in cities like Alexandria (which the emperor never visited), an alternative explanation is necessary.

Remarkably, nearly all the coins (with the exception of those from Juliopolis) show the *quadriga* frontally, whereas imperial coinage almost exclusively shows the *quadriga* in profile.[100] The coins of Anazarbus and Hierapolis-Castabala are so alike that one is tempted to see them as products of the same travelling mint (that is, the work of specialist die-engravers who travelled through the provinces supplying their services to numerous cities).[101] Both cities were in Cilicia; hence this theory is attractive.

The similarity of the iconography on the provincial coins suggests that the types were all inspired by a common imagery. Herodian, who records that a painting of Elagabalus was created while the emperor was in Nicomedia, provides a possible candidate.

[98] Elagabalus married Aquilia Severa (a Vestal Virgin) in AD 220. He divorced her in AD 221 in favour of Annia Faustina, but had returned to Aquilia by the end of AD 221 (Frey 1989: 87–92; Icks 2006: 174).

[99] On the identification of the second bust as Severus Alexander see Meshorer 1989: 47.

[100] Meshorer 1989: 49.

[101] For travelling mints see Kraft 1972.

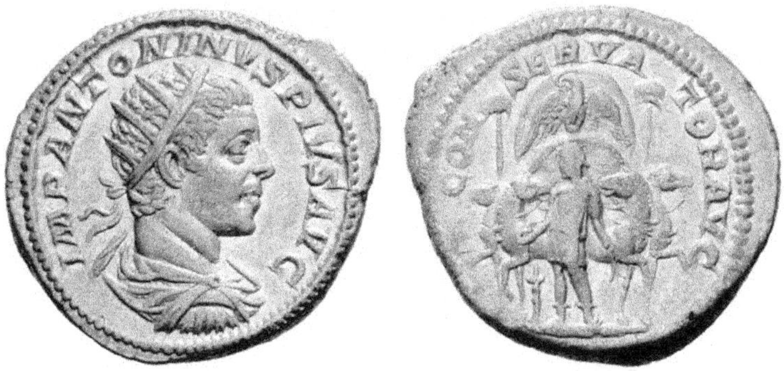

Figure 61: Antoninianus of Elagabalus with the Emesene stone in a *quadriga* and Elagabalus sacrificing in front. The reverse legend reads CONSERVATOR AVG.

> ... he [Elagabalus] was anxious that the senate and people of Rome should get used to seeing his dress, and to test out their reactions to the sight before he arrived. So an enormous picture was painted of him as he appeared in public performing as a priest. Also in the picture was a portrait of the Emesene god, to whom he was represented making a favourable sacrifice. The picture was sent to Rome with orders that it should hang right in the middle of the senate house, very high up over the head of the statue of Victory.[102]

Zimmermann suspected that Herodian invented this painting in order to strengthen his discussion of the emperor's strange and exotic clothing, which the author uses to underscore the 'otherness' of Elagabalus.[103] Though Herodian may have tailored his account to flag the foreignness of the emperor, we need not automatically dismiss the notion that public images and paintings of the emperor as high priest of Elagabal were sent to Rome and the rest of the empire. Baldus was the first to connect Herodian's description of a painting with a coin released by the imperial mint showing Elagabalus in the act of sacrifice, with the Emesene stone on a *quadriga* behind him (Figure 61).[104] The emperor's stance, holding a branch and *patera*, echoes other imagery that portrays the young emperor as priest of the god (discussed below). Baldus suggested that what was shown on the coin was an approximate representation of what was on the imperial painting, and that this was the source of the similar iconography seen throughout the empire. We cannot be certain that this was the precise image. But the similarities between the representations of the god Elagabal across the empire suggest that there was imagery circulating, which Herodian played with in his work to demonstrate the character of the emperor.

[102] Hdn. 5.5.6. [103] Zimmermann 1999b: 224–30. [104] Baldus 1989: 469–72.

Portraits of emperors regularly circulated throughout the empire, in sculpture, paintings and other visual media, though it is uncertain how commonly these portraits included a deity.[105] If the official image of Elagabalus included the Emesene stone, it would explain the close association that developed between the emperor and his god: they were visually linked with each other.

There are variations in the provincial representation of the god as imperial imagery was incorporated into local culture. The coins of Neapolis combine the god with Mt Gerizim, making the image a statement of the connection of the city to the imperial power. The coins of Laodicea add a crescent to the scene. Meshorer is undoubtedly correct in attributing this variance to the celestial aspect of the Emesene deity: it was a sun god, which could then have associations with the moon.[106] That the god Elagabal only appears on the coinage of select cities suggests that its promulgation in this manner was voluntary.

The type from Juliopolis, showing the *quadriga* in profile, is to current knowledge unique among the provincial representations of the stone. The type is extremely similar to that released by the imperial mint. Price observed that imperial coin types might have influenced the mint of Juliopolis.[107] Elagabalus likely had an active mint while he wintered in Nicomedia, relatively close to Juliopolis (both cities were in Bithynia). The city may have obtained its image of the Emesene god directly from the imperial coins; hence this unique provincial representation.

Since the date and geography of many of these coins prohibits association with the journey of the emperor Elagabalus to Rome, another explanation of the iconography is necessary. There need not be any single event that occasioned their issue, since the coins were struck at different times. Juliopolis' issues, for example, date to the second half of AD 219. Price noted an obverse die link between this coin and others (the emperor on horseback, the emperor holding a legionary standard and spear) and suggested that the coin was part of a series struck to commemorate the marriage of the young emperor.[108] Likewise, the appearance of the Emesene god on coinage of Alexandria in AD 221 may have been part of a series of coins struck to celebrate the marriage to Aquilia Severa. If this was the case, these coins would provide valuable testimony to the close association between the emperor and the god – one evoked the other.

[105] Albertson 2004: 259–306. [106] Frey 1989: 45–6; Meshorer 1989: 49.
[107] Price 1971: 127. [108] Price 1971: 127.

But the portrayal of the Emesene god may also have reflected the introduction of the Emesene cult to the cities concerned. Civic coinage focused on local cults, events and culture, as well as the relationship of the city to the emperor.[109] Consequently, the introduction of the iconography of Elagabal to the coinage of a city may well signify the introduction of the Emesene cult. This explanation accords with the fact that many of these coins were struck late in Elagabalus' reign: the introduction of a foreign cult would not have been immediate.

Other evidence attests to the worship of the god Elagabal beyond the city of Rome. Sardis, for example, celebrated a festival called the *Elagabalia* in this period.[110] The *Historia Augusta* also suggests the cult was introduced in Faustinopolis:

> He [Caracalla] has a temple, he has a board of Salii, he has an Antonine brotherhood, he who himself took from Faustina not only her temple but also her name as a goddess – that temple, at least, which her husband had built her in the foot-hills of the Taurus, and in which this man's son Elagabalus Antoninus afterwards made a shrine, either for himself or the Syrian Jupiter (the matter is uncertain) or for the sun.[111]

The temple at Faustinopolis was built in honour of Marcus Aurelius' wife Faustina after she suddenly died in the area in AD 176.[112] The shrine mentioned by the author was probably for the god Elagabal, who was a sun god and the head of the pantheon in Emesa (consequently akin to Jupiter).[113] The god's name, identical to the nickname of the emperor 'Elagabalus', may have created the confusion about the dedicatee of the temple.

The veracity of the *Historia Augusta* here (as elsewhere) is problematic. The ultimate source of this statement (if any) remains unknown.[114] No evidence survives to suggest Caracalla had *sodales* or *salii*, but the shrine in Faustinopolis is mentioned twice in the work, in two different biographies.[115] If the tale is true, the installation of a shrine to Elagabal in a temple of Caracalla would have underlined the connection between one Marcus Aurelius Antoninus and the next. After all, Elagabalus claimed to be the son of Caracalla.

In Pamphylia, a dedication to a sun god on behalf of the *boule* and *demos* is preserved. Close analysis of the inscription reveals an erasure after the

[109] Butcher 2006: 54; Harl 1987: 14; Howgego 2005: 2.

[110] Burrell 2004: 111; Robert 1989: 51–2.

[111] *SHA M. Ant.* 11.6–7; *SHA Marcus Aurelius* 26.4.9.

[112] *SHA Marcus Aurelius* 26.4; Robert 1964: 81–2. [113] Frey 1989: 45.

[114] Meckler 1994: 67.

[115] There were, however, *sodales Antoniniani* for Antoninus Pius and *sodales Aureliani Antoniniani* for Marcus Aurelius (*CIL* 5.3223). Given Caracalla's official name of Marcus Aurelius Antoninus, the author may have been confused.

word *helios*; the traces that remain allow this erasure to be restored as *elegabalō*.[116] That the dedication was made by the *demos* and the *boule* suggests the cult of Elagabal had been officially incorporated into the city; this is not the dedication of an individual.

In AD 221 a *templum* to the god Elagabal was built by the *possessores* of Altaua in Mauretania for the health and prosperity of the emperor.[117] Elagabalus may have settled these *possessores*, and their gratitude to the emperor probably resulted in the construction of a temple or shrine to the favoured god of their patron.

It is thus apparent that the cult of Elagabal spread beyond Rome and Emesa in the years AD 218–222. This was by no means the first time the empire had been exposed to the cult: native Emesenes had been erecting inscriptions to their deity many decades before.[118] The Emesene military cohort in particular has left a significant epigraphic record of cultic activity.[119] The unit was probably formed in AD 167–169 or thereabouts, and spent a significant period of time at Intercisa in Pannonia Inferior.[120] Epigraphic evidence attests to the construction and completion of a temple to Elagabal by the cohort, likely attached to the unit's fort at Intercisa and dedicated on the occasion of the visit of Severus and his two sons to the area in AD 202.[121] Under Septimius Severus there was also Emesene cultic activity in Rome (discussed in more detail below).

The appearance of the cultic stone on the coinage of several provincial cities, however, suggests a rapid spread of the cult as a result of imperial devotion. The implementation of the cult was probably done with the assistance of a widely circulated iconography, which was interpreted at a local level. The reigns of Severus and Caracalla have illustrated the potential impact of the imperial presence on the provincial reception of imperial ideology. The same phenomenon may have continued under Elagabalus. Robert believed that the procession of the emperor through the empire induced many cities to introduce the worship of a god who was held in the highest imperial esteem.[122] Such an explanation does not account for the

[116] Robert 1964: 80; *Bull. Épigr.* 1948, 229.

[117] *AE* 1985, 976. There is also a dedication to Elagabal in Pannonia Inferior (*AE* 1975, 704) but the inscription does not furnish any information about the circumstances in which it was erected.

[118] *AE* 1994, 1285 (Laurium in Germania Inferior); Cumont 1924: 342–5 (Corduba in Spain, AD 171)

[119] *AE* 1975, 704; *AE* 1910, 133; AE 1910, 141; *RIU* 1106–1107, 1230; *RHP* 326. Dedications of the Emesene cohort to Sol: *AE* 1992, 1850 (Numidia, reign of Caracalla); *AE* 1933, 26 (Numidia); *AE* 1933, 47 (Numidia).

[120] Fitz 1972; Mann 1974: 259.

[121] *AE* 1973, 437; *RIU* 1104; Alföldy 1997: 238–9; Fishwick 2000: 318.

[122] Robert 1989: 49–50.

presence of the Emesene god in cities that Elagabalus never visited, such as Alexandria and Aelia Capitolina. However, the obvious devotion of the emperor to the deity may have encouraged cities to introduce the cult in hope of imperial favour, or in gratitude for benefactions received. The adoption of the cult and/or its iconography may also have been motivated by a desire to express a close connection with the ruling power. Alexandria remains a special case since the mint was under imperial control; this may explain the *quadriga* type released by the city.

Herodian suggests that the emperor had an active role in the dissemination of the cult of Elagabal, and records that the emperor issued instructions that the god's name be placed before that of any other god during public sacrifices.[123] Herodian does not specify whether these orders were confined to the magistrates and citizens of Rome, or whether the order applied to the entire empire. His statement, however, is not borne out by the surviving epigraphic evidence. There is not a single example of the god Elagabal preceding other deities in the epigraphic record of votive offerings from this period. Moreover, if the provincial numismatic representations of the god reflected a widespread imperial policy, one would expect more cities to have struck coins showing the sacred Emesene stone.

Radnóti believed that the imperial command mentioned by Herodian was implemented, and points to a dedication set up *deo p[atrio] Soli Ela[gabalo]* by the governor of Raetia, C. Iulius Avitus Alexianus.[124] The inscription is fragmentary and its interpretation is more complicated than appears at first glance. Onomastically, it is likely that Alexianus was an Emesene.[125] It is more likely that Alexianus was acting according to his own local culture, rather than under orders from the emperor. The fact that the dedication is *deo patrio Soli Elagabalo*, to the god of the homeland, argues strongly in favour of this interpretation.[126]

The evidence intimates that the Emesene cult was adopted in the provinces voluntarily. Sardis (which celebrated the *Elagabalia*) was granted its third neokorate under Elagabalus. The city may have adopted Elagabal's worship to win favour with the emperor, in gratitude for the privilege or as

123 Hdn. 5.5.7.

124 Radnóti 1961: 383–412. The inscription was found with several others in Augsburg. It dates to either the reign of Caracalla or Elagabalus (Radnóti 1961: 391–2).

125 Radnóti 1961: 402.

126 This is how the god is described in inscriptions set up by the *Cohors Hemesenorum*, the military unit from Emesa (e.g. AE 1910, 33).

part of the neokorate cult.[127] Given the close association between the emperor and his chief deity, the introduction of the cult of the Emesene stone may have seemed a natural accompaniment to the cult of the emperor. The neokorate was later withdrawn under Severus Alexander, along with several others granted by Elagabalus.

Competition for honours amongst provincial cities was fierce, a fact highlighted by the case study of Anazarbus. Anazarbus' titles under Elagabalus advertised that the city was 'the first, the greatest and most beautiful', an honour granted by Elagabalus and abbreviated to AMK on the city's coinage.[128] The emperor became a civic demiurge (the first time this had occurred in the city) and it appears that games normally held in Tarsus were transferred to the town.[129] Indeed, the privileges granted to Anazarbus all seem to have been at the expense of its rival, Tarsus.[130] The adoption of the cult of Elagabal may have further emphasised the close ties between the city, the emperor and Rome, underlining the new status of the polis. During Elagabalus' reign Anazarbus also struck coinage showing Romulus and Remus, and the emperor himself.[131]

Like Severus, Elagabalus honoured his *patria*: Emesa was granted the privilege of holding games that were called the *Helia Pythia*.[132] The city may also have received the title of *metrocolonia* (a modification of the more common *metropolis*).[133] The poor preservation of ancient Emesa in the present day means we are unable to tell whether the emperor sponsored any building programmes in the city.

It is evident that worship of Elagabal was adopted in some cities outside Rome, but to envisage an empire-wide implementation of the cult is unwarranted. The surviving evidence suggests a piecemeal adoption done to highlight a connection to the emperor, and performed within a dialogue of imperial favour. To what extent the rituals associated with the cult of Elagabal in the provinces reflected its cultic origins in Emesa is uncertain.

[127] Burrell 2004: 111. It has been suggested that Elagabalus granted a neokorate to Sardis, Ephesus and Nicomedia because he wed the god Elagabal to Kore, Artemis and Demeter, the respective tutelary goddesses of these cities (Robert 1989: 49–56). Robert also hypothesised that the presence of Elagabal at Faustinopolis was due to the lunar associations of *Diva* Faustina. This idea was furthered by Johnston, who argued that Elagabalus granted honours to cities with prominent cults to Apollo, whom he identified as a sun god comparable to Elagabal (Johnston 1984: 52–80). These theories have since been rightly dismissed by Burrell (Burrell 2004: 137). There is inadequate evidence to support these claims, particularly since Elagabalus also granted neokoria to cities without large solar or lunar cults.

[128] Ziegler 2004: 84. 'A' stood for first, M and K for μεγίστη and καλλίστη.

[129] ANS 75.219.7; Harl 1987: 66; Ziegler 1993: 283 numbers 461–5, 467; Ziegler 2004: 82.

[130] Ziegler 1993: 24, 116–17. [131] Ziegler 1993: 117. [132] Seyrig 1971: 340.

[133] Butcher 2004: 221.

It may be that this foreign deity was interpreted along traditional Graeco-Roman lines. Provincial interpretations of the god and the cult are considered below.

Negotiating the foreign and *interpretatio Romana*

Close examination of the documentary evidence reveals the way in which the Emesene cult was visualised in the wider empire. It is evident that the reception and interpretation of the cult and its iconography was complex, and differed from one region of the empire to another.

The official titles of Elagabalus that indicated his position as high priest (*sacerdos amplissimus dei inuicti Solis Elagabali*) are only found in Latin, not in Greek (though few Greek inscriptions from the reign of Elagabalus survive).[134] Future findings may change this situation, but the fact remains that Elagabalus' priestly titles were not adopted to the same extent in the Greek-speaking world. Latin inscriptions from this period describe the emperor as *Imperator Caesar M. Aurelius Antoninus Pius Felix Augustus sacerdos amplissimus dei inuicti Solis Elagabali pontifex maximus*. The title *sacerdos amplissimus dei inuicti Solis Elagabali* is absent from Greek epigraphy. Even Greek inscriptions erected by government officials do not mention the emperor's position as the high priest of Elagabal.[135] No attempt was made to translate the titles or incorporate them into the emperor's titulature. But Greek inscriptions also largely ignored the emperor's usual religious title *Pontifex Maximus*. The absence of Elagabalus' titles from Greek epigraphy may thus be in keeping with a divergence of epigraphic habit between the two languages. It is also symbolic of cultural differences between the Latin- and Greek-speaking worlds. For the latter, the proclamation of the emperor's new and unusual religious position was not as apparent (or perhaps it was not thought as significant) as in the Latin-speaking world.

The complete absence of these titles from Greek epigraphy may have meant that the radical transformation of the person of the emperor was not as pronounced as in Latin-speaking regions. Though living under the same ruler, the conventions of language and culture meant that, as with previous emperors, the perception and the description of Elagabalus in the East were slightly different from those presented in the official language of Rome.

[134] Of the 153 inscriptions noted by Arrizabalaga y Prado, only 18 are in Greek (Arrizabalaga y Prado 2010: 109).

[135] For example *AE* 1991, 1594 (a legate in Arabia).

Similarly, the 'horn' that characterises Elagabalus' later portraiture, likely connected to the emperor's rôle as high priest of Elagabal, never appears on provincial coinage. The significance of the appendage is discussed below, but key to the discussion here is that this particular attribute was not adopted in the provinces. Perhaps the significance of the appendage was not apparent, though this is unlikely. Its absence here highlights the fact that the emperor did not enforce the iconography associated with his Emesene priesthood, and that provincial cities did not feel the urge to reproduce it. For the most part, provincial die-cutters were autonomous, free to adapt the emperor's portraiture and not particularly constrained by models issued from above.[136] Provincial coin portraits often added solar rays or lunar crests to the imperial family, or other attributes of local significance.[137] At some level there was a decision not to transfer the 'horn' of Elagabalus' imperial portraiture, despite the fact that the emperor's portrait was arguably the most important part of the coin, guaranteeing its status as legal tender.[138] We might also note here that although some cities adopted the imagery of the god Elagabal for their local currencies, the image of the emperor as high priest of Elagabal was not, to current knowledge, transferred to provincial coinage. Considering the large emphasis this image had on official imperial coinage (23 per cent, Figure 56), its absence in provincial contexts is significant.

The *Elagabalia* celebrated by Sardis suggests that the god was incorporated into traditional Greek cultic practices.[139] The iconography employed on the city's coinage recording the festival is traditionally Greek (agonistic vases). The situation is more complicated than it appears at first sight, however: in Emesa itself the god was hellenised and worshipped with traditional Greek rituals. The *Helia Pythia* celebrated in Emesa in this period is probably a reference to the god Elagabal. Other material from Emesa suggests that Elagabal could be conceptualised as Sol.[140] Inscriptions indicate that *Sol Elagabal* was a title for the god within the city of Emesa itself.[141]

It is possible that the god's solar aspects encouraged the imperial mint to place an emphasis on Sol throughout Elagabalus' reign. The hoard analysis suggests that Sol constituted about 8 per cent of the emperor's silver reverse types (Figure 56). This is not to equate the god Elagabal with Sol or Sol

[136] Butcher 2006: 30–3.

[137] For example Mikocki 1995: 70 (Domna with cornucopia) and 71 (Domna with quiver).

[138] Duncan-Jones 2005: 461. [139] Ziegler 2004: 78.

[140] *BMC Syria* (Emesa) 21; Butcher 2003: 343; Millar 1993: 301 (who cites a Greek dedication from the Tell of Homs to 'Theos Helios Elagabalos'); Seyrig 1971: 337–73.

[141] *AE* 1962, 229; *AE* 1973, 437a; *AE* 1994, 1285; *AE* 1910, 133; *AE* 1910, 141.

Invictus; Hijmans has illustrated the fallacy involved in this rather simplistic approach.[142] Rather, the Roman mint, recognising the Sol aspect inherent within the cult of Elagabal, may have interpreted the deity according to the traditional Roman pantheon. It can be no coincidence that a significant proportion of Elagabalus' types display the image of Sol, the Roman god who could most closely be associated with Elagabal.

The sacred stone of Emesa is described on some imperial coin issues as CONSERVATOR AVG (Figure 61), a legend also placed on coins displaying Sol.[143] Commodus had previously bestowed the title on Sarapis,[144] but otherwise the title (numismatically at least) was associated with Jupiter. This did not completely cease under Elagabalus: coins struck with the image of Jupiter are accompanied by the legend IOVI CONSERVATORI.[145] But the bestowal of the epithet *conservator* on Elagabal, and on Sol, may reflect the attempts of the Roman mint to communicate this new deity to the populace. The challenge faced by the Roman mint in representing this foreign deity may have resulted in the adoption of Latin epithets that communicated the deity's close relationship to the emperor. An epithet borrowed from Jupiter, the head of the Roman pantheon (just as Elagabal was head of the Emesene pantheon) is understandable in this context.

This discussion has highlighted the mechanisms by which various aspects of the Emesene cult were (or were not) adopted by Romans under the emperor Elagabalus. The diversity in which the cult was (or was not) adopted strengthens the suggestion that the introduction of the worship of Elagabal in the provinces was a voluntary affair. When the provincial evidence is considered in conjunction with material from the Roman mint, one gains the impression that the Emesene god was at times subjected to *interpretatio Romana* in order to more easily communicate the relationship of Elagabal to the emperor, as well as the god's addition to the Roman pantheon. We now turn from the provinces to a consideration of the implementation of the cult of Elagabal inside Rome itself.

Transforming a city: Elagabalus and Elagabal in Rome

Herodian records that when the young emperor arrived in Rome in AD 219 he was dressed in an exotic fashion.[146] Herodian may have been inspired

[142] Hijmans 1996: 115–50. [143] *RIC* IV.2 *Elagabalus* 61–3. [144] *RIC* III *Commodus* 261.
[145] *RIC* IV.2 *Elagabalus* 89–91.
[146] Hdn. 5.5.7–8. Dio also comments that Elagabalus did not dress appropriately (Dio 80.8.3, 80.8.1).

somewhat by Dio, but probably also by the trope of an eastern and luxurious ruler.[147] Here again we see Herodian's use of dress to characterise Elagabalus as a ruler influenced by foreign *paideia*. In another section Herodian provides a vivid image of Elagabalus for his reader:

> He wore the most expensive type of clothes, woven of purple and gold, and adorned himself with necklaces and bangles. On his head he wore a crown in the shape of a tiara glittering with gold and precious stones. The effect was something between the sacred garb of the Phoenicians and the luxurious apparel of the Medes.[148]

Coins struck to mark the entry of the new emperor into the capital do not show him in this religious apparel, but instead employ a traditional *adventus* motif (the emperor on horseback with raised right arm).[149] It is likely that the mint used a conventional image for the *adventus* in order to communicate the message to the greatest audience. The use of traditional imagery need not reflect a public reaction to the clothing of the emperor as postulated by Turcan, nor need it reflect the reality of what the emperor wore the day he entered Rome.[150] In the Roman language of images the emperor on horseback unambiguously communicated an imperial *adventus*; the dies for the coins may have been prepared in advance. Deviation from the established, standard type would endanger the 'readability' of the image.[151]

Monumentalising the foreign: the temples to Elagabal in Rome

Literary evidence informs us that Elagabalus built two temples to his Emesene god in Rome: one on the Palatine Hill and the other in the suburbs of the city. In this respect Elagabalus followed Severan tradition: Severus and Caracalla had probably both monumentalised their particular form of divine support in the city's landscape, which was constantly changing to reflect the discourse of imperial power. In this sense, we should not see the construction of a temple to the god Elagabal as an outrage to Roman religion, but as part of a larger Severan (and imperial) tradition that utilised building programmes to communicate on a monumental scale the piety of the emperor and his unwavering divine support.

[147] Zimmermann 1999b: 311. Zimmermann (*ibid.* p. 227) suggests that Herodian's description here is derived from Dio's account of Commodus (73.17.3), but the motif of extravagant clothing was a common one, and we need not see any direct use of Dio here.

[148] Hdn. 5.5.4. [149] *RIC* IV.2 *Elagabalus* 57–8, with the legend ADVENTVS AVGVSTI.

[150] Turcan 1997: 97. [151] Hedlund 2008: 23–4.

The *Elagabalium* on the Palatine

The *Historia Augusta* records that a temple to Elagabal was located on the Palatine, *iuxta aedes imperatorias* ('close to the imperial palace').[152] Earlier in the *Vita* we are told that a temple was founded on a site that had once contained a shrine to Orcus.[153] This may be a reference to an otherwise unknown structure on the Palatine, or to the location of the second temple to Elagabal, or the text may have been invented or corrupted. Manuscript B of the text reads EDESORTI, manuscript P reads EDESORCI, and various emendations have been suggested: EDESBELI (*aedes Beli*, referring to a shrine to Bel in the suburbs), EDESMARCI (referring to an earlier structure on the Palatine built under Marcus Aurelius), and *Adonidis horti*, an emendation that stretches the imagination to the limit.[154] Each suggestion has been made to support a particular archaeological reconstruction of the area, not on the basis of the manuscripts themselves.[155] A shrine to Orcus may have existed in antiquity, though no hint of it has survived. The difficulties associated with this passage mean that it should not be used as definitive evidence in locating the temples to Elagabal in Rome.

Dio does not mention a temple on the Palatine, but Herodian (not providing the location) notes that the emperor 'built an enormous and magnificent temple to his new god, around which he set up many altars'.[156] The *Chronicle* of Jerome states that a temple to Elagabal was dedicated in AD 220.[157] Aurelius Victor records that the emperor transported his god to Rome and 'set up an altar in the innermost parts of the palace'.[158] Here we might glimpse some of the fourth century rhetoric that linked Elagabalus to Constantine. Victor's statement that the temple to Elagabal was deep inside the palace sounds strikingly similar to the location of the Constantinian church of Santa Croce in Gerusalemme, which was located inside the Sessorian Palace.[159] Victor thus may also reflect the parallels drawn between Constantine and Elagabalus in the late fourth century.

The temple, or *Elagabalium* has now been identified fairly securely with the archaeological remains on the Vigna Barberini, which sits atop a platform on the Palatine near the imperial palaces (Figures 62–3). Access to the

[152] *SHA Heliogab.* 3.4–5. [153] *SHA Heliogab.* 1.6.

[154] Cecamore 1999: 340; Chausson 1995b: 706–7, 711; Chausson 1997: 66.

[155] Editors of the text have refrained from any speculation on or emendation of this line.

[156] Hdn. 5.5.8.

[157] Jer. *Ad. Abr.* 296g (Helm). While the entry is present in Jerome, it is not present in the Armenian manuscript of Eusebius' work (Karst 1911). This suggests that it is an addition by Jerome (Helm 1956: 214), perhaps part of his desire to make the *Chronicle* more Roman in focus.

[158] Aur. Vict. *Caes.* 23: 'in palatii penetralibus altaria constituit'. [159] Krautheimer 1983: 25.

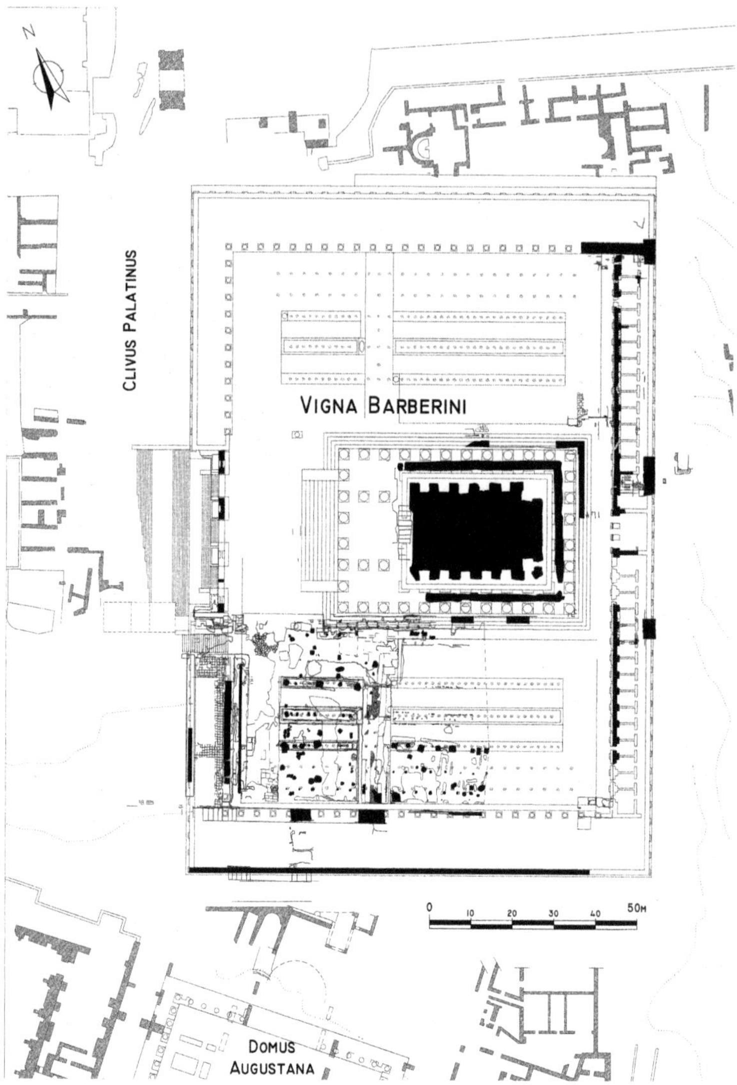

Figure 62: The Vigna Barberini complex. Drawing by N. André in collaboration with F. Villedieu, CNRS, France.

complex was through a monumental gate or *propylaeum* that faced the *clivus Palatinus,* the street that led to the Palatine palatial complex. The temple was thus closely linked with the imperial house. When seen from street level below the temple might have seemed like an extension of the palatial façade. This proximity would have highlighted the close association between the emperor and his god, an alignment that would later lead to the conflation of their names.

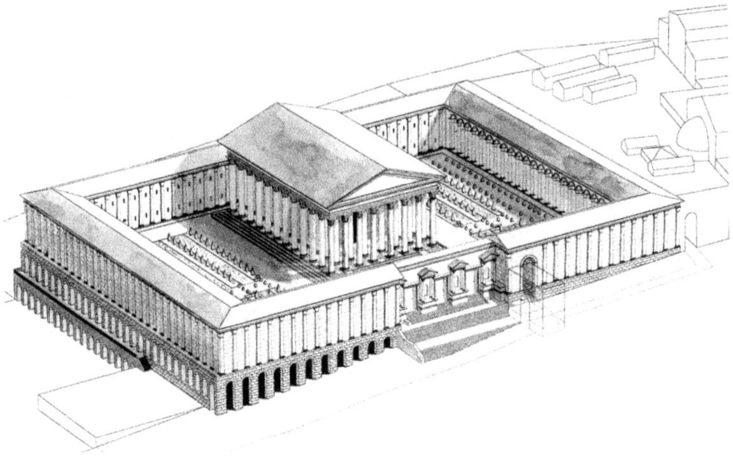

Figure 63: Reconstruction of the *Elagabalium* complex. Drawing by P. Veltri in collaboration with F. Villedieu, CNRS, France.

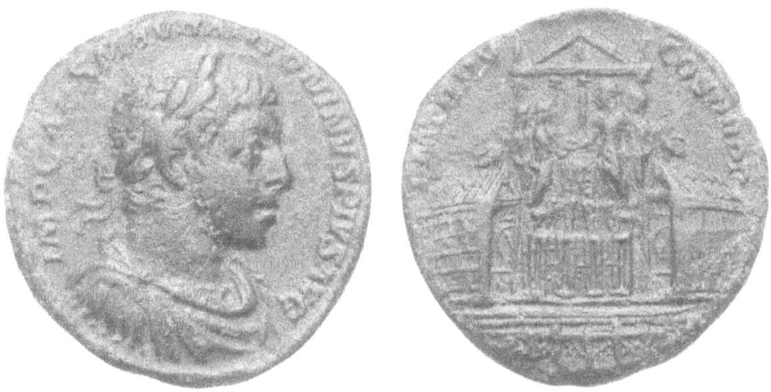

Figure 64: Medallion of Elagabalus showing the *Elagabalium* on the Palatine with the legend P M TR P V COS IIII P P. (Münzkabinett der Staatlichen Museen zu Berlin, Object Number 18205364).

The *Elagabalium* is portrayed on a small medallion of Elagabalus now in the Münzkabinett of the Staatlichen Museen in Berlin (Figure 64).[160] The piece shows four figures sacrificing in front of a temple that is surrounded by porticoes and possesses a *propylaeum*. The figures likely represent Elagabalus (the largest figure), and perhaps Severus Alexander and the imperial women or sacrificial attendants. The mention of Elagabalus' fourth

160 Münzkabinett der Staatlichen Museen zu Berlin Object No. 18205364 (24mm, 10.69g) = Dressel 1973: no. 105. This same piece is also published in Gnecchi 1912: (vol. 3) 41 no. 6, pl. 152 no. 11 (erroneously attributed to his collection); Sambon, Canessa et al. 1907: no. 2546, pl. XXXII; and *RIC* IV.2 *Elagabalus* 339.

consulship dates the coin to the final months of Elagabalus' reign, between December AD 221 and March AD 222. Nothing on the piece identifies the temple as the *Elagabalium*, though this is the likeliest interpretation. The layout of the temple on the medallion matches the archaeological remains of the temple excavated on the Vigna Barberini.

The scene is also similar to a larger medallion that has recently come to light on the market.[161] This piece is also dated to Elagabalus' fourth consulship, and so is likely contemporary with the smaller medallic piece. This image suggests that representations of the cult stone (*agalma*) were placed above the monumental gate. The cult stone itself may be represented on the ornate, multi-tiered altar, at which the emperor, dressed as high priest of Emesa, is offering sacrifice. The medallion indicates that the monumental gate had three doors (shown closed), which archaeological excavations on the Vigna Barberini site have confirmed.[162] The medallion also shows a monumental staircase with a fence in front, and porticoes surrounding the enclosure. There is little doubt that what is shown is the *Elagabalium* on the Palatine, both on this piece and on the smaller medallion.

The multi-tiered altar shown on the piece has certain similarities to the altar of the stone shown on the provincial coinage of Emesa. On civic coinage of the city the stone is shown on a two-tiered altar, decorated with three sets of arches containing different figures.[163] This same configuration is seen on the altar of the large medallion, suggesting an Emesene influence in the Roman temple.[164]

The imagery of four figures sacrificing to the Emesene stone also appears on another *aes* medallion.[165] On this piece there is no temple, but the Emesene stone is clearly shown (Figure 65). The obverse shows two confronted busts, rare for the imperial coinage of Elagabalus. The poorly preserved state of the medallion prohibits precise identification, but the only other known example of confronted busts under Elagabalus shows the emperor with Aquilia Severa.[166] It is thus probably Aquilia who is represented here, dating the medallion after AD 220.

The representation of the temple appears only to occur on medallic issues, intended to form imperial gifts. Imperial coinage intended for

161 The piece went through the Classical Numismatic Group. It is 36mm, 46.25g, and has a die axis of 12 h. The piece is now in a private collection. http://www.cngcoins.com/Coin.aspx?CoinID=155774.

162 Villedieu 2007: 376.

163 *BMC Syria* (Emesa) 9–12.

164 Civic coinage of Emesa also shows the temple to Elagabal with a monumental staircase (*BMC Syria* (Emesa) 15–17). This may have inspired the monumental staircase of the Palatine temple.

165 BM 1992, 0509.364.

166 Gnecchi 1912: (vol. 3) 79 no. 1.

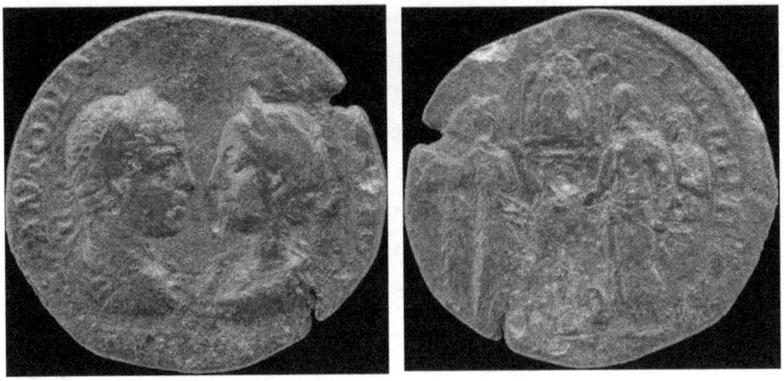

Figure 65: Medallion of Elagabalus with four individuals sacrificing to the Emesene stone and the legend [CONSERVAT]OR IMPERII.

circulation showed the god Elagabal in a *quadriga*, or the emperor as high priest of the god (discussed in more detail below). The two medallions showing the temple date to the end of Elagabalus' reign. One might expect the representation of a temple to occur on issues close to the time the structure was completed. For example, coins commemorating the completion of the arch of Septimius Severus in the Roman forum were struck in AD 204, the same year as the dedication.[167] However, this is not a universal rule, and since the precise date of many imperial buildings is reliant on the coin evidence (and vice versa), it is difficult to establish a precise relationship between the completion of a structure and its representation on coinage. A delay of two years is not impossible, if Jerome is correct in recording the dedication date as AD 220.

The representation of the temple in the numismatic evidence corresponds closely to the archaeological remains on the Vigna Barberini, which have been the subject of excavations by the *École Française de Rome*.[168] These excavations have uncovered the remains of a Flavian terrace on the site measuring 180m × 120m.[169] This was built over older Julio-Claudian houses, perhaps annexes to the imperial palaces.[170] The Flavian terrace likely housed a 'hanging garden', though more recently Villedieu has proposed a Flavian temple in the area.[171] There remains little evidence,

[167] *RIC* IV.2 *Elagabalus* 764.

[168] The results of the excavations have been regularly published in the *Mélanges de l'École Française de Rome*. A summary of the excavations and their findings can be found in Villedieu 2007. See also Broise and Thébert 1999: 729–47; Cecamore 1999: 311–49; Chausson 1995b: 661–765; Chausson 1997: 31–85; De Rossi 2000: 413–502; Grenier and Coarelli 1986: 230–53; Morel and Villedieu 2002: 74–96; Royo 1986: 707–66; Royo 1997: 3–30; Villedieu et al. 1992; Villedieu, Broise et al. 1998; Villedieu, Morel et al. 1997; Villedieu, Pergola et al. 1996.

[169] Broise and Thébert 1999: 730.

[170] Morel and Villedieu 2002: 74–96.

[171] Hanging gardens: André, Villedieu et al. 2004: 112–23. Temple: Villedieu 2007: 379–89.

however, to support Villedieu's suggestion that an older temple must have preceded the Severan temple. Recent finds during excavations on the site have been interpreted as the remains of the 'rotating dining room' of Nero's Golden House. It remains to be seen how this discovery will influence the understanding of the topography of the site.

The excavations on the Vigna Barberini uncovered a burn layer, which Villedieu reasonably connected with the fire under Commodus in AD 191/2.[172] The ceramics from this phase date to this period, and Villedieu suggests that the area may have held the palatial archives and libraries that Dio and Galen mention as being destroyed in the blaze.[173] These libraries (*bibliotheca ad Apollinis*) are represented on the Severan marble plan, indicating that Severus rebuilt them after the fire.[174]

The Severan temple remains on the Vigna Barberini suggest a single, coherent structure, constructed extremely rapidly in two stages temporally close to each other.[175] Villedieu suggested that the renovation of the area and the construction of the temple on the site began under Septimius Severus, with Elagabalus later renovating the area for conversion to the *Elagabalium.*[176] Broise and Thébert suggested Elagabalus as the initiator of the work, with modifications by Severus Alexander. This theory was based on the large number of anepigraphic bricks on the site (the use of which began under Caracalla) and other materials that suggested a date in the second half of the Severan period.[177] However, Thébert has more recently acknowledged the evidence in favour of an initial building campaign around the turn of the third century.[178] We are thus presented with a dilemma: either Severus, as part of his wider rebuilding of the Palatine, constructed a temple for which we have no other evidence, which was then modified by Elagabalus to house the cult statue of Elagabal, or the building site lay dormant for about thirty years, enabling the complex to be finalised under Elagabalus, and modified by Severus Alexander when he rededicated the complex to another god after Elagabalus' fall. The more reasonable interpretation of the evidence is that Septimius Severus began the construction of the complex, and that it was renovated under Elagabalus to house his cultic god. It is hard to imagine that an area so close to the imperial palace lay dormant for over thirty years, and Villedieu assigns the monumental

[172] Villedieu 2007: 250–63.

[173] Dio 78.24.2; Galen *De compositione medicamentorum* I (ed. Kuehn, XIIII, 362); Villedieu 2007: 263.

[174] Lusnia 1998: 214. [175] Broise and Thébert 1999: 736–45. [176] Villedieu 2007: 263–377.

[177] Broise and Thébert 1999: 740. [178] André, Villedieu et al. 2004: 128–9.

gate to the second phase of the construction.[179] It is this monumental gate that is shown on the coins of Elagabalus, so the second construction phase occurred under his reign. The archaeological evidence suggests only that the first phase of building took place in the period between AD 190–210/20, and the second sometime between the years AD 210/220–240.[180] If Elagabalus converted an existing structure, then this fact helps in explaining Jerome's dedication date of AD 220, just a year after the emperor arrived in Rome.

If Septimius Severus completed and dedicated a temple on the Vigna Barberini before the reign of Elagabalus, no suggestion of it can be found in the other source evidence. Hill believed Elagabalus transformed an earlier structure dedicated to Jupiter into his *Elagabalium*.[181] Others have since adopted this theory with some variations.[182] Rededicating an existing temple would have been an affront to religious sensibilities and may explain Dio's statement that the emperor placed the god before Jupiter.[183] But Hill may have interpreted the numismatic evidence too literally.[184] This will be discussed more fully in the following chapter. But the topography of the site under Septimius Severus remains elusive.

The final temple complex after the second phase of building consisted of a temple surrounded by porticoes and gardens (Figures 62–3). As well as the plant beds, the excavations uncovered several large pits that may have housed statuary or, as Villedieu suggested, the numerous altars mentioned by Herodian.[185] A church to St Sebastian now stands on part of the site. The account of Sebastian's martyrdom records that he spoke to the emperor Diocletian 'on the steps of Elagabalus' (*et stans super gradus Heliogabali, venientibus imperatoribus dixit*), perhaps an allusion to the *Elagabalium*.[186] Despite the rededication of the *Elagabalium* by Severus Alexander, the area seems to have retained a memory of its heritage; the problems associated with the historical reliability of the *Acta* (it is unlikely St Sebastian met Diocletian) do not detract from its topographical evidence. The mention of Elagabalus in a work written well after his death and *damnatio* highlights the complex connection between space and memory in Rome.

179 Villedieu 2007: 376–8. 180 Villedieu 2007: 374. 181 Hill 1960a: 119–20.

182 Castagnoli 1979: 331–47; Hill 1960a: 117–20; Richardson 1992: 142; Steinby 1996: 10–11; Turcan 1997: 121–4.

183 Dio 80.11.1.

184 Rowan 2009: 123–35. Villedieu 2007: 379–89 is perhaps also too literal in his interpretation of the numismatic evidence in his discussion of what the temple of Severus might have housed.

185 Villedieu 2007: 370; Hdn. 5.5.8. 186 Acta S. Sebastiani Martyris 23 (*PL* 17.Col 1056B).

Hill noted that in the medieval period the region was called the *regio Palladii*, perhaps a reference to the alleged transferral of the *Palladium* to the *Elagabalium*.[187] Herodian records that the god Elagabal was married to the *Palladium*, though it is doubtful whether this event ever actually occurred.[188] But the tale may reflect a popular belief that it did. This may have led to the name *regio Palladii*. The area is close to the *mundus*, a hole where Romulus had allegedly thrown the first fruits of agricultural prosperity for the foundation of Rome. This hole was later consecrated to the *Manes*, which may explain the *Historia Augusta*'s comment about Orcus. Ultimately, though, the statement in the *Historia Augusta* remains puzzling.[189]

The Vigna Barberini is also close to the Roman forum, where a capital was found showing the Emesene cult stone decorated with an eagle, with two goddesses on either side (Figure 66).[190] Along one side of the capital is a scene of Victory sacrificing a bull. Studniczka identified the goddess on the left of the stone as Pallas/Minerva, because of the figure's *aegis* and helmet. The goddess on the right is more mutilated, but Studniczka suggested Urania as a possibility, noting Herodian's comment that the sacred stone was married not only to Pallas/Minerva, but also to Urania.[191] The identification of Minerva seems secure, but the identity of the goddess on the left remains speculative. Juno is a good guess: the god Elagabal would thus be portrayed between Minerva and Juno, a play on the traditional Capitoline triad. The column is relatively small (56 × 37cm). Hülsen suggested it may have come from a chapel in the forum, Butler postulated that it may have come from a chapel dedicated to Elagabal and Vesta, and von Domaszewski suggested that it might have originated from a *statio* of Emesenes.[192] Given the size of the capital, a secondary location in the Roman forum consecrated to Elagabal is a possibility. On a more solid note, the juxtaposition of the sacred stone with traditional Roman goddesses suggests that the god was intended to amalgamate with existing religious practices rather than supplant them.

[187] *CIL* 10.6441 also gives this name to the area (Hill 1960a: 118). [188] Hdn. 5.6.3.

[189] Turcan 1997: 121.

[190] Arrizabalaga y Prado 2004–5; Studniczka 1901: 273–82; von Mercklin 1962: 154 no. 383. One section of the capital was found in the vicinity of the temple of Castor, the other reportedly 'on the foundations of the arch of Augustus'.

[191] Hdn. 5.6.3.

[192] Arrizabalaga y Prado 2004–5; Butler 1908: 81; Hülsen 1902: 67; and von Domaszewski 1909: 201 n.3.

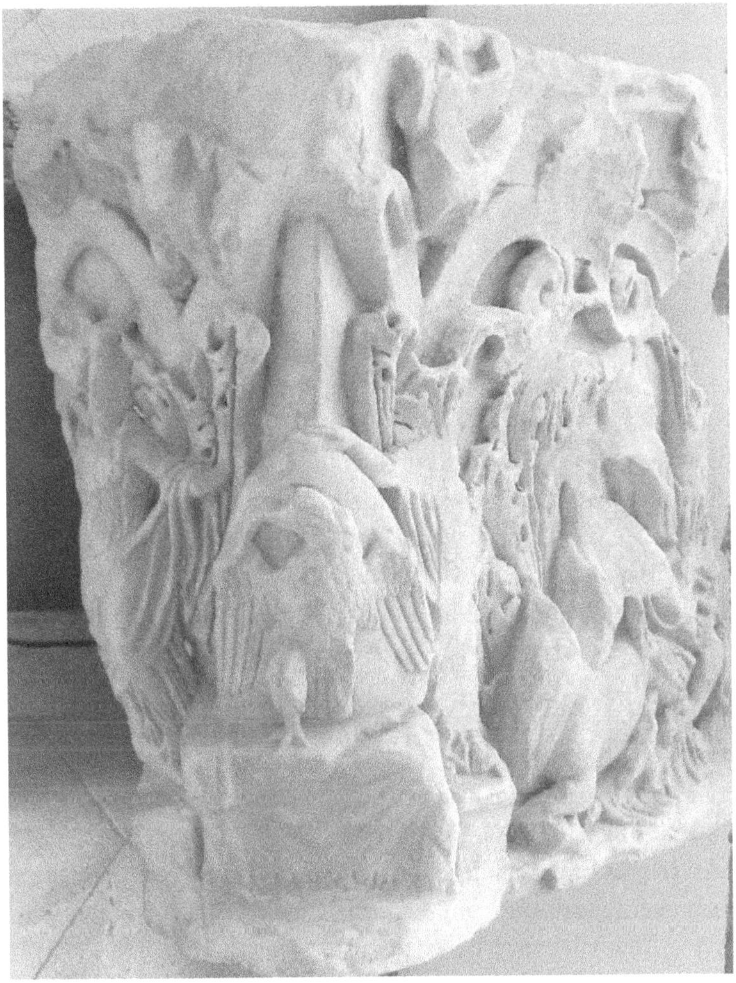

Figure 66: Capital of Elagabal.

The second temple to Elagabal

Herodian provides a description of a second temple to Elagabal:

In the outlying district of the city he constructed a vast, magnificent temple to which he brought the god each year at midsummer. He instituted many different festivals and constructed circuses (for horse-racing) and theatres, imagining that, if he provided chariot races and all kinds of spectacles and entertainments, and if he feasted all night long, he would be popular.[193]

[193] Hdn. 5.6.6.

The location of this second temple is the subject of debate, but the most probable location is the Sessorian Palace in the *horti spei veteris.* The *Historia Augusta* records that Elagabalus withdrew to the area.[194] The *horti* may have once belonged to Elagabalus' father Sextus Varius Marcellus.[195] They became imperial property under Severus, when construction began on an imperial palace complex.[196] The area remained in imperial possession well after the Severan period; Constantine's mother Helena inhabited the complex, and the church of Santa Croce in Gerusalemme was built on the site.[197]

The Severan complex consisted of a residential quarter, connected by a large corridor or *portus triumphalis* to an amphitheatre and circus.[198] In this respect it was similar to the Augustan palace on the Palatine, which was adjacent to the Circus Maximus, as well as the later complex of Maxentius on the Appian Way. Excavations on the site have revealed that the Circus was shortened under Elagabalus, creating a large quadrangular space in front of the imperial residence.[199] It is possible that this and other alterations to the complex executed at this time were connected with the second temple to Elagabal mentioned by Herodian.[200] The suggestion is made more attractive by the obvious parallel with the complex on the Palatine Hill, where the temple was adjacent to the imperial palace. The site also fits well with Herodian's mention of spectacles, circuses and theatres.[201] Several other comments by ancient authors make better sense when viewed within the context of this suburban imperial residence. Dio notes that Elagabalus played the charioteer at home, and the *Historia Augusta* records that the emperor brought *quadrigae* from the circus into his banqueting rooms or porticoes.[202] The latter may well be based on the monumental corridor joining the imperial residence with the circus.[203] These literary tropes thus may have been inspired by the design of the palatial complex.

Paterna suggested that the temple to Elagabalus at the Sessorian Palace might have been converted into a temple to Sol under Severus Alexander.[204] The existence of a temple to Sol may explain the circuitous route of the Aurelian wall that was later constructed in the area: it may have been

[194] *SHA Heliogab.* 13.5.

[195] Borgia, Colli et al. 1998: 243; Colli 1996: 777; Optendrenk 1969: 87; Turcan 1997: 136–7.

[196] Guidobaldo 2004: 12; Lusnia 1998: 219; Paterna 1996: 817, 847. [197] Colini 1955: 174.

[198] Paterna 1996: 853. [199] Borgia, Colli et al. 2008; Paterna 1996: 851.

[200] Paterna 1996: 851.

[201] Colini 1955: 170–3; Matern 2002: 33; Richardson 1992: 142; Steinby 1996: 10; Turcan 1997: 136. Steinby suggests that the temple might be identified with one of the larger structures of the *Sessorium.*

[202] Dio 80.14.2; *SHA Heliogab.* 27.1. [203] Paterna 1996: 820. [204] Paterna 1996: 851–2.

designed to encompass the temple within the city's new boundaries. Under Constantine the Severan atrium of the complex was converted into the basilica of Santa Croce in Gerusalemme.[205] Constantine and Elagabalus are brought into direct parallel again. That both Constantine and Elagabalus built structures for their new cults in the same outlying area may have encouraged the connection between the two seen in the *Historia Augusta*.

The actions of both Elagabalus and Constantine are indicative of the conscious connection in the Roman mind between space and cult. Constantine's early Christian buildings, located at the edge of Rome and on imperial property, were consciously inoffensive.[206] Elagabalus too may have been careful in his placement of the cult of Elagabal. If we are correct in placing the second temple of Elagabal in Rome in the *horti spei veteris*, then the imperial residence was once again visibly juxtaposed with the residence of the divine; the emperor and god remained closely connected. It would be fitting for the suburban temple to mirror the Palatine. Indeed, if the temple were constructed on land owned by the emperor himself, it would be a politic way to erect a monument to a foreign cult in a space-poor city: no person or deity need be displaced.

Elagabal in Alsium

A third cultic place for the god Elagabal in Italy might be found in Alsium on the coast of Etruria, at the Villa di Marina di San Nicola. A *fistula* was discovered in the area inscribed on one side with the phrase *dei Solis invicti magni Elagabal*, and *dei Sol* on the other.[207] The genitive indicates that the water carried within the pipe was meant for the god Elagabal (as is apparent in other cultic sites) and suggests an Emesene cult in the area. Bruun suggested that the villa was owned by a member of the élite, who became a supporter of the cult under Elagabalus, or that the emperor himself owned the villa.[208] In the latter case, the emperor may once again have converted his own land into a cultic site for his god.

The two temples to Elagabal in Rome continued the negotiation between local and imperial culture apparent under the earlier Severan dynasty, a dialogue played out in a spatial and geographical framework.[209] The Severan temples to provincial deities within Rome, and large-scale imperial building programmes outside the capital are monumental remnants of a dialogue in which the power of the Severan emperors was conceptualised. Elagabalus should be seen as part of this wider phenomenon, not as an aberration.

[205] Colli 1996: 777–81. [206] Krautheimer 1980: 24; Krautheimer 1983: 23–5.
[207] Bruun 1997: 1. [208] Bruun 1997: 1–5. [209] Petsalis-Diomidis 2007: 252.

Tiberius Julius Balbillus: an Emesene in Rome

Palmer proposed the Janiculum Hill in Trastevere as an alternative possibility for the second temple of Elagabal.[210] This area has yielded several inscriptions to eastern deities and several to the god Elagabal erected by an individual named Tiberius Julius Balbillus.[211] These inscriptions date from the earlier Severan period, and Palmer believed they indicated the existence of a temple to the god Elagabal in the area.[212] Balbillus is an unusual name, suggestive of a native Emesene (a princess under Hadrian, related to the dynasty at Emesa, was named Balbilla).[213] Balbillus may have been an Emesene, perhaps coming to Rome under Severus and Julia Domna.[214] His epigraphic activity thus need not indicate a temple to Elagabal, let alone an imperial one. The majority of the dedications found in this area are to Palmyrene gods; hence it was probably a Palmyrene cultic place that Balbillus appropriated for his own religious needs.[215] The fact that the inscriptions diminish under Elagabalus, and are concentrated within a very specific period of time (AD 199–215), suggests the activity of a single individual under Septimius Severus and Caracalla. It is not indicative of an imperial temple.

Though Trastevere is unlikely to be the location of the second temple to Elagabal, Balbillus provides a valuable insight into the Emesene cult in the absence of a large body of material from Emesa itself.[216] In dated inscriptions Balbillus is characterised as *sacerdos Solis*, priest of the Sun.[217] In two undated inscriptions, the sun god of Balbillus' devotion is further described as *Elagabal*; Balbillus is *sacerdos Solis Elagabali.*[218] Palmer suggested that these undated inscriptions were contemporary with the reign of Elagabalus; the advent of the Emesene emperor to Rome manifested itself in a change of

[210] Arrizabalaga y Prado and Marcos 2005: 90; Matern 2002: 33–4; Palmer 1981: 377–80. Optendrenk 1969: 87 suggested the second temple might have been a temporary structure dismantled after Elagabalus' death.

[211] *CIL* 6.708, 6.1027, 6.1603, 6.2129, 6.2130, 6.2269, 6.2270; Palmer 1981: 368–97.

[212] Matern 2002: 34 suggests that the Emesene sacred stone was housed in this sanctuary in Trastevere until the temple on the Palatine was completed.

[213] Matern 2002: 34. [214] Chausson 1995b: 701, 715; Matern 2002: 34.

[215] Chausson 1995b: 663–701.

[216] Very little remains of ancient Emesa (modern Homs) today. On the city and its archaeological remains see Dieudonne 1906: 132–55; King 2002: 39–58; Millar 1993: 300–9; Philip 2005: 21–42; Seyrig 1952–3: 204–50; Seyrig 1959: 184–92; Sullivan 1977: 198–219; and von Domaszewski 1908: 223–42.

[217] *CIL* 6.1027 (AD 199), 6.1603 (AD 201), 6.2129 (AD 201), 6.2130 (AD 215), 6.2270 (AD 199).

[218] *CIL* 6.2269, 6.708.

titles for Balbillus.[219] The theory, while possible, is not probable. There is no evidence to suggest that Balbillus was still in Rome during the reign of Elagabalus (the last securely dated inscription is AD 215), and if these inscriptions dated to AD 218–222, then Balbillus would possess the same titles as the emperor. A better explanation of the evidence is that Balbillus was active in Rome during the early Severan dynasty, and that his position as *sacerdos* of Elagabal in Rome was superseded by the emperor Elagabalus. The epigraphic record of Balbillus, however, illustrates that Elagabalus' titles were established ones utilised by priests of Emesa.

The midsummer procession

In his work Herodian describes a religious procession that took place between the two temples to Elagabal in Rome.

> The god was set up in a chariot studded with gold and precious stones and driven from the city to the suburb. The chariot was drawn by a team of six large, pure white horses that had been decorated with lots of gold and ornamented discs. No human ever sat in the chariot or held the reins, which were fastened to the god as though he were driving himself. Antoninus ran along in front of the chariot, but facing backwards as he ran looking at the god and holding the bridles of the horses. He ran the whole way backwards like this looking up at the front of the god.[220]

Herodian then goes on to undermine this image of an imperial procession by adding that to stop the emperor falling over as he ran backwards, sand was put down along the route.[221] This ironic undertone also emerges when Herodian describes the gifts distributed by the emperor: in the scramble to get the riches people were trampled to death or impaled on the spears of soldiers.[222] In this section of this work Herodian builds up an image of the emperor, going on to note that Elagabalus was often seen driving chariots or dancing, and that he often wore make-up.[223] How much of Herodian's description of the midsummer festival is truth, then, remains difficult to discern.

Frey has argued that this festival was one transferred from Emesa, perhaps ultimately deriving from the Babylonian New Year festival, with which it has parallels.[224] There is no evidence from Emesa itself for such a festival, but this does not automatically disprove the existence of one, or of a

[219] Palmer 1981: 378. [220] Hdn. 5.6.6–7. [221] Hdn. 5.6.8. [222] Hdn. 5.6.10.
[223] Hdn. 5.6.10. [224] Frey 1989: 48.

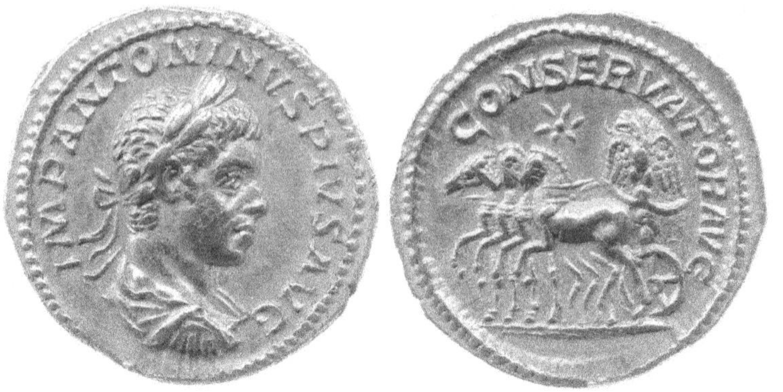

Figure 67: Aureus of Elagabalus with the Emesene stone in a *quadriga* and the legend CONSERVATOR AVG.

procession in Rome. If we accept that there were two temples to Elagabal in the city, presumably the god had to travel in some ceremonial form from one to the other.

Baldus believed that the imperial coinage showing the Emesene stone in a *quadriga* referred to the midsummer procession. There are two varieties of this *quadriga* type: one with what have been labelled 'parasols' (Figure 57) and one without (Figure 67). Baldus suggested that the pieces struck without the 'parasols' commemorated the return of the sacred stone to the Palatine temple in winter, when it would not need protection from the sun. Those coins with 'parasols' illustrated the midsummer procession.[225] As discussed above, however, these pieces with 'parasols' come from a mint outside Rome and were struck early in the emperor's reign. It is hard to connect coins struck in Antioch or Nicomedia in a period before the emperor had even entered the capital with a ceremonial procession in Rome.

Since the cultic stone was a solar god, it is also unlikely that it needed protection from the sun. The 'parasols' identified by Baldus and others are more likely to be cultic standards or *semeia*, pieces described by Lucian in *De Dea Syria*.[226] Similar standards are known in the cult of Jupiter Dolichenus and in temples at Carrhae, Dura, Hatra and Palmyra.[227] On local coins of Emesa the objects are portrayed beside the stone within the temple (they are not providing shade). They thus had a cultic function,

225 Baldus 1991: 175–8.

226 Lucian *Syr. D.* 33; Frey 1989: 59–63; Oden 1997: 109–22; Rowan 2006: 114–19. On *semeia* in eastern religious contexts see Caquot 1955: 59–69; Ingholt 1954: 18; Lightfoot 2004: 540; and Rostovtzeff 1942: 98–105. On religious standards in general see Henig 1983: 109–12.

227 Iuppiter Dolichenus: Speidel 1978: 55–66; Carrhae and Hatra: Rostovtzeff 1942: 98; Dura: Ingholt 1954: 18; Palmyra: Gawlikowski 1984.

making *semeia* the likeliest explanation.[228] Here we should note that a coin type was struck for Elagabalus showing the emperor in priestly dress, sacrificing over an altar with two standards behind him. These two standards may in fact represent the sacred standards of the god Elagabal.[229]

As for the types without *semeia*, there is no need to connect their release with a processional festival.[230] The coins carry no precise indication of date. The legend accompanying the image, CONSERVATOR AVG, bears no reference to a festival. If we are to trust the representation of the Palatine *Elagabalium* shown on the imperial medallions, the image of the stone on the *quadriga* was placed on the monumental gate of the complex and was thus probably a well-known cult representation of the god in this period. A more likely explanation is that these coin types took the existing iconography associated with the god Elagabal (displayed on paintings and other media), and incorporated it into a type that communicated the protective capacity of Elagabal for the new régime.

The procession described by Herodian in all likelihood only took place once, in AD 221.[231] By this year both temples in Rome would have been completed, and Elagabalus fell from power before midsummer the following year. If the procession was a one-off event, that may explain the absence of the spectacle from Dio's account.

Though the procession from one temple to another may have derived from an eastern cultic context,[232] Herodian describes it in the language of a Roman triumph.[233] In Herodian's account the stone was placed in a golden chariot drawn by white horses, an apparatus normally associated with the ceremony of triumph, though it also had connections to the chariots of Jupiter and Sol.[234] Herodian records that before the cultic stone went 'images of all other gods and valuable or precious temple dedications and all the imperial standards or costly heirlooms'.[235] This recalls the *spolia* that preceded the emperor in a military triumph. The Roman army was also involved in the procession.[236] Herodian records that the people ran alongside the procession showering wreaths and flowers on the emperor. He never directly equates the procession of Elagabal to that of a triumph, but it is apparent that either the procession had these overtones, or that Herodian chose to portray the event along these lines.

The numismatic representation of the sacred stone in a chariot (Figure 67) would have also recalled an imperial triumph, which was often visualised with

[228] Rowan 2006: 114–19. [229] *RIC* IV.2 *Elagabalus* 48–50.
[230] *RIC* IV.2 *Elagabalus* 61–2, 64–5. [231] Frey 1989: 71; Turcan 1997: 138.
[232] Frey 1989: 47–9. [233] Icks 2008a: 147. [234] Beard 2007: 234. [235] Hdn. 5.6.8.
[236] Hdn. 5.6.8.

the emperor in a *quadriga*.[237] The presentation of Elagabal using the iconography of a ritual closely associated with the emperor and confined to him (a triumph), would have served to reinforce the connection between the emperor and the god in the minds of the populace.

As mentioned above, Herodian describes festivals in connection with the procession, noting the numerous gifts bestowed on the populace and recording that the emperor himself participated in the chariot racing.[238] Dio also records that numerous games and spectacles took place in Elagabalus' reign.[239] An inscription from Delphi attests to the existence of an *Antonineia Pythia* in Rome.[240] The inscription details the victories of two individuals; the placement of the *Antonineia Pythia* at the top of the inscription may reflect the fact that it was given a significant place in the hierarchy of festivals of this kind. Though the inscription could refer to a celebration under Caracalla or Elagabalus, Robert believed it was connected with the games celebrated under Elagabalus and described by Herodian and Dio. Elagabalus may thus have introduced a new Greek festival to Rome.[241] Greek-style games were rare, though not unheard of, in the city of Rome; the *Capitolia* was a permanent fixture within the city, and Nero had also celebrated Greek games called the *Neronia*.[242] Robert observed that the epigraphic reference to the *Antonineia* suffered mutilation, more in keeping with the *damnatio* of Elagabalus than with Caracalla.[243] Though the inscriptional evidence indicates a festival in honour of the emperor (Antoninus) rather than the god himself, the close connection between the two suggests that the cultic stone might have been associated with the celebrations in some way. If this were the case, the god's protection and support of the régime (and consequently the entire Roman Empire) was reinforced through ritual to the wider Roman populace. A similar phenomenon has already been explored under Septimius Severus.

(Mis)reading imperial iconography and the implementation of the Emesene cult

The offence consisted, not in his introducing a foreign god into Rome or in his exalting him in very strange ways, but in his placing him even before Jupiter himself and causing himself to be voted his priest...[244]

[237] *RIC* IV.2 *Elagabalus* 26, 35–6, 54–5, 170, 174–5A, 180, 182–3, 296–8, 308–13, 316–17, 331, 337–8.

[238] Hdn. 5.6.6–10. [239] Dio 80.10.2–3. [240] Robert 1970: 20. [241] Robert 1970: 26.

[242] Suet. *Ner*. 12.7; Robert 1970: 7. [243] Robert 1970: 24. [244] Dio 80.11.1.

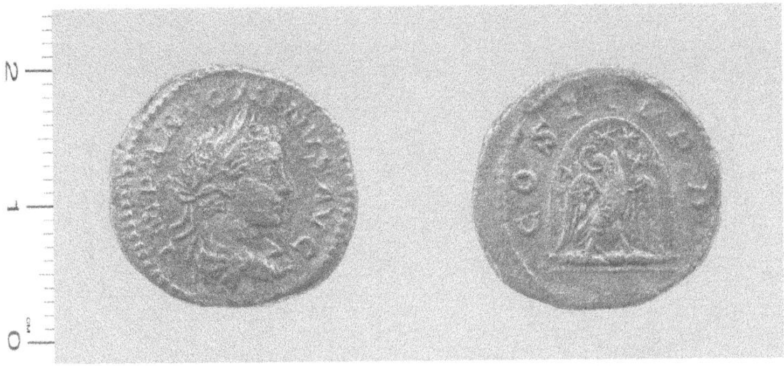

Figure 68: Denarius of Elagabalus displaying the Emesene stone decorated with stars and an eagle on a thunderbolt. The reverse legend reads COS III P P.

The documentary evidence does not support Dio's claim that Elagabalus attempted to remove Jupiter from the head of the Roman pantheon. The surviving *Acta* of the Arval brothers for this period suggest that the sacrifices and festivals of the empire proceeded uninterrupted.[245] In this aspect of Roman religious life, at least, the cult of Elagabal seems to have had no impact at all.

The quantitative numismatic evidence also reveals that the emperor's public image was by no means monotheistic. Mars constituted 4% of the silver coinage in the emperor's name, Sol 8% and Jupiter 2% (Figure 56). Though both Sol and Jupiter could have been associated with Elagabal through *interpretatio Romana*, their presence on the emperor's coinage suggests that Elagabalus did not intend to usurp or destroy the existing Roman pantheon.

The epithets and iconography employed in association with the sacred stone, however, may have signalled to the Roman populace that the Emesene god was aligned with Jupiter. In particular, the eagle on the stone would have suggested an amalgamation between the god and Jupiter. This may or may not have been intentional, as it is clear that the eagle was part of local Emesene iconography.[246] One particular representation of Elagabal highlights the potential for misunderstanding (Figure 68).[247] The sacred stone is shown decorated with stars and with an eagle on a thunderbolt carrying a wreath in its beak.[248] For the Romans, this image (and others like it) may have been (mis)'read' as a statement of the Jovian pretensions of the Emesene deity.[249]

[245] Optendrenk 1969: 98–100; Scheid 1998a: 293–309.

[246] Cumont 1910: 119–64 on the eagle in Syrian contexts.

[247] *RIC* IV.2 *Elagabalus* 176.

[248] Hdn. 5.3.5 describes markings that were on the stone.

[249] Freedberg 1989: 19–20 on how one image can elicit a variety of responses.

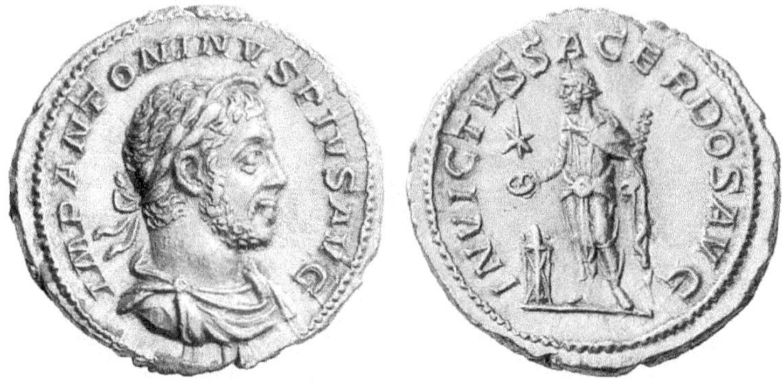

Figure 69: Aureus of Elagabalus. The obverse shows a portrait of the emperor with a 'horn', the reverse displays the emperor in his capacity as high priest of Elagabal with the legend INVICTVS SACERDOS AVG.

The 'horn' of Elagabalus

The portraiture of Elagabalus changes in AD 221, with the emperor being given more mature features and an item that has traditionally been identified as a 'horn' (Figure 69). Mattingly and Sydenham suggested that 'here the horn is used symbolically as representing the solar rays emanating from the head of Elagabalus'.[250] Frey rightly questioned this interpretation and instead believed the appendage was either an amulet of the kind described by Dio (79.11.3) or an index finger.[251] Krengel suggested that Elagabalus is depicted wearing the phallus of a bull.[252] The appendage does differ in length, and in some cases, does possess a bulge at the end reminiscent of a phallus.

Krengel and Frey are correct in asserting that the appendage does not point upwards like a horn. But the interpretation of a bull's phallus remains problematic since it has no parallel in the ancient world. Statues of Jupiter Heliopolitanus in Syria are occasionally given this attribute, but there are no parallel representations of people or priests. If the attribute is a phallus, one would expect it to be erect – a far more powerful statement of fertility and power.[253] The complete absence of comment in a hostile ancient literary record suggests that it must be something else. (One imagines that if the emperor did indeed parade about Rome wearing a phallus on his head, this would have been ideal fodder for authors attempting to condemn the ruler).

[250] Mattingly, Sydenham et al. 1938: 26.

[251] Frey 1989: 69 n. 4. Frey stated that he had seen what appeared to be a fingernail on a well-preserved coin, but provides no image or reference.

[252] Krengel 1997: 53–72 with discussions by Arrizabalaga y Prado 2010: 71–3; Brendle 2001: 411–14; Icks 2006: 173; Kaizer 2005: 190; and Weiser 2000: 53–6.

[253] This is the case on the statues of Jupiter Heliopolitanus.

Examining a series of numismatic portraits of the emperor reveals that this attribute does not appear to come out of the emperor's head, but rather from his laurel wreath (it is rarely if at all seen in conjunction with the radiate crown). The feature could also be rendered with considerable diversity – its length and shape were subject to change. Kaizer believed this was indicative of a series of different phalli.[254] This diversity in representation, however, is also seen in the portrayal of other paraphernalia associated with the Emesene cult: the sacred stone on the *quadriga* and the *semeia*. Such diversity is probably more indicative of the fact that the trappings of the Emesene cult did not have an established Roman iconography.[255] The varying portrayals of the appendage more likely reflect the negotiation of a foreign iconography by the Roman mint, not a series of changing portraits of the emperor himself.

An analysis of the reverse types which accompany this 'horn' show that it occurs in conjunction with two main types: Elagabalus in a *quadriga* holding a branch and sceptre, and Elagabalus sacrificing at an altar as high priest of Emesa.[256] The 'horn', though, does not appear on every portrait used for these types.

A more likely interpretation of the appendage can perhaps be sought in the headgear of priests of the Near East. Unfortunately the scarcity of material remains from Emesa makes a direct comparison with priests from this city extremely difficult. It is also dangerous to draw too many conclusions from the practices of other Near Eastern religions.[257] Kaizer, however, observes that though there was no 'theological orthodoxy' in Near Eastern religions, there was an 'orthodoxy of iconography'.[258] In this context we might note that Palmyrene priests were often depicted with items attached to the front of their headwear. These could include oval cabochons, rosettes, or even a miniature bust.[259] Only sculptural representations of the Palmyrene decorations are known, so there can be no direct comparison with the profile view present on the coins of Elagabalus. But one might cautiously suggest that perhaps priests in Emesa wore something to this effect, which was then represented on Elagabalus' numismatic portraiture. None of the surviving sculpture of Elagabalus shows him with any such appendage (though most of Elagabalus' sculpture was destroyed or re-cut to resemble Severus Alexander).[260] The absence might also reflect the fact that none of the paraphernalia associated with Elagabalus' religious activities seems to have

[254] Kaizer 2005: 190. [255] Rowan 2006: 118.

[256] There are some exceptions to this general rule: *RIC* IV.2 *Elagabalus* 342 (an *adventus* type with Elagabalus on a horse) and *BMCRE* V *Elagabalus* 255 (a reverse showing Victory).

[257] Kaizer 2006: 26–47. [258] Kaizer 2006: 41. [259] Colledge 1976: 140.

[260] Varner 2004: 156. On the surviving sculpture of Elagabalus see Fittschen 2008: 109–15.

been adopted on a universal scale. The appendage on Elagabalus' coinage may be the 'amulet' mentioned by Dio, but like many other problems associated with this ruler's iconography, it remains a mystery.

Elagabal as head of the Roman pantheon?

Frey postulated that the proclamation of Elagabal as the chief deity of the empire occurred in AD 220, coinciding with the emperor's decision to officially adopt the titulature of the high priest of Emesa and to represent himself as an Emesene priest on coins.[261] Prior to this, Frey argued, the worship of the Emesene god was restrained, perhaps through the influence of the imperial women.[262] This model of restrained worship followed by an outbreak of religious zeal in AD 220 has been attractive for many scholars since it explains how the Roman state 'suffered' the rule of Elagabalus for four years. Reading the account of Dio, it seems inconceivable that Romans tolerated the behaviour of the emperor for any extended period of time. An easy explanation is that the extremes of Elagabalus' religious activities only surfaced towards the end of his reign, directly resulting in his overthrow.[263] As already noted, however, it is apparent that not all inhabitants of the empire shared Dio's prejudice. The Jekyll-and-Hyde model of the emperor does not account for the nuances in the remaining evidence and is too heavily reliant on the vision of Elagabalus presented in the literary evidence.

Elagabalus as *summus sacerdos Elagabali* on imperial coinage

From the end of AD 219 coins were struck showing the emperor as high priest of Elagabal (Figure 69). Though there were numerous variants, the reverse type was essentially the same: the emperor standing, sacrificing over a lighted altar and holding a *patera*, usually with a star in the field.[264] Elagabalus is clothed in eastern attire, the jewels and pantaloons noted by

[261] Frey 1989: 80–6. [262] Frey 1989: 75. [263] Birley 1990: 511.

[264] Variants to this general theme were the presence of a standard(s) (perhaps *semeia*) (*RIC* IV.2 *Elagabalus* 48–51), a bull (*RIC* IV.2 *Elagabalus* 88, 191) and a horn (*RIC* IV.2 *Elagabalus* 87). The star often shown in the field of Elagabalus' coinage has traditionally been interpreted as a representation of the solar aspects of the Emesene cult, but considering that this star moves around in the field, does not appear to be an obligatory part of the design, and was present on imperial coinage before and after Elagabalus' reign (e.g. *RIC* III *Commodus* 233–7, 241, 244 and *RIC* IV.2 *Severus Alexander* 262–4, 266, 274, 284–7, 300–1), it might be better seen as an *officina* mark. That it occurs more frequently under Elagabalus may be because the emperor's coinage had fewer types (focused as it was on the production of coinage showing the emperor as high priest), making it difficult to distinguish each *officina* or workshop on the basis of reverse type alone. The system of *officina* marks introduced later may have been based on this more parsimonious system.

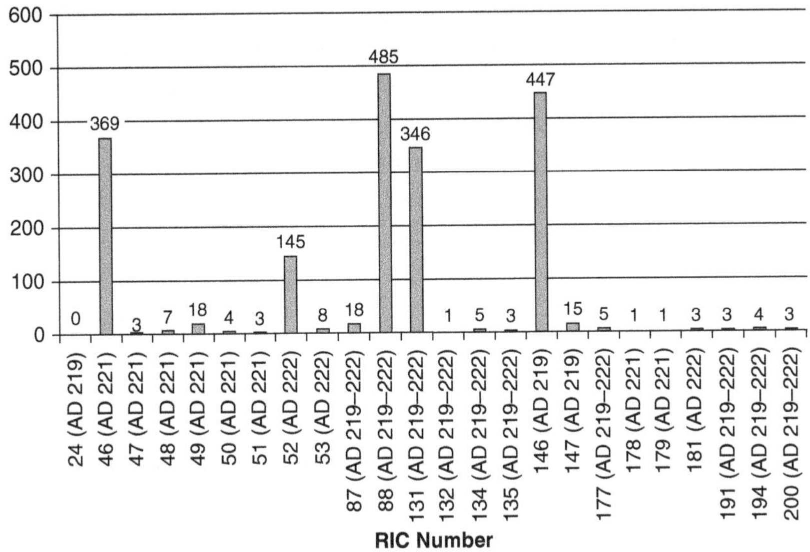

Figure 70: Silver types showing Elagabalus as Emesene high priest, as represented in hoards.

Herodian and Dio in their accounts.[265] The emperor is also shown holding something at his left side, described as a club or a branch. Instead of a branch it is more likely that Elagabalus is holding a bundle of twigs, a common attribute of Syrian priests (for example, at Palmyra).[266] Once again, there are varying representations of the object, but this may reflect the uncertainty of Roman die-cutters in trying to establish an iconography for a foreign cult, rather than any actual variation in the object itself. These coin types were struck in large quantities, constituting approximately 23 per cent of Elagabalus' total silver coinage in the hoard sample (Figures 56, 70).

The absence of *RIC* IV.2 *Elagabalus* 24 from the sample seems to confirm suspicions regarding this coin's authenticity.[267] Dated earlier than the other types showing Elagabalus as an Emesene high priest, it may have simply

[265] Dio 80.11.12; Hdn. 5.3.6, 5.5.3–4; Dirven 2007: 21–36. Zimmermann 1999b: 226 suggested that the divergence between Herodian's description of Elagabalus' dress and the representation of it in the numismatic evidence indicated that Herodian had never seen a picture of the emperor in this garb. However, the mint struggled to represent the foreign iconography of the new emperor, as discussed above, and thus may not have been strictly accurate in its representation. Moreover, Herodian may have taken an image of Elagabalus and modified it to align the emperor more closely with Roman visions of eastern priests. This modification for rhetorical effect does not necessarily mean that the author had not seen a picture of the emperor as high priest of Emesa.

[266] Krumeich 2000/1: 111. A particularly well-preserved statue of a Palmyrene priest holding twigs is now in the National Museum in Damascus, Syria.

[267] Mattingly 1950: 545 notes that the coin is doubtful.

been misreported by earlier collectors. The relatively small number of eastern issues (*RIC* IV.2 *Elagabalus* 177–200) may reflect the smaller minting capacity of the East, but also may reflect problems in the hoard publications. The same coin type has been assigned to two different mints on the basis of style, and students of the relevant hoards may not always have been able to distinguish between Rome and Antioch/Nicomedia. It is thus likely that some eastern issues are present in the numbers attributed to Rome (*RIC* IV.2 *Elagabalus* 46, 147).

The total quantity of coins is extraordinary, particularly when one compares it to the paucity of coins found in the hoard sample displaying the god Elagabal. There was obviously a large visual focus in Elagabalus' reign on his position as high priest. There were several major issues of this type: *RIC* IV.2 *Elagabalus* 46, 88/191, 131 and 146. The sheer quantity of these coin types, released from the end of AD 219 to Elagabalus' death in AD 222, seems to support Frey's suggestion that Elagabalus, or the mint, began a concentrated religious programme during these years.

Epigraphic evidence, however, provides a different perspective. Surviving inscriptions do not support the argument that Elagabalus only publicly assumed the titles of an Emesene priest in AD 220/1.[268] An inscription from Italy in AD 219 is dedicated to the emperor, *sacerdoti amplissimo dei inuicti Solis Elagabali.*[269] An inscription found in the amphitheatre of Tarragone, dated to the second half of AD 218, describes Elagabalus as *sacerdos amplissimus dei invicti Solis Elagabali.*[270] In many inscriptions Severus Alexander is described as *nobilissimus Caesar imperi et sacerdotis.*[271] No mention is made of the Emesene god. In others Elagabalus is given the title *sacerdos*, but Alexander is described in more traditional terms as *nobilissimus Caesar.*[272] Other pieces demonstrate that even after AD 220 there was not universal recognition or implementation of Elagabalus' priestly titles. A milestone from Cappodocia dating to AD 221 does not make any reference to the emperor's position as high priest, nor does a milestone of Asia Minor from AD 222.[273] These may be exceptions; certainly most inscriptions conform to Frey's general rule that the representation of Elagabalus as high priest of Emesa was 'unleashed' from AD 220. But these examples indicate that Elagabalus' religious 'programme' was neither as centralised, nor as organised, as once thought. It is worth recalling that

[268] Frey 1989: 81. [269] *AE* 2001, 938. The inscription is fragmentary. [270] *AE* 1990, 654.

[271] *AE* 2000, 1203 (Császár, Pannonia Superior); *AE* 1995, 1565 (Doliche(?), Syria); *AE* 1966, 339 (military diploma from Moesia); *AE* 1964, 269 (military diploma of uncertain origin).

[272] *AE* 1995, 1641 (Golas, Tripolitania); AE 1936, 85 (Virunum).

[273] Cappodocia: *AE* 1993, 1565. Asia Minor: *AE* 1989, 731 (this text is admittedly confused).

Elagabalus' priestly titles are never found in Greek, nor is the 'horn' ever seen on provincial coinage.

It is evident from the combined literary, numismatic and epigraphic evidence that Elagabalus proclaimed Elagabal as a patron deity from the outset of his reign. If we are correct in believing that coinage showing the Emesene stone was destroyed after Elagabalus' death, there may have been a greater numismatic emphasis on the cult in the emperor's early years than our current evidence suggests. Types showing the emperor as high priest of Emesa are released from the end of AD 219 according to Thirion.[274] This need not reflect a period of restraint followed by excess, but may simply be the result of the emperor's long journey to Rome. If the emperor arrived in Rome in July AD 219, and coin types showing him in Emesene religious dress began later that same year, this is not a significant delay. We should not see a period of restraint followed by excess, but rather a reign in which the emperor's religious activities were subject to regional interpretations and representation. None of the material remains suggests a concerted policy implemented from above; changes to the emperor's portrait and titulature seem to have been implemented throughout the empire in a haphazard way. Either the emperor did not enforce a universal adoption of his Emesene cult, or the mechanics of the Roman Empire did not allow such an implementation to take place.

Blurring boundaries: Elagabal(us)

In Philostratus' *Life of Apollonius of Tyana*, Apollonius visits an Indian king who refuses to engage in philosophy. Apollonius asks the king what he has gained from this refusal, and the king replies 'the whole of virtue and the identification of myself with the Sun'.[275] This may be an allusion to Elagabalus.[276] The association between the emperor and his god became so close that their names eventually aligned and the deity suffered a *damnatio* along with the emperor. This was an extraordinary act.

The close association between the emperor and his god is most evident in the account of the *Historia Augusta*. It is here that the emperor is named *Heliogabalus*, a Latinised play on the god's name Elagabal.[277] The author

[274] Thirion 1968: 20. [275] Philostr. *VA* 3.26.

[276] Anderson 1989: 143; Flinterman 1995: 220–1. Morgan suggests that Heliodorus' *Ethiopia*, like Philostratus' vision of India, is also an analogue or cipher for the city of Emesa (Morgan 2009: 265–81).

[277] *SHA Heliogab.* 1.6.

may have been picking up on an earlier tradition – the *Historia Augusta* was reliant on Marius Maximus for at least some material.[278] Aurelius Victor also mentions the nickname, suggesting it came from a common source.[279] Whether the nickname was contemporary with Elagabalus' reign, or whether it was created later is impossible to discern. It does not occur in Dio or Herodian.

The nickname, whether posthumous or not, was likely inspired by the unusual alignment between emperor and god. The emperor's titles (*sacerdos amplissimus dei Solis Elagabali*) reinforced the connection to the deity, reiterated again and again. The sacred stone of Emesa was described as CONSERVATOR AVG and a large proportion of the emperor's coinage highlighted his role as *sacerdos* of the god.[280] This connection was also apparent elsewhere, particularly in the location of the temples to Elagabal. Though the imagery of the Emesene cult and the emperor's role as high priest is today largely preserved on coins, it is highly likely that the iconography was displayed on other media as well.

The marriages of Elagabalus and Elagabal

The marriages of both god and emperor would have served only to heighten the connection between the two. During his short rule Elagabalus was married four times to three different women: Julia Cornelia Paula (of Roman nobility), Julia Aquilia Severa (a Vestal Virgin whom Elagabalus married twice) and Annia Faustina (descended from the Antonine imperial family).[281] Similarly the god Elagabal was reportedly married to Urania of Carthage and to the Roman Palladium.[282] Frey dismisses the last marriage as fiction,[283] but its invention may have been motivated by the close alignment between god and emperor. Elagabalus's marriage to a Vestal may have spawned the story that the god married the Palladium, a divine equivalent.

The reasons behind the multiple marriages of Elagabalus are difficult to uncover. Butler suggested that the marriages were aimed at securing connections to the Roman nobility, while more recently Icks has suggested the marriages, particularly to the Vestal Aquilia Severa, were aimed at forging strong bonds between the Emesene religion and that of Rome.[284]

[278] *SHA Heliogab.* 11.7. [279] Aur. Vict. *Caes* 23. [280] *RIC* IV.2 *Elagabalus* 61–2, 64–5.

[281] Dio 80.5.4, 80.9.1–4; Hdn. 5.6.1; *SHA Heliogab.* 6.6–9. The marriage to Faustina once again highlights the continuing connection to the Antonine dynasty in this period.

[282] Urania of Carthage: Dio 80.12.1; Hdn. 5.6.4; *SHA Heliogab.* 7.1; *Palladium*: Hdn. 5.6.3; *SHA Heliogab.* 3.4, 6.6–9 (though with obvious references to Christianity).

[283] Frey 1989: 53–4. [284] Frey 1989: 54; Icks 2006: 175; Petsalis-Diomidis 2007: 251.

Both Dio and Herodian reflect an association between the human and the divine marriages in their narratives. Dio notes that during the marriage of the Emesene god to Urania, Elagabalus collected wedding gifts for the goddess 'as he had done in the case of his own wives'.[285] Herodian juxtaposes his accounts of the marriages, discussing the emperor's wives before progressing to those of the Emesene god, observing that 'it was not just human marriage that he made a mockery of'.[286] Both forms of marriage (the human and the divine) also seem to have been accompanied by large celebrations, which would reinforce the connection.[287]

The little evidence that survives concerning the marriages suggests that Elagabalus may have desired to create a divine dynasty, in which high priest (himself) and priestess (the Vestal Aquilia Severa) would give birth to the next generation of emperors and high priests. Dio presents this idea, which is also hinted at in Herodian.[288] If this were the case, the emperor and his advisors may have been trying to alter the basis of Roman imperial power, using divine sanction as *the* underlying force behind the throne. Caution must be exercised in accepting these accounts however; the numismatic types of Elagabalus' wives in no way suggest a dynastic priesthood. The coinage of the imperial wives in this period is noteworthy only in that it continues largely to display traditional Roman reverse types.

Venus Caelestis and Julia Soaemias

One coin type may allude to the marriage of the god Elagabal to Urania of Carthage. Coin types struck for Aquilia Severa (Elagabalus' second wife) and Julia Soaemias display a legend hitherto not seen on Roman coinage: VENVS CAELESTIS.[289] Urania was identified with Dea Caelestis and Aphrodite/Venus in the Graeco-Roman world. Mattingly suggested that the epithet *Caelestis* indicates it is Urania who is represented on the coins here.[290] No Venus Caelestis types struck with the portrait of Aquilia Severa were present in the hoard sample; hence Mattingly was correct in classifying the type as a hybrid, 'the reverse belonging strictly to Julia Soaemias'.[291] This is starkly underlined by the fact that the type constituted approximately 96 per cent of Soaemias' coinage in the hoards (Figure 71). That the mother of the emperor should be represented in such an exclusive manner is

[285] Dio 80.12.1–2. [286] Hdn. 5.6.3. [287] Dio 80.9.1–3; Hdn. 6.4.5.
[288] Dio 80.11.3–4; Hdn. 5.6.2. [289] *RIC* IV.2 *Elagabalus* 230, 240–5, 402–8.
[290] Mattingly 1950: ccxxxiii; Whittaker LCL, 50 n. 1. [291] Mattingly 1950: ccxxxvii.

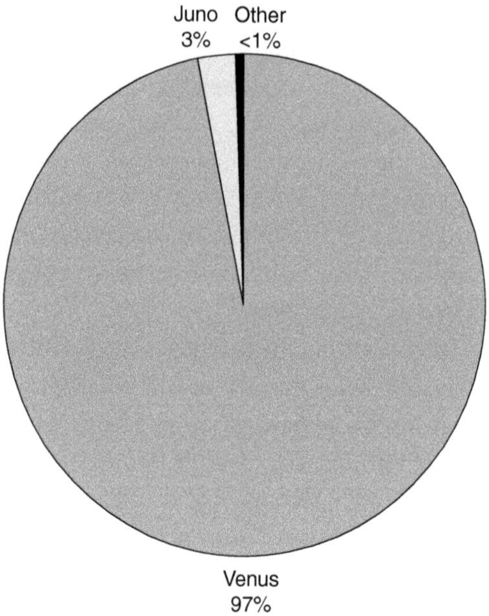

Figure 71: Reverse silver types of Julia Soaemias as represented in hoards (n = 619).

extraordinary; Elagabalus' grandmother Julia Maesa has a much larger repertoire of imagery on her coinage (Figure 72).

The singularity of Soaemias' numismatic image suggests that the type was used from the beginning of Elagabalus' reign, prior to the marriage of the Emesene stone to Urania. We might then be better advised to view this type as an *interpretatio Romana* of an Emesene goddess.[292] Frey observes that an Aphrodite figure did exist in the Emesene pantheon.[293] The gods Azizos and Monimos, Venus as the morning and evening star, were also worshipped in the city.[294] The unusual numismatic image of the empress may reflect her support of the Emesene cult during Elagabalus' rule. While Elagabalus' grandmother Mamaea survived into Severus Alexander's reign, Soaemias was murdered with her son, and her body was dragged through Rome along with the emperor.[295] Varner observes that Soaemias is the only empress to suffer such a drastic form of public abuse.[296] Her treatment here may reflect a significant public role in Elagabalus' religious activities.

[292] Mattingly 1950: ccxliv. [293] Frey 1989: 50. [294] Drijvers 1980: 148–52.
[295] Dio 80.20.2; Hdn. 5.8.8–9. [296] Varner 2001: 49.

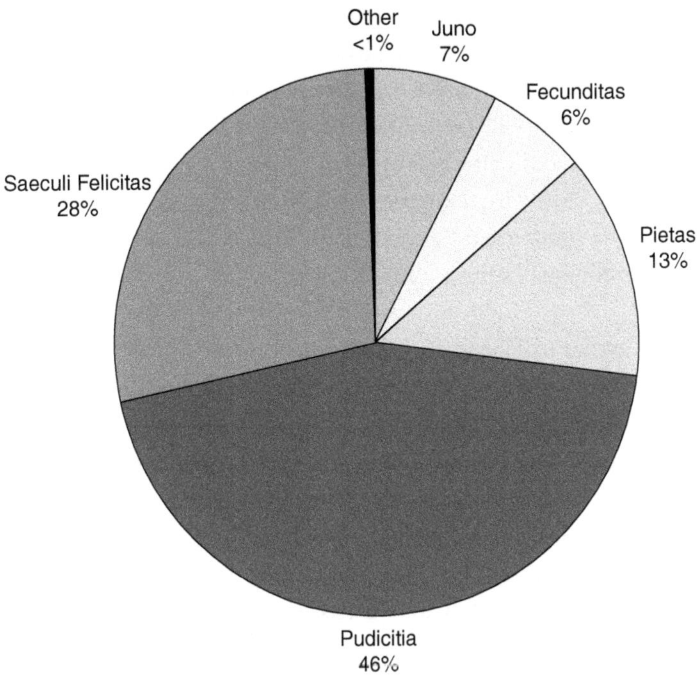

Figure 72: Reverse silver types of Julia Maesa as represented in hoards (n = 2,220).

The *damnatio memoriae* of Elagabal(us)

The alignment between god and emperor was likely the cause of the double *damnatio*. Though gods and festivals (particularly foreign ones) were often subject to political sanction (for instance the *Bacchanalia* in 186 BC), the *damnatio* of a god and his expulsion from the city was extremely uncommon. The conversion of the temple of Elagabal on the Palatine by Severus Alexander must also be seen in this context: though sanctuaries and gods might be added to existing temples, complete conversion was extremely unusual. It is a testament to the close alignment between the emperor and his god that the sanctions imposed on Elagabalus after his death were also imposed upon a deity. Like the implementation of the Emesene cult, these sanctions were probably not overarching, nor exhaustive, but the evidence that remains is illuminating. The residents of Altaua, for example, having constructed a temple or shrine to Elagabal, must have destroyed or rededicated it after the fall of the emperor (at least, the erasure of the god's name from the inscription suggests that this was the case).[297] A similar process

[297] *AE* 1985, 976.

must have occurred for the other cultic centres throughout the empire. Even in inscriptions erected prior to Elagabalus' reign (for instance by the Emesene Balbillus) Elagabal's name was subject to erasure.[298] The politics involved in a *damnatio* will be considered more fully in the following chapter. The unusual and extreme implementation of Elagabalus' tutelary deity was met with a similarly extreme reaction. Severus Alexander would be forced to actively condemn the actions of his predecessor, something that defined his own religious claims to power.

The religious activities of Elagabalus might thus be seen as part of a wider Severan emphasis on the divine sanction of imperial rule, but there are also significant new developments during the emperor's rule. Like the earlier Severan rulers, Elagabalus associated himself with a particular deity who had a provincial cult centre. In constructing two temples to his god in Rome Elagabalus was also following a precedent that dated back to Augustus. But in publicly representing himself as high priest of the god, in addition to his role as *pontifex maximus*, Elagabalus differed significantly from what had gone before, or from what would follow. In maintaining his Emesene religious office after he had become emperor Elagabalus and his advisors created a new and modified image of a Roman ruler. Indeed, the emperor and his council may have been trying to alter the nature of imperial rule by creating a system in which the emperor would rule through divine sanction as high priest of the Emesene god. If we are to interpret the reign of Elagabalus as an experiment in the foundations of Roman imperial power, however, it was a failure. This is more than demonstrated in the ideology that followed Elagabalus' fall. The rule of Elagabalus' successor, Severus Alexander, would be characterised by an emphasis on Roman precedent and tradition.

[298] *CIL* 6.2269.

6 Severus Alexander and the re-founding of Rome

Elagabalus was overthrown in AD 222, reportedly beheaded and dragged through the city before being thrown into the Tiber. His cousin, Severus Alexander, succeeded him. Dio reports that no one associated with Elagabalus' rule survived.[1] This set of circumstances, the *damnatio* of one emperor as another rose to power, has shaped visions of Alexander's reign from antiquity through to the modern day. From the beginning of his reign Alexander closely aligned himself with Jupiter, and also with Romulus and Augustus. This was a pointed contrast to the rule of his predecessor. Having suffered the rule of Elagabalus, Rome was to be 're-founded'.

Dio's account breaks off under Severus Alexander, and the portrayal of the emperor by both Herodian and the *Historia Augusta* makes any reconstruction of the reign difficult. Herodian's account characterises Alexander as an emperor dominated by women. This topos is particularly apparent in Herodian's narrative of Alexander's Persian and German campaigns.[2] The account presented in the *Historia Augusta* is by contrast largely positive, and may have been written as a direct response to Herodian's work.[3] In the *Historia Augusta* the emperor is portrayed as an ideal prince, an image that served as inspiration for authors of the more modern age, particularly in the work of Sir Thomas Elyot and Guevara's *Decadas de las vidas de los X Cesares*.[4] The different presentations of Severus Alexander might be seen as part of a broader divergence between the Greek and Latin traditions on the Persian Wars under Alexander's reign, and on the effectiveness of Alexander as a leader.[5] The circumstances of Alexander's reign have complicated the historical accounts; his overthrow by Maximian would doubtless have led to a negative historical tradition, while the pro-Alexander stance of those involved in the revolution of AD 238 would have created or resuscitated a more positive view.[6]

1 Dio 80.20.2–21.3. 2 Hdn. 6.1.5, 6.5.8–9, 6.9.8.

3 Evident from the work itself (*SHA Alex. Sev.* 52.2–3). See also Bertrand-Dagenbach 1990: 126 and Ferrero 1999: 191–216.

4 Lascelles 1951: 305–18. See also Whetstones 1584.

5 Edwell 2008: 160–7. Latin sources claim the emperor was victorious in these wars, whereas the Greek accounts report a failure.

6 Edwell 2008: 51.

The *Vita* of Severus Alexander in the *Historia Augusta* is largely fictional, shaped by the concerns and culture of the fourth century.[7] Alexander represents the author's vision of a model ruler for his own time. He is surrounded by a good and faithful council, banishes eunuchs from the court and consequently achieves good rule in spite of his Syrian background.

The *Historia Augusta* presents Alexander's reign as a contrast to Elagabalus, a comparison sustained throughout the entire *Vita*. Explicit attention is drawn, for example, to the fact that Alexander removed the jewels from the footwear Elagabalus had favoured, and that Alexander forbade anyone to worship him, although Elagabalus had allowed *proskynesis*. Elagabalus wasted the grain supply while Alexander bought grain at his own expense, Elagabalus had been the slave of eunuchs but Alexander limited their number, and so on, *ad nauseam*.[8] The *Historia Augusta* may have emphasised the contrast for its own purpose(s), but the tradition might have developed out of the focus on change and renewal that Alexander fostered at the beginning of his reign. The numismatic evidence and the *damnatio memoriae* of Elagabalus, discussed in more detail below, suggest that Alexander's rule was to a certain extent defined by an explicit contrast with his predecessor.

An uncritical reading of the *Historia Augusta* has led some to believe Alexander's reign heralded a new dawn of religious syncretism, an idea that dates back to the work of Réville.[9] In the *Vita* Alexander refers to Marna and has household *Lares* that included Apollonius of Tyana, Christ, Abraham and Orpheus. The emperor also reportedly wished to build a temple to Christ but was prevented from doing so out of concern that all men would then become Christians.[10] Needless to say, these statements tell us more about the world of the author than the religious activities of Alexander.[11] As Bertrand-Dagenbach has illustrated, these references were literary allegories with contemporary significance aimed at the author's readers.[12] The statement that the emperor may have worshipped Christ or supported the Christians can be dismissed as fiction, though fiction that might have derived from a tolerant religious atmosphere in this period.[13]

[7] For modern discussions of this topic see Edwell 2008; Birley 1991: 345–6; Blázquez 1990: 25–36; Chauvot 1994: 285–91; Ferrero 1999: 191–216; Hönn 1911; Jardé 1925; Penella 1977: 229–30; and Straub 1970: 247–72.

[8] *SHA Alex. Sev.* 4.2, 18.4, 11.9, 13.6.

[9] Bregman 1982: 58–72; Halsberghe 1984: 2191; Réville 1886: 23. Against this idea see Chauvot 1994: 285–91.

[10] *SHA Alex. Sev.* 17.4, 29.2, 43.6–7. [11] Ruggini 1991: 133.

[12] Bertrand-Dagenbach 1990: 41. The mention of Marna is a pun on Cic. *Cat* 1.1.2; the temple to the god was also closed in AD 401.

[13] *SHA Alex. Sev.* 22.4, 39.2, 44.6; Euseb. *Hist. eccl.* 6.21.3–4; Birley 1991: 345; Cameron 1965: 245–8; Cross 2002: 6; McKechnie 1999: 440–1; Sterz 1977: 700–3.

Herodian's presentation of Alexander introduces the reader to a new complexity in his larger exploration of *paideia*. Alexander receives a Greek and Latin education, but the effect of this is undermined by the influence of his mother, whose actions betray her lack of *paideia*. As Sidebottom demonstrates, Herodian presents an image of *paideia* paradoxically undermined by the very person who was trying to instil it.[14] For example, Mamaea removes all corrupting influences from her son (6.1.5), but then Herodian goes on to detail her obsession with money (6.1.8), an obsession which displays an absence of the virtues brought about by *paideia*. Herodian here blames Alexander's character: though he had received an appropriate education and disapproved of Mamaea's actions, his mildness meant that he remained under her corrupting influence (6.1.10, 6.9.8). This adds a level of complexity to Herodian's exploration of *paideia* and suggests to the reader that Greek education cannot completely overcome inherent character traits.

Herodian's vision of an emperor dominated by women has been transferred into some of the modern scholarship that focuses on Severus Alexander's reign.[15] Alexander, like his cousin Elagabalus, was fourteen when he came to power. His *consilium* and advisors might thus have informally included his mother Julia Mamaea and grandmother Julia Maesa. But when Alexander died in AD 235 he would have been about twenty-seven. Though the imperial women *might* have been influential at the beginning of the emperor's reign, it is impossible to identify whether this influence continued as Alexander grew older. As has been explored for Elagabalus, if the imperial women were the true powers behind the throne, then this reality was not communicated to the public through the imperial coinage or other official media.

Upon Alexander's accession the Emesene god was banished from Rome and Herodian records that the statues of the gods were restored to their traditional places.[16] Alexander's emphasis on Jupiter signalled to the populace the return of a principate that conformed to expectations and precedent.

This theme of restoration was not restricted to the sphere of cult and religion. The renovation and repair of buildings in Rome (recorded on coinage and in the *Historia Augusta*) also played a rôle in the ideology of renewal.[17] Alexander completed the necessary renovations of the

[14] Sidebottom 1998: 2811. [15] Cleves 1982; Kosmetatou 2002: 398–414.

[16] Hdn. 6.1.3; Dio 80.21.2; *SHA Alex. Sev.* 6.2.

[17] *RIC IV.2 Severus Alexander* 58–9, 499–51, 453 (*thermae Alexandri*), 410–11 (Colosseum) as well as the temple of Jupiter Ultor, which is discussed in more detail below. See *SHA Alex. Sev.* 24.3–4, 25.3–9, 27.7–11, 28.6, 45.8 with discussion by Benario 1961: 281–90 and Coarelli 1987: 429–56.

Colosseum after it had been struck by lightning, and renovated and completed several bath and theatre complexes.[18] This interest in public works of a utilitarian nature targeted at the wider populace of Rome is reminiscent of the building emphases of the Flavian dynasty after Nero. Coarelli also suggests that Alexander was responsible for the renovation of the Arval Grove at Magliana, and the construction of the *umbilicus urbis Romae*, a structure in the Roman forum which was believed to mark the centre of the empire and from which all distances were measured.[19] If this structure is to be connected with the *milliarium aureum*, or monumental milestone of Augustus erected in the forum near the Temple of Saturn, then we may have an explicit connection to Augustus created by Alexander.[20] At the very least, the *umbilicus* must have referenced or evoked the Augustan structure. Though the archaeological remains of the Arval Grove complex in Magliana can only suggest a date for renovations in the first half of the third century, Alexander's focus on religious renewal and traditionalism makes him a good candidate for the work.

Alexander's coinage also communicated the virtues and benefits of his rule to the empire.[21] Alexander may even have been proclaimed as *sacerdos urbis* on a coin of Antioch, a pointed contrast to Elagabalus' title as *sacerdos* of the god Elagabal.[22] The emperor's silver types also had a significant emphasis on Mars and Jupiter (Figure 73).

It is clear these two gods were closely associated with Alexander's rise to power as well as the military campaigns against Persia that would later shape his reign. Severus Alexander initially assumed the rôle of princeps as the avenger of Roman morals, Roman culture and Roman religion. This vengeance would develop into claims of military prowess as the Roman borders came under siege in AD 230.

[18] Coarelli 1987: 433; Ramsay 1935: 419–47. *P. Oxy.* 3.412 preserves part of Julius Africanus' *Kestoi*, which was dedicated by the author to Severus Alexander. In the preserved fragment Africanus discusses the location of a text 'near the baths of Alexander, in the beautiful library at the Pantheon which I myself designed for the emperor' (*P. Oxy.* 3.412, lines 59–66).

[19] Coarelli 1987: 433–4, 443; Scheid and Broise 1983: 202–11.

[20] Richardson 1992: 404 suggests that the two structures are associated since it is unlikely that two centres of Rome existed so close to each other at the same time.

[21] Amongst the virtues and personifications Annona constituted 6% of the emperor's silver coinage in the hoard sample, Aequitas 5%, Fides, Spes and Providentia 3% each, Libertas and Liberalitas 2% each.

[22] *RIC* IV.2 *Severus Alexander* 297, though the coin is irregular and may not have been an official issue.

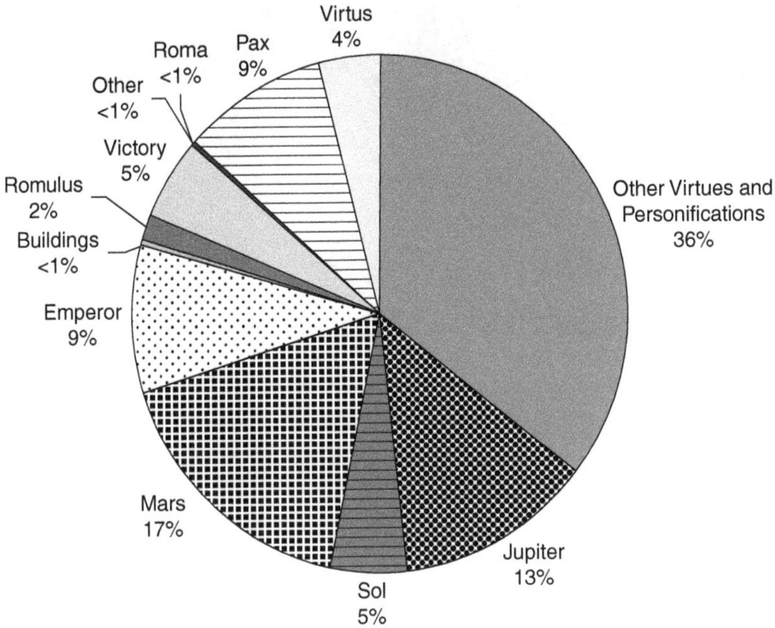

Figure 73: Reverse silver types of Severus Alexander as represented in hoards (n = 12,225).

The temple of Jupiter Ultor and the Jovian ideology of power

The death of Elagabalus and the banishment of the Emesene deity meant that the temple of Elagabal on the Palatine no longer had an occupant. It is likely that Severus Alexander transformed the *Elagabalium* into a temple to Jupiter Ultor (Jupiter the Avenger). Jupiter's 'restoration' was proclaimed in a pointed and monumental fashion, leaving the population in no doubt as to the differences between Alexander and his predecessor. The evidence for the conversion of the *Elagabalium* is primarily numismatic (Figure 74).

Coins of Severus Alexander with the legend IOVI VLTORI display a structure remarkably similar to that seen on the medallion of Elagabalus (Figure 64).[23] The similarities between these images have formed the basis for the theory that the *Elagabalium* was converted. The pieces of both emperors show a temple with a large area in front, surrounded by porticoes with a colonnade or gateway. All also show evidence of *opus quadratum*. One might even suggest that the die-engravers were conscious of Elagabalus' earlier issue and set out to communicate the use of the same

[23] *BMCRE* VI *Severus Alexander* 208*, 209*, 210*; *RIC* IV.2 *Severus Alexander* 413; Gnecchi 1912: (vol. 2) no. 7.

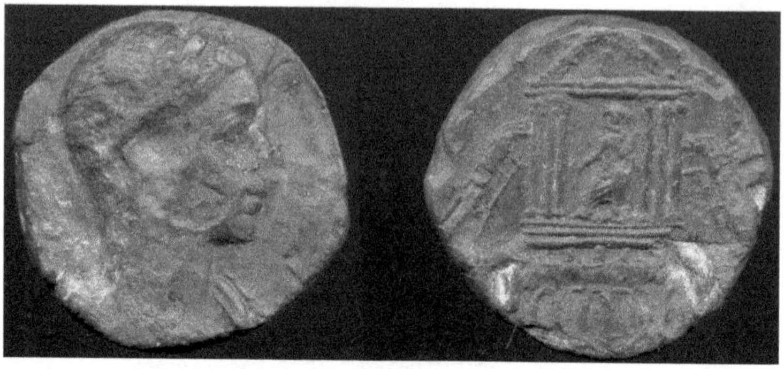

Figure 74: Medallion of Severus Alexander showing the Temple of Jupiter Ultor with the legend IOVI VLTORI P M TR P III COS P P S C.

structure for a purpose more in keeping with 'traditional' Roman religion, highlighting the conversion of sacred space. The epithet given to Jupiter in this instance is significant: VLTOR or avenger, reflecting Severus Alexander's redress of Elagabalus' infractions. Normally an epithet of Mars, the word Ultor is only recorded in connection with Jupiter on one earlier coin, an aureus of Commodus (though the existence of this coin is uncertain).[24] Ultor did occur as a title of Jupiter on inscriptions before Alexander's reign, though it remained unusual.[25]

The complete rededication of a Roman temple on the Palatine may have been unusual, but the conversion of a building of an emperor who had suffered a *damnatio* had precedent. One of the more notable examples of the phenomenon is Nero's *domus aurea*, the extravagance of which was seen as a reflection of Nero's selfishness and the transgressions of his régime.[26] Successive emperors went to considerable efforts to cover areas of Nero's palace with pointedly utilitarian public buildings: Vespasian rebuilt the temple of *Divus Claudius* and the Colosseum, Titus constructed baths, Domitian a gladiatorial school, and Trajan also erected baths.[27]

Not every structure of a 'bad' emperor was subjected to this treatment: Domitian had a large public building programme, of which a great many monuments can still be identified, suggesting that these were not subjected to a later conversion.[28] Rather, the actions surrounding the *damnatio* were

[24] *RIC* III *Commodus* 200, reliant on Cohen 261. Cohen recorded that the specimen was in the British Museum, but the *BMCRE* reports that it is not. Cohen may have misread VLTORI for VICTORI.

[25] Angeli 1971: 151–2, also incidental evidence for the easy confusion between the epithets VICTOR and VLTOR.

[26] Suet. *Ner.* 31; Tac. *Ann.* 15.42; Griffin 1984: 137–8. [27] Griffin 1984: 137. [28] Jones 1992: 85.

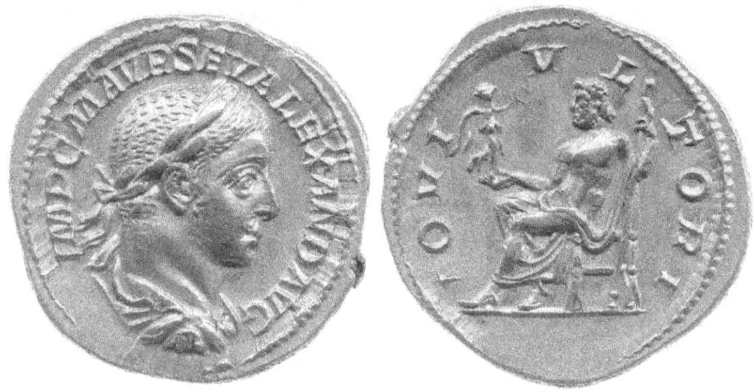

Figure 75: Aureus of Severus Alexander with Jupiter and the legend IOVI VITORI.

targeted towards the person of the emperor himself and the monuments that encapsulated his vices. The equestrian statue of Domitian erected in the Forum, for example, *was* destroyed after his death.[29] Nero's golden palace was connected with the questionable morals of the emperor, so it too was converted. Within this context the public transformation of the temple of Elagabal can be seen as further evidence of how closely the emperor Elagabalus and his deity were aligned; the *damnatio* of one necessarily entailed the *damnatio* of the other. The conversion of the temple was as necessary as the overthrow of the emperor, for the wrongs of the régime were inherently connected with the structure.

The precise nature of the cult that was installed in the converted *Elagabalium* has been the subject of debate. The most influential theory has been that of Hill, who suggested that Alexander re-installed the cult of Jupiter that had originally occupied the area.[30] Hill's hypothesis was largely reliant on the numismatic evidence. Coin types struck for Alexander show the image of Jupiter Victor holding Victory and a sceptre, accompanied by the legend IOVI VLTORI (Figure 75). Regionary catalogues mention a temple to Jupiter Victor on the Palatine, and Hill concluded that Elagabalus must have converted a temple of Jupiter Victor, which was then restored under Alexander.[31]

Hill's use of the numismatic evidence presents problems. The coinage of Alexander proclaimed IOVI VLTORI, not IOVI VICTORI. For Hill, the imagery of Jupiter Victor on Alexander's coinage meant that the pieces had

[29] Jones 1992: 85.

[30] Hill 1960a: 117–20; Hill 1960b: 208–10; most recently reiterated in Stewart 2003: 213.

[31] Notitia, Regio X, Palatium 11: *aedem Iovis victoris.*

to refer to this particular form of the god. Yet the legends and imagery on imperial coinage were more nuanced than this: different statue types of Jupiter could be paired with different legends.[32] Hill believed that the legend IOVI VICTORI had to be accompanied by the well-known statue type of Jupiter seated, holding Victory and a sceptre. In many instances this is the case.[33] But the epithet is also found paired with other Jovian cult statues, for example Jupiter Ammon.[34] Conversely, the iconography of Jupiter Victor appears on Roman coinage not only with the legend IOVI VICTORI and IOVI VLTORI, but with the legends IOVI CONSER(vatori), IOVI CAP (itolino) PR(aesidi) VRB(is), IOVI INVICTO, IOVI PRAE(senti) and IOVI PRAE(sidi) OR(bis).[35] The image and the legend on a Roman coin did not have to be in exact correspondence.

A numismatic legend could differ from the iconography it accompanied, and the Roman mint came to utilise this to great effect, expanding the possible interpretations and associations of a particular image. In this sense, the legend guided the viewer in the interpretation of the coin.[36] The legend on the Alexander type is a clear indication that the Roman mint intended to communicate the idea of Jupiter the Avenger. To the Roman mind Jupiter could operate in any number of ways, but the act of giving an epithet to a deity suggested that he had acted in that capacity.[37] IOVI VLTORI suggests that Jupiter had acted in revenge, not that Jupiter *Victor* had acted in this capacity.

This nuanced relationship between legend and image on coinage may have been more apparent on Jupiter types due to the close association between the princeps and Jupiter. Jupiter was increasingly given very specific epithets on coin types, titles that often alluded to the situation of the imperial person. This is particularly marked from the reign of Commodus, who also visually aligns himself with the deity.[38] For example, Jupiter is shown on Commodus' coinage holding a thunderbolt and sceptre with the legend IOVI IVVENI, alluding to the youthful rule of Commodus

32 Rowan 2009: 128–35.

33 For example: *RIC* I^2 *Vitellius* 68; *RIC* II *Domitian* 253; *RIC* II *Hadrian* 251; *RIC* III *Commodus* 291; *RIC* III *Marcus Aurelius* 1612; *RIC* IV.1 *Septimius Severus* 441B; *RIC* IV.1 *Caracalla* 200.

34 *RIC* IV.1 *Septimius Severus* 272. For other imagery see *RIC* IV.1 *Clodius Albinus* 25–7 and *RIC* IV.1 *Septimius Severus* 204, and discussion in Rowan 2009.

35 CONSERVATORI: *RIC* IV.1 *Pescennius Niger* 42, *RIC* IV.1 *Septimius Severus* 111A, 130, 504A; IOVI CAP PR VRB: Bland, Burnett et al. 1987: 68, Group II no. 4; INVICTO: *RIC* IV.1 *Septimius Severus* 480; PRAE(sens): Classical Numismatic Group, Mail Bid Sale 61 (25 September 2002) 1850; IOVI PRAE OR: Fritz Rudolf Künker Münzenhandlung, Auction 83 (17 June 2003) 1018.

36 Bryson 1981: 4, and 5: 'language enormously shapes and delimits our reception of images'.

37 Rives 2007: 15.

38 Bergmann 1998: 265; Hekster 2002: 102; Rowan 2009: 131–2.

himself.[39] After the fall of Cleander in AD 191, Jupiter is shown on the imperial coinage as the defender of the imperial *salus* and the emperor's security.[40] This connection between the emperor and Jupiter is not surprising; both were the supreme rulers of their respective kingdoms.

The alignment between the emperor and Jupiter was also increasingly expressed in numismatic imagery. Under Septimius Severus, for example, Jupiter is shown towering over two children, presumably meant to represent Caracalla and Geta.[41] As discussed in the third chapter, an aureus of Severus shows Jupiter seated between Liber Pater and Hercules.[42] Their portrayal with Jupiter, a unique numismatic type, was a result of their strong connection to Severus, who himself was associated with Jupiter.[43]

The Jupiter Ultor types of Severus Alexander thus allude to the cult of Jupiter Ultor, and communicate the role of Alexander as the avenger of Elagabalus' régime. The young emperor closely aligned himself with Jupiter from the very beginning of his reign: his *dies imperii* is recorded in the *Feriale Duranum* as 13 March, a day holy to Jupiter and in the *Chronography of 354* mentioned as a day sacred to Jupiter Cultor. Chausson suggests this may be a corruption of the epithet Ultor.[44] Coarelli points out that this is a different date from the cult day of Jupiter Victor, which is 13 April.[45] This again suggests that we should not align the cults of Jupiter Victor and Jupiter Ultor. Severus Alexander's connection to Jupiter was thus announced from the beginning of his rule and was continuously communicated by the imperial mint throughout his reign, with the epithets of Jupiter changing to reflect contemporary imperial circumstances. In many senses this was a continuation of earlier tradition, but Alexander's pointed association with Jupiter meant a new variety of Jovian types were struck, as well as an increased quantity of Jupiter coinage. The god's sanction of Alexander's reign signalled a pointed return to the Jovian language of power.

Looking for a precise context behind Alexander's Jovian types is difficult since much of the emperor's coinage does not list his tribunician power (the easiest and most secure method for dating Roman imperial coinage). However, the chronology and dates deduced by Carson in the British Museum catalogue of coins for Alexander provides a general idea of the date of many issues. When this chronology (based on portraiture, coin

[39] *RIC* III *Commodus* 499, 525, 532. [40] *RIC* III *Commodus* 255, 256, 597.

[41] *RIC* IV.1 *Septimius Severus* 226, 233, 243. This type is also present on a medal of Marcus Aurelius (Gnecchi 1912: (vol. 2) 52, pl. 63.3), though presumably here the two figures represent Aurelius and Lucius Verus.

[42] Hill 1982: 159–60. [43] Rowan 2009. [44] Chausson 1995b: 739. [45] Coarelli 1987: 437.

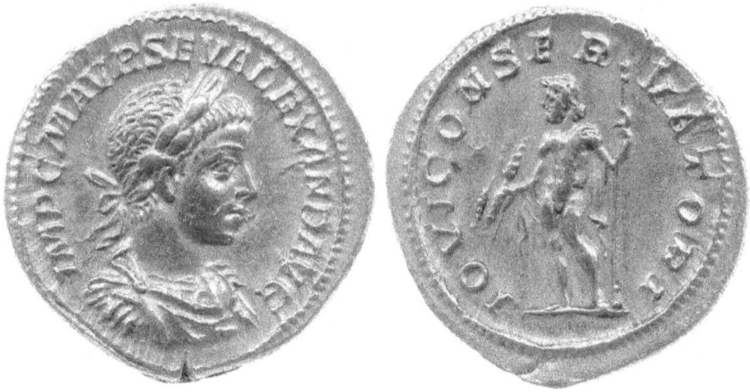

Figure 76: Aureus of Severus Alexander with Jupiter holding thunderbolt and sceptre and the legend IOVI CONSERVATORI.

hoards and type) is followed, the close relationship between Alexander and Jupiter is fully revealed.[46]

Jupiter appeared on Alexander's coinage from the beginning of his reign, initially without an epithet, then with the legend IOVI CONSERVATORI (Figure 76).[47] The epithet of Jupiter here likely has reference to the ideology surrounding Severus Alexander's succession. Both Dio and Herodian describe a plot of Elagabalus against his younger cousin, the failure of which led directly to Alexander's coming to the throne.[48] Whether or not these accounts reflect the truth of the situation, there must have been an immediate justification behind the murder of Elagabalus, and a plot against Alexander's life is a likely candidate. *Conservator* signalled Alexander's escape from this plot; his preservation from his cousin's murderous intent is attributed to the protection of Jupiter, who became the tutelary god of the young emperor's entire reign. CONSERVATOR may also have possessed a secondary meaning. Elagabalus had bestowed this nominally Jovian title on the Emesene god Elagabal.[49] The restoration of the epithet to Jupiter may thus have signified Jupiter's return to supremacy in the early years of Severus Alexander's reign. The hoard evidence suggests that there was a heavy emphasis on Jupiter at the beginning of the emperor's reign (Figure 77). The stress on this particular type makes sense when one considers its thematic connection to Alexander's accession.

46 For a fuller discussion see Rowan 2009.

47 Without an accompanying legend: *RIC* IV.2 *Severus Alexander* 4, 5, 387 (AD 222), 18–20 (AD 223), 34–5 (AD 224). The legend *Iovi Conservatori: RIC* IV.2 *Severus Alexander* 140–1 (AD 222).

48 See Dio 80.19.1 and following; Hdn. 5.8.3.

49 *RIC* IV.2 *Elagabalus* 61–2, 64–5; Numismatica Ars Classica, Auction 29 (11 May 2005) 596.

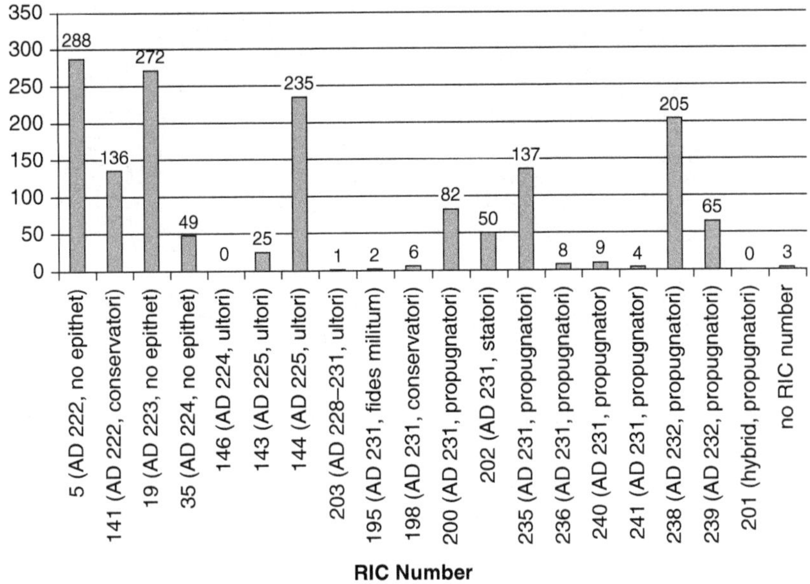

Figure 77: Silver Jupiter types of Severus Alexander as represented in hoards.

In AD 224, coin types were released showing the temple of Jupiter Ultor (Figure 74), with one type appearing on a silver denarius.[50] The following year (according to the chronology of Carson) the IOVI VLTORI type showing the imagery of Jupiter Victor was struck (Figure 75).[51] The denarius temple type was completely absent from the hoard analysis, suggesting that it was a very small issue.[52] It may have been struck to mark the completion of the transformation of the *Elagabalium*. Although small in quantity, one might argue that the very act of striking this type was an important means of marking and recording the transformation of urban space. By contrast, the silver issue with the imagery of Jupiter Victor (*RIC* IV.2 *Severus Alexander* 143–4) has a stronger presence in hoards, constituting about 23 per cent of the emperor's denarii struck in AD 225. The well-known image of Jupiter Victor was employed to communicate the religious restoration of the empire, and for the literate the accompanying legend made a powerful statement about Severus Alexander's imperial ideology.

In AD 230, news reached Rome of the invasion of Ardarshir, King of Persia, and in AD 231 Alexander embarked on a campaign against the Persians.[53] The decision to issue coinage with the image of Jupiter at this juncture, after a gap of six years, is telling. Carson identifies five types of

[50] *RIC* IV.2 *Severus Alexander* 146, 412–13. [51] *RIC* IV.2 Severus Alexander 142–5.
[52] *RIC* IV.2 Severus Alexander 146. [53] Dio 80.3.1–5.3; Hdn. 6.2.1–7.1.1.

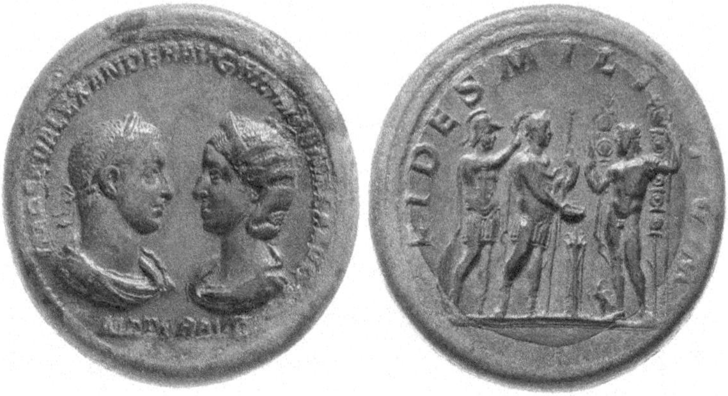

Figure 78: Medallion of Severus Alexander showing the emperor sacrificing to Jupiter while being crowned by Virtus (or Mars) with the reverse legend FIDES MILITVM.

Jupiter struck in this year. Jupiter again appears as *Conservator*, though this time the god is given a new military context.[54] This martial aspect was articulated through the release of coins and medallions showing the emperor and Jupiter accompanied by the legend FIDES MILITVM (Figure 78).[55] A bronze medallion was also struck with the legend IOVI CONSERVATORI, showing Severus Alexander, Jupiter, and a soldier holding two standards.[56] The emphasis on the loyalty of the soldiers may have been particularly poignant in AD 231: Dio mentions that many of the troops in the east had revolted and were joining the invading Persian army.[57] Only two examples of the *fides militum* type were found in the hoard sample; it must have been a small issue. Again, the mere act of designing and striking the image of Jupiter protecting the emperor and ensuring the loyalty of the Roman army may have been the most significant aspect of this type. Coin types bearing the legend IOVI PROPVGNATORI (Jupiter the Defender) with an image of Jupiter hurling a thunderbolt were minted from AD 231 to 232 according to the chronology of Carson (Figure 79).[58] This epithet has clear military overtones and was struck in relatively large numbers (Figure 77).

Also in AD 231 a type was struck for Severus Alexander showing Jupiter Stator on the reverse.[59] Jupiter Stator had last appeared on the coinage of

[54] *RIC* IV.2 *Severus Alexander* 197–200, 558–9.
[55] *RIC* IV.2 *Severus Alexander* 195, 555–6, 662; *BMCRE VI Severus Alexander* 734–6.
[56] *BMCRE VI Severus Alexander* 736*; Gnecchi 1912: (vol. 2) 84 no 5.
[57] Dio 80.4.1–2.
[58] AD 231: *RIC* IV.2 *Severus Alexander* 234–6, 240–1, 628–30. AD 232: *RIC* IV.2 *Severus Alexander* 237–9, 631–4.
[59] *RIC* IV.2 *Severus Alexander* 773, 927.

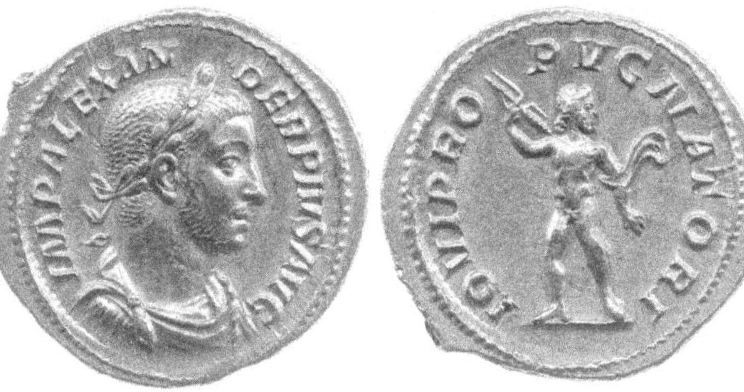

Figure 79: Aureus of Severus Alexander with Jupiter hurling a thunderbolt and the legend IOVI PROPVGNATORI.

Antoninus Pius, but the god had possessed a connection with Rome from its very foundation.[60] According to Roman tradition, a temple was vowed to Jupiter Stator by Romulus at a critical moment in the battle against the Sabines.[61] The Roman army was losing the battle and had begun to flee, but returned under the auspices of Jupiter Stator (Jupiter 'the Stayer'). This particular temple was never constructed, but M. Atilius Regulus later made a similar vow that he fulfilled in the war against the Samnites.[62] For this reason Jupiter Stator has been interpreted as the god who stays panic in battle.

The appearance of the god on the coinage of Antoninus Pius has been connected with his military activities in Britain in AD 142,[63] but the coin is better seen as part of the imagery marking significant events in the early history of Rome, in all likelihood part of a programme connected with the construction of the temple of Venus at Rome.[64] Many of Pius' types between AD 140 and 144 display myths and legends from Rome's early history, for example, Aeneas, Anchises, Rhea Silvia and the she-wolf and twins.[65] The Jupiter Stator type should be viewed within this context;

[60] *RIC* III *Antoninus Pius* 72, 607, 773, 927. [61] Livy 1.12.3–6; Ov. *Fast.* 6.794.

[62] Livy 10.36.11, 10.37.15. [63] Strack 1937: 53.

[64] *RIC* III *Antoninus Pius* 609. The temple was likely built in association with the *Romaia*. On the connection of the festival to the temple see Ath. *Deip.* 8.361f. Both Hadrian and Pius show the temple of Venus and Rome on their coinage, suggesting it was begun under Hadrian and completed by Pius sometime around AD 144. See Strack 1937: 69; *RIC* II *Hadrian* 783–4 (AD 134–8); *RIC* III *Antoninus Pius* 543 (AD 139), 622–3, 651–2, 664 (AD 140–4).

[65] Toynbee 1925: 170–3. Apollo: *RIC* III *Antoninus Pius* 598; Jupiter Stator: *RIC* III *Antoninus Pius* 72, 607, 773, 927; Romulus: *RIC* III *Antoninus Pius* 90, 149, 624, 645, 665; Aeneas: *RIC* III *Antoninus Pius* 91, 615, 627; she-wolf and twins: *RIC* III *Antoninus Pius* 94–6, 630–4, 648–50, 718, 734–5, 788, 986, 997; sow: *RIC* III *Antoninus Pius* 629, 722, 733; *Romae Aeternae*: *RIC* III *Antoninus Pius* 621–2, 664.

particularly since Romulus' intended temple and Regulus' actual building had become conflated in the Roman mind.[66]

In view of the mythical associations of Jupiter Stator and the god's appearance under the religiously conservative Antoninus Pius, the type of Severus Alexander has particular significance. It alludes to the religious restoration and traditionalism of the emperor through a connection with Romulus, while at the same time making reference to the upcoming military campaign. The type only appears on a single denarius, and is present in very small numbers in the hoard analysis (Figure 77).[67]

Also struck in this period (AD 228–231) was another IOVI VLTORI issue.[68] This may have been a 'commemorative' like that postulated by Hill for the earlier Severans (though in his examples the issues were struck the following year).[69] It is more likely that Jupiter 'the Avenger' was used in conjunction with the upcoming war. Like Jupiter Stator, Jupiter Ultor was used to connect the religious conservatism of the emperor to the Persian campaign: Stator and Ultor conveniently encapsulated Alexander's religious activities while simultaneously referring to military ideology. The issue is present in small numbers in the hoard sample (Figure 77). Just as the emperor's image and ideology could change according to contemporary circumstances, so too could the associations of particular deities. The visual language of Rome was a living language, constantly changing and evolving.

It is clear that Jupiter functioned as a protective deity of Alexander throughout his reign, and different epithets of the god were used to express divine assistance in contemporary contexts. The particular emphasis of Severus Alexander on the cult of Jupiter can be quantified through a comparison with the earlier Severan dynasty (Figures 7, 37–8, 56, 73). Jupiter was more heavily represented on the coinage of Severus Alexander than any other Severan emperor. Under Septimius, types of Jupiter constituted approximately 5% of silver types struck in the emperor's name, and for his co-ruler Caracalla, the amount was less than 1%. During Caracalla's sole rule Jupiter constituted about 9% of the emperor's denarii, perhaps reflecting the increased visual emphasis given to the divine on this emperor's coinage. A decline is seen under Elagabalus, with Jupiter types falling to a mere 2%. It is apparent that the types released by the Roman mint, and their respective quantities, reflected the religious emphases of particular emperors. During the reign of Severus Alexander Jupiter types rise to

[66] Mattingly and Sydenham 1930: 6. For the conflation between the two temples see Cic. *Cat.* 1.13.33.

[67] *RIC* IV.2 *Severus Alexander* 202. [68] *RIC* IV.2 *Severus Alexander* 203. [69] Hill 1964: 173.

approximately 13% of the emperor's total silver coinage. We can thus quantify the religious polarity of Elagabalus and Severus Alexander through numismatics. Although many of the individual Jovian issues of Severus Alexander were struck in small quantities, together they combine to generate a significant portion of Alexander's silver coinage. Jupiter would have been a significant part of the overall message communicated to those using Alexander's currency.

Mars Ultor, Romulus and Augustus in Alexander's principate

The quantitative perspective provided by coin hoards reveals that another deity had a significant presence throughout Severus Alexander's reign. Mars featured on about 17 per cent of the emperor's silver coinage (Figure 73). Here we might recall that Ultor was the epithet traditionally associated with Mars. Augustus had vowed a temple to Mars Ultor before his campaign against Caesar's assassins, but only dedicated the structure after the recovery of Roman standards from the Parthians.[70] Thus although it was conceived in vengeance for Caesar's murder, the temple and cult of Mars Ultor came to have broader associations with revenge and victory over Roman enemies. This dual association fitted perfectly with the reign of Alexander: he too had overcome a 'civil' enemy (Elagabalus), and then undertook military campaigns in the East.

Mars types were struck in large quantities in the early period of Alexander's reign, when the themes of revenge and restoration were most prominent (Figure 80). Unlike the Jupiter types of Alexander, the majority of Mars coin types did not include an epithet for the god. Instead, the titles of the emperor formed the reverse legend (e.g. P M TR P COS P P). This only underlines the significance of the very specific Jupiter epithets discussed above. Three main iconographic types of Mars grace Alexander's coinage: Mars with an olive branch and reverse spear, Mars carrying a spear and trophy, and Mars carrying a spear and resting a hand on a shield. The 'olive branch' types were struck in large quantities at the beginning of Alexander's reign (Figure 80). One of Alexander's coins showing Mars with an olive branch carries the reverse legend MARTI PACIFERO.[71] If these types are connected with Elagabalus' overthrow, this adds an

[70] Barchiesi 2002: 1–22; Morawiecki 1981: 29–37; Simpson 1977: 91–4; Zanker 1988: 194. For the architecture of the temple see Ganzert 1985: 201–19; Ganzert 1996; and Kockel 1983: 421–48.

[71] *RIC* IV.2 *Severus Alexander* 159–60.

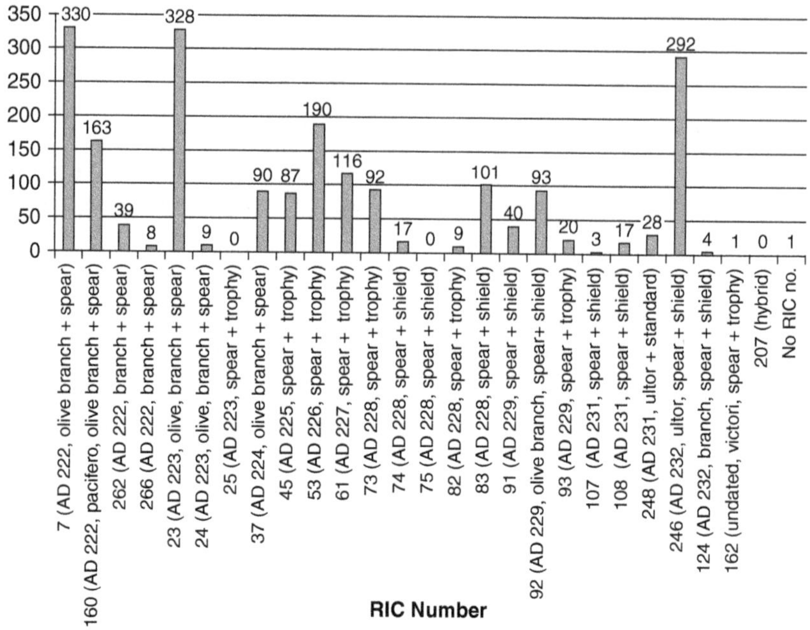

Figure 80: Silver Mars types of Severus Alexander as represented in hoards.

interesting martial aspect to the imperial ideology of this time. The spear-and-trophy iconographic type of Mars then appear to have formed a focus from AD 225 to 228.

An additional type portrays Mars with a shield and spear, with a standard resting on his left arm.[72] Carson dates this type, as well coin types displaying Jupiter Propugnator and Sol, to AD 231.[73] They probably all have reference to the Persian War. In AD 232, significant quantities of Mars Ultor types were struck (Figure 80).[74] Mars, as well as Jupiter, formed an important ideological aspect of Alexander's Persian campaign. The god's association with earlier successes against the Parthians makes the reference to Mars at this juncture fitting; it is apparent that in other areas the Romans responded to the Persian threat by using the motifs and procedures that had been employed previously against the Parthians.[75] Mars thus functioned in Alexander's reign as a god associated with Elagabalus' overthrow as well as Alexander's foreign wars.

The temple to Mars Ultor was located in the Augustan forum and had strong associations with Romulus.[76] Ovid records that Augustus had the scene of Romulus dedicating the *spolia opima* engraved on the door of the new temple.[77] By this action Augustus (who allegedly had considered taking

[72] *RIC* IV.2 *Severus Alexander* 248, 638. [73] *BMCRE* VI *Severus Alexander* 802–6, 830–53.
[74] *RIC* IV.2 *Severus Alexander* 246–8. [75] Edwell 2008: 160.
[76] On the possibility of an earlier structure to Mars Ultor on the capital see Hannah 1998: 422–33.
[77] Ov. *Fast.* 5.559–566; Springer 1954: 27–32.

the name of Romulus) visually underlined his connection to the mythical hero and his own position as the second founder of the city. The temple's connection to both Romulus and Augustus fits well with the public image Alexander (or his council) cultivated as a ruler. Alexander was associated with Romulus and Augustus and his principate witnesses an emphasis on the renewal and re-foundation of the city after Elagabalus. Mars, and the associations of his cult in Rome, formed an important part of this ideology.

The *Historia Augusta* records that Alexander set up colossal statues of the deified emperors in the Forum of Nerva 'after the example of Augustus, who erected in his forum marble statues of the most illustrious men, together with the record of their achievements'.[78] Ovid provides some detail about the Augustan forum complex: one of the central niches was occupied by a statue of Romulus carrying the *spolia opima*, and the other central niche was filled with a statue group of Aeneas and Anchises.[79] If the *Historia Augusta*'s statement can be trusted here, then Alexander pointedly imitated Augustus in the forum adjacent to his.[80] One could travel directly from Augustus' forum, containing the temple of Mars Ultor, the statues of Romulus, Aeneas and the *summi viri*, to Nerva's forum with Alexander's own 'hall of fame'. Whether or not this statement reflects historical fact, the conscious alignment between Alexander and Augustus in the *Historia Augusta* reflects an association that was probably promoted during Alexander's reign.

Romulus appears on the imperial coinage under Severus Alexander for the first time during the Severan dynasty. The type first emerges in AD 228 and thereafter retains a presence on the emperor's coinage.[81] Romulus is shown walking right, carrying a spear and trophy, the *spolia opima* of the statue in the Augustan forum. The association of Romulus with Severus Alexander is taken a step further when this image is paired with the legend VIRTVS AVG. (Figure 81).[82] By adding this legend to the image, the viewer is left uncertain as to whether the figure is Romulus or the emperor; the carefully crafted ambiguity casts Alexander as a founder of Rome, assimilated to Romulus.[83] Alexander, as restorer of Roman culture after

[78] *SHA Sev. Alex.* 28.6.

[79] Ov. *Fast.* 5.563–6. See also Suet. *Aug.* 31.5; Geiger 2008: 99; Zanker 1988: 210.

[80] On the forum see Bauer 1976: 117–50; Bauer 1988: 41–57; and D'Ambra 1993: 20.

[81] *RIC* IV.2 *Severus Alexander* 85–6, 96–7, 103–4.

[82] *RIC* IV.2 *Severus Alexander* 223–5, 625–6.

[83] Indeed, the ambiguity between the two images meant that Cohen, and consequently the *RIC*, lists two different coin types: 'Romulus, bareheaded, walking r., carrying spear and trophy' (*RIC* IV.2 *Severus Alexander* 223–4), and the 'emperor in military dress, walking r., carrying spear and trophy' (*RIC* IV.2 *Severus Alexander* 225). Inspection of the coins concerned suggests that this is the same image, a conclusion also reached by Carson, who described the type (and indeed all the 'Romulus' types) as 'Severus Alexander as Romulus' (*BMCRE* VI *Severus Alexander* 481–2).

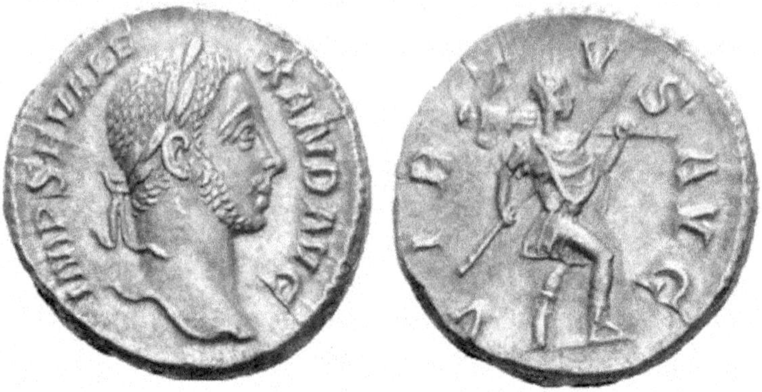

Figure 81: Denarius of Severus Alexander showing Romulus (or the emperor) carrying spear and trophy, with the legend VIRTVS AVG.

Elagabalus, is akin to the founders of Rome. The Romulus and Severus Alexander as Romulus types only had a small presence on the silver coinage of the princeps (2 per cent, Figure 73). Nonetheless the association between the original founder of Rome and the last of the Severan emperors likely reflected a wider visual and ideological programme that would have been communicated through other media. Alexander's building activities, detailed above, would have formed one such medium.

The politics of *damnatio memoriae* and the Persian war in the provinces

The *damnatio* of Elagabalus and the politics of renewal and re-founding that characterised Alexander's principate had a direct effect on the cities that had received honours under Elagabalus. Cities that had been granted neokorates under Elagabalus lost the honour, as well as associated status and prestige. Though cities were quick to acknowledge the ascent of Alexander as sole emperor, the imagery and titles used by these cities throughout Alexander's reign reflects the uncertainty and confusion that must have followed in the aftermath of Elagabalus' death.

Eight cities were granted the honour of a neokorate under Elagabalus. All of them eventually had this title withdrawn under Severus Alexander, though the process may have been a lengthy one.[84] Philippopolis in Thrace was one of the cities affected, but the neokorate title was retained

[84] Burrell 2004: 295.

on inscriptions well into Severus Alexander's reign, so that there was a delay of several years before the honour was finally withdrawn, or before the city publicly acknowledged its loss in status.[85] Hierapolis in Phrygia also seems to have delayed somewhat in updating its titulature; a statue of Julia Mamaea, Alexander's mother, still mentions the neokorate of Elagabalus.[86] The city also ceased to strike coinage, though it had minted abundantly during Elagabalus' reign. This may be because the need for small change had diminished, or perhaps, as Burrell suggests, the abstinence from minting may reflect chagrin at the loss of status.[87] Beroia in Macedonia also delayed in removing its neokorate title, though Ephesus acted more quickly.[88] The uncertainty that must have been present at the time is encapsulated in a unique inscription from Sardis. Having been granted a third neokorate by Elagabalus, the city erected an inscription under Severus Alexander describing itself as 'many times neokoros of the Augusti by the decrees of the sacred senate'.[89] By refraining from mentioning the precise number of neokoria, the Sardinians managed to get around the problem of not knowing whether their Elagabalian neokorate was still valid. Or perhaps this phraseology was created so that the loss of the neokorate did not have to be explicitly stated. The city of Cyzicus in Mysia changed its titles from 'two times neokoros' to simply 'neokoros', indicating that their honour had also been withdrawn.[90] However, it appears that the honour was regranted late in Alexander's reign, since the city again begins to call itself 'twice neokoros', striking coins showing two agonistic tables and two prize crowns with the busts of Severus Alexander and Julia Mamaea.[91]

Miletos in Ionia was granted a second neokorate by Elagabalus, and the embarrassment or uncertainty surrounding the loss of this title may explain why no coin of Miletos mentions its neokorate status during Alexander's rule. By contrast, neighbouring Magnesia seems to have capitalised on Miletos' fall from grace by striking coins advertising its position as neokoros of Artemis Leukophyrene, an honour awarded by Alexander.[92] One coin describes Miletos as the 'metropolis' of Ionia, and shows Alexander shaking hands with the *boule* of the city.[93]

A similar situation is seen in Cilicia with the cities of Anazarbus and Tarsus, which were in constant competition over status. This rivalry

[85] Burrell 2004: 244–5. [86] Burrell 2004: 138. [87] Burrell 2004: 138.

[88] Burrell 2004: 194, 138. [89] Burrell 2004: 111.

[90] Burrell 2004: 96, *BMC Mysia* (Cyzicus) 262–3.

[91] *SNG von Aulock* 1281. Also *BMC Mysia* (Cyzicus) 264, a very complex reverse type, but which may record a ceremony involving the lighting of palms.

[92] Burrell 2004: 58, 142–3; *BMC Ionia* (Magnesia ad Meandrum) 73. [93] *SNG von Aulock* 7928.

continued throughout the Severan period, and was mentioned in the previous chapter on Elagabalus. Both cities had received honours under Septimius Severus. Anazarbus, however, won particular favour under Elagabalus when the emperor became a demiurge in the city.[94] It was during the reign of Elagabalus that the abbreviation normally seen on Tarsus' coinage, AMK ('first, greatest, most beautiful'), also appears on Anazarbus' issues. The title then disappears from Anazarbus' coinage early in Severus Alexander's reign.[95] Under Severus Alexander Tarsus may have gained the upper hand in the on-going rivalry, since the city was granted honours as the emperor made his way East to fight the Persians in AD 231. At this time Tarsus released coinage showing the emperor wearing the demiurge crown on the obverse and a ship on the reverse.[96] The demiurge was traditionally responsible for grain supply to the city, and Ziegler is probably correct in supposing that Severus Alexander assumed the position and offered free or heavily subsidised grain to the city in order to alleviate the burden of having to support the imperial retinue and troops. A similar act had been performed by Caracalla as he went east in AD 215; on both occasions the city marked the event with the ship coin type.[97]

A gold medallion of Severus Alexander was also found in the city of Tarsus, as part of a hoard that also contained some of the 'Alexander' medallions mentioned in the chapter on Caracalla.[98] The medallion was struck in AD 230, and likely was a gift presented by the emperor as he made his way east. The emperor is shown on the obverse in full military attire, holding in his right hand a Victory with trophy, and in his left the end of a sword. The reverse of the medallion shows the emperor seated and being crowned by Victory, with Virtus in front and a shield inscribed VOT X. The piece speaks to the military image of Alexander as he embarked on the Persian War. The civic officials of Anazarbus were no doubt aware of Alexander's ideology in this period. In AD 230/1 the city struck coins showing Victory on a globe, a military trophy with the emperor on the right and Nike on the left, and a type showing the emperor sacrificing before a temple while being crowned by Nike, who is shown above the temple pediment (Figure 82).[99]

In eastern campaigns troops often had to be moved from the Danubian regions through Asia Minor and Cilicia to the eastern *limes*.[100] As

[94] Ziegler 1985: 86–90. [95] Burrell 2004: 217. [96] *BMC Cilicia* (Tarsus) 213.
[97] Ziegler 1977: 29–67.
[98] Gnecchi 1912: (vol. 1) 5 no. 2, pl. 1 no. 9; Longpérrier 1868: 322; Ziegler 1977: 47.
[99] Ziegler 1993: nos. 626–8; *SNG Levante Supp.* 344; ANS 1973.191.143.
[100] Ziegler 1996: 119–34.

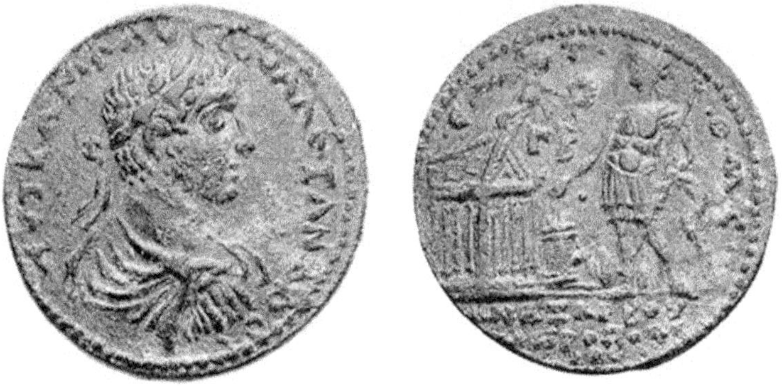

Figure 82: Coin of Anazarbus showing Severus Alexander sacrificing before a temple with Nike standing on the *acroterion* offering a wreath to the emperor.

Alexander went to meet the Persian threat he, like Caracalla and Severus before him, travelled through Cilicia, prompting the cities to strike coinage. This coinage probably had two purposes: to ensure that enough small change existed to meet the increased need generated by the emperor and his retinue, and to record any imperial honours and the imperial presence in the city. In addition to Tarsos and Anazarbus, the city of Aegeae in Cilicia also struck coinage, marking the bestowal of its first neokorate.[101]

Severus Alexander was more reticent than Elagabalus in granting neokorate honours, while at the sametime curtailing grants that had been bestowed by his predecessor.[102] However, the emperor's Persian campaign appears to have formed a context for the bestowal of some imperial privileges. Aegeae, a strategic port town, was granted a neokorate, probably in AD 230/1.[103] It is likely that Alexander became Aesculapius' cult partner, just as Caracalla was Aesculapius' cult partner at Pergamum. Coins struck commemorating the honour show the emperor with the serpent-entwined staff of Aesculapius, with the title 'greatest chief priest of the world and of Aesculapius'.[104] In addition to this type, Aegeae struck coinage showing the emperor on horseback, a warship and a transport ship with four figures waiting to receive it.[105] These types underline the military context of Alexander's benefaction to the city.

The Persian War, more than the divine ideology used by Severus Alexander throughout his reign, seems to have had a significant rôle in the provincial representations of the emperor. This may also be a result of the fact that Alexander removed more honours than he bestowed, so that

[101] Burrell 2004: 230. [102] Burrell 2004: 208, 296. [103] Burrell 2004: 230.
[104] Burrell 2004: 230–2; Woodward 1963: 5–7; Ziegler 1985: 93; Ziegler 2003: 205–18.
[105] Weiss 1982: 202.

there was less opportunity for ideological and iconographic dialogue between the emperor and individual cities. The adoption of the cult of Elagabal in the provinces, Elagabalus' bestowal of numerous honours on provincial cities, in addition to the fact that for the majority of his rule Elagabalus remained inside the city of Rome, also may have meant that the 'outrages' of Elagabalus were not a concern outside the city of Rome. If this were the case, the ideology of the restoration and re-founding of Rome may have been largely targeted at the city of Rome itself.

Alexander's Persian campaign, however, created ample opportunities for provincial cities to interact with their leader and his ideology. The examples of Tarsus and Anazarbus have already been cited in this regard. Since their coinage carries precise dates, it is easier to connect specific iconography with historical circumstances. Other cities also struck 'military' types (for example Seleucia ad Calycadnum in Cilicia struck several types of Nike holding a sign proclaiming *eleutheria* or 'freedom'), but with no secure way to date these issues we cannot connect them with Alexander's Persian War.

We might connect Alexander's presence in Antioch, however, with an extraordinary type released by the city.[106] Antioch struck a coin type showing Tyche seated on a rock with the river god Orontes swimming below, with another Tyche on the left holding a rudder and cornucopia, and a military figure on the right, crowning the seated Tyche with a wreath (Figure 83).[107] The image is similar to a statue described by Malalas that was erected in the theatre of Antioch under Trajan. Malalas records that a bronze statue of a seated girl dressed as the city's Tyche was erected with the Orontes shown swimming below. The girl/Tyche was shown being crowned by Seleucus and Antiochus, who completed the statue group.[108] The image struck under Severus Alexander has significant differences to this prototype: only one figure in military dress is shown, and on the left another Tyche is added instead. Butcher believed that since the figure on the right is shown with long hair on some of the specimens, the figure should be identified with a Hellenistic ruler instead of Alexander.[109] However, the alterations made by the die-engraver to the established Trajanic sculpture group suggest that the coin is communicating an activity of Alexander himself, albeit one where he is aligned with the Hellenistic founders of the city. As in Rome with Romulus and Augustus, Alexander is closely aligned with the very beginnings of the city of Antioch. Bellinger interpreted the

[106] On Alexander in Antioch see Hdn. 6.4.3–5, 6.6.3–6; *SHA Sev. Alex.* 53.1–7.

[107] ANS 1944.100.66076; McAlee 2007: 304.

[108] Malalas 276 (=11.10). Also Pausanias 6.2.7, who notes that Eutychides made a statue of Tyche for the Antiochenes. For discussion see Butcher 2004: 298–9 and McAlee 2007: 304.

[109] Butcher 2004: 299.

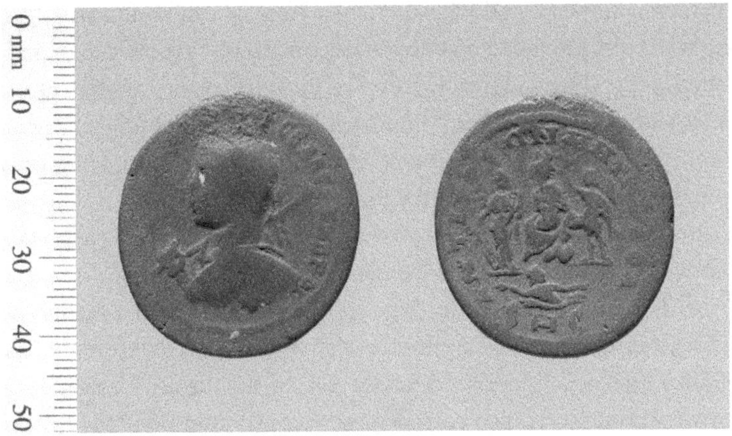

Figure 83: Coin of Antioch showing Tyche seated on a rock being crowned by a figure in military dress, with the river Orontes swimming below and a Tyche with cornucopia and rudder on the left.

scene as one that represented Alexander as the successor of Seleucus, crowning the Tyche of Antioch, with the second Tyche representing the citizenry involved in the dedication.[110] Fortuna or Tyche carrying a rudder and cornucopia, however, was often characterised on Roman coinage (including Roman coinage struck in Antioch) as 'Fortuna Redux', or the Tyche of Return.[111] Thus the image may present the Tyche of the city with Fortuna Redux and Alexander on either side. The coin may have commemorated the presence of the emperor in the city and perhaps also honours granted.

The other cities to be granted a neokorate by Severus Alexander were Neocaesarea in Pontus, and Caesarea in Cappadocia.[112] Notably, these were both in regions where no city had had an Elagabalian neokorate withdrawn. Their coinage does not draw on the divine ideology utilised by Severus Alexander in his rule. Again, this ideology may have had more resonance in the city of Rome.

Dispelling the 'oriental' myth: Sol under the Severans

Given the solar nature of Elagabal, the presence of Sol on Alexander's coinage may appear unusual at first glance (Figure 73). But we should not

[110] Bellinger 1939: 6; Butcher 2004: 299.

[111] E.g. *RIC* IV.1 *Pescennius Niger* 25–6 (Antioch); *RIC* IV.2 *Severus Alexander* 196, 232.

[112] Neocaesarea: Burrell 2004: 208; Waddington, Babelon et al. 1925: 37–49. Caesarea: Burrell 2004: 249, *SNG von Aulock* 6509, 6511.

conflate the Emesene god with the larger Roman cult to the sun.[113] This thought process has led to the erroneous conclusion that the cult of Sol was quashed under Alexander only to be re-introduced by Aurelian after his conflict with the Palmyrenes.[114] Romans had their own indigenous cult of the god, and as Hijmans has demonstrated, this cult did not necessarily equate with the solar deities of the Roman East.[115]

There is no denying the visual presence Sol had during the Severan period (Figures 7, 37–8, 56, 73). Lichtenberger has highlighted the close connection between Sol and Septimius Severus, seen in both the visual media of the Roman government as well as those created in provincial contexts.[116] Under Septimius the god appears on about 2% of the denarii struck for the emperor, during Caracalla's co-rule the god constituted 7% of the emperor's silver coinage, during Caracalla's sole rule 5%, and under Elagabalus 8%. We should refrain, however, from attributing this to the 'provincial' background of the dynasty,[117] as it is clear that Sol was associated with the imperial régime well before the Severan period.[118] Indeed, comparison of a living ruler with the sun had been an established theme since Hellenistic times.[119]

A close examination of representations of Sol on imperial coinage suggests that the god could have a very specific context. From Trajan, and perhaps even before, Sol was invoked in battles and victories in the east.[120] The god functioned on coinage as an expression of eastern conquest, of the emperor's military strength and success in a specific geographical area.[121] Quantitative analysis of Alexander's coinage illustrates that this was the context for the representations of the god in his reign. Though Sol types were struck from the beginning of Alexander's rule, it is only from AD 230 (when the Persian king Ardarshir rose to power) that Sol came to be minted in significant numbers from year to year (Figure 84).

No examples of the coin issues struck in either AD 222 or AD 228 were found in the hoard analysis, though types struck from AD 230 are found in significant quantities. On the basis of Carson's chronology and the hoard sample, it appears that Sol types constituted about a third of all denarii

[113] An error made in Halsberghe 1972 and Halsberghe 1984: 2182–201.

[114] Mainly based on the evidence of *SHA Aurel.* 25.4–6. [115] Hijmans 1996: 115–50.

[116] Lichtenberger 2011: 219–79.

[117] Golfetto 2002; Palmer 1978: 1085–6; Williams 1999: 309.

[118] See discussions in Alföldi 1935: 107; Bergmann 1998; Berrers 2004: 39–42; di Palma 1999: 333–4; Fears 1976: 494–6; and Hedlund 2008: 191–2.

[119] Fears 1976: 495.

[120] Kantorowicz 1963: 126. Sol may also have been used to allude to the East in the Republican period (Ryan 2005: 81–9).

[121] Berrers 2004: 40.

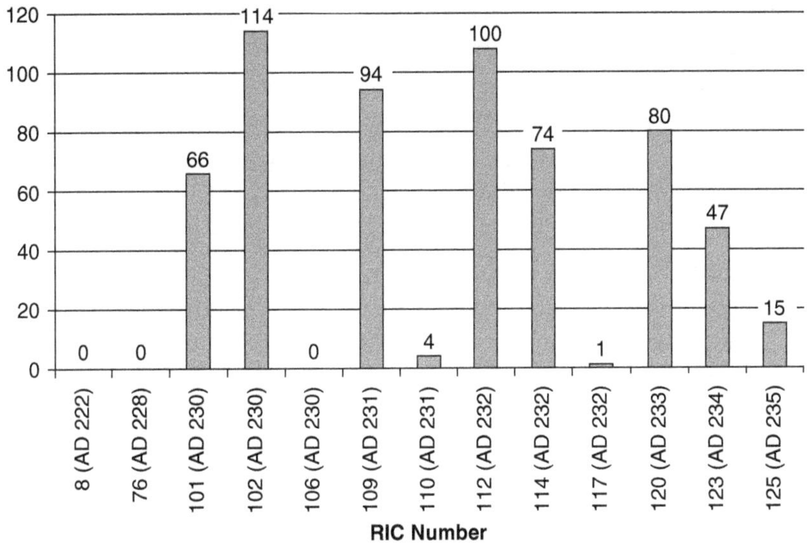

Figure 84: Silver Sol types of Severus Alexander as represented in hoards.

struck in AD 230, a prominence that continued until AD 233, when Alexander returned 'triumphant' from the East.[122] The iconography of Sol probably formed part of a wider imperial ideology of victory and was intricately connected to the circumstances at hand.

The first appearance of Sol on Roman imperial coinage was under Vespasian, who restruck a Republican type that may have been connected with a Parthian conflict in 42 BC.[123] The type was struck between AD 69 and 71, and formed part a wider 're-release' of old types in this period.[124] Sol next appears under Trajan, probably in connection with the Parthian War (AD 114–117). Trajan's Sol coins display the emperor's new title of *Parthicus* and were struck contemporaneously with other types detailing the emperor's victory.[125] Sol is also present on the young Hadrian's coinage in AD 117–118 with the legend ORIENS, perhaps a pun on the eastern victories and Hadrian's emergence as emperor.[126] The god also appears on an eastern coin of Hadrian in AD 123 (?) and on *aes* coinage in the period AD 125–128, then on a coin of Commodus in AD 186.[127] The god's next appearance

[122] A medallion (*BMCRE* VI *Severus Alexander* 949) struck in this year shows Alexander being crowned by Victory with the Tigris and Euphrates at his feet. This demonstrates that whatever the literary controversy surrounding Alexander's Persian campaign, the emperor officially claimed victory.

[123] *RIC* II *Vespasian* 28, a restitution type of L. Mussidius Longus, Crawford 494/43a.

[124] Mattingly and Sydenham 1926: 6; Buttrey 1972b: 89–109.

[125] *RIC* II *Trajan* 326–30, 341–2. [126] *RIC* II *Hadrian* 16, 20, 43.

[127] *RIC* II *Hadrian* 145, 167–8, 661; *RIC* III *Commodus* 119.

under Septimius Severus would mark the beginning of a more frequent connection with the imperial régime.

Sol appears on Severus' coinage from AD 197, and then frequently appears on types issued for himself and his two sons for the rest of his reign.[128] The god, as well as his consort Luna, were associated with the *aeternitas* of the dynasty.[129] But Sol also maintained his associations with conquest in the East. Dio's account of Severus' failure to take the city of Hatra during the second Parthian War in AD 198 ascribes Severus' decision to pull back from the attack to the famous civic sun cult Shamash.[130] The account has striking similarities to Dio's narrative of Trajan's attempt to seize Hatra, when the sun god sent a plague of flies to defeat the emperor.[131] This may be more than coincidence: after his Parthian victories Severus consciously aligned himself with Trajan. An aureus struck in this period shows Severus on a horse holding a spear with the legend S P Q R OPTIMO PRINC, a clear reference to his claimed ancestor.[132] The *Feriale Duranum* records that the celebration of Severus' victories was on 28 January AD 198, the *dies imperii* of Trajan.[133] It is within this concerted effort to align his actions with those of Trajan that we might understand some of the Sol imagery that appears on Septimius' coinage. Though new iconography of Sol was introduced to the Roman mint under the Severans,[134] the Trajanic type of the bust of Sol was retained, underscoring the connection between the ruling dynasty and Trajan.[135] The military overtones of this image are implicit in the fact that Sol (and Severus by implication) is hailed as PACATOR ORBIS. Sol was not a disruptive intrusion into the existing Roman pantheon, but was used within an established and acceptable tradition.[136]

[128] *RIC* IV.1 *Septimius Severus* 101–2, 115, 117, 217, 282, 489, 492, 742, 744, 749; *RIC* IV.1 *Caracalla* 163; *RIC* IV.1 *Geta* 50, 108.

[129] Berrers 2004: 42.

[130] Dio 76.12.2. Panel IV of the Severan arch may portray the military actions against Hatra, though Brilliant remained doubtful (Brilliant 1967: 174; Rubin 1975a: 426–31).

[131] Dio 68.31.2, where the comparison between Severus and Trajan is even more explicit. The similarities in the accounts of the sieges of Hatra recalls the similarities between the 'weather miracles' of Marcus Aurelius in his war against the Quadammi, and those experienced by Severus in his battle against Niger at Issus. See Lusnia 1998: 65 for a discussion. It may be that Severus made conscious use of these tales in order to underscore his connection to the Antonine dynasty.

[132] *RIC* IV.1 *Septimius Severus* 169; Rubin 1975a: 437.

[133] *Feriale Duranum* col.1, II, 14–16; Birley 1988: 130; Rubin 1975a: 455.

[134] A standing Sol with whip and raised right hand (Berrers 2004: 40–1).

[135] For example *RIC* IV.1 *Septimius Severus* 282.

[136] Berrers 2004: 39–49; Williams 1999: 309.

We should see the increased presence of Sol during the Severan period not as an eastern 'orientalising' influence, but partly as a reflection of the increased presence of this dynasty along the eastern frontier. Trajan had utilised Sol as a signifier of eastern victories, and the god was consequently called upon by those successors who followed in his footsteps. Severus developed the iconography to highlight the eternity of the Severan dynasty, but this too had established precedents.

Severus Alexander's reign was one that emphasised renewal and restoration. The visual representation of the divine support of the emperor was crafted so as to reflect these themes and to tie the young ruler to Romulus and Augustus. One might despair of the complicated literary tradition for this period. But it is in this reign, more than that of any other Severan emperor, that we can see how coin imagery functioned as a language, how particular representations of gods in particular capacities, and with particular epithets, were used to signify the position of the emperor and the empire as a whole. A better understanding of this language provides an insight into why particular gods were represented at particular times and opens up a new understanding of how the Romans visualised both the divine and the principate. A renewed emphasis on Jupiter and Mars signalled a conspicuous return to traditional Roman religion, a reaction to the reign of Elagabalus. The types of Sol marked the new threat posed by the Persians and confronted by the emperor's campaigns in the East. From an examination of the gods who were associated with the régime we can see that Alexander was cast in the mould of a founder, a restorer of the city of Rome and its cultural, moral and religious traditions.

This dialogue is difficult to find, however, on the provincial coin types of the empire. Instead civic types participated in the ideology of victory and military prowess that surrounded Severus Alexander's eastern campaign. The removal of many provincial honours granted under Elagabalus may have resulted in a more reticent numismatic and epigraphic output. On the other hand, the activities of Elagabalus in Rome and Alexander's response may not have held the same resonance in the provinces as the emperor's military campaigns. The Persian threat, Alexander's journey east, and the resources expected from provincial cities in support of this, may have 'spoken' more immediately to the wider empire.

Conclusion: Divine ideology in the Severan dynasty

The preceding examination has illustrated the dynamism of the divine ideology employed by the Severan dynasty. Each emperor of the dynasty emphasised divine sanction, but the particular form this sanction took changed from reign to reign. The flexibility of divine sanction and the emperor's public image as a whole is underlined by Neptune's role in the British war of Severus. While Liber Pater and Hercules had been associated with the emperor and his rule from the beginning of Severus' reign, the particular context of the British war meant that the divine ideology shifted at this juncture to a god more fitting to the circumstances at hand. The imperial image would shift again with Caracalla's assumption of the throne. The emperor's association with healing deities might have arisen from an imperial illness, but it would later assist with the literary construction of an emperor consumed by fratricidal guilt. In this respect, Caracalla demonstrates how the image of an emperor might be modified by his subjects, particularly after death. The flexibility of the divine sanction utilised in the Roman principate was pushed beyond the acceptable boundaries under Elagabalus. Elagabalus' image was so far removed from the expected and established notion of a princeps that he was overthrown. This demonstrates that although the image of the princeps could shift and change, this had to occur within a recognisable set of boundaries and cultural norms.

Liber Pater and Hercules provided the ideology of divine support necessary for Severus as an emperor. They had a small, though significant presence on Severus' denarii, forming part of a wider imperial image whose main focus was on military victory and the benefits this brought to the empire. Nonetheless, however small, the presence of these deities is significant. They appear on Severus' coinage before Jupiter, in conjunction with the celebration of the saecular games, and as part of a stunning series of aurei. Severus likely constructed a temple to the deities in Rome, and if this can be connected to the colossal remains on the Quirinal, the monument would have formed an imposing statement. Severus did not act without precedent. Augustus had also built a new temple to his patron deity Apollo on the Palatine and had also incorporated his tutelary deity into the saecular games.

That these deities operated within a wider, evolving visual language is suggested by the fact that the legends accompanying the images of Hercules and Liber Pater on the coinage of Severus changed over time, reflecting Severus' civil wars, the celebration of the saecular games and perhaps the construction of a temple to the deities in Rome. The multifaceted nature of the imperial image is also evident in the fact that, with the exception of Lepcis Magna, the imagery of Liber and Hercules is really not adopted in provincial cities on a large scale. Within Lepcis, the presence of Liber and Hercules was as much connected to local culture as to the person of the princeps. The two deities formed an avenue through which the city could communicate its close connection with the emperor and his success. Other provincial and private media focused on the image of Severus as a military leader and as a member of the Antonine dynasty. Severus' patron deities were part of a wider, complex imperial image, reflecting the long history of the principate, and the complexity of Severus himself and his heritage. This complexity is revealed again under Severus' successor.

Caracalla emphasised throughout his rule the support of the god Sarapis. The god appears on the emperor's coinage from the very beginning of his reign and maintains a significant presence throughout the rest of his rule. A range of iconography of Sarapis was employed on the imperial coinage to communicate the god's diverse rôle: as a *conservator* of the emperor (with raised right hand, recalling the deity's protection of Commodus), as a god who supported and sanctioned the imperial rule and its associated abundance (carrying a wreath or ears of corn), and as the host of the emperor in the sanctuary at Alexandria (the seated 'Alexandrian' type).

Apollo and Aesculapius are also shown on the imperial coinage, but only for a discrete period. Caracalla paid homage to Apollo Grannus while on campaign in Germany, and probably consulted the oracle of Apollo of Claros at Colophon. Caracalla also stayed in the sanctuary of Aesculapius in Pergamum. Here the imperial patronage had a direct effect on the city concerned: Pergamum was awarded the honour of a third neokorate. The coin types of the Roman mint were connected to these particular activities. The adoption of 'provincial' imagery by the mint at Rome had already been seen under Severus with the iconography of Baal Hammon, the god Eshmun and the portrayal of Liber and Hercules together. The phenomenon continued under Caracalla, communicating the emperor's journey east and the divine support he enjoyed. Again, the emphasis on Alexander the Great apparent during Caracalla's rule demonstrates the multidimensional nature of the imperial image.

This image would make one of its most radical changes under Elagabalus. An exploration of Elagabalus' reign highlights the unusually close association that existed between Elagabalus and the deity from Emesa. It is difficult to assess whether the introduction of the Emesene god to Rome was intended to transform the foundations of Roman imperial power (from a monarchy that emphasised military prowess to one largely justified by divine sanction), or whether the importation of the cult to Rome was merely a religious desire of the emperor that would have unforeseen repercussions in the Roman world.

It is clear, though, that the cult of Elagabal was not forced on the wider empire. Although the emperor constructed two temples to his god in Rome, and conspicuously declared his devotion to the cult stone, the surviving evidence does not suggest that the emperor was seeking to supplant Jupiter as head of the Roman pantheon. Rather, provincial cities voluntarily adopted a cult that was obviously favoured by the emperor as part of the on-going dialogue between ruler and subject. An important part of this discourse was status, and it is perhaps no surprise that many of the cities that contain evidence for cults to Elagabal were also awarded privileges by the emperor. The appearance of Caracalla's divine ideology on provincial coinage had also occurred within the context of imperial favour. The adoption of the Emesene cult was done to suit local taste, and was not subjected to an overarching set of rules, though the iconography seems to have originated from a central source. As a result, though there is a common iconography employed for the god Elagabal in the provinces, the emperor's 'horn' is never translated to provincial issues, nor are the emperor's Emesene titles found in Greek epigraphy.

The reign of Severus Alexander drew on what might be seen as more traditional motifs of power, no doubt in reaction to the reign of his cousin Elagabalus. Jupiter was closely aligned with the emperor, and the god's protection and support of Alexander was communicated through the use of changing epithets that reflected contemporary circumstances. This was not an innovation, but the continuation of an existing tradition that had become particularly marked from Commodus on. The alignment between the head of the empire and the head of the Roman pantheon may have facilitated a creativity and flexibility within the mint that allowed Jovian numismatic types to be subtly modified through differing iconography and select legends, communicating the special relationship between man and god. It is apparent that word and image interacted in complex and nuanced ways on imperial coinage, and the Roman mint used both to create an overall effect.

Alexander also emphasised the renewal of Rome through building projects in the city and by connecting himself to the famous founders of Rome, Augustus and Romulus. The best evidence for this in a reign with little reliable literary evidence is the emperor's coinage. Mars Ultor (a cult associated with Romulus and Augustus) and Jupiter Ultor have a significant presence on the emperor's coinage. But this imperial ideology seems to have featured on civic coinage and epigraphy much less than during the rule of previous Severan emperors. This may have been because the ideology of renewal after Elagabalus may have been most relevant for the city of Rome and its élite. The removal of Elagabalian imperial honours from cities in the empire may have resulted in a reluctance to continue epigraphic and numismatic output, whereby a city's loss of status might be made both public and permanent. Many of those cities that did receive honours under Severus Alexander were granted them during the emperor's Persian campaign, and their coinage reflects the military context of the grant.

Alongside diversity in the imperial image was continuity. All four of the Severan emperors advertised their virtues and the benefits of their régime on coinage. Religious ceremonies, like those of the Arval brothers, remained unchanged even under Elagabalus.[1] Though some cities were influenced by the religious ideologies of the different emperors, the majority continued in their established civic calendars and culture. The Severan emperors, with the exception of Elagabalus, continued to 'look' like Roman emperors. They went to war and participated in traditional public festivals and ceremonies. The dynasty was associated with deities that had provincial cult centres, but these gods also had Roman cultic contexts (Hercules, Dionysus, Apollo and even Aesculapius and Sarapis). In the proclaimed and sustained connection to a particular deity or deities, the Severans were following a precedent that had been established by Augustus and which had been developing since the days of the Republic, with the divine associations of Marius, Sulla, Pompey and Caesar.

The divine ideology invoked by each emperor had an effect on the landscape of Rome. Severus built a temple to Liber Pater and Hercules, probably to be connected with the colossal temple on the Quirinal Hill. Caracalla built or renovated a structure to Sarapis, perhaps adjacent to the colossal temple of his father on the Quirinal. The enormous bath complex begun under Caracalla may also have referenced the divine ideology of the Severan dynasty through its sculptural decoration. Elagabalus constructed two structures to his god in Rome, both probably to be connected to imperial

[1] Scheid 1998a: 277–324.

palace complexes. The temple on the Vigna Barberini visibly juxtaposed the imperial residence and the residence of the divine, and was very probably a factor in the close association between Elagabalus and the god Elagabal that would metamorphose into the nickname *Heliogabalus*. The other structure might be located in the Sessorian Palace complex, its presence suggested by the quadrangular negative space left by the Aurelian wall at this point. Severus Alexander converted the *Elagabalium* into a temple to Jupiter Ultor, a cult title that served as a reminder and warning of Elagabalus' misdeeds. One imagines that Alexander also converted to other uses the second temple to Elagabal. That each emperor felt obliged to monumentalise his divine support in the capital of the empire underlines the importance attached to divine support in the visualisation of power in this period. It also highlights the continuing significance of the city of Rome as the centre of power.

The effect of Severan patron deities outside the city of Rome was more mixed. Provincial cities in this period adopted the religious ideologies of the emperor to express status and to underline their connection to the imperial person. This could be motivated by a variety of factors: the presence of the emperor in the city or surrounding area (for instance Caracalla in Pergamum), imperial benefaction (the granting of games or neokoria), or inter-city rivalry (between Nicomedia and Nicaea, and between Tarsus and Anazarbus). This religious sphere connected and overlapped with other areas of contact between the emperor and his subjects. In this context the ideology of war and military success also formed a key arena.[2] The reception of the imperial image and ideology was never simple, but was negotiated within private and local cultural contexts for different purposes. The reign of Elagabalus demonstrates this well: the iconography and titulature of the emperor as high priest of Emesa was never adopted by Greek-speaking cities, though several adopted the imperial iconography of the god Elagabal.

The transmission of the imperial image could be achieved in a number of different ways. Imperial ideology, whether it incorporated divine support, military victories or great figures from the past such as Alexander the Great, was communicated to the wider populace by buildings, paintings, sculpture, coinage and other visual media. Imitations of official imagery (for example the iconography of Elagabal by provincial die-engravers) illustrate this procedure in action. This was not a one-way process; the adoption of provincial iconography by the Roman mint, particularly under Caracalla and Elagabalus, demonstrates that imagery and ideology could also travel

[2] Harl 1987: 40.

from the provinces to Rome. Dispatches to the Senate and works penned by the princeps himself (known for Septimius Severus and Caracalla) would also have contributed to the dissemination of the public image of the emperor.[3] Less formal routes of communication also existed, particularly the movement of people, imperial officials and the emperor himself. Noticeable here is the epigraphic activity of Modestus, whose altars in Petra recalled the deities associated with the Severan saecular games.

A consideration of the archaeological contexts of numismatic finds, and their description in contemporary literary sources, provides an insight into the *Nachleben* or afterlife of coins and medallions.[4] Though primarily intended to circulate as currency, coins were often appropriated for other uses, reflecting their secondary function as mementoes and monuments of events, and of the emperor himself. The incorporation of coins in jewellery, particularly gold types, highlights that the aureus was viewed as a status symbol.[5] The tendency to treat medallions, whether struck in the provinces or by the mint in Rome, as heirlooms or 'souvenirs' of a particular event highlights their owners' emotional attachment to these objects.

Using a hoard analysis to view an emperor's coinage in its totality enables a reassessment of the numismatic image of each princeps. Though such an analysis can only be performed on the silver issues of the Severan emperors, the results are nonetheless revealing. The relatively small presence of Liber Pater and Hercules in Severus' coinage has been ascertained, as well as the large emphasis on deities under Caracalla. The perspective provided by hoards has uncovered the visual weight given to Elagabalus' rôle as high priest of the Emesene stone, as well as the increased presence of Jupiter on the coinage of Severus Alexander. We can in fact quantify the differing religious emphases of Alexander and his cousin Elagabalus: 13 per cent of Alexander's silver coinage had Jovian imagery, whereas under Elagabalus the figure was only 2 per cent. The hoard evidence highlights the changes in the composition of imperial coinage from emperor to emperor, which in turn reflects the weight given to coinage as a medium that reflected and conveyed imperial ideology.

The importance of coinage as a medium of record and communication is also underscored by the constant change in coin types from year to year. Newly minted coins would have communicated specific ideas to targeted audiences. Perhaps one of the most revealing examples here is the emphasis on Sol during the Persian campaigns of Severus Alexander. The large quantity of the coinage being struck at the end of Severus Alexander's

[3] Sidebottom 2007: 55. [4] Rowan 2010. [5] Vermeule 1975: 5–32.

reign was likely to finance the Persian Wars, and the large iconographic emphasis on Sol would have underlined the support of a deity traditionally associated with Roman conquests in the East. The saecular games coinage of Severus and his predecessors also suggests the possibility that there was an archive of coin types in Rome. This suggestion leads to the idea that the coin types struck from year to year formed an official record of each emperor's rule. This collection of imperial annals were obviously accessed when need arose; this would explain the similarities between the saecular coin types of Augustus, Domitian and Severus, as well as the 'restitution' coinage which was struck intermittently throughout the imperial period. An archive of coin types may also help in explaining the fact that the Roman mint continued to strike small numbers of 'commemorative' types that detailed the sacrifices, celebrations and other events that occurred throughout an emperor's reign. These may have been intended to contribute to an official record of a reign, and viewing the numismatic evidence from this perspective can lead to fruitful results for the historian.

Divine support formed one basis through which emperors could justify their right to rule. The support of a particular deity or deities provided a mechanism by which emperor and subject alike could visualise imperial power and its manifestations. Yet there was more to an emperor than his religious support; military prowess remained central to imperial ideology. The material remains from the reign of Severus Alexander demonstrate this vividly: the Persian War was a major factor in the emperor's interaction with his subjects. Ultimately, the failure of Severus Alexander to stem invasions from the east and the north, and his inability to win the support of the soldiers, meant the end of the Severan dynasty.[6] Dio records that Severus realised the vital importance of the military as a base of power, reportedly advising his sons 'be harmonious, enrich the soldiers and scorn all other men'.[7] Even if this statement is little more than a reflection of Dio's ideas about the Roman army and Severus as an emperor, ultimately it would be the army that decided the fate of the Severan dynasty.

[6] Hdn. 6.8.1–6.9.8. [7] Dio 77.152.

Appendix 1

Silver reverse types of the emperors Trajan to Severus Alexander based on the contents of the Reka-Devnia hoard. (Analysis incorporates sole rules only.)[1]

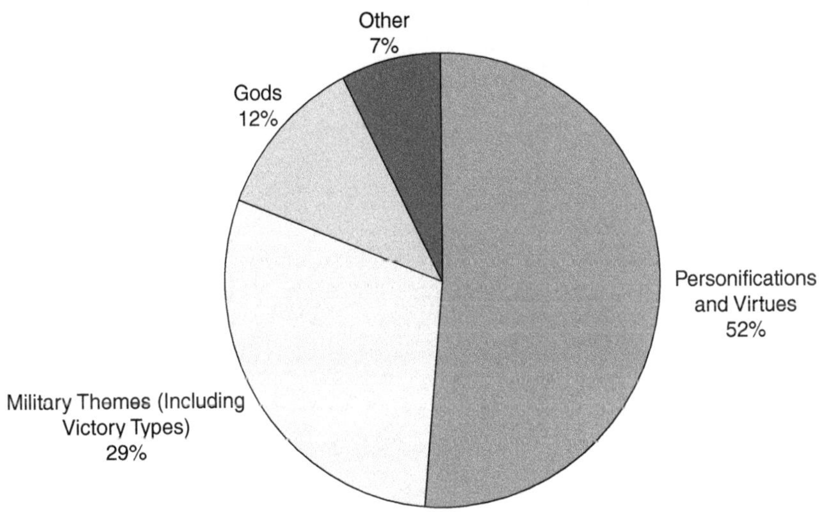

Figure 85: Trajan.

[1] The 'gods' category for Elagabalus includes coin types showing the emperor in his capacity as high priest of Elagabal.

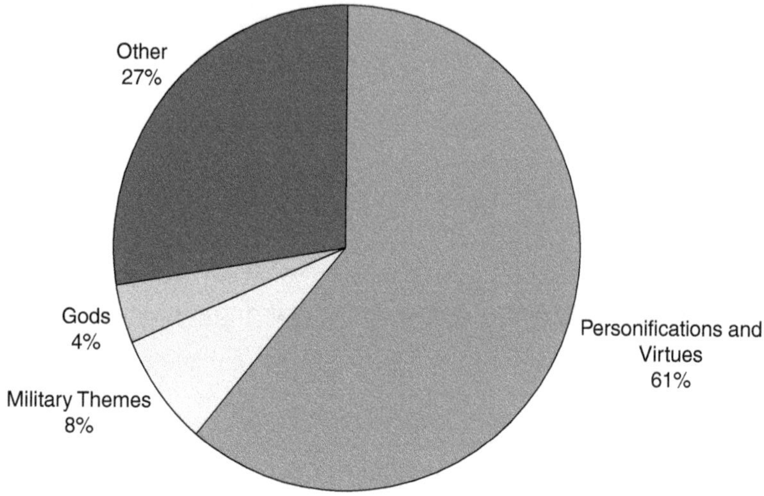

Figure 86: Hadrian.

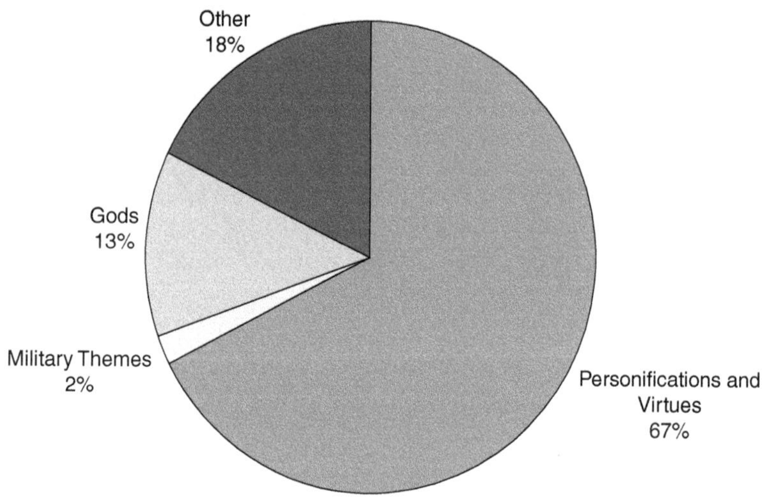

Figure 87: Antoninus Pius.

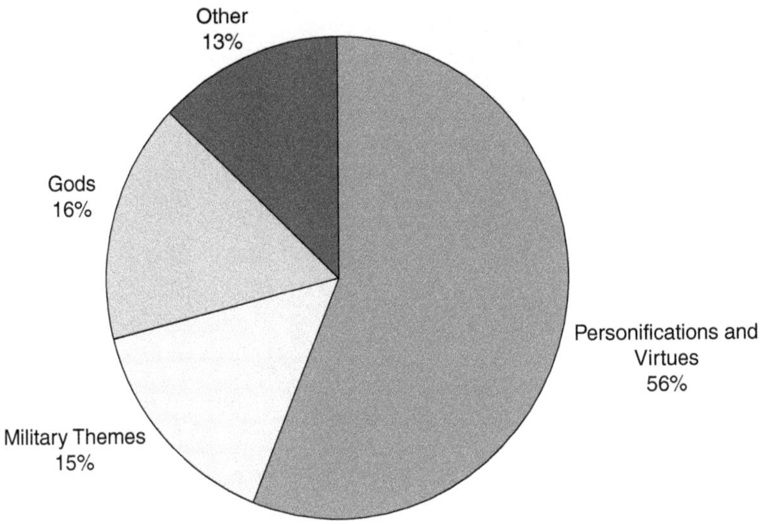

Figure 88: Marcus Aurelius.

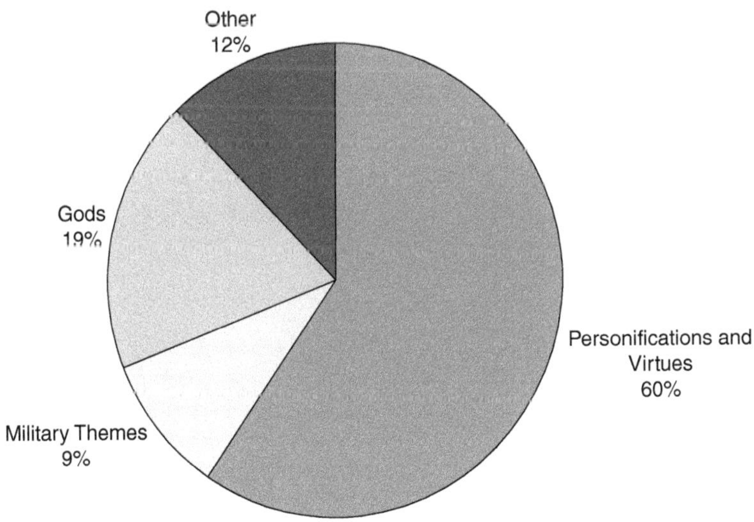

Figure 89: Commodus.

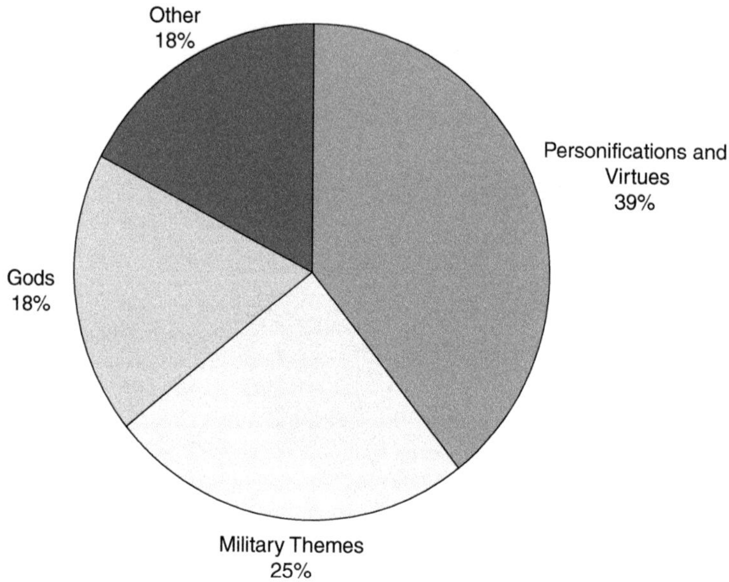

Figure 90: Septimius Severus.

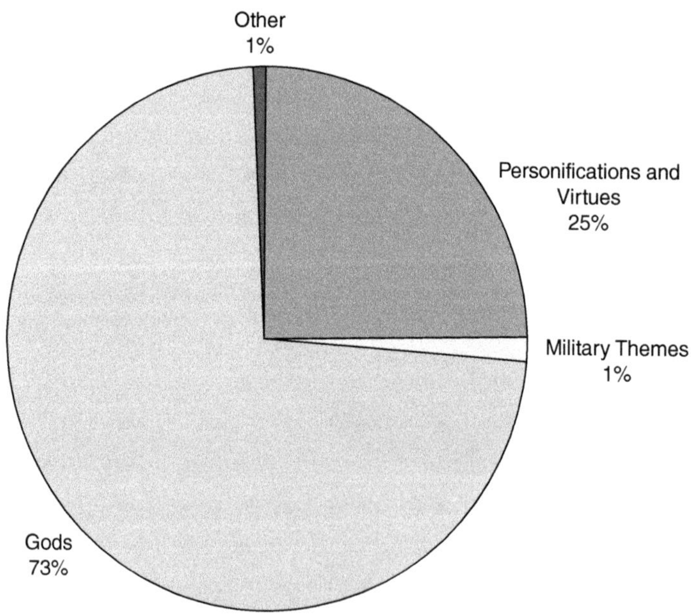

Figure 91: Caracalla.

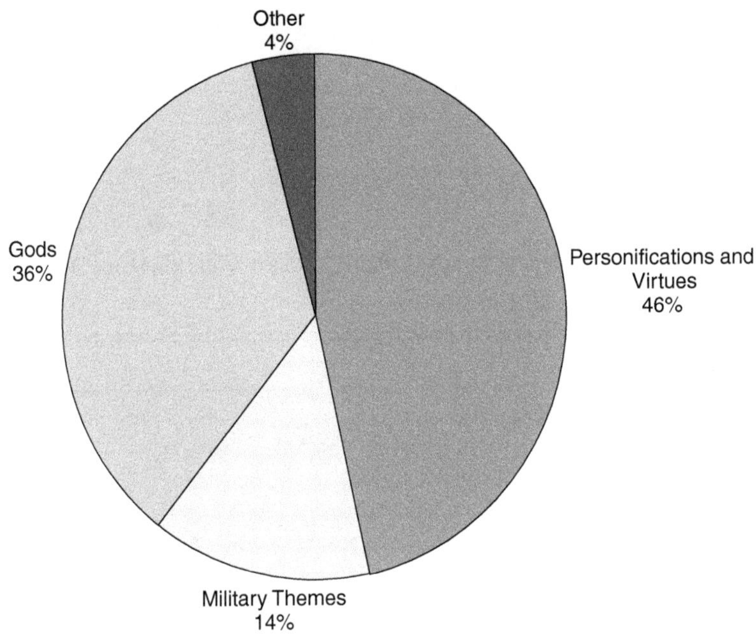

Figure 92: Elagabalus.

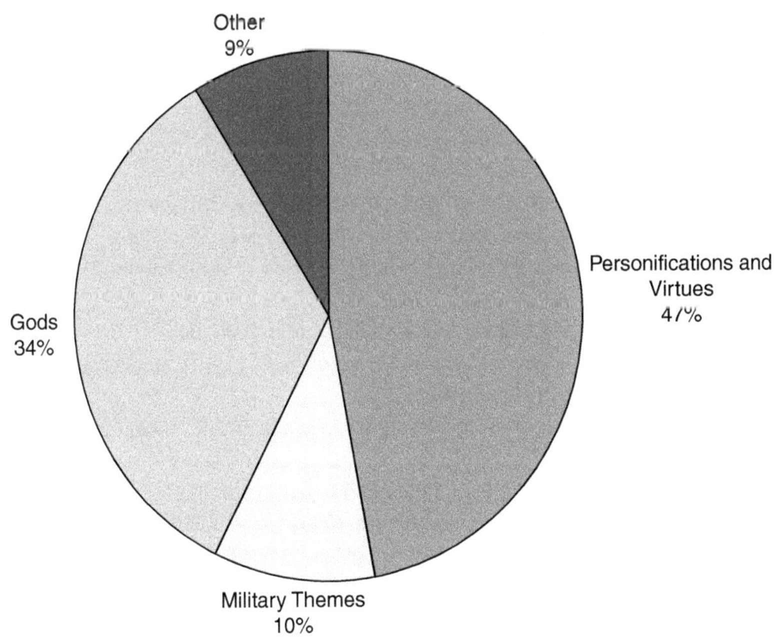

Figure 93: Severus Alexander.

Appendix 2

Preliminary collection of reverse silver dies of the 'stone on quadriga' type (RIC IV.2 Elagabalus 144, 195–6, 197).

Die	Examples
1	J. Vinchon (6–7 May 1959) 320
2	a) Münzen und Medaillen (2–4 December 1957) 531
	b) Gemini LLC, Auction V (6 January 2009) 821
	c) Gorny & Mosch Münzhandlung, Auction 165 (17 March 2008) 2132
	d) Gorny & Mosch Giessener Münzhandlung, Auction 134 (11 October 2004) 2949
3	a) CNG, Mail Bid Sale 66 (19 May 2004) 1560
	b) Fritz Rudolf Kunker GmbH & Co. KG, Auction 111 (18 March 2006) 6908
4	a) J. Schulman (10–13 June 1974) 1883
	b) CNG Triton XI (8 January 2008) 957
	c) Gorny & Mosch Giessener Münzhandlung, Auction 138 (7 March 2005) 2263
	d) Numismatik Lanz München, Auction 97 (22 May 2000) 801
5	Münzen und Medaillen (6–7 December 1968) 497
6	Gorny & Mosch Giessener Münzhandlung, Auction 159 (8 October 2007) 447
7	a) CNG Mail Bid Sale 64 (24 September 2003) 1158
	b) CNG Mail Bid Sale 75 (23 May 2007) 1102
8	Helbing 63 (29 April 1931) 1041
9	Hirsch 18 (1907) 1188
10	Gorny & Mosch Münzhandlung, Auction 160 (9 October 2007) 2047
11	Gorny & Mosch Münzhandlung, Auction 118 (15 October 2002) 2299
	(=Gorny & Mosch Giessener Münzhandlung, Auction 125 (13 October 2003) 541)
12	a) British Museum (RIC IV.1 pl 3.2; BMCRE pl. 91.8)
	b) Numismatik Lanz München, Auction 128 (22 May 2006) 604
	c) Gorny & Mosch Giessener Münzhandlung, Auction 142 (10 October 2005) 2770
13	a) Baranowsky Fx Pr 1934 pt 3, 4812
	b) Gorny & Mosch Giessener Münzhandlung, Auction 160 (9 October 2007) 2408
14	Spink Sale 4018 (6 October 2004) 244
15	a) Münzen und Medaillen (16–17 June 1967) 97
	b) Numismatik Lanz München, Auction 100 (20 November 2000) 131
16	Dr Busso Peus Nachfolger, Auction 376 (29 October 2003) 1011
17	Numismatik Lanz München, Auction 123 (30 May 2005) 706
18	Gorny & Mosch Giessener Münzhandlung, Auction 176 (10 March 2009) 2426
19	a) Grabow XIV (27 July 1939) 1051
	b) CNG, Mail Bid Sale 72 (14 June 2006) 1593
20	British Museum (BMCRE pl. 91.7)

Die	Examples
21	a) Egger 39 (1912) 1149
	b) CNG Triton VI (14 January 2003) 1053
22	a) Rauch (4–5 June 1971) 252
	b) Numismatik Lanz München, Auction 112 (25 November 2002) 722
23	a) A. Tkalec AG Auction 2001 (19 February 2001) 329
	b) A. Tkalec Auction 2003 (24 October 2003) 342
	c) Gerhard Hirsch Nachfolger, Auction 248–9 (6 February 2007) 2063
24	Dr Busso Peus Nachfolger, Auction 384 (2 November 2005) 729
25	a) Gorny & Mosch Giessener Münzhandlung, Auction 114 (4 March 2002) 367
	b) Fitzwilliam Museum CM.BU.322-R
26	a) Münzen und Medaillen (12–13 November 1970) 404
	b) Poindessault (29–30 May 1972) 281
	c) Münzen und Medaillen Deutschland, Auction 13 (9 October 2003) 730
27	Münzen und Medaillen (2–3 December 1975) 679
28	Münzkabinett Berlin 18206708
29	Dmitry Markov Coins and Medals, New York Sale IV (17 January 2002) 384
30	Numismatik Lanz München, Auction 120 (18 May 2004) 438
31	Hamburger (17 June 1908) 1391
32	Fritz Rudolf Kunker GmbH & Co. KG, Auction 111 (18 March 2006) 6907
33	UBS Gold & Numismatics, Auction 78 (9 September 2008) 1792
34	a) Münzhandlung Basel, Auction 10 (15 March 1938) 695
	b) Gorny & Mosch Giessener Münzhandlung, Auction 130 (8 March 2004) 2270
	c) Auktionhaus HD Rauch GmbH Summer Auction 2007 (11 September 2007) 775
	d) Gorny & Mosch Giessener Münzhandlung, Auction 117 (14 October 2002) 635
35	Basel Münzhandlung VI (18 March 1936) 1875 (= Glendining (29–30 October 1975) 635
36	Fitzwilliam Museum CM.3.20–1991
37	Fitzwilliam Museum CM 3.19–1991

Appendix 3
List of hoards used

Britain

Bristol (AD 208, 1,480 coins)
Mattingly, H. and Pearce, B. W. (1938) 'The Bristol hoard of denarii, 1937', *NC* 18: 85–98.

Muswell Hill, London (AD 210, 654 coins)
Mattingly, H. (1929) 'Muswell Hill', *NC* 9: 315–19.

Darfield II, South Yorkshire (AD 215, 500 coins)
Corder, P. (1948) 'A second hoard of Roman denarii from Darfield', *NC* 8: 78–80.

Edston, Peeblesshire, Scotland (AD 222, 290 coins)
Holmes, N. and Hunter, F. (1997) 'Edston, Peebles-Shire', *CHRB* 10: 149–68.

Shapwick Villa, Somerset (AD 224, 9,238 coins)
Abdy, R. and Minnitt, S. (2002) 'Shapwick Villa', *CHRB* 11: 169–233.

Denbighshire, Wales (AD 226, 507 coins)
Mattingly, H. (1923) 'Find of Roman denarii in Denbighshire', *NC* 3: 152–5.

St Mary Cray, Bromley (AD 228, 376 coins)
Robertson, A. S. (1935) 'The St. Mary Cray hoard', *NC* 15: 62–6.

East England (AD 230, 3,169 coins)
Evans, J. (1898) 'A hoard of Roman coins', *NC* 18: 126–84.

Falkirk, Scotland (AD 230, 1,925 coins)
MacDonald, G. (1934) 'A hoard of Roman denarii from Scotland', *NC* 14: 1–30.

Cambridge (AD 248, 193 coins)
Boyd, W.C. (1897) 'A find of Roman denarii near Cambridge', *NC* 17: 119–26.

Darfield, South Yorkshire (AD 250, 481 coins)
Walker, J. (1946) 'The Darfield hoard of Roman denarii.' *NC* 6: 147–50.

Brickendonbury, Hertfordshire (AD 250, 430 coins)
Evans, J. (1896) 'Roman coins found at Brickendonbury, Hertford', *NC* 16: 191–208.
Stevenage, Hertfordshire (AD 263, 387 coins)
Bland, R. (1988) 'Stevenage, Hertfordshire', in *The Normanby Hoard and Other Roman Coin Hoards*, ed. R. Bland and A. Burnett. London: 43–71.
Caistor by Yarmouth, Norfolk (*c.* AD 270, 847 coins)
Jenkins, G. K. (1947) 'The Caister by Yarmouth hoard', *NC* 7: 175–9.

France

Aïn, Rhône-Alpes (AD 215, 446 coins)
Salama, P. (2001/2002) 'Le trésor de deniers d'Aïn Témouchent et ses satellites dans l'Afrique romaine', *TM* 20: 185–222.
Viuz-Faverges (AD 252, 2,306 coins)
Pflaum, H. G. (1981) 'Le trésor de Viuz-Faverges', *TM* 3: 33–76.
Nanterre, Paris (AD 254, 1,968 coins)
Gentilhomme, P. L. (1947) 'La trouvaille de Nanterre', *RN* 9: 15–114.
Eauze, Gers (AD 261, 28,003 coins)
Schaad, D., Agrinier, P., et al. (1992) *Le trésor d'Eauze*. Toulouse.

Belgium

Elligines-Sainte-Anne (AD 240, 276 coins)
Lallemand, J. (1968) 'Le trésor d'Elligines-Sainte-Anne: deniers de Marc-Aurèle à Gordien III', *RBN* 114: 138–68.
Clavier, Liège (AD 255, 1,680 coins)
Lallemand, J. (1969) 'Le trésor de Clavier III: deniers et antoniniens de Commode à Valérien-Gallien', *RBN* 115: 263–331.

Italy

Vicenza, Veneto (AD 235, 110 coins)
no. 45/3(1) in *RMRVe* IV.1
Via Tritone, Rome (AD 244, 828 coins)
Cesano, L. (1925) 'Nuovi ripostigli di denari di argento dell' 'impero romano.' *Atti e Memorie dell'Istituto Italiano di Numismatica* 5: 57–72.

Germany

Welzheim, Baden-Württemburg, (AD 225, 652 coins)
no. 4596 in *FMRD* II.4.
Baden-Baden, Baden-Württemburg (AD 228, 611 coins)
no. 2196 in *FMRD* II.2.
Mainz, Rhineland-Palatinate (AD 228, 186 coins)
no. 1153 in *FMRD* IV.1.
Eining, Bavaria (AD 235, 73 coins)
no. 2034 in *FMRD* I.2.
Kirchmatting, Bavaria (AD 235, 1,318 coins)
no. 2116 in *FMRD* I.2.
Kempten Lindenberg III (AD 235, 640 coins)
no. 7186 in *FMRD* I.7.
Pfünz (AD 235, 94 coins)
no. 5042 in *FMRD* I.5.
Wiggensbach, Bavaria (AD 235, 401 coins)
no. 7199 in *FMRD* I.7.
Cologne (AD 238, 4,169 coins)
no. 1004 3a-b in *FMRD* VI.1.1.
Niederaschau, Bavaria (AD 238, 766 coins)
no. 1229 in *FMRD* I.1.
Wiesbach, Rhineland-Palatinate (AD 254, 402 coins)
no. 1082 in *FMRD* III.
Linsberg (AD 238, 286 coins)
Dembski, G. (2007) 'Ein römischer Münzschatzfund aus Linsberg, Gem. Erlach, BH wieder Neustadt', *NZ* 115: 33–55.
Gunzenhausen, Bavaria (AD 244, 510 coins)
no. 5057 in *FMRD* I.5.

Romania

Ghirişa, Beltiug (AD 198, 151 coins)
no. 141 in Depeyrot, G. and Moisil, D. (2008) *Les trésors de deniers de Trajan à Balbin en Roumanie*. Wetteren.
Frânceşti, Vâlcea (AD 219, 1,365 coins)
Depeyrot, G. and Moisil, D. (2004) *Le trésor Frânceşti (Roumanie)*. Wetteren.

Munteneşti, Valsui (AD 228, 742 coins)
no. 183 in Depeyrot, G. and Moisil, D. (2008) *Les trésors de deniers de Trajan à Balbin en Roumanie*. Wetteren.
Barza, (AD 235, 1,337 coins)
no. 174 in Depeyrot, G. and Moisil, D. (2008) *Les trésors de deniers de Trajan à Balbin en Roumanie*. Wetteren.
Taga (AD 239, 962 coins)
Protase, D. and Crişan, I. H. (1968), 'Tezaurul de monede imperiale Romane de la Ţaga.' *Studii şi Cercetări de Numismatică* 4: 139–73.

Hungary

Kecel, Bács-Kiskun (AD 215, 255 coins)
Katalin, B. S. (1986) 'A keceli éremlelet', *Cumania* 9: 27–74.
Ercsi, Fejér (AD 228, 386 coins)
Soproni, S. (1964) 'Az ercsi éremlelet', *Numizmatikai közlöny* 62/63: 9–17.
Börgöndi, Székesfehérvár (AD 235, 587 coins)
Aladár, R. (1936) 'A börgöndi éremlelet', *Numizmatikai közlöny* 34/35: 24–7.

Slovenia

Leskovec (AD 236, 122 coins)
no. 408 in *FMRSlow* II.
Postojna, Carniola (AD 238, 339 coins)
no. 91.2 in *FMRSlow* I.
Gračič, Zreče (AD 253, 431 coins)
no. 176 in *FMRSlow* III.

Bulgaria

Nicolaévo (AD 249, 936 coins)
Seure, G. (1923) 'Trésors de monnaies antiques en Bulgarie III: Le trésor de Nicolaévo', *RN* 26: 111–53.
Rustschuk (AD 249, 1,602 coins)
Muschmov, N. A. (1918) 'Münzfunde aus Bulgarien', *NZ* 11: 43–51.
Reka-Devnia, Devnya (AD 251, 81,096 coins)
Mouchmov, N. A. (1934) *Le trésor numismatique de Réka-Devnia (Marcianopolis)*. Sofia.

Depeyrot, G. (2004) *La propagande monétaire (64–235) et le trésor de Marcianopolis* (251). Wetteren.

Plevna (AD 259, 3,296 coins)

Mattingly, H. and Salisbury, F. S. (1924) 'A find of Roman coins from Plevna in Bulgaria', *NC* 4: 210–38.

Macedonia

Usküb (Skopje) (AD 249, 1,022 coins)

Kubitschek, W. (1908) 'Ein Denarfund aus der Gegend von Usküb', *NZ* 41: 37–47.

Serbia

Singinudum, Belgrade (AD 254, 2,445 coins)

Kondic, V. (1969) *The Singinudum Hoard of Denarii and Antoniniani (Septimius Severus–Valerian)*. Belgrade.

Turkey

South East Turkey (AD 251, 1,911 coins)

Bendall, S. (1966) 'An eastern hoard of Roman imperial silver', *NC* 6: 165–70.

Haydere, Aydin (AD 264, 2,330 coins)

Ashton, R. (1991) 'The Haydere hoard and other hoards of the mid-third century from Turkey', in *Recent Turkish Coin Hoards and Numismatic Studies*, ed. C. S. Lightfoot. Oxford: 91–180.

Syria

Syria (AD 212, 261 coins)

Cesano, L. (1925) 'Nuovi ripostigli di denari di argento dell'impero romano.' *Atti e Memorie dell'Istituto Italiano di Numismatica* 5: 57–72.

Dura Europos III and IV (AD 218, 402 coins)

Bellinger, A. R. (1949) *The Excavations at Dura Europos, Volume 6: The Coins*. New Haven.

Bibliography

Aalders, G. J. D. (1986) 'Cassius Dio and the Greek world', *Mnemosyne* 39: 282–304.

Ahmed, S. S. (1968) *Southern Mesopotamia in the Time of Ashurbanipal.* Paris.

Aitken, E. B. (2004) 'Why a Phoenician? A proposal for the historical occasion for the *Heroikos*', in *Philostratus's Heroikos: Religion and Cultural Identity in the Third Century C.E.*, ed. E. B. Aitken and J. K. B. Maclean. Atlanta: 267–84.

Aitken, E. B., and Maclean, J. K. B. (2004) 'Introduction', in *Philostratus's Heroikos: Religion and Cultural Identity in the Third Century C.E.*, ed. E. B. Aitken and J. K. B. Maclean. Atlanta: xvii–xxiv.

Albertson, F. C. (2004) 'The creation and dissemination of Roman imperial portrait types: the case of Marcus Aurelius type IV', *JDAI* 119: 259–306.

Alcock, S. E. (2004) 'Material witness: an archaeological context for the *Heroikos*', in *Philostratus' Heroikos: Religion and Cultural Identity in the Third Century C.E.*, ed. E. B. Aitken and J. K. B. Maclean. Atlanta: 159–68.

Alföldi, A. (1935) 'Insignien und Tracht der römischen Kaiser', *MDAI(R)* 50: 3–171.

(1938–1941) 'Tonmodel und Reliefmedaillons aus den Donauländern', in *Laureae aquincenses, memoriae Valentini Kuzsinszky dicatae. Aquincumi baberagak, Kuzsinszky Balint emlekenek szenteli Budapest szekesfovaros kozonsege es a Pazmany-Egyetem rem-s Rgisgtani Intzete.* Dissertationes Pannonicae Series 2, 10. Budapest: 312–41.

(1977) 'From the *Aion Plutonios* of the Ptolemies to the *saeculum frugiferum* of the Roman emperors', in *Greece and the Eastern Mediterranean in Ancient History and Prehistory*, ed. K. H. Kinzl. Berlin: 1–30.

Alföldi, M. R.-. (1999) *Bild und Bildersprache der römischen Kaiser.* Mainz.

Alföldy, G. (1960) 'Pannoniciani augures', *Acta Antiqua* 8: 145–64.

(1971) 'Herodians Person', *Ancient Society* 2: 204–33.

(1974) 'The crisis of the third century as seen by contemporaries', *GRBS* 15: 89–112.

(1976a) 'Das neue *Saeculum* des Pescennius Niger', in *Bonner Historia-Augusta Colloquium 1972/1974.* Bonn: 1–10.

(1976b) 'Zwei Schimpfnamen des Kaisers Elagabal: *Tiberinus* und *Tractaticius*', in *Bonner Historia-Augusta Colloquium 1972/1974.* Bonn: 11–21.

(1996) '*Nox dea fit lux*! Caracallas Geburtstag', in *Historiae Augustae Colloquium Barcinonense*, ed. G. Bonamente and M. Mayer. Bari: 9–36.

(1997) 'Die Großen Götter von Gorsium', *ZPE* 115: 225–41.

Amandry, M. and Hollard, D. (1997) 'Le trésor de bronzes romains de Plaisians (Drôme)', *TM* 16: 21–3.

Ameling, W. (1997) 'Griechische Intellektuelle und das Imperium Romanum: das Beispiel Cassius Dio', *ANRW* II.34.3: 2472–96.

Anderson, G. (1986) *Philostratus: Biography and Belles Lettres in the Third Century AD*. London.

(1989) 'The *pepaideumenos* in action: sophists and their outlook in the early Roman empire', *ANRW* II.33.1: 79–208.

Ando, C. (2000) *Imperial Ideology and Provincial Loyalty in the Roman Empire*. Berkeley.

André, N., Villedieu, F. et al. (2004) 'Vom "schwebenden Garten" zum Tempelbezirk – Die Untersuchungen der École Française de Rome in der Vigna Barberini', in *Die Kaiserpaläste auf dem Palatin in Rom*, ed. A. Hoffmann and U. Wulf. Mainz: 112–43.

Andreau, J. (2008). 'The use and survival of coins and of gold and silver in the Vesuvian cities', *The Monetary Systems of the Greeks and Romans*, ed. W. V. Harris. Oxford: 208–225.

Angeli, M. G. B. (1971) 'A proposito di un'epigrafe da Ciunia di recente riedita', *Epigrafica* 33: 150–2.

Arrizabalaga y Prado, L. d. (2003) 'Iter Principis: Elagabal's route from Emesa to Rome?' *Area Studies Tsukuba* 21: 59–100.

(2004–5) 'Anaglyptica Variana: column capitals with sculptural relief, and associated fragments, related to the cult of Elagabal', *Tsukuba Studies in Literature and Linguistics* 43–6: 111–258.

(2010) *The Emperor Elagabalus: Fact or Fiction?* Cambridge.

Arrizabalaga y Prado, L. d. and Marcos, R. F. (2005) 'The site of the Varian temple of Elagabal in Rome: a topographical and astronomical approach to the question', *Tsukuba Studies in Literature and Linguistics* 47: 89–124.

Asso, P. (2002) 'The function of the fight: Hercules and Antaeus in Lucan', *Vichiana: Rassegna di studi classici* 4: 57–72.

Aurigemma, S. (1940) 'L'elefante di Leptis Magna e il commercio dell'avorio e delle *ferae libycae* negli *emporia* Tripolitani', *Africa Italiana* 7: 67–86.

Babelon, E. (1903) 'Les monnaies de Septime Sévère, de Caracalla et de Geta relatives à l'Afrique', *RIN* 16: 157–74.

Baharal, D. (1989) 'Portraits of the emperor L. Septimius Severus (193–211 A.D.) as an expression of his propaganda', *Latomus* 48: 566–80.

(1994) 'Caracalla and Alexander the Great: a reappraisal', *Studies in Latin Literature and Roman History* 7: 524–67.

(1996) *Victory of Propaganda. The Dynastic Aspect of the Imperial Propaganda of the Severi: the Literary and Archaeological Evidence AD 193–235*. Oxford.

(2000) 'Public image and women at court in the era of the adoptive emperors (AD 98–180). The case of Faustina the Younger', *Studies in Latin Literature and Roman History* 10: 318–27.

Baldus, H. R. (1971) *Uranius Antoninus. Münzprägung und Geschichte.* Bonn.

(1989) 'Das "Vorstellungsgemälde" des Heliogabal. Ein bislang unerkanntes numismatisches Zeugnis', *Chiron* 19: 467–76.

(1991) 'Zur Aufnahme des Sol Elagabalus-Kultes in Rom, 219 n. Chr', *Chiron* 21: 175–8.

Baldwin, B. (1981) 'Acclamations in the Historia Augusta', *Athenaeum* 59: 138–49.

(1989) 'Some aspects of Commodian', *ICS* 14: 331–46.

Balsdon, J. P. V. D. (1951) 'Sulla Felix', *JRS* 41: 1–10.

Bandinelli, R. B., Caffarelli, E. V. et al. (1966) *The Buried City: Excavations at Lepcis Magna.* New York.

Barchiesi, A. (2002) 'Martial arts. Mars Ultor in the Forum Augustum: A verbal monument with a vengeance', in *Ovid's Fasti. Historical Readings at its Bimillenium*, ed. G. Herbert-Brown. Oxford: 1–22.

Barker, D. (1996) 'The Golden Age is proclaimed'? The Carmen Saeculare and the renascence of the Golden Race', *CQ* 46: 434–46.

Barnes, T. D. (1967) 'The family and career of Septimius Severus', *Historia* 16: 87–107.

(1968) 'Pre-Dacian acta martyrum', *JThs* 19: 509–31.

(1970) 'The lost Kaisergeschichte and the Latin historical tradition', in *Bonner Historia-Augusta-Colloquium 1968/69*: 13–43.

(1972) 'Ultimus Antoninorum', in *Bonner Historia-Augusta Colloquium 1970.* Bonn: 53–74.

(1975) 'Frank Kolb: Literarische Beziehungen zwischen Cassius Dio, Herodian und der Historia Augusta. Bonn: Habelt 1972. XII, 196 S', *Gnomon* 47: 368–73.

(1978) *The Sources of the Historia Augusta.* Brussels.

(1984) 'The composition of Cassius Dio's *Roman History*', *Phoenix* 38: 240–54.

Bartoccini, R. (1932) 'L'arco quadrifonte dei Severi a Lepcis (Leptis Magna)', *Africa Italiana* 4: 32–152.

Barton, I. M. (1977) 'The inscriptions of Septimius Severus and his family at Lepcis Magna', *Mélanges offerts a Léopold Sédar Senghor*: 3–12.

(1977/8) 'The effects of imperial favour: Septimius Severus and Lepcis Magna', *Museum Africum* 6: 60–3.

Barton, T. (1994) 'The *inventio* of Nero: Suetonius', in *Reflections of Nero: Culture, History and Representation*, ed. J. Elsner and J. Masters. London: 48–63.

Bassett, E. L. (1955) 'Regulus and the serpent in the *Punica*', *CPh* 50: 1–20.

Bauer, H. (1976) 'Il foro transitorio e il tempio di Giano', *RPAA* 49: 117–50.

(1988) 'Der Urplan des Forum Transitorum', in *Bathron. Beiträge zur Architektur und verwandten Künsten für Heinrich Drerup zu seinem 80. Geburtstag*, ed. H. Büsing and F. Hiller. Saarbücken: 41–57.

Baynes, N. (1926) *The Historia Augusta. Its Date and Purpose*. Oxford.
Beard, M. (1985) 'Writing and ritual: a study of diversity and expansion in the Arval acta', *PBSR* 53: 114–62.
(2007) *The Roman Triumph*. Cambridge, Mass.
Beard, M., North, J. et al. (1998) *Religions of Rome*. Cambridge.
Behr, C. A. (1968) *Aelius Aristides and the Sacred Tales*. Amsterdam.
(1981) *P. Aelius Aristides. The Complete Works*, 2 vols. Leiden.
Bellinger, A. R. (1939) 'The eighth and ninth Dura hoards', *Numismatic Notes and Monographs* 85: 1–92.
(1958) 'Roman and Byzantine medallions in the Dumbarton Oaks collection', *DOP* 12: 127–56.
(1961) *Troy: The Coins*. Princeton.
Benabou, M. (1976) *La résistance africaine à la romanisation*. Paris.
Benario, H. W. (1954) 'The dediticii of the constitutio Antoniniana', *TAPhA* 85: 188–96.
(1959) 'The titulature of Julia Soaemias and Julia Mamaea: Two Notes', *TAPhA* 90: 9–14.
(1961) 'Severan Rome and the Historia Augusta', *Latomus* 20: 281–90.
Benedum, C. (2001) 'Betrachtungen zu Asklepios und dem Aesculapius der Römer', *WJA* 25: 187–204.
Benoist, S. (1999) 'Le retour du prince dans la cité (juin 193-juillet 326)', *CCG* 10: 149–75.
(2005) *Rome, le prince et la Cité. Pouvoir impérial et cérémonies publiques (1er siècle av. – début du IVe siècle apr. J.-C.)* Paris.
Bergmann, M. (1998) *Die Strahlen der Herrscher. Theomorphes Herrscherbild und politische Symbolik im Hellenismus und in der römischen Kaiserzeit*. Mainz.
Bernal, M. (1987–2006) *Black Athena: the Afroasiatic Roots of Classic Civilisation*. New Brunswick, N.J.
(2001) *Black Athena Writes Back: Martin Benal Responds to his Critics*. Durham, N.C.
Bernhard, O. (1926) 'Aesculapius und die Asklepiaden auf römischen Münzen', *SNR* 24: 129–41.
Berrers, S. (2004) *Sonnenkult und Kaisertum von den Severern bis zu Constantin I*. Stuttgart.
Bertrand-Dagenbach, C. (1990) *Alexandre Sévère et l'Histoire Auguste*. Brussels.
Besnier, M. (1902) *L'Île Tibérine dans l'antiquité*. Paris.
Bickerman, E. (1926) *Das Edikt des Kaisers Caracalla in P. Giss*. 40. Berlin.
Bickford-Smith, R. A. (1994/5) 'The imperial mints in the East for Septimius Severus: it is time to begin a thorough reconsideration', *RIN* 96: 53–71.
Birley, A. R. (1969) 'Coups d'état of the year 193', *BJ* 169: 247–80.
(1971) *Septimius Severus, The African Emperor*. London.
(1988) *Septimius Severus, The African Emperor* (2nd edn). London.

(1990) 'Review: Martin Frey: Untersuchungen zur Religion und zur Religionspolitik des Kaisers Elagabal. (Historia Einzelshriften, 62.) Pp. 125. Stuttgart: Franz Steiner, 1989. DM 36', *CR* 40: 510–11.

(1991) 'Alexander Severus in the Historia Augusta', *CR* 41: 345–6.

(1994) 'Further notes on the HA Severus', in *Historiae Augustae Colloquium Genevense*, ed. G. Bonamente and F. Paschoud. Bari: 19–42.

(1998) 'A new tombstone from Vindolanda', *Britannia* 29: 299–306.

Birley, E. (1932) 'Roman garrisons in the north of Britain', *JRS* 22: 55–9.

(1953) 'Senators in the Emperor's service', *PBA* 39: 197–214.

(1974) 'Cohors I Tungrorum and the oracle of the Clarian Apollo', *Chiron* 4: 511–13.

Bland, R. (1996) 'The Roman coinage of Alexandria, 30 BC – AD 296: interplay between Roman and local designs', in *Archaeological Research in Roman Egypt: The Proceedings of the Seventeenth Classical Colloquium of the Department of Greek and Roman Antiquities, British Museum*, ed. D. M. Bailey. Ann Arbor. JRA Suppl. 19: 113–27.

Bland, R. and Abdy, R. (2002) 'Hoards of the Severan period from Roman Britain', *CHRB* 11: 19–46.

Bland, R. F., Burnett, A. M., et al. (1987) 'The mints of Pescennius Niger in the light of some new *aurei*', *NC* 147: 65–83.

Blázquez, J. M. (1990) 'Alejandro Magno, modelo de Alejandro Severo', *Latomus* 208: 25–36.

Bloch, H. (1943) 'A dream of Septimius Severus', *Classical Weekly* 37: 31–2.

Boatwright, M. (1987) *Hadrian and the City of Rome*. Princeton.

Bober, P. P. (1943) 'The sculptures of the Arch of Septimius Severus at Leptis Magna'. Master of Arts Thesis, New York University.

Bolin, S. (1958) *State and Currency in the Roman Empire to 300 AD*. Stockholm.

Bonanno, A. (1976) *Portraits and Other Heads on Roman Historical Relief up to the Age of Septimius Severus*. Oxford.

(1976–7) 'The Severan commemorative relief at Cyrene. The portraiture', *Society for Libyan Studies Annual Report* 8: 19–26.

Boon, G. C. (1958) 'A Roman pastrycook's mould from Silchester', *AntJ* 38: 237–40.

Borgia, E., Colli, D. et al. (1998) 'Roma, S. Croce in Gerusalemme. Nuove acquisizioni topografiche', *BCAR* 99: 243–50.

(2008) '*Horti spei veteris* e *Palatium sessorianum*: nuove acquisizioni da interventi urbani 1996–2008. Parte I', *Fasti Online* (www.fastionline.org/).

Bosch, C. (1935) *Die kleinasiatischen Münzen der römischen Kaiserzeit*. Stuttgart.

Bosworth, B. (2007) 'Rider in the chariot: Ptolemy, Alexander and the elephants', in *Alexander the Great and the Hellenistic Kingdoms*, ed. K. Sheedy. Sydney: 17–22.

Boucher, B. (2000) 'Nature and antique in the work of Andrea Palladio', *Journal of the Society of Architectural Historians* 59: 296–311.

Bowersock, G. W. (1975) 'Herodian and Elagabalus', *YCS* 24: 229–36.

(1985) 'Cassius Dio and Herodian', in *Cambridge History of Classical Literature I: Greek Literature*, ed. P. E. Easterling and B. M. W. Knox. Cambridge: 710–13.

Braund, D. (2000) 'Athenaeus, *On the Kings of Syria*', in *Athenaeus and his World*, ed. D. Braund and J. Wilkins. Exeter: 514–22.

Bregman, J. (1982) 'Pagan religious syncretism and symbolism on the Greek imperials of the early third century', *Dionysius* 6: 58–72.

Brendle, T. (2001) 'Die Religionspolitik Kaiser Elagabals im Spiegel seiner Münzen', *NNB* 50: 411–14.

Brilliant, R. (1967) *The Arch of Septimius Severus in the Roman Forum*. Rome.

Broise, H. and Thébert, Y. (1999) 'Élagabal et le complexe religieux de la Vigna Barberini', *MEFRA* 3: 729–47.

Brouquier-Reddé, V. (2003) 'Le temple de la Victoire Germanique de Caracalla à Dougga', in *La place du sanctuaire de la Victoire Germanique de Caracalla à Dougga dans la typologie de l'architecture religieuse païenne de l'Afrique romaine*, ed. M. Khanoussi. Tunisia: 457–89.

Brown, F. E. (1951) 'Cosa I: history and topography', *MAAR* 20: 7–113.

Bruhl, A. (1953) *Liber Pater*. Paris.

Bruun, C. (1997) 'Kaiser Elagabal und ein neues Zeugnis für den Kult des Sonnengottes Elagabalus in Italien', *Tyche* 12: 1–5.

Bruun, P. M. (1991) 'The charm of quantitative studies in numismatic research', in *Die Münze. Bild-Botschaft-Bedeutung. Festschrift für Maria R.-Alföldi*, ed. H. Noeske and H. Schubert. Frankfurt: 65–83.

Bryson, N. (1981) *Word and Image. French Painting of the Ancien Régime*. Cambridge.

Buraselis, K. (1989) *Studies on the Policy of the Severans and the Constitutio Antoniniana*. Athens.

Burnett, A. (1999) 'Buildings and monuments on Roman coins', in *Roman Coins and Public Life under the Empire*, ed. G. M. Paul and M. Ierardi. Ann Arbor, Mich.: 137–64.

Burnett, A., Amandry, M. et al. (1992) *Roman Provincial Coinage*, vol 1. London.

Burrell, B. (2004) *Neokoroi: Greek Cities and Roman Emperors*. Leiden.

Butcher, K. (1988) 'The colonial coinage of Antioch-on-the-Orontes *c.* AD 218–53', *NC* 148: 63–75.

(2003) *Roman Syria and the Near East*. London.

(2004) *Coinage in Roman Syria*. London.

Butcher, M. S. (2006) *Roman Provincial Coinage*, vol. 7.1. London.

Butler, O. F. (1908) *Studies in the life of Heliogabalus*. New York.

Buttrey, T. V. (1972a) 'A hoard of *sestertii* from Bordeaux and the problem of bronze circulation in the third century A.D.', *ANSMS* 18: 33–58.

(1972b) 'Vespasian as moneyer', *NC* 12: 89–109.

(1992) 'The denarii of Pescennius Niger', *NC* 152: iv–xxii.

(1993) 'Calculating ancient coin production: facts and fantasies', *NC* 153: 335–51.

(1994) 'Calculating ancient coin production II: why it cannot be done', *NC* 154: 341–52.

Cadotte, A. (2003) 'Frugifer en Afrique du Nord: épithète divine ou dieu à part entière?' *ZPE* 143: 187–200.

Calabria, P. (1992) 'La monetazione di L. Rubrius Dossenus', *RIN* 94: 65–80.

Calicó, X. (2003) *The Roman Aurei*, vol 2: *From Didius Julianus to Constantinus I (193AD–335AD).* Barcelona.

Cameron, A. (1965) 'Review: Heidnische Geschichtsapologetik in der christlichen Spätantike. Untersuchungen über Zeit und Tendenz der Historia Augusta', *JRS* 55: 240–50.

Capai, C. F. (1991) 'Il culto di Asclepio da Epidauro a Roma: medicina del tempio e medicina scientifica', *CCC* 12: 271–84.

Caquot, A. (1955) 'Note sur le *semeion* et les inscriptions Araméennes de Hatra', *Syria* 32: 59–69.

Carlson, C. W. A. (1969) 'The "laetitia temporum" reverses of the Severan dynasty', *Journal of the Society for Ancient Numismatics* 1: 20–1.

(1971–2a) 'Ludi Saeculares rites of the Roman imperial coinage (Part I)', *Journal of the Society for Ancient Numismatics* 3: 9–11.

(1971–2b) 'Ludi Saeculares rites of the Roman imperial coinage (Part II)', *Journal of the Society for Ancient Numismatics* 3: 27–9.

Carradice, I. (1998) 'Towards a new introduction to the Flavian coinage', in *Modus Operandi. Essays in Honour of Geoffrey Rickman*, ed. M. Austin, J. Harries and C. Smith. London: 93–118.

Carrubba, R. W. (1966) 'The curse on the Romans', *TAPhA* 97: 29–34.

Carson, R. A. G. (1956) 'System and product in the Roman mint', in *Essays in Roman Coinage Presented to Harold Mattingly*, ed. R. A. G. Carson and C. H. V. Sutherland. London: 227–39.

(1983) 'Coin hoards and Roman coinage of the third century AD', in *Studies in Numismatic Method Presented to Philip Grierson*, ed. C. N. L. Brooke, B. H. I. Stewart, J. G. Pollard and T. R. Volk. Cambridge: 65–74.

Càssola, F. (1968) *Storia dell'impero romano dopo Marco Aurelio*. Florence.

Castagnoli, F. (1979) 'Su alcuni problemi topografici del Palatino', *NSA* 34: 331–47.

Castritius, H. (1988) 'Caracalla, Augustus und Alexander? Zu Cassius Dio 77,7,2', in *Zu Alexander d. Gr. Festschrift G. Wirth zum 60. Geburtstag am 9.12.86*, vol. II, ed. W. Wolgang. Amsterdam: 879–84.

Cecamore, C. (1999) '*Faustinae aedemque decernerent (SHA, Marcus*, 26). Les fragments 69–70 de la *Forma Urbis* et la première dédicace du temple de la Vigna Barberini', *MEFRA* 111: 311–49.

Chastagnol, A. (1984). 'Les jubilés décennaux et vicennaux des empereurs sous les Antonins et les Sévères', *Revue Numismatique* 26: 104–24.

Chausson, F. (1995a) 'L'autobiographie de Septime Sévère', *REL* 73: 183–98.

(1995b) '*Vel Iovi Vel Soli*: quatre études autour de la Vigna Barberini (191–354)', *MEFRA* 107: 661–765.

(1997) 'Le site de la Vigna Barberini de 191 à 455', in *La Vigna Barberini (Roma Antica 3)*. Rome: 31–85.

Chauvot, A. (1994) 'La notion de "Syrien" dans l'*Histoire Auguste* et le cas d'Alexandre Sévère', *Ktèma* 19: 285–91.

Cheung, A. (1998) 'The political significance of Roman imperial coin types', *GNS* 191: 53–61.

Christiansen, E. (1988) *The Roman Coins of Alexandria, Quantitative Studies: Nero, Trajan, Septimius Severus*. Aarhus.

Christol, M. (1971) 'Un écho des jeux séculaires de 204 après Jésus-Christ en Arabie sous le gouvernement de Q. Aiacius Modestus', *REA* 73: 124–40.

Clark, A. J. (2007) *Divine Qualities. Cult and Community in Republican Rome*. Oxford.

Clauss, M. (2001) *Kaiser und Gott. Herrscherkult im römischen Reich*. Leipzig.

Clay, C. L. (1976) 'Roman imperial medallions: The date and purpose of their issue', in *Actes du 8e Congrès International de Numismatique*, ed. H. A. Cahn and G. L. Rider. Paris: 253–65.

Clerc, G. and Leclant, J. (1994) 'Sarapis', *LIMC* VII.1: 666–92.

Cleves, R. L. (1982) *Severus Alexander and the Severan Women*. Los Angeles.

Coarelli, F. (1987) 'La situazione edilizia di Roma sotto Severo Alessandro', in *L'Urbs. Espace urbain et histoire (1er siècle av. J.-C.- IIIe siècle ap. J.-C.)*. Rome: 429–56.

Coleman, K. M. (1990) 'Fatal charades: Roman executions staged as mythological enactments', *JRS* 80: 44–73.

Colini, A. M. (1955) 'Horti spei veteris, Palatium Sessorianum', *RPAA* 8: 137–77.

Colledge, M. A. R. (1976) *The Art of Palmyra*. London.

Colli, D. (1996) 'Il palazzo sessoriano nell'area archeologica di S. Croce in Gerusalemme: ultima sede imperiale a Roma?' *MEFRA* 108: 771–815.

Cooley, A. (2007) 'Septimius Severus: the Augustan emperor', in *Severan Culture*, ed. S. Swain, S. Harrison and J. Elsner. Cambridge: 385–400.

Cordovana, D. (2007) *Segni e immagini del potere tra antico e tardantico: I Severi e la provincia Africa Proconsularis*. Catania.

Cotton, H. M. and Eck, W. (1997) 'Ein Ehrenbogen für Septimius Severus und seine Familie in Jerusalem', *Electrum* 1: 11–20.

Crawford, M. H. (1974) *Roman Republican Coinage* (2 vols.). Cambridge.

(1983) 'Roman imperial coin types and the formation of public opinion', in *Studies in Numismatic Method Presented to Philip Grierson*, ed. C. N. L. Brooke, B. H. I. Stewart, J. G. Pollard and T. R. Volk. Cambridge: 47–64.

Crook, J. (1955) *Consilium Principis*. New York.

Cross, F. M. (2002) 'The Hebrew inscriptions from Sardis', *HThR* 95: 3–19.

Cumont, F. (1910) 'L'aigle funéraire des Syriens et l'apothéose des Empereurs', *RHR* 62: 119 61.

(1911) *Oriental Religions in Roman Paganism*. New York.

(1924) 'Une dédicace à des dieux syriens trouvée a Cordoue', *Syria* 5: 342–5.

Daguet-Gagey, A. (2000) *Septime Sévère. Rome, l'Afrique et l'Orient.* Paris.

(2004) 'Septime Sévère et ses fils, *Restitutores Vrbis*. La personnalisation des mérites impériaux', *RN* 160: 175–99.

(2005) 'L'arc des Argentiers, à Rome', *RH* 635: 499–516.

Dahmen, K. (2007) *The Legend of Alexander the Great on Greek and Roman Coins.* London.

(2008). 'Alexander in gold and silver: reassessing third ventury AD medallions from Aboukir and Tarsos', *American Journal of Numismatics* 20: 493–546.

D'Ambra, E. (1993) *Private Lives, Imperial Virtues. The Frieze of the Forum Transitorium in Rome.* Princeton.

Damsky, B. L. (1990) 'The stadium aureus of Septimius Severus', *AJN* 2: 77–105.

Dareggi, G. (1994) 'Severo Alessandro, *Romanus Alexander*, e il complesso santuariale di Thugga', *Latomus* 53: 848–58.

Dattari, A. (1901–2) *Nummi Augg. Alexandri*, 2 vols. Cairo.

Davis, P. J. (2001) 'The fabrication of tradition: Horace, Augustus and the secular games', *Ramus* 30: 111–27.

de Blois, L. (1998) 'Emperor and empire in the works of Greek-speaking authors of the third century AD', *ANRW II.* 34.4: 3391–443.

(2003) 'The perception of Roman imperial authority in Herodian's work', in *The Representation and Perception of Roman Imperial Power*, ed. L. d. Blois, P. Erdkamp, O. Hekster, G. d. Kleijn and S. Mols. Amsterdam: 148–56.

(2006) 'Emperorship in a period of crises. Changes in Emperor worship, imperial ideology and perceptions of imperial authority in the Roman Empire in the third century A.D.', in *The Impact of Imperial Rome on Religions, Ritual and Religious Life in the Roman Empire*, ed. L. de Blois, P. Funke and J. Hahn. Leiden: 268–78.

de Callataÿ, F. (1995) 'Calculating ancient coin production: seeking a balance', *NC* 155: 289–311.

De Rossi, G. (2000) 'Rome: le Palatin (Vigna Barberini)', *MEFRA* 112.1: 413–502.

Degrassi, D. (1987) 'Interventi edilizi sull'Isola Tiberina nel I sec. a.c.: nota sulle testimonianze letterarie, epigrafiche ed archeologiche', *Athenaeum* 75: 521–7.

Delaine, J. (1987) 'The "cella solearis" of the baths of Caracalla: A reappraisal', *PBSR* 55: 147–56.

(1997) *The Baths of Caracalla. A study in the Design, Construction, and Economics of Large-Scale Building Projects in Imperial Rome.* Portsmouth.

Desnier, J.-L. (1993) '*Omina et realia*. Naissance de l'*Urbs sacra* sévérienne (193–204 ap. J.-C.)', *MEFRA* 105.2: 548–620.

(1994) 'Septime Sévère, rassembleur de l'Orbis Romanus', in *L'Afrique, la Gaule, la religion à l'époque romaine. Mélanges à la mémoire de Marcel Le Glay*, ed. Y. L. Bohec. Brussels: 752–66.

(1997) 'On the bridge on a coin of Septimius Severus', *NC* 157: 191–3.

di Palma, S. (1999) 'Evoluzione dei culti solari a Roma: Il *Sol Invictus* da Settimio ad Alessandro Severo', in *Gli Imperatori Severi*, ed. E. Covolo and G. Rinaldi. Rome: 333–6.

Di Vita, A. (1975) 'La ricostruzione dell'arco dei Severi a Leptis Magna in un disegno di C. Catanuso ed esistenza e significato di un tetrapilo preseveriano', *QAL* 7: 3–26.

(1977) 'Ancora del tetrapilo precedente l'arco dei Severi a Leptis Magna: una messa a punto', *QAL* 9: 135–43.

Di Vita, A., Di Vita-Evrard, G. et al. (1999) *Libya: the Lost Cities of the Roman Empire*. Cologne.

Diehl, E. (1932) 'Zu den neuen Acta ludorum saecularium septimorum des Jahres 204 n. Chr.', *Sitzungsberichte der Preussischen Akademie der Wissenschaften, philologisch-historische Klasse* 27: 762–94.

Dietz, K. (1985) 'Zwei neue Meilensteine Caracallas aus Gundelfingen, Ldkr. Dillingen a.d. Donau, Reg.-Bez. Bayerisch-Schwaben', *Germania* 63: 75–86.

Dieudonne, A. (1906) 'Numismatique syrienne. Emese', *RN* 10: 132–55.

Dirven, L. (2007) 'The emperor's new clothes: a note on Elagabalus' priestly dress', in *Der christliche Orient und seine Umwelt: gesammelte Studien zu Ehren Jürgen Tubachs anlässlich seines 60. Geburtstags*, ed. J. Tubach, G. Vashalomidze and L. Greisiger. Wiesbaden: 21–36.

Downey, G. (1937) 'Malalas on the history of Antioch under Severus and Caracalla', *TAPhA* 68: 141–56.

Dressel, H. (1973) *Die römischen Medaillone des Münzkabinetts der staatlichen Museen zu Berlin*. Zürich.

(1981) 'Fünf Goldmedaillons aus dem Funde von Abukir', in *The Coinages of Alexander the Great*, ed. S. Gardiakos. Chicago: 1–130.

Drexler, W. (1889) 'Der Isis- und Sarapis-Cultus in Kleinasien', *NZ* 11: 1–234.

Drijvers, H. J. W. (1980) *Cults and Beliefs at Edessa*. Leiden.

Drinkwater, J. F. (2007) *The Alamanni and Rome 213–496 (Caracalla to Clovis)*. Oxford.

Duncan-Jones, R. (1993) 'Empire-wide patterns in Roman coin hoards', in *Coin Finds and Coin Use in the Roman World*, ed. C. E. King and D. G. Wigg. Berlin: 139–52.

(1994) *Money and Government in the Roman Empire*. Cambridge.

(2001) 'The denarii of Septimius Severus and the mobility of Roman coin', *NC* 161: 75–89.

(2002) 'The denarii of Septimius Severus and the mobility of Roman coin: further comment', *NC* 162: 342–5.

(2003) 'Roman coin circulation and the cities of Vesuvius', in *Credito e moneta nel mondo romano. Atti degli incontri capresi di storia dell'economica antica*, ed. E. Lo Cascio. Bari: 161–80.

(2005) 'Implications of Roman coinage: debates and differences', *Klio* 87: 459–87.

(2006) 'Crispina and the coinage of the empresses', *NC* 166: 223–8.

Eastmond, A. (2003) 'Between icon and idol: The uncertainty of imperial images', in *Icon and Word. The Power of Images in Byzantium. Studies Presented to Robin Cormack*, ed. A. Eastmond and L. James. Aldershot: 73–85.

Edwell, P. (2008) *Between Rome and Persia: The Middle Euphrates, Mesopotamia and Palmyra under Roman Control.* London.

Ehrhardt, C. T. H. R. (1984) 'Roman coin types and the Roman public', *JNG* 34: 41–54.

Eingartner, J., Eschbaumer, P. et al. (1993) *Faimingen-Phoebiana I. Der römische Tempelbezirk in Faimingen-Phoebiana.* Mainz.

El-Khachab, A. E.-M. (1961) 'O "Karakallos" Kosmokrator', *JEA* 47: 119–33.

Elsner, J. (2005) 'Sacrifice and narrative on the arch of the Argentarii at Rome', *JRA* 15: 83–98.

Erkell, H. (1969) 'Ludi Saeculares und Ludi Latini Saeculares. Ein Beitrag zur römischen Theaterkunde und Religionsgeschichte', *Eranos* 67: 166–74.

Ermanno, A. and Arslan, A. (1995) *Il ripostiglio di Biassono (Milano) 1975.* Milan.

Espinosa, U. (1990) 'La alejandrofilia de Caracala en la antigua historiografia', *Neronia IV (Latomus)* 209: 37–51.

Euzennat, M. (1976) 'Une dédicace volubilitaine a l'Apollon de Claros', *Antiquités Africaines* 10: 63–8.

Fähndrich, S. (2005) 'Zum urbanen Kontext des severischen Quadrifons in Lepcis Magna', in *Urbanistik und städtische Kultur in Westasien und Nordafrika unter den Severern*, ed. D. Kreikenborn, K.-U. Mahler and T. M. Weber. Worms: 29–45.

Fantham, E. (1992) *Lucan: De Bello Civili Book II.* Cambridge.

Fears, J. R. (1976) 'The solar monarchy of Nero and the imperial panegyric of Q. Curtius Rufus', *Historia* 25: 494–6.

(1977) *Princeps a Diis Electus: The Divine Election of the Emperor as a Political Concept at Rome.* Rome.

(1981) 'The cult of Jupiter and Roman imperial ideology', *ANRW* II.17.1: 3–141.

Fejfer, J. (1992) 'Divus Caracalla and Julia Domna. A note', in *Ancient Portraiture: Image and Message*, ed. T. Fischer-Hansen, J. Lund, M. Nielsen and A. Rathje. Copenhagen: 207–19.

Fentress, E., Bodel, J. et al. (2003) 'Cosa V: An intermittent town, excavations 1991–1997', *MAAR*, Supplementary Vol. 2: 1–400.

Fernando, G. (1992) 'Septimo Severo en Anazarbo', *Emerita* 60: 235–9.

Ferrero, I. M. (1999) 'Severus Alexander's *severitas* and the composition of the life', in *Historiae Augustae Colloquium Genevense*, ed. F. Paschoud. Bari: 191–216.

Fishwick, D. (1984) 'Coins as evidence: some phantom temples', *EMC* 27: 263–70.

(1987) *The Imperial Cult in the Latin West.* Leiden.

(2000) 'The sacred area at Gorsium', *Phoenix* 54: 309–31.

Fittschen, K. (2008) 'Elagabal aus dem Steinhaufen', *BCAR* 109: 109–15.

Fitz, J. (1972) *Les Syriens a Intercisa.* Brussels.

Flinterman, J. (1995) *Power, Paideia and Pythagoreanism.* Amsterdam.

Flower, H. I. (2000) '*Damnatio memoriae* and epigraphy', in *From Caligula to Constantine. Tyranny and Transformation in Roman Portraiture*, ed. E. R. Varner. Atlanta: 58–69.

(2006) *The Art of Forgetting. Disgrace and Oblivion in Roman Political Culture.* Chapel Hill, N.C.

Freedberg, D. (1989) *The Power of Images. Studies in the History and Theory of Response.* Chicago.

Frend, W. H. C. (1975) 'A Severan persecution? Evidence of the Historia Augusta', in *Forma futuri: studi in onore del cardinale Michele Pellegrino.* Turin: 470–80.

Frey, M. (1989) *Untersuchungen zur Religion und zur Religionspolitik des Kaisers Elagabal.* Stuttgart.

Frothingtham Jr, A. L. (1886) 'Archaeological news', *AJA* 2: 203–33.

Gagé, J. (1934) 'Les jeux séculaires de 204 ap. J.-C. et la dynastie des Sévères', *Mélanges d'archéologie et d'histoire* 51: 33–78.

(1975) 'Alexandre le Grand en Macédonie dans la Ière moitié du IIIe siècle ap. J.-C.', *Historia* 24: 1–16.

Gaifman, M. (2008) 'The aniconic image of the Roman Near East', in *The Variety of Local Religious Life in the Near East in the Hellenistic and Roman Periods*, ed. T. Kaizer. Leiden: 37–72.

Gambato, M. (2000) 'The female-kings. Some aspects of the representation of Eastern Kings in the *Deipnosophistae*', in *Athenaeus and his World*, ed. D. Braund and J. Wilkins. Exeter: 227–30.

Ganzert, J. (1985) 'Der Mars-Ultor-Tempel auf dem Augustusforum in Rom', *MDAI(R)* 92: 201–19.

(1996) *Der Mars-Ultor-Tempel auf dem Augustusforum in Rom.* Mainz.

Gardner, A. (1886) 'La religion à Rome sous les Sévères', *English Historical Review* 1: 550–5.

Garnsey, P. (2004) 'Roman citizenship and Roman law in the late Empire', in *Approaching Late Antiquity*, ed. S. Swain and M. Edwards. Oxford: 133–55.

Gasparri, C. (1983–4) 'Sculture provenienti dalle terme di Caracalla e di Diocleziano', *Rivista dell'Istituto nazionale d'archeologia e storia dell'arte* 6–7: 133–50.

Gatti, G. (1943/4) 'Topografia dell'Iseo campense', *RPAA* 20: 117–63.

Gawlikowski, M. (1984). *Palmyre*, vol 8. Warsaw.

Geiger, J. (2008) *The First Hall of Fame. A Study of the Statues in the Forum Augustum.* Leiden.

Genière, J. d. l. (1992) 'Le sanctuaire d'Apollon à Claros, découvertes récentes', *Académie des Inscriptions et Belles-Lettres, Comptes Rendus*: 195–210.

Gentilhomme, P. L. (1943) 'Catalogue des 93 *aurei* trouvés à Rennes en 1774', *RN* 7: 29–43.

Ghazoul, F. J. (2004) '*Orientalism*: clearing the way for cultural dialogue', *Religion* 34: 123–7.

Ghedini, F. (1984) *Giulia Domna. Tra Oriente e Occidente.* Rome.

Gilles, K.-J. and Weisser, B. (2006/7) '*Griechische Souvenirs*: antike Münzen aus Philippopolis und Perinth aus der Mosel bei Trier', *TZ* 69/70: 127–36.

Gilliam, J. F. (1965) 'Dura rosters and the *constitutio Antoniniana*', *Historia* 14: 74–92.

(1969) 'On *divi* under the Severi', *Latomus* 102: 284–9.

Gitler, H. and Ponting, M. (2003) *The Silver Coinage of Septimius Severus and his Family (193–211 AD). A Study of the Chemical Composition of the Roman and Eastern Issues.* Milan.

Gnecchi, F. (1912) *I medaglioni romani* (3 vols.). Milan.

Goddio, F., Bernand, A. et al. (1998) 'L'épigraphie sous-marine dans le Port Oriental d'Alexandrie', *ZPE* 121: 131–43.

Golfetto, A. (2002) *Rom im Bann des Sonnengottes.* Driesen.

Golvin, J.-C., Khanoussi, M. et al. (2005) *Dougga. Études d'architecture religieuse. Les sanctuaires des Victoires de Caracalla, de "Pluton" et de Caelestis.* Bordeaux.

Goodfellow, C. E. (1935) 'Roman citizenship: a study of its territorial and numerical expansion from the earliest times to the death of Augustus'. Ph.D. dissertation, Bryn Mawr University, Bryn Mawr.

Gorrie, C. (2002) 'The Severan building program and the secular games', *Athenaeum* 90: 461–81.

(2007) 'The restoration of the porticus Octaviae and Severan imperial policy', *G&R* 54: 1–17.

Graf, F. (2009) *Apollo.* London.

Grant, M. (1957) 'The border-line between Roman coins and medallions', *Congrès International de Numismatique* 2: 167–74.

Gregory, A. (1994) '"Powerful images": responses to portraits and the political uses of images in Rome', *JRA* 7: 80–99.

Grenier, J. C., and Coarelli, F. (1986) '*(Porticus) Adonaea, aedes Heliogabali, aedes Iovis Ultoris.* La tomba di Antinoo?' *MEFRA* 98: 230 53.

Griffin, M. T. (1984) *Nero. The End of a Dynasty.* London.

Grossardt, P. (2009) 'How to become a poet? Homer and Apollonius visit the mound of Achilles', in *Theios Sophistes. Essays on Flavius Philostratus' Vita Apollonii*, ed. K. Demoen and D. Praet. Leiden: 75–94.

Grueber, H. A., and Poole, R. S. (1874) *Roman Medallions in the British Museum.* London.

Guidobaldo, F. (2004) '*Sessorium* e Laterano. Il nuovo polo cristiano della Roma Costantiniana', *MEFRA* 116: 11–15.

Haight, E. H. (1918) 'An "inspired message" in the Augustan poets', *AJPh* 39: 341–66.

Hajjar, Y. (1990) 'Divinités oraculaires en Syrie et en Phénicie', *ANRW* II.18.4: 2236–320.

Hall, A. S. (1978) 'The Klarian oracle at Oenoanda', *ZPE* 32: 263–8.

Hall, L. J. (2004) *Roman Berytus: Beirut in Late Antiquity.* London.

Halsberghe, G. H. (1972) *The Cult of Sol Invictus.* Leiden.

(1984) 'Le culte de Deus Sol Invictus à Rome au 3e siècle après J.C.' *ANRW* II.17.4: 2182–201.

Hamilton, C. D. (1969) 'The tresviri monetales and the Republican cursus honorum', *TAPhA* 100: 181–99.

Hammond, M. (1932) 'The significance of the speech of Maecenas in Dio Cassius, book LII', *TAPhA* 63: 88–102.

(1940) 'Septimius Severus, Roman bureaucrat', *HSPh* 51: 137–73.

Handler, S. (1971) 'Architecture on the Roman coins of Alexandria', *AJA* 75: 57–74.

Hannah, R. (1998) 'Games for Mars and the temples of Mars Ultor', *Klio* 80: 422–33.

Hannestad, N. (1988) *Roman Art and Imperial Policy.* Aarhus.

Harker, A. (2008) *Loyalty and Dissidence in Roman Egypt. The Case of the Acta Alexandrinorum.* Cambridge.

Harl, K. W. (1981) 'Caracalla or Elagabalus? The imperial imago at the Greek mint of Magnesia ad Meandrum', *ANSMN* 26: 163–84.

(1987) *Civic Coins and Civic Politics in the Roman East AD 180–275.* Berkeley.

Hart, G. D. (2000) *Asclepius the God of Medicine.* London.

Hasebroek, J. (1921) *Untersuchungen zur Geschichte des Kaisers Septimius Severus.* Heidelberg.

Haynes, D. E. L., and Hirst, P. E. D. (1939) *Porta Argentariorum.* London.

Haywood, R. M. (1940) 'The African policy of Septimius Severus', *TAPhA* 71: 175–85.

(1941) 'The Oil of Leptis', *CPh* 36: 246–56.

(1962) 'A further note on the African policy of Septimius Severus', *Hommages à Albert Grenier.* Brussels: 786–90.

Hecht, R. E. (1968) 'Some Greek imperial coins in my collection', *NC* 8: 27–35.

Hedlund, R. (2008) "*... achieved nothing worthy of memory*". *Coinage and Authority in the Roman Empire c. AD 260–295.* (Studia Numismatica Upsaliensia 5). Uppsala.

Heichelheim, F. M. (1940) 'The text of the *constitutio Antoniniana* and the three other decrees of the emperor Caracalla contained in Papyrus Gissensis 40', *JEA* 26: 10–22.

Heil, M. (2006) 'Clodius Albinus und der Bürgerkrieg von 197', in *Staatlichkeit und politisches Handeln in der römischen Kaiserzeit*, ed. H.-U. Wiemer. Berlin: 55–85.

Hein, H. (1991) 'Herrscherkult im römischen Ägypten und Damnatio Memoriae Getas. Überlegungen zum Berliner Severertondo und zu Papyrus Oxyrhynchus XII 1449', *MDAI(R)* 98: 263–98.

Hekster, O. (2002) *Commodus. An Emperor at the Crossroads.* Amsterdam.

(2003) 'Coins and messages. Audience targeting on coins of different denominations?' in *The Representation and Perception of Roman Imperial Power*, ed. L. de Blois, P. Erdkamp, O. Hekster, G. de Kleijn and S. Mols. Amsterdam: 20–35.

Hekster, O. and Manders, E. (2006) 'Kaiser gegen Kaiser: Bilder der Macht im. 3 Jahrhundert', in *Transformationsprozesse des römischen Reiches im 3. Jahrhundert und ihre Rezeption in der Neuzeit*, ed. K.-P. Johne, T. Gerhardt and U. Hartmann. Stuttgart: 135–44.

Helm, R. (1956) *Die Chronik des Hieronymus.* Berlin.

Henig, M. (1983) 'A question of standards', *OJA* 2: 109–12.

(1986) 'Caracalla as Hercules? A new cameo from South Shields', *AntJ* 66: 378–80.
Herrero, S. M. (1989) 'Un oráculo del Apolo de Claros en Galicia', *Anejos de Gerión II: E studios sobre la Antigüedad en homenaje al Profesor Santiago Montero Díaz.* Madrid: 357–64.
Herrmann, P. (1972) 'Überlegungen zur Datierung der " Constitutio Antoniniana"', *Chiron* 2: 519–30.
Herzog, R. (1934) 'Ein Asklepios-Hymnus des Aristeides von Smyrna', *Sitzungsberichte der Preussischen Akademie der Wissenschaften, philologisch-historische Klasse* 21: 753–70.
Hijmans, S. E. (1996) 'The sun which did not rise in the East: the cult of Sol Invictus in the light of non-literary evidence', *Babesch* 71: 115–50.
Hill, P. V. (1960a) 'Aspects of Jupiter on coins of the Rome mint, AD 65–318', *NC* 20: 113–28.
(1960b) 'The temples of Augustus and Elagabalus and the identity of the temples of the Divi and of "Jupiter Ultor"', *NCirc* 68: 208–10.
(1962) 'The temples and statues of Apollo in Rome', *NC* 2: 125–42.
(1964) 'Notes on coinage of Septimius Severus and his family AD 193–217', *NC* 4: 169–88.
(1982) 'A new gold type of Septimius Severus', *NCirc* 90: 159–60.
Holden, A. (2008) 'The abduction of the Sabine women in context: the iconography on late antique contorniate medallions', *AJA* 112: 121–42.
Hollstein, W. (1994) 'Apollo und Libertas in der Münzprägung des Brutus und Cassius', *JNG* 44: 113–33.
Hölscher, T. (2004) *The Language of Images in Roman Art.* Cambridge.
(2006) 'The transformation of victory into power: from event to structure', in *Representations of War in Ancient Rome*, ed. S. Dillon and K. E. Welch. Cambridge: 27–48.
Hombert, P. (1945) 'Sarapis *Kosmokrator* et Isis *Kosmokrateira.* A propos de quelques terres cuites inédites', *AC* 14: 319–29.
Hönn, K. (1911) *Quellenuntersuchungen zu den Viten des Heliogabalus und des Severus Alexander.* Leipzig.
Hornbostel, W. (1973) *Sarapis.* Leiden.
(1978) 'Sarapiaca I', in *Hommages à Maarten J. Vermaseren*, vol. 2, ed. M. B. de Boer and T. A. Edridge. Leiden: 501–18.
Howe, S. (1999) *Afrocentrism: Mythical Pasts and Imagined Homes.* London.
Howgego, C. (1985) *Greek Imperial Countermarks.* London.
(1993) 'The circulation of silver coins, models of the Roman economy, and the crisis of the third century AD: some numismatic evidence', in *Coin Finds and Coin Use in the Roman World*, ed. C. E. King and D. G. Wigg. Berlin: 119–236.
(2005) 'Coinage and identity in the Roman provinces', in *Coinage and Identity in the Roman Provinces*, ed. C. Howgego, V. Heuchert and A. Burnett. Oxford: 1–18.
Hülsen, C. (1894) 'Zur Topographie des Quirinals', *RhM* 49: 379–423.

(1902) 'Die Ausgrabungen auf dem Forum Romanum 1898–1902', *MDAI(R)* 17: 1–97.

Hülsen, C. H., Michaelis, A., et al. (1906) *Codex Escurialensis. Ein Skizzenbuch aus der Werkstatt Domenico Ghirlandaios*. Vienna.

Hurter, S. (1980) 'Ein neuer Aureus des Caracalla', *GNS* 117: 39–41.

Icks, M. (2006) 'Priesthood and imperial power. The religious reforms of Heliogabalus, 220–222 AD', in *The Impact of Imperial Rome on Religions, Ritual and Religious Life in the Roman Empire*, ed. L. de Blois, P. Funke and J. Hahn. Leiden: 169–78.

(2008a) 'Images of Elagabalus'. D.Phil. thesis. Radboud Universiteit, Nijmegen.

(2008b) 'Kakos. Badness and anti-value in classical antiquity', in *Heliogabalus, a Monster on the Roman Throne: the Literary Construction of a 'Bad' Emperor*, ed. I. Sluiter and R. M. Rosen. Leiden: 476–88.

(2009) 'Empire of the Sun? Civic responses to the rise and fall of Sol Elagabal in the Roman empire', in *Ritual Dynamics and Religious Change in the Roman Empire*, ed. O. Hekster, S. Schmidt-Hofner and C. Witschel. Leiden: 111–20.

Inan, J. and Rosenbaum, E. (1966) *Roman and Early Byzantine Portrait Sculpture in Asia Minor*. London.

Ingholt, H. (1954) *Parthian Sculptures from Hatra*. New Haven.

Ioppolo, G. (1968) 'Una nuova iscrizione monumentale presso l'arco dei Severi a Leptis Magna', *LibAnt* 5: 83–92.

Jacques, F. (1992) 'Les *nobiles* exécutés par Septime Sévère selon l'*Histoire Auguste*: liste de proscription ou énumération fantaisiste?' *Latomus* 51: 119–44.

Jardé, A. (1925) *Études critiques sur la vie e le règne de Sévère Alexandre*. Paris.

Jarrett, M. G. (1994) 'Non-legionary troops in Roman Britain: part one, the units', *Britannia* 25: 35–77.

Jenewein, G. (2008) *Die Architekturdekoration der Caracallathermen*. Vienna.

Jenkins, G. K. (1973–4) 'Some ancient coins of Libya', *Society for Libyan Studies Annual Report* 5: 29–35.

Johnston, A. (1982) 'Caracalla or Elagabalus? A case of unnecessary mistaken identity', *ANSMN* 27: 97–147.

(1983) 'Caracalla's path: the numismatic evidence', *Historia* 32: 58–76.

(1984) 'Hierapolis revisited', *NC* 144: 52–80.

Jones, A. H. M. (1936) 'Another interpretation of the "constitutio Antoniniana"', *JRS* 26: 223–35.

(1956) 'Numismatics and history', in *Essays in Roman Coinage Presented to Harold Mattingly*, ed. R. A. G. Carson and C. H. V. Sutherland. Oxford: 13–33.

Jones, B. W. (1992) *The Emperor Domitian*. London.

Jones, C. P. (2001) 'Philostratus' Heroikos and its setting in reality', *JHS* 121: 141–9.

(2005) 'Ten dedications "to the gods and goddesses" and the Antonine plague', *JRA* 18: 293–301.

(2006) 'Cosa and the Antonine plague?' *JRA* 19: 368–9.

Kádár, Z. (1986) 'L'importance religieuse et artistique du culte d'Asklepios-Aesculapius sur les médailles de Caracalla à Pergamon', *ACD* 22: 31–5.

Kadman, L. (1956) *The Coins of Aelia Capitolina*. Jerusalem.

Kaizer, T. (2005) 'Kingly priests in the Roman Near East?' in *Imaginary Kings. Royal Images in the Ancient Near East, Greece and Rome*, ed. O. Hekster and R. Fowler. Stuttgart: 177–92.

(2006) 'In search of oriental cults. Methodological problems concerning the particular and the general in Near Eastern religion in the Hellenistic and Roman periods', *Historia* 55: 26–47.

Kampmann, U. (1992/3) 'Asklepios mit Omphalos in der römischen Reichsprägung. Zu einem Beispiel der Beeinflussung der Reichsprägung durch Lokalmünzen', *JNG* 42/43: 39–48.

Kantorowicz, E. H. (1963) 'Oriens Augusti – lever du roi', *DOP* 17: 117–77.

Karst, J. (1911) *Die Chronik des Eusebius: aus dem armenischen übersetzt*. Leipzig.

Keita, M. (2000) 'The politics of criticism: "Not out of Africa" and "Black Athena" revisited', *Journal of World History* 11: 337–45.

Keltanen, M. (2002) 'The public image of the four empresses – ideal wives, mothers and regents?' in *Women, Wealth and Power in the Roman Empire*, ed. P. Setälä, R. Berg, R. Hälikkä et al. Rome: 105–46.

Kemmers, F. (2006) *Coins for a Legion. An Analysis of the Coin Finds from the Augustan Legionary Fortress and Flavian Canabae Legionis at Nijmegen*. Mainz.

Kemmers, F. and Myrberg, N. (2011) 'Re-thinking numismatics: the archaeology of coins', *Archaeological Dialogues* 18: 87–108.

Keresztes, P. (1970) 'The constitutio Antoniniana and the persecutions under Caracalla', *AJPh* 91: 446–59.

Kettenhofen, E. (1979) *Die syrischen Augustae in der historischen Überlieferung*. Bonn.

Khanoussi, M. (2003) 'Le temple de la Victoire Germanique de Caracalla à Dougga', in *L'Afrique du Nord antique et médiévale*, ed. M. Khanoussi. Tunisia: 447–56.

Kindler, A. (1980) 'The "damnatio memoriae" of Elagabal on city-coins of the Near East', *GNS* 30: 3–7.

King, C. (2003) 'The organization of Roman religious beliefs', *ClAnt* 22: 275–312.

King, G. R. D. (2002) 'Archaeological fieldwork at the citadel of Homs, Syria: 1995–1999', *Levant* 34: 39–58.

Kinney, D. (1986) 'Spolia from the baths of Caracalla in Sta. Maria in Trastevere', *ABull* 68: 379–97.

Kleiner, D. E. E. (1992) *Roman Sculpture*. New Haven, Conn.

Kockel, V. (1983) 'Beobachtungen zu dem Tempel des Mars Ultor und zum Forum des Augustus', *MDAI(R)* 90: 421–48.

Kolb, F. (1972) *Literarische Beziehungen zwischen Cassius Dio, Herodian und der Historia Augusta*. Bonn.

(1976) 'Herodian in der Historia Augusta', in *Bonner Historia-Augusta-Colloquium 1972/1974*. Bonn: 143–52.

(1995) 'Cassius Dio, Herodian und die Quellen der Historia Augusta', in *Historiae Augustae Colloquium Maceratense*, ed. G. Bonamente and G. Paci. Bari: 179–91.

Kolev, K. (1991) 'Kopien griechischer Skulpturen auf Münzen von Philippopolis', *Klio* 73: 510–25.

Komnick, H. (2001) *Die Restitutionsmünzen der frühen Kaiserzeit*. Berlin.

Kosmetatou, E. (2002) 'The public image of Julia Mamaea. An epigraphic and numismatic inquiry', *Latomus* 61: 398–414.

Kotula, T. (1985) 'Septime-Sévère, a-t-il visité l'Afrique en tant qu'empereur?' *Eos* 73: 151–65.

Kraft, K. (1972). *Das System der kaiserzeitlichen Münzprägung in Kleinasien*. Berlin.

Krautheimer, R. (1980) *Rome: Profile of a City, 312–1308*. Princeton.

(1983) *Three Christian Capitals. Topography and Politics*. Berkeley.

Krengel, E. (1997) 'Das sogenannte "Horn" des Elagabal – die Spitze eines Stierpenis. Eine Umdeutung als Ergebnis fachübergreifender Forschung.' *JNG* 47: 53–72.

Krumeich, R. (2000/1) 'Der Kaiser als syrischer Priester: Zur Repräsentation Elagabals als *sacerdos dei Solis Elagabali*', *Boreas* 23/4: 107–12.

Kulikowski, M. (2007) 'Marius Maximus in Ammianus and the *Historia Augusta*', *CQ* 57: 244–56.

Kunisz, A. (1983) 'Udzial Zlotego Pieniadza W Cyrkulacji Na Terytorium Egiptu W I–III W. N.E.', *Wiadomos´ci Numizmatyczne* 27: 121–65.

Kushnir-Stein, A. (2000) 'Septimius Severus and cities in Samaria: rewards and punishments', *SCI* 19: 149–54.

La Rocca, E. (1984) *La riva a mezzaluna. Culti, agoni, monumenti funerari presso il Tevere nel Campo Marzio occidentale*. Rome.

Lange, C. H. (2009) *Res Publica Constituta. Actium, Apollo and the Accomplishment of the Triumviral Assignment*. Leiden.

Lascelles, M. (1951) 'Sir Thomas Elyot and the legend of Alexander Severus', *Review of English Studies* 2: 305–18.

Lefkowitz, M. (1996) *Not out of Africa: How Afrocentrism Became an Excuse to Teach Myth as History*. New York.

Lefkowitz, M. R. and Maclean Rogers, G., (eds.) (1996) *Black Athena Revisited*. Chapel Hill, N.C.

Leigh, M. (2000) 'Lucan and the Libyan tale', *JRA* 90: 95–109.

Lembke, K. (1994) *Das Iseum Campense in Rome*. Heidelberg.

Lendon, J. E. (1990) 'The face on the coins and inflation in Roman Egypt', *Klio* 72: 106–34.

Lenfant, D. (2001) 'De Sardanapale à Élagabal: les avatars d'une figure du pouvoir', in *Images et représentations du pouvoir et de l'ordre social dans l'antiquité*, ed. M. Molin. Paris: 46–55.

Letta, C. (1989) 'Le dediche dis deabusque secundum interpretationem oraculi Clarii Apollinis e la constitutio Antonin', *SCO* 39: 265–80.

(1994) 'Il "naufragio" di Caracalla in Cassio Dione, nell'Historia Augusta e nei commentari degli Arvali', *ZPE* 103: 188–90.

Levick, B. (1969) 'Caracalla's path', in *Hommages à Marcel Renard*, ed. J. Bibauw. Brussels: 426–46.

(1982) 'Propaganda and the imperial coinage', *Antichthon* 6: 104–16.

(1999) 'Messages on the Roman coinage: types and inscriptions', in *Roman Coins and Public Life under the Empire*, ed. G. M. Paul. Ann Arbor: 41–60.

(2007) *Julia Domna Syrian Empress*. London.

Lichtenberger, A. (2007) 'Severus Pius Augustus. Studien zur sakralen Repräsentation und Rezeption der Herrschaft des Septimius Severus und seiner Familie (193–211 n. Chr.)', Habilitationsschrift, Wilhelms-Universität, Münster.

(2011) *Severus Pius Augustus. Studien zur sakralen Repräsentation und Rezeption der Herrschaft des Septimius Severus und seiner Familie (193–211 n. Chr.)*. Leiden.

Lightfoot, J. L. (2004) *Lucian: On the Syrian Goddess*. Oxford.

Lipinski, E. (1993) 'Les *dii patrii* des Leptis Magna', *AncSoc* 24: 41–50.

Lo Cascio, E. (2005) 'The age of the Severans', in *The Cambridge Ancient History*, vol. 12, ed. A. K. Bowman, P. Garnsey and A. Cameron. Cambridge: 137–55.

(2008) 'The function of gold coinage in the monetary economy of the Roman Empire', in *The Monetary Systems of the Greeks and Romans*, ed. W. V. Harris. Oxford: 160–73.

Longpérrier, A. (1868) 'Trésor de Tarse', *RN* 13: 309–36.

Longtin, R. (2000) 'Constantine and Christianity: The numismatic evidence', *Journal of the Classical and Medieval Numismatic Society* 1: 5–27.

L'Orange, H. P. (1982) *Apotheosis in Ancient Portraiture*. New York.

Lorcin, P. M. E. (2002) 'Rome and France in Africa: recovering colonial Algeria's Latin past', *French Historical Studies* 25: 295–329.

Lukaszewicz, A. (1992) 'Antoninus the *koryphos* (note on P. Oxy XLVI 3298.2)', *JJP* 22: 43–6.

Lusnia, S. (1995) 'Julia Domna's coinage and Severan dynastic propaganda', *Latomus* 54: 119–39.

(1998) 'The Building Program of Septimius Severus at Rome, A.D. 193–211', Ph.D. dissertation, University of Cincinnati.

(2004) 'Urban planning and sculptural display in Severan Rome: reconstructing the Septizodium and its role in dynastic politics', *AJA* 108: 517–44.

(2006a) 'Battle imagery and politics on the Severan arch in the Roman Forum', in *Representations of War in Ancient Rome*, ed. S. Dillon and K. E. Welch. Cambridge: 272–99.

(2006b) 'Redating the Septizodium and Severan propaganda', in *Proceedings of the XVIth International Congress of Classical Archaeology, Boston, August 23–26, 2003. Common Ground: Archaeology, Art, Science and Humanities*, ed. C. C. Mattusch, A. A. Donohue and A. Brauer. Oxford: 196–9.

Maclean, J. K. and Aitken, E. B. (2001) *Flavius Philostratus: Heroikos*. Atlanta.

Madaule, J. (1924) 'Le monument de Septime Sévère au *Forum Boarium*', *MEFRA* 41: 111–50.

Mader, G. (2005) 'History as carnival, or method and madness in the *Vita Heliogabali*', *ClAnt* 24: 131–72.

Maderna, C. (2005) 'Zur Gigantomachie des sogenannten Tempels der Gens Septimia in Lepcis Magna', in *Urbanistik und städtische Kultur in Westasien und Nordafrika unter den Severern*, ed. D. Kreikenbom, K. U. Mahler and T. M. Weber. Worms: 61–82.

Magie, D. (1953) 'Egyptian deities in Asia Minor in inscriptions and on coins', *AJA* 57: 163–87.

Mancini, G. (1926) 'Rome', *Notizie degli scavi di antichità* 1: 229–43.

Manders, E. (2008) 'Coining images of power. Patterns in the representation of Roman emperors on imperial coinage AD 193–284'. D.Phil. thesis, Radboud University, Nijmegen.

Mann, J. C. (1974) 'Review: J. Fitz, Les Syriens a Intercisa (Collection Latomus, vol. 122)', *JRA* 64: 259–60.

(2002) 'The settlement of veterans discharged from auxiliary units stationed in Britain', *Britannia* 33: 183–8.

Marasco, G. (1998) 'Erodiano e la crisi dell'impero', *ANRW* II.34.4: 2837–927.

Marsden, A. B. (1997) 'Between Principate and Dominate: imperial styles under the Severan dynasty and the divine iconography of the imperial house on coins, medallions and engraved gemstones AD 193–235.' *JBAA* 150: 1–16.

Marsden, A. and Henig, M. (2002) 'Caracalla as Hercules on an intaglio found near Lincoln', *OJA* 21: 419–22.

Marvin, M. (1983) 'Freestanding sculptures from the baths of Caracalla', *AJA* 87: 347–84.

Matern, P. (2002) *Helios und Sol. Kulte und Ikonographie des griechischen und römischen Sonnengottes*. Istanbul.

Mattingly, D. J. (1994) *Tripolitania*. Ann Arbor.

(1996) 'From one colonialism to another: imperialism and the Maghreb', in *Roman Imperialism: Post-Colonial Perspectives*, ed. J. Webster and N. J. Cooper. Leicester: 49–69.

Mattingly, H. (1932) 'The coinage of Septimius Severus and his times. Mints and chronology.' *NC* 12: 177–98.

(1950) *Coins of the Roman Empire in the British Museum V: Pertinax to Elagabalus*. London.

Mattingly, H. and Sydenham, E. A. (1926) *The Roman Imperial Coinage II: Vespasian to Hadrian*. London.

(1930) *The Roman Imperial Coinage III: Antoninus Pius to Commodus*. London.

(1936) *The Roman Imperial Coinage IV.1: Pertinax to Geta*. London.

Mattingly, H., Sydenham, E. A. et al. (1938) *The Roman Imperial Coinage IV.2: Macrinus to Pupienus*. London.

(1949) *The Roman Imperial Coinage IV.3. Gordian III – Uranius Antoninus*. London.

Mayer, E. (2010) 'Propaganda, staged applause, or local politics? Public monuments from Augustus to Septimius Severus', in *The Emperor and Rome. Space, Representation and Ritual*, ed. B. C. Ewald and C. F. Noreña. Cambridge: 111–34.

McAlee, R. (2007) *The Coins of Roman Antioch*. London.

McCann, A. M. (1968) *The Portraits of Septimius Severus*. Rome.

McKechnie, P. (1999) 'Christian grave-inscriptions from the *familia Caesaris*', *JEH* 50: 427–41.

McKenzie, J. (2007) *The Architecture of Alexandria and Egypt*. New Haven.

McKenzie, J. S., Gibson, S. et al. (2004) 'Reconstructing the Serapeum in Alexandria from the archaeological evidence', *JRS* 94: 73–121.

Meadows, A. and Williams, J. (2001) 'Moneta and the monuments: coinage and politics in Republican Rome', *JRS* 91: 27–49.

Meckler, M. (1999) 'Caracalla the intellectual', in *Gli Imperatori Severi*, ed. E. d. Covolo and G. Rinaldi. Rome: 39–46.

(2005) 'Caracalla's sense of humour and Cassius Dio's Latinity', in *Historiae Augustae Colloquium Barcinonense*, ed. G. Bonamente and M. Mayer. Bari: 221–31.

Meckler, M. L. (1994) 'Caracalla and his late antique biographer'. Ph.D. dissertation, University of Michigan.

Mennen, I. (2006) 'The image of an emperor in trouble (legitimation and representation of power by Caracalla)', in *The Impact of Imperial Rome on Religions, Ritual and Religious Life in the Roman Empire*, ed. L. de Blois, P. Funke and J. Hahn. Leiden: 253–67.

Merkelbach, R. and Stauber, J. (1996) 'Die Orakel des Apollon von Klaros', *EA* 27: 1–53.

Meshorer, Y. (1989) *The Coinage of Aelia Capitolina*. Tel Aviv.

Metcalf, W. E. (1996a) *The Silver Coinage of Cappadocia, Vespasian–Commodus*. New York.

(1996b) 'Roman dies in modern studies', in *Italiam fato profugi Hesperinaque venerunt litora*. Louvain-La-Neuve: 253–8.

(1999) 'Coins as primary evidence', in *Roman Coins and Public Life under the Empire*, ed. G. M. Paul and M. Ierardi. Ann Arbor: 1–18.

(2002) 'The Reka Devnia hoard re-examined', in *Ritrovamenti monetali nel mondo antico: problemi e metodi*, ed. G. Gorini. Padua: 145–50.

(2006) 'Roman imperial numismatics', in *A Companion to the Roman Empire*, ed. D. S. Potter. Oxford: 35–44.

Michaelis, A. (1885) 'Sarapis standing on a Xanthian marble in the British Museum', *JHS* 6: 287–318.

Mierse, W. E. (2004) 'The architecture of the lost temple of Hercules Gaditanus and its Levantine associations', *AJA* 108: 545–75.

Mikocki, T. (1995) *Sub specie deae: Les impératrices et princesses romaines assimilées à des déesses*. Rome.

Millar, F. (1962) 'The date of the *constitutio Antoniniana*', *JEA* 48: 124–31.

(1964) *A Study of Cassius Dio*. Oxford.

(1991) 'Les congiaires à Rome et la monnaie', in *Nourrir la plèbe: actes du colloque tenu a Genève les 28 et 29 Sept 1989 en hommage à Denis van Berchem*, ed. A. Giovannini. Basle: 143–59.

(1993) *The Roman Near East 31 BC – AD 337*. Cambridge.

(2004) 'Rome in Greek culture: Cassius Dio and Ulpian', in *La cultura storica nei primi due secoli dell'impero romano*, ed. L. Troiani and G. Zecchini. Milan: 17–40.

Miller, J. (2009) *Apollo, Augustus and the Poets*. Cambridge.

Milne, J. G. (1941) *Kolophon and Its Coinage: A Study*. New York.

(1971) *Catalogue of Alexandrian Coins*. Oxford.

Mitchell, S. (2002) 'The cult of Theos Hypsistos between Pagans, Jews and Christians', in *Pagan Monotheism in Late Antiquity*, ed. P. Athanassiadi and M. Frede. Oxford: 81–148.

(2003) 'Inscriptions from Melli (Kocaaliler) in Pisidia', *AS* 53: 139–59.

Molinari, M. C. (2002) 'Alcune riflessioni sui ritrovamenti di medaglioni e di grandi bronzi provinciali a Roma', *RIN* 103: 203–17.

Moore, G. F. (1903) 'Baetylia', *AJA* 7: 198–208.

Morawiecki, L. (1981) 'The beginnings of the cult of Mars Ultor', *Prace Historyczne* 70: 29–37.

Morel, J.-P. and Villedieu, F. (2002) 'La Vigna Barberini à l'époque néronienne', in *Neronia VI (Latomus): Rome à l'époque néronienne*, ed. J.-M. Croisille and Y. Perrin. Brussels: 74–96.

Morgan, J. R. (2009) 'The Emesan connection: Philostratus and Heliodorus', in *Theios Sophistes. Essays on Flavius Philostratus' Vita Apollonii*, ed. K. Demoen and D. Praet. Leiden: 265–81.

Morstein-Marx, R. (2004) *Mass Oratory and Political Power in the Late Roman Republic*. Cambridge.

Moscovich, M. J. (2004) 'Cassius Dio's palace sources for the reign of Septimius Severus', *Historia* 53: 356–68.

Mrav, Z. (2000) 'Der Besuch Caracallas und der Deus Invictus Serapis-Kult in Pannonien', *Communicationes archaeologicae Hungariae* 2000: 67–97.

Mundle, I. (1957) 'Untersuchungen zur Religionspolitik des Septimius Severus (Herkules, Bacchus, Jupiter, Juno)'. D.Phil. dissertation, Freiburg Universität, Freiburg.

(1961) 'Dea Caelestis in der Religionspolitik des Septimius Severus und der Julia Domna', *Historia* 10: 228–37.

Munzi, M. (2001) *L'epica del ritorno. Archeologia e politica nella Tripolitania Italiana*. Rome.

Musurillo, H. A. (1954) *The Acts of the Pagan Martyrs*. Oxford.

Newby, Z. (2007) 'Art at the crossroads? Themes and styles in Severan art', in *Severan Culture*, ed. S. Swain, S. Harrison and J. Elsner. Cambridge: 201–49.

Newell, E. T. (1910) 'The gold medallions of Abukir', *AJN* 44: 128–30.

Newman, R. (1990) 'A dialogue of power in the coinage of Antony and Octavian', *AJN* 2: 33–67.

Nock, A. D. (1929) 'Clarian Apollo', *CR* 43: 126.

(1972) 'The Emperor's divine *comes*', in *Essays on Religion in the Ancient World*, vol. 2, ed. Z. Stewart. Oxford: 653–75.

Noreña, C. F. (2001) 'The communication of the Emperor's virtues', *JRS* 91: 146–68.

(2003) 'Medium and message in Vespasian's templum pacis', *MAAR* 48: 25–43.

Nutton, V. (2004) *Ancient Medicine*. London.

Oden, R. A. (1997) *Studies in Lucian's De Dea Syria*. Michigan.

Oesterheld, C. (2008) *Göttliche Botschaften für zweifelnde Menschen. Pragmatik und Orientierungsleistung der Apollon-Orakel von Klaros und Didyma in hellenistisch-römischer Zeit*. Göttingen.

Oliver, J. H. (1940) 'Julia Domna as Athena Polias', in *Athenian Studies Presented to William Scott Ferguson*. Cambridge: 521–30.

(1989) *Greek Constitutions of Early Roman Emperors from Inscriptions and Papyri*. Philadelphia.

Optendrenk, T. (1969) *Die Religionspolitik des Kaisers Elagabal im Spiegel der Historia Augusta*. Bonn.

Osborne, J. (1983) 'The earliest antiquarian description of Caracalla's Sarapeum on the Quirinal Hill in Rome', *EMC* 7: 220–5.

Palagia, O. (1986) 'Imitation of Herakles in ruler portraiture. A survey, from Alexander to Maximinus Daza', *Boreas* 9: 137–51.

Palmer, R. E. A. (1978) 'Severan ruler-cult and the moon in the city of Rome', *ANRW* II.16.2: 1085–120.

(1981) 'The topography and social history of Rome's Trastevere (southern sector)', *PAPhS* 125: 368–97.

Parke, H. W. (1985) *The Oracles of Apollo in Asia Minor*. London.

Parr, P. J. and Starcky, J. (1962) 'Three altars from Petra', *Annual of the Department of Antiquities in Jordan* 6–7: 13–20.

Paterna, C. (1996) 'Il circo Variano a Roma', *MEFRA* 108: 817–53.

Penella, R. J. (1977) 'S.H.A., Alexander Severus 43, 6–7: two Emperors and Christ', *VChr* 31: 229–30.

(1980) 'Caracalla and his mother in the "Historia Augusta"', *Historia* 29: 382–4.

Pera, R. (1979) 'Probabili significati della scritta *INDULGENTIA AVGG IN CARTHAGINEM* ed *INDULGENTIA AVGG IN ITALIAM* su alcune monete di Settimio Severo e Caracalla', *RIN* 81: 103–26.

Petsalis-Diomidis, A. (2007) 'Landscape, transformation, and divine epiphany', in *Severan Culture*, ed. S. Swain, S. Harrison and J. Elsner. Cambridge: 250–89.

Philip, G. (2005) 'Settlement and landscape development in the Homs Region, Syria. Report on work undertaken during 2001–2003', *Levant* 37: 21–42.

Picard, C. (1922) *Éphèse et Claros*. Paris.

Piccioli, A., (ed.) (1926) *La rinascita della Tripolitania: memorie e studi sui quattro anni di governo del conte Giuseppe Volpi di Misurata*. Milan.

Picozzi, M. G. and Valeriani, R. (1999) *Palazzo Colonna*. Rome.

Pietrzykowski, M. (1986) 'Die Religionspolitik des Kaisers Elagabal', *ANRW* II.16.3: 1806–25.

Pighi, I. (1965) *De ludibus saecularibus populi Romani Quiritum*. Amsterdam.

Pink, K. (1933) 'Der Aufbau der römischen Münzprägung in der Kaiserzeit I. Die Zeit des Septimius Severus', *NZ* 66: 17–54.

(1934) 'Der Aufbau der römischen Münzprägung in der Kaiserzeit II. Von Caracallas Regierungsantritt bis zum Tode Elagabals', *NZ* 67: 3–17.

(1946) 'Die Triumviri monetales unter Augustus', *NZ* 71: 113–25.

Platnauer, M. (1965) *The Life and Reign of the Emperor Lucius Septimius Severus*. Rome.

Polley, A. R. (2003) 'The date of Herodian's history', *AC* 72: 203–8.

Pollini, J. (1990) 'Man or god: divine assimilation and imitation in the late Republic and early Principate', in *Between Republic and Empire. Interpretations of Augustus and his Principate*, ed. K. A. Raaflaub and M. Toher. Berkeley: 334–57.

Possenti, L. D. (1995) 'Le divinità comites', *AFLM* 28: 141–70.

Potter, D. S. (2004) *The Roman Empire at Bay AD 180–395*. London.

(2008) 'Septimius Severus', in *Lives of the Caesars*, ed. A. A. Barrett. Malden, Mass.: 204–27.

Price, M. J. (1971) 'Greek imperial coins. Some recent acquisitions by the British Museum', *NC* 11: 121–34.

Price, S. R. F. (1979) 'The divine right of emperors', *CR* 29: 277–9.

(1984) *Rituals and Power: The Roman Imperial Cult in Asia Minor*. Cambridge.

Putnam, M. C. J. (2000) *Horace's Carmen Saeculare: Ritual Magic and the Poet's Art*. New Haven, Conn.

Radnóti, A. (1961) 'C. Julius Avitus Alexianus', *Germania* 39: 383–412.

Raeder, J. (1992) 'Herrscherbildnis und Münzpropaganda: zur Deutung des "Serapistypus" des Septimius Severus', *JDAI* 107: 175–96.

Ramage, E. S. (1989) 'Juvenal and the establishment. Denigration of predecessor in the "Satires"', *ANRW* II.33.1: 640–707.

(1991) 'Sulla's propaganda', *Klio* 73: 93–121.

Ramsay, H. G. (1935) 'A third century A.C. building program', *AC* 4: 419–47.

Rawson, B. (1970) 'Pompey and Hercules', *Antichthon* 4: 30–7.

Rea, J. R. (1968) *The Oxyrhynchus Papyri*, vol. 46. London.

Reece, R. (1987) *Coinage in Roman Britain*. London.

(2003) 'The "normal" hoard', in *Roman Coins and Archaeology*. Wetteren: 283–8.

Reed, N. (1978) 'Pattern and purpose in the Antonine itinerary', *AJPh* 99: 228–54.

Renberg, G. H. (2006/7) 'Public and private places of worship in the cult of Asclepius at Rome', *MAAR* 51: 87–172.

Reusch, W. (1938) 'Griechische Münzen und Inschriften der römischen Kaiserzeit aus Köln', *Germania* 22: 166–75.

Réville, J. (1886) *La religion à Rome sous les Sévères*. Paris.

Reynolds, J. M. (1996) 'Libya', in *Oxford Classical Dictionary*, 3rd edn, ed. S. Hornblower and A. Spawforth. Oxford: 855–6.

Ricci, A. (1982) 'Una conferma all'Historia Augusta', *SCO* 32: 179–87.

Rich, J. W. (1998) 'Augustus's Parthian honours, the temple of Mars Ultor and the arch in the Forum Romanum', *PBSR* 66: 71–128.

Richardson, L. (1992) *A New Topographical Dictionary of Ancient Rome*. London.

Ridley, R. (1982) *Zosimus, New History. A Translation with Commentary*. Canberra.

(1989) 'The fate of an architect: Apollodoros of Damascus', *Athenaeum* 67: 551–66.

Rives, J. B. (1995) *Religion and Authority in Roman Carthage from Augustus to Constantine*. Oxford.

(2007) *Religion in the Roman Empire*. Oxford.

Robert, L. (1964) *La déesse de Hiérapolis Castabala (Cilicie)*. Paris.

(1970) 'Deux concours Grecs à Rome', *CRAI* 114: 6–27.

(1989) 'Une fête à Sardes', *Opera Minora Selecta* 6: 49–56.

Roesch, P. (1982) 'Le culte d'Asclepios à Rome', in *Médecins et Médecine dans l'Antiquité*, ed. G. Sabbah. Saint-Étienne: 171–9.

Romanelli, M. P. (1931) 'Notizie degli scavi', *NSA* 7: 313–45.

Roos, A. G. (1915) 'Herodian's method of composition', *JRS* 5: 191–202.

Rostovtzeff, M. (1942) 'Vexillum and victory', *JRS* 32: 92–106.

Rowan, C. (2006) 'The procession of Elagabalus and the problem of the parasols', *Journal of the Numismatic Association of Australia* 17: 114–19.

(2009) 'Becoming Jupiter: Severus Alexander, the temple of Jupiter Ultor and Jovian iconography on Roman imperial coinage', *AJN* 21: 123–50.

(2010) 'Slipping out of circulation: the afterlife of coins in the Roman world', *Journal of the Numismatic Association of Australia* 20: 1–14.

(2011) 'The public image of the Severan women', *PBSR*: 241–73.

(in press) 'Communicating a consecratio: The deification coinage of Faustina I', *Proceedings of the XIVth International Numismatic Congress, Glasgow*.

Rowe, A. (1946) *Discovery of the Famous Temple and Enclosure of Serapis at Alexandria*. Cairo.

Royo, M. (1986) 'Topographie ancienne et fouilles sur la *Vigna Barberini*', *MEFRA* 98: 707–66.

(1997) 'Constructions et aménagements antiques antérieurs au grand temple "Sévérien"', in *La Vigna Barberini (Roma Antica 3)*. Rome: 3–30.

Rubin, Z. (1971) 'Supernatural and Religious Sanction of the Emperors' Rule Under the Severi, 193–217'. D.Phil. thesis, Oxford.

(1975a) 'Dio, Herodian and Severus' Second Parthian war', *Chiron* 5: 419–41.

(1975b) 'Further to the dating of the *constitutio Antoniniana*', *Latomus* 34: 430–6.

(1976/7) 'The *felicitas* and the *concordia* of the Severan house', *SCI* 3: 153–72.
(1980) *Civil-War Propaganda and Historiography*. Brussels.
Ruggini, L. (1991) 'Elagabalo, Constantino e i culti 'Siriaci' nella *Historia Augusta*', in *Historiae Augustae Colloquium Parisinum*, ed. G. Bonamente and N. Duval. Macerata: 123–46.
Rutherford, I. (2009) 'Black sails to Achilles: the Thessalian pilgrimage in Philostratus' Heroicus', in *Philostratus*, ed. E. Bowie and J. Elsner. Cambridge: 230–47.
Ryan, F. (2005). 'Der Sonnengott auf den Münzen der Römischen Republik', *Revue Suisse de Numismatique* 84: 81–9.
Säflund, G. (1968) 'Zur Ikonographie des Kaisers Septimius Severus', *Opuscula* 5: 119–34.
Saller, R. P. (1982) *Personal Patronage under the Early Empire*. Cambridge.
Salzmann, D. (2001) 'Alexanderschilde – Numismatische Zeugnisse für die Alexanderverehrung Caracallas', in *Wissenschaft mit Enthusiasmus. Beiträge zu antiken Bildnissen und zur historischen Landeskunde*, ed. J. Bergmann. Rahden: 173–91.
Sambon, A., Canessa, C. et al. (1907) *Collections Martinetti & Nervegna, médailles grecques et romaines aes grave*. Bologna.
Santangeli Valenziani, R. (1991) 'Osservazioni sul tempio di piazza del Quirinale', *BCAR* 94: 7–16.
Santangelo, F. (2007a) 'Pompey and religion', *Hermes* 135: 228–33.
(2007b) *Sulla, the Elites and the Empire*. Leiden.
Santangelo, M. (1941) 'Il Quirinale nell'antichità classica', *Atti della Pontificia Accademia Romana di Archeologia, Memorie* 5: 77–214.
Scheid, J. (1987) 'Polytheism impossible; or, the empty gods: reasons behind a void in the history of Roman religion', *The Inconceivable Polytheism* (History and Anthropology 3): 303–25.
(1998a) *Commentarii fratrum arvalium qui supersunt. Les copies épigraphiques des protocoles annuels de la confrérie Arvale (21 av. – 304. ap. J.-C.)*. Rome.
(1998b) 'Déchiffrer des monnaies. Réflexions sur la représentation figurée des jeux séculaires', in *Images romaines: actes de la table ronde organisée à l'Ecole normale supérieure, 24–26 Octobre 1996*, ed. F. Dupont and C. Auvray-Assayas. Paris: 13–35.
(1998c) 'Le protocole Arvale de l'année 213 et l'arrivée de Caracalla à Nicomédie', in *Epigrafia Romana in Area Adriatica*, ed. G. Paci. Pisa: 439–51.
Scheid, J. and Broise, H. (1983) 'Les fouilles de la Magliana: Le *lucus* et l'*aedes Deae Diae*', *Il Lazio nell'antichità romana* 12: 173–213.
Scheithauer, A. (1990) 'Die Regierungszeit des Kaisers Elagabal in der Darstellung von Cassius Dio und Herodian', *Hermes* 118: 335–56.
Schmidt, M. G. (1997) 'Die "zeitgeschichtlichen" Bücher im Werke des Cassius Dio – von Commodus zu Severus Alexander', *ANRW* II.34.3: 2591–649.

Schmitz, T. A. (1999) 'Performing history in the Second Sophistic', in *Geschichtsschreibung und politischer Wandel im 3. Jh. n. Chr.*, ed. M. Zimmermann. Stuttgart: 71–92.

Schneider, M. (2000) 'Sardanapal(l)os/Sardanal(l)us: Gleanings from ancient Assyria in Cicero', *AClass* 43: 119–27.

Scott, K. (1936) *The Imperial Cult under the Flavians*. Stuttgart.

Seelentag, G. (2004) *Taten und Tugenden Traians. Herrschaftsdarstellung im Principat*. Munich.

Seyrig, H. (1952–3) 'Antiquités de la necropole d'Emese', *Syria* 29–30: 204–50.

(1959) 'Caractères de l'histoire d'Emese', *Syria* 36: 184–92.

(1971) 'Le culte de Soleil en Syrie a l'époque romaine', *Syria* 48: 337–73.

Sharples, J. (1981) 'The Denarii of the Mint of Rome, AD 193–211'. Masters thesis, University of Manchester, Manchester.

Shayegan, M. R. (2004) 'Philostratus' *Heroikos* and the ideation of late Severan policy towards Arsacid and Sasanian Iran', in *Philostratus's Heroikos: Religion and Cultural Identity in the Third Century C.E.*, ed. E. B. Aitken and J. K. B. Maclean. Atlanta: 285–315.

Sherman, C. L. (1928) 'The constitutio Antoniniana in the light of the *gnōmōm tou idiou logou*', *TAPhA* 59: 33–47.

Sherwin-White, A. N. (1973) 'The tabular of Banasa and the Constitutio Antoniniana', *JRS* 63: 86–98.

Sidebottom, H. (1997) 'The date of the composition of Herodian's *History*', *AC* 66: 271–6.

(1998) 'Herodian's historical methods and understanding of history', *ANRW* II.34.4: 2775–836.

(2007) 'Severan historiography: evidence, patterns, and arguments', in *Severan Culture*, ed. S. Swain, S. Harrison and J. Elsner. Cambridge: 52–82.

Sillar, S. (2001) 'Caracalla and the senate: the aftermath of Geta's assassination', *Athenaeum* 89: 407–23.

Simpson, C. J. (1977) 'The date of the dedication of the temple of Mars Ultor', *JRS* 67: 91–4.

Snijder, G. S. (1940) 'Kaiser Hadrian und der Tempel der Venus und Roma', *JDAI* 55: 1–11.

Sobocinski, M. G. (2006) 'Visualizing ceremony: The design and audience of the ludi saeculares coinage of Domitian', *AJA* 110: 581–602.

Sommer, M. (2004) 'Elagabal – Wege zur Konstruktion eines "schlechten" Kaisers', *SCI* 23: 95–110.

Spawforth, T. (2006) '"Macedonian times": Hellenistic memories in the provinces of the Roman Near East', in *Greeks on Greekness. Viewing the Greek Past under the Roman Empire*, ed. T. Whitmarsh, C. Kelly and J. Warren. Cambridge: 1–26.

Speidel, M. P. (1978) *The Religion of Iuppiter Dolichenus in the Roman Army*. Leiden.

(1994a) *Die Denkmäler der Kaiserreiter. Equites Singulares Augusti*. Cologne.
(1994b) *Riding for Caesar. The Roman Emperors' Horse Guards*. London.
Springer, L. A. (1954) 'The cult and temple of Jupiter Feretrius', *CJ* 50: 27–32.
Squarciapino, M. F. (1974) *Sculture del foro Severiano di Leptis Magna*. Rome.
Stambaugh, J. E. (1972) *Sarapis Under the Early Ptolemies*. Leiden.
Starcky, J. and Bennett, C.-M. (1968) 'Les inscriptions du téménos', *Syria* 45: 41–66.
Steinby, E. M. (1996) *Lexicon Topographicum Urbis Romae*, vol. 3: H–O. Rome.
Sterz, S. A. (1977) 'Christianity in the Historia Augusta', *Latomus* 36: 694–715.
Stewart, P. (2003) *Statues in Roman Society. Representation and Response*. Oxford.
Strack, P. L. (1937) *Untersuchungen zur römischen Reichsprägung des zweiten Jahrhunderts III: Die Reichsprägung zur Zeit des Antoninus Pius*. Stuttgart.
Straub, J. (1970) 'Severus Alexander und die Mathematici', in *Bonner Historia-Augusta-Colloquium 1968–1969*. Bonn: 247–72.
Streck, M. (1916) *Assurbanipal und die letzten assyrischen Könige bis zum Untergange Niniveh's*. Leipzig.
Strenski, I. (2002) 'Durkheim, disciplinarity, and the "*sciences religieuses*"', in *Disciplinarity at the Fin de Siècle*, ed. A. Anderson and J. Valente. Princeton: 153–76.
Strocka, M. (1972) 'Beobachtungen an den Attikareliefs des severischen Quadrifons von Lepcis Magna', *AntAfr* 6: 147–72.
Strong, D. E. (1972/3) 'Septimius Severus at Lepcis Magna and Cyrene', *Society for Libyan Studies Annual Report* 4: 27–35.
Studniczka, F. (1901) 'Ein Pfeilercapitell auf dem Forum', *MDAI(R)*16: 273–82.
Sullivan, R. D. (1977) 'The dynasty of Emesa', *ANRW* II.8: 198–219.
Sumi, G. S. (2002) 'Spectacles and Sulla's public image', *Historia* 51: 414–32.
Sutherland, C. H. V. (1986) 'Compliment or complement? Dr Levick on imperial coin types', *NC* 146: 85–93.
Svoronos, J. N. (1904–8). *Ta nomismata tou kratous ton Ptolemaion*. Athens.
Swain, S. (1999) 'Defending Hellenism: Philostratus, *In Honour of Apollonius*', in *Apologetics in the Roman Empire*, ed. M. Edwards, M. Goodman and S. Price. Oxford: 157–96.
(2007) 'Introduction', in *Severan Culture*, ed. S. Swain, S. Harrison and J. Elsner. Cambridge: 1–26.
Syme, R. (1971) *Emperors and Biography*. Oxford.
(1972) 'The son of the emperor Macrinus', *Phoenix* 26: 275–91.
Taylor, L. R. (1934) 'New light on the history of the secular games', *AJPh* 55: 101–20.
Taylor, R. (2004) 'Hadrian's Serapeum in Rome', *AJA* 108: 223–66.
Thiel, W. (2005) 'Lohn und Strafe – Zur Situation der Städte im Osten des römischen Reiches während des Bürgerkrieges zwischen Septimius Severus und Pescennius Niger', in *Urbanistik und städtische Kultur in Westasien und Nordafrika unter den Severern*, ed. D. Kreikenborn, K.-U. Mahler and T. M. Weber. Worms: 103–18.
Thirion, M. (1968) *Le monnayage d'Élagabale (218–222)*. Amsterdam.

Thomas, E. (2007) 'Metaphor and identity in Severan architecture: the Septizodium at Rome between "reality" and "fantasy"', in *Severan Culture*, ed. S. Swain, S. Harrison and J. Elsner. Cambridge: 327–76.

Tocchi, A. (1956) 'Il culto seculare dei Gemini e i tipi monetari Severiani con Bacco ed Ercole', *RIN* 58: 3–20.

Tod, N. (1942) 'A bilingual dedication from Alexandria', *JEA* 28: 53–6.

Tomlin, R. S. O. (1980) 'Fairy gold: monetary history in the Augustan History', in *Imperial Revenue, Expenditure and Monetary Policy in the Fourth Century AD* (BAR International Series 76), ed. C. E. King. Oxford: 255–69.

Touratsoglou, I. (2008) 'Tarsos, Aboukir, etc.; before and after. Once again', *American Journal of Numismatics* 20: 479–92.

Townsend, P. W. (1938) 'The significance of the arch of the Severi at Lepcis', *AJA* 42: 512–24.

(1955) 'The revolution of AD 238. The leaders and their aims', *YCS* 14: 49–105.

Toynbee, J. M. C. (1925) 'Some "programme" coin-types of Antoninus Pius', *CR* 39: 170–3.

(1944a) *Roman Medallions*. New York.

(1944b) 'Roman medallions: their scope and purpose', *NC* 4: 27–44.

Tran, V. (1983) *Sérapis debout: corpus des monuments de Sérapis debout et étude iconographique*. Leiden.

Trapp, M. B. (1997) *Maximus of Tyre. The Philosophical Orations*. Oxford.

Traversari, G. (1956) 'Monete commemorative dei "*ludi saeculares Septimi*" con scena teatrale a "*siparia*"', *RIN* 4: 21–30.

Turcan, R. (1978) 'Le culte impérial au IIIe siècle', *ANRW* II.16.2: 996–1084.

(1984) 'Les premières effigies monétaires d'Elagabal: problèmes politiques et dynastiques', in *Ritratto ufficiale e ritratto privato: atti della II conferenza internazionale sul ritratto romano*. Rome: 535–9.

(1988) 'Héliogabale précurseur de Constantin?' *BAGB* 1: 38–52.

(1997) *Héliogabale et le sacre du Soleil*. Paris.

Vagi, D. L. (1995) 'Propaganda and the Pythian games: Caracalla as Alexander Novus', *Celator* 9 (12): 6–10.

van Berchem, M. D. (1973) 'L'itinéraire Antonin et le voyage en Orient de Caracalla (214–215)', *CRAI*: 123–6.

van Buren, A. W. (1911) 'A medallion of Antoninus Pius', *JRS* 1: 187–95.

van Heesch, J. (1978) 'Les ateliers monétaires de Pescennius Niger', *RBN* 124: 57–72.

Vanni, F. M. (1990) 'La monetazione di Leptis Magna', *RIN* 92: 33–73.

Várhelyi, Z. (2001) 'Magic, religion, and syncretism at the oracle of Claros', in *Between Magic and Religion. Interdisciplinary Studies in Ancient Mediterranean Religion and Society*, ed. S. R. Asirvatham, C. O. Pache and J. Watrous. Lanham: 13–31.

Varner, E. R. (2001) 'Portraits, plots and politics: "damnatio memoriae" and the images of imperial women', *MAAR* 46: 41–93.

(2004) *Mutilation and Transformation. Damnatio Memoriae and Roman Imperial Portraiture.* Leiden.

Vermeule, C. C. (1975) 'Numismatics in antiquity', *SNR* 54: 5–32.

(1977) 'Commodus, Caracalla and the tetrarchs: Roman emperors as Hercules', in *Festschrift für Frank Brommer*, ed. U. Hockmann and A. Krug. Mainz: 289–94.

(1982) 'Alexander the Great, the emperor Severus Alexander and the Aboukir medallions', *SNR* 61: 61–79.

Vicenzo, F. et al. (2000) 'L'ipogeo di "Roma Vecchia" al IV miglio della Via Latina. Scavi e restauri 1996–1997', *RAC* 76: 3–179.

Vidman, L. S. (1986) 'Caracalla e Sarapide in una iscrizione di Efeso', *StudClas* 24: 143–7.

Villedieu, F. (2007) *La Vigna Barberini* II. Rome.

Villedieu, F. et al. (1992) 'Activités de l'École Française de Rome: Rome Le Palatin (Vigna Barberini)', *MEFRA* 104: 465–93.

Villedieu, F., Broise, H. et al. (1998) 'Rome: Le Palatin (Vigna Barberini)', *MEFRA* 110: 473–549.

Villedieu, F., Morel, J. P. et al. (1997) 'Rome: Le Palatin (Vigna Barberini)', *MEFRA* 109: 417–40.

Villedieu, F., Pergola, P. et al. (1996) 'Rome: Le Palatin (Vigna Barberini)', *MEFRA* 108: 423–51.

Visscher, F. d. (1961) 'La constitution Antonine et la dynastie africaine des Sévères', *RIA* 8: 229–42.

von Domaszewski, A. (1908) 'Die politische Bedeutung der Religion von Emesa', *Archiv für Religionwissenschaft* 11: 223–42.

(1909) *Abhandlungen zur römischen Religion.* Leipzig.

von Henneberg, K. (1994) 'Tripoli: Piazza Castello and the making of a fascist colonial capital', in *Streets: Critical Perspectives on Public Space.* Berkeley: 135–50.

von Mercklin, E. (1962) *Antike Figuralkapitelle.* Berlin.

Vout, C. (2007) *Power and Eroticism in Imperial Rome.* Cambridge.

Waddington, W. H., Babelon, E. et al. (1925) *Recueil général des monnaies grecques d'Asie Mineure.* Paris.

Wagenvoort, H. (1956) 'The crime of fratricide', in *Studies in Roman Literature, Culture and Religion.* New York: 169–83.

Walda, H. and Walker, S. (1984) 'The art and architecture of Lepcis Magna: marble origins by isotopic analysis', *Libyan Studies* 15: 81–95.

Walker, D. (1988) 'The Roman coins', in *The Temple of Sulis Minerva at Bath*, ed. B. Cunliffe. Oxford: 281–358.

Wallace-Hadrill, A. (1981a) 'Galba's aequitas', *NC* 141: 20–39.

(1981b) 'The Emperor and his virtues', *Historia* 30: 298–323.

(1986) 'Image and authority in the coinage of Augustus', *JRS* 76: 66–87.

Walters, H. B. (1926) *Catalogue of the Engraved Gems and Cameos, Greek, Etruscan and Roman, in the British Museum.* London.

Ward-Perkins, J. B. (1948) 'Severan art and architecture at Lepcis Magna', *JRS* 38: 59–80.

(1951) 'The arch of Septimius Severus at Lepcis Magna', *Archaeology* 4: 226–31.

(1993) *The Severan Buildings of Lepcis Magna*. London.

Warren, P. (1990) 'Of Baetyls', *OAth* 18: 193–206.

Weber, G. (1978) 'Reste römischer Steinarchitektur in Faimingen. Bestandteile des Apollo-Grannus-Heiligtums?' *Germania* 56: 511–21.

Webster, J. (2001) 'Creolizing the Roman Provinces', *AJA* 105: 209–25.

Weir, R. (2004) *Roman Delphi and its Pythian Games*. Oxford.

Weiser, W. (1983) *Katalog der Bithynischen Münzen der Sammlung des Instituts für Altertumskunde der Universität zu Köln*, I: *Nikaia*. Opladen.

(2000) 'Elagabal mit Stierpenis-Hütchen – Animalphallokrat oder Weichteil-Wolpertinger?' *Geldgeschichtliche Nachrichten* 196: 53–6.

Weiss, P. (1982) 'Ein Altar für Gordian III, die älteren Gordiane und die Severer aus Aigeai (Kilikien)', *Chiron* 12: 191–205.

(2005) 'The cities and their money', in *Coinage and Identity in the Roman Provinces*, ed. C. Howgego, V. Heuchert and A. Burnett. Oxford: 57–68.

Weisser, B. (1995) 'Die kaiserzeitliche Münzprägung von Pergamon'. D.Phil. dissertation, Ludwig Maximilians Universität, Münster.

(2005) 'Pergamum as paradigm', in *Coinage and Identity in the Roman Provinces*, ed. C. Howgego, V. Heuchert and A. Burnett. Oxford: 135–42.

Weissert, D. (1963) 'Bemerkungen zum Wortlaut des P. Giss. 40 I', *Hermes* 91: 239–50.

Welles, C. B. (1962) 'The discovery of Sarapis and the foundation of Alexandria', *Historia* 11: 271–98.

Whetstones, G. (1584) *A Mirour for Magestrates of Cyties*. London.

Whitmarsh, T. (2007) 'Prose literature and the Severan dynasty', in *Severan Culture*, ed. S. Swain, S. Harrison and J. Elsner. Cambridge: 29–51.

(2009) 'Performing heroics: language, landscape and identity in Philostratus' Heroicus', in *Philostratus*, ed. E. Bowie and J. Elsner. Cambridge: 205–29.

Whittaker, C. R. (2004) *Rome and its Frontiers*. London.

Widmer, W. (1967) *Kaisertum, Rom und Welt in Herodian's Meta Markon Basileias Istoria*. Zürich.

Wiegand, T. (1932) *Zweiter Bericht über die Ausgrabungen in Pergamon 1928–32: das Asklepieion*. Berlin.

Wilhem, A. (1933) 'Zu neuen Inschriften aus Pergamon', *Sitzungsberichte der Preussischen Akademie der Wissenschaften, philologisch-historische Klasse* 20: 836–59.

Will, E. (1988) 'Eshmoun', in *LIMC* IV.1: 23–4.

Williams, J. H. C. (1999) 'Septimius Severus and Sol, Carausius and Oceanus: two new Roman acquisitions at the British Museum', *NC* 159: 307–13.

Williams, W. (1979) 'Caracalla and the authorship of imperial edicts and epistles', *Latomus* 38: 67–89.

Wilson, A. (2007) 'Urban development in the Severan empire', in *Severan Culture*, ed. S. Swain, S. Harrison and J. Elsner. Cambridge: 290–326.

Wirth, G. (1975) 'Caracalla in Franken', *Festschrift für Gerhard Pfeiffer (Jahrbuch für fränkische Landesforschung)* 34/35: 39–74.

Wiseman, T. P. (2008) *Unwritten Rome*. Exeter.

Wolff, H. (1976) 'Die Constitutio Antoniniana und Papyrus Gissensis 40 I'. D.Phil. dissertation, University of Cologne.

Wolters, R. (1999) *Nummi Signati*. Munich.

(2001) 'Bronze, silver or gold? Coin finds and the pay of the Roman army', *Zephyrus* 53/4: 579–88.

(2003) 'Die Geschwindigkeit der Zeit und die Gefahr der Bilder: Münzbilder und Münzpropaganda in der römischen Kaiserzeit', in *Propaganda-Selbstdarstellung-Repräsentation im römischen Kaiserreich des 1. Jhs. n. Chr.*, ed. G. Weber and M. Zimmermann. Stuttgart: 175–204.

Woodward, A. M. (1963) 'The neocorate at Aegeae and Anazarbus in Cilicia', *NC* 3: 5–10.

Woolf, G. (2003) 'Seeing Apollo in Roman Gaul and Germany', in *Roman Imperialism and Provincial Art*, ed. S. Scott and J. Webster. Cambridge: 139–52.

Worden, V. (2001) 'Image and symbol in Severan state portrait cameos', in *Archaeology of the Roman Empire*, ed. N. J. Higham. Oxford: 343–55.

Wroth, W. (1882) 'Telesphoros', *JHS* 3: 283–300.

Xella, P. (1991) *Baal Hammon. Recherches sur l'identité et l'histoire d'un dieu phénico-punique*. Rome.

Zanker, P. (1988) *The Power of Images in the Age of Augustus*. Ann Arbor.

Zarrow, E. M. (2003) 'Aeneas or the Catanean brothers', *NC* 163: 123–35.

Zehnacker, H. (1964) 'Le monnayage de L. Rubrius Dossennus et la victoire d'Esculape', in *Hommages à Jean Bayet*, ed. M. Renard and R. Schilling. Bruxelles: 739–48.

Ziegler, R. (1977) 'Münzen Kilikiens als Zeugnis kaiserlicher Getreidespenden', *JNG* 27: 29–67.

(1978) 'Antiochia, Laodicea und Sidon in der Politik der Severer', *Chiron* 8: 493–514.

(1985) *Städtisches Prestige und kaiserliche Politik*. Düsseldorf.

(1993) *Kaiser, Heer und Städtisches Geld. Untersuchungen zur Münzprägung von Anazarbos und anderer ostkilikischer Städte*. Vienna.

(1996) 'Civic coins and imperial campaigns', in *The Roman Army in the East*, ed. D. L. Kennedy. Ann Arbor: 119–34.

(2003) 'Asklepioskult und Kaiserkult im kilikischen Aigeai um die Mitte des 3. Jahrhunderts n. Chr.', *Olba* 7: 205–18.

(2004) 'Der Burgberg von Anazarbos in Kilikien und der Kult des Elagabal in den Jahren 218 bis 222 n. Chr.', *Chiron* 34: 59–85.

Zimmermann, M. (1999a) 'Herodians Konstruktion der Geschichte und sein Blick auf das stadtrömische Volk', in *Geschichtsschreibung und politischer Wandel im 3. Jh. n. Chr.*, ed. M. Zimmermann. Stuttgart: 119–43.

(1999b) *Kaiser und Ereignis*. Munich.

Zinsli, S. C. (2005) 'Gute Kaiser, schlechte Kaiser. Die eusebische Vita Constantini als Referenztext für die Vita Heliogabali', *WS* 118: 117–38.

Ziolkowski, A. (1992) *The Temples of Mid-Republican Rome and Their Historical and Topographical Context*. Rome.

Zwierlein-Diehl, E. (1986) *Glaspasten im Martin-von-Wagner-Museum der Universität Würzburg I: Abdrücke von antiken und ausgewählten nachantiken Intagli und Kameen*. Munich.

Index

Lightning Source UK Ltd.
Milton Keynes UK
UKHW030716091220
374876UK00006B/38

9 781107 020122